The Wild Beach

& Other Stories

Edited by Helena Goscilo & Byron Lindsey

Ardis

First paperback edition 1993

Ardis Publishers
2901 Heatherway
Ann Arbor, Michigan 48104

ISBN 0-679-74893-8

Distributed by Vintage Books,
a division of Random House, Inc.

Contents

From the Editors

"Society and government are yesterday, but language and literature are always today. Sometimes they may be even tomorrow!" the poet Joseph Brodsky said recently. These words can serve as an epigraph to this collection, which appears at a time of epic developments in Russian history. Although the social and political system that prevailed when this "baker's dozen" of stories were written already clearly belongs to yesterday, the works themselves, "pure fiction," belong very much to the present, in two different, perhaps especially Russian ways.

The first is Brodsky's poetic and universal context: the act of reading recreates that strange synthesis—memories of sound and light—literature. Each reader will reanimate a text in his own way and reconstitute it to reflect his own profile. This process may touch the connecting rods of perceptions and passions, producing, in Marianne Moore's phrase, "imaginary gardens with real toads in them." Russian literature, along with its many visible toads and promised gardens, has a loyal constituency of readers, both at home and abroad. For two centuries Russian culture has been super-European, with a special interest in the Western literary heritage. Yet, it is also a culture with strong infusions of Eastern, inwardly focused values. The readership of belles lettres in Russia has been high and discerning. And come what may, despite the present flood of the prurient and petty through new channels of uncensored publishing, this is unlikely to change soon. In Russia, literature is ingrained as the primary set of credentials for belonging, however remotely, to the world of civilized values and, beyond that, for aspiring to the prestigious traditions of the old intelligentsia. Abroad too, Russian literature has a strong, long-standing constituency. Surely all responsible for this anthology—the writers, editors, and translators—hope that it will find similar appeal among the many English language readers for whom the act of reading fiction is an affirmation of genuine experience, however imaginary and varied the process of restitution.

The second way this fiction belongs to the present is more circumstantial and informative: it tells us about Russia today, describing, in particular, the social and moral conditions of its discontent. The two alternating functions—the poetic and the civic—are characteristic of Russian literature since the nineteenth century: they often intertwine and overlap during the same period, as the journalistic supports the artistic and vice versa. In fact Russian literature during glasnost seems especially kindred in spirit to that rich and diverse period at the end of the nineteenth century, similarly reform-minded and relatively unhindered by censorship. Tolstoy's polemics, fictional and otherwise, appeared alongside Chekhov's finely crafted psychological portraits, which were often journalistic in their attention to sociological background, and the satires of Gleb Uspensky and Saltykov-Shchedrin alternated with the pre-modernistic inner voyages of Vsevolod Garshin and the humanistic lyricism of Vladimir Korolenko.

The writers gathered here reflect severe but familiar twentieth-century experiences. They write about betrayals, greed, deception, and disdain for the natural environment, conditions that often lead to violence. Although they do not comprise a literary generation, their works, freed from censorship, provide reliable sources for understanding the recent dramatic impulses for change.

Reading between the lines is a particularly Russian art, and translation extends the opportunities of this exercise to all who are concerned about the destiny of Russia and its role in our world. Translation, in fact, has been the primary task in this project—*The Wild Beach* and its earlier companion volume, *Glasnost*. Our approach has been meticulous, painstaking, thorough—and, probably best of all in matters of translation, collective. In general, it has been an endeavor of many, beginning and essentially ending, with the writers themselves.

* * *

To my partners in the project, Helena Goscilo and all the translators, especially those who waited to see their work appear in this second volume, my first thanks for their efforts in bringing our project to completion; their professional talents, dedication, and patient understanding produced this anthology. Helena's boundless expertise, intellectual energy, and inspired editing permeate the anthology. Vyacheslav Davidenko, professor of English at the Institute of Foreign Languages in Alma-Ata, Kazakhstan, used his dexterity with both English and Russian to check the texts for accuracy and stylistic faithfulness, line by line; almost all of the translations reflect his enormous bilingual talent and selfless dedication to the project. Thanks to the authors I was able to interview—Gennady Golovin, Mikhail Kuraev, Vitaly Moska-lenko, Vyacheslav Pyetsukh, Valery Popov, Tatyana Tolstaya; they gave me valuable perspectives as well as important factual details; apologies to Golovin and Pyetsukh for the involuntary misnomers in *Glasnost*. Mary Ann Szporluk at Ardis has been the editors' editor, and the final English texts are indelibly printed with her keen and sensitive touch. In fact, her perspective and guidance on every aspect of the project has been vital to its realization. A very special thanks to my friend Robert M. Gordon, poet and stylist supreme, for his careful reading and skillful emendations of my own translations. Tania Grigorieva Lindsey, my wife, has lived with the project since its inception and at every stage has made critical contributions in choosing the works, re-searching "the right word" in translations, and deflecting the "academic" din that interfered. Her analytical insights and moral support were essential. The University of Illinois at Champaign-Urbana has been my research base, whether in residence, thanks to its Summer Research Laboratory, or from a distance, through the remarkable outreach of the scholars and professional staff who comprise its Center for Slavic and East European Studies and Slavic and East European Library. They all were my colleagues in this endeavor.

Byron Lindsey
Albuquerque, New Mexico
January 1992

* * *

Since the publication of our *Glasnost: An Anthology of Russian Literature under Gorbachev* in September 1990, the pace of change in the Soviet Union has accelerated so frenetically that any observation about today's events is vir-tually guaranteed obsolescence by the time it appears in print. That threat of imminent irrelevance applies, *pace* Gorbachev, to both parts of the very term "Soviet Union." The unpredictability that, paradoxically, has been the single stable factor in Soviet history from its inception continues to thrive in Russian culture, which remains as implicated as ever in politics. A mere year ago who could have foreseen that the editorial board of *Ogonyok* and *Literaturnaya gazeta* would relieve Vitaly Korotich and Fyodor Burlatsky, respectively, of their positions as chief editors—on political grounds? Or that publication of the officious newspaper *Pravda* would be suspended at the same time as *The New World* (*Novy mir*), the liberal monthly that launched Solzhenitsyn's career, prepared drastic cuts in its circulation? The impact of the shortlived, thwarted

August coup by Party diehards seems to be enacting the domino effect, whereby the fall of one cadre topples another, in an endless series of debacles that has made strange bedfellows, to say the least, of Korotich, the former chief editor of *Ogonyok*, erstwhile Foreign Minister Alexander Bessmertnykh, and Dmitry Urnov, conservative ex-editor of *Questions of Literature* (*Voprosy literatury*). Yet even before the cataclysmic shocks of the coup's demise made themselves felt, a less violent but equally consequential revolution was well under way: the marginalization of High Culture by both popular culture (spontaneously generated) and the implacable forces of market economics (partially imposed).

Of all the mothballed myths to have perished during the battle of the book and the buck, perhaps the hardiest is that of Russians' vaunted unique love of Culture. With the removal of the prohibitions that vouchsafed authors like Anna Akhmatova, Boris Pasternak, and Alexander Solzhenitsyn the status of cult figures, the artificially stimulated clamor for their works evaporated. Starting this year, volumes of Solzhenitsyn, Osip Mandelstam, Vladimir Vysotsky, and other legendary symbols of opposition languish in bookstores and kiosks. Easy access has effectively killed desire, in a process that, as Serge Schmemann accurately observed in *The New York Times*, "reflects a normalization rather than a disruption." Now subject to the supply and demand of a market economy, Culture has lost its capitalization and its audience. Poetry readings, lectures on literature, and classical concerts attract only small groups. Skyrocketing costs of production and a shortage of paper have caused Pushkin House to worry about the feasibility of its projected series of nineteenth-century classics in authoritative editions and the prestigious critical journal *Questions of Literature* to contemplate closing down, yet pseudonymous erotica and pornography sporting naked women on their covers flood the streets. Currently, the most sought after items in Moscow are detective fiction, tales of adventure, "how to" manuals, pornography, and rock recordings. Not Anna Akhmatova, but Agatha Christie is the most popular woman writer in Moscow; not political allegory, but blueprints for financial success absorb the thousands who pore over Dale Carnegie's *How to Win Friends and Influence People*; not Andrei Tarkovsky's lugubrious cinematic ruminations on life's meaning, but videos of explicit sex acts enjoy a mass popularity. As authors haggle fiercely over contracts and porn-peddlers negotiate prices for their wares, the post-glasnost era of decentralized enterprise shows Soviet culture emulating Donald Trump's art of "the deal."

While this year has witnessed the demythologizing of Culture on Russian soil, the tumult that kept Americans riveted to their televisions for reports about the coup and its aftermath has only intensified Western curiosity about any and all recent developments in Soviet life, its C/culture included. In this disjunction between the insider's and the outsider's perspective, then, a second volume of glasnost fiction might be welcome in the West, yet appear to verge on quixoticism or quaintness within the changed Soviet context. But our project, coincidentally, has its Russian counterpart, undertaken by Sergei Kaledin, author of "The Humble Cemetery" ("Smirennoe kladbishche," 1987) and editor of a collection that anticipated ours in more ways than one: *The Last Floor* (*Poslednii etazh*, 1989). The companion volume, tentatively titled *The Fifth Corner* (*Piatyi ugol*), was scheduled to appear in late 1991.

The overlap between Kaledin's first volume and ours is telling: both include Kuraev's *Captain Dikshtein* and Petrushevskaya's "Our Crowd." Both contain selections by Shmelyov, Golovin, Iskander, and Tolstaya. Although Evgeny Popov, Okudzhava, and Kaledin himself are represented in his collection and not in ours, they originally were slated for inclusion in *Glasnost*. Only the unavailability of rights to the stories we wanted forced us to exclude them.

No other sizable anthologies with comparable contents have appeared in the Soviet Union, unless one counts the anomalous *Glas: New Russian Writing*, edited by Natasha Perova and Andrew Bromfield, who clearly hope to break the Western monopoly on English translations of recent Russian literature. Printed by an independent company in Moscow called Russlit, the anthology of 264 pages attempts to give English-speaking readers a sense of the latest developments in contemporary Russian letters. Presumably the first in a continuing series, *Glas* more properly belongs to the venerable Russian genre of the thick journal—a format that currently finds itself imperiled by the unstable financial conditions of the Soviet publishing industry, which lacks a strong, confident sense of what to publish in a free market economy. Anyone who has tracked Soviet publication patterns in the last couple of years will have noticed that announced projects fail to materialize (see Interbook's phantom list), while other items may be released simultaneously by several publishers (e.g., earlier, Nabokov's prose; now, translations of Western mysteries), and so on, in an atmosphere peculiarly combining sluggishness and near-frenzy.

If Soviet publishers are seeking Western readers (=hard currency), then Western publishers reciprocate by courting Soviet editors (=cultural authority or "native" expertise). Witness the two anthologies of primarily glasnost fiction issued in the West over the last three years: Abbeville Press's *The New Soviet Fiction* (1989), under Sergei Zalygin's editorship, and *Dissonant Voices: The New Russian Fiction* (1991), the first of Harvill's "Leopard" series in England, assembled by Oleg Chukhontsev. Both contain stories by Village Prose writers, a category consciously omitted from *The Last Floor* and *Glasnost*. Moreover, Abbeville's *The New Soviet Fiction* has a translation from

Azerbaijani and one from Georgian. Yet a comparison of the available anthologies reveals more similarities than differences. Although Petrushevskaya is the sole writer represented in all four, the same names tend to recur (Bitov, Grekova, Makanin, Okudzhava, E. Popov, Tolstaya), as do narratives about war experiences (whether the Second World War or the recent Soviet intervention in Afghanistan). The Chukhontsev collection offers the richest diversity of texts, which, however, are confined to the short story, hence almost all very brief. The other three collections opt for fewer, but longer, narratives. Taken together, the four anthologies provide a reliable picture of what interests that dwindling minority of Russians who have retained faith in Culture.

According to Kaledin, one of his own short stories, works by Tolstaya, Ivan Goncharov, Eduard Limonov, and several "unknown" writers will comprise his second volume. Whereas Kaledin decided its contents after his first compilation was already in print, our second collection consists of those texts we chose in 1987-88 but could not encompass in a single volume owing to limitations of space. Our only subsequent addition to the original list is Lyudmila Ulitskaya's "Happy," whose novelty resides in its open treatment of Soviet Jewish life.

Thematically and stylistically, the entries in *The Wild Beach* span a wide range, from the modernist abstraction of Ivanchenko's protracted existentialist meditation, to the journalistic factography of Granin's historical re-creation. The recuperation of a specific moment in history preoccupies not only Granin, but also Tendryakov and Kondratiev, whereas Moskalenko, Pyetsukh, Shorokhov, and Ekimov spotlight a brand of antihero that has gained a firm foothold in recent fiction: the amoral, destructive, self-seeking egotist who acknowledges no legitimate restraints on his behavior other than the limits of his own appetite. In a more innocent time such a type might have been dubbed antisocial, although the epithet seems grotesquely euphemistic, incommensurate with a readiness to commit murder for fun or profit. Of all the narratives, only Sukhanova's pro-natalist "Delos" recalls Village Prose in both manner and ideological orientation as it grapples with moral issues. Its artlessness contrasts with Trifonov's compact text, whose autobiographically grounded, ambiguous exploration of moral betrayal with the intriguingly unreliable aid of memory condenses the characteristic features of his novellas.

For the sake of consistency, *The Wild Beach* preserves the format and transliteration of *Glasnost*. I hope that it omits, however, the errors of its predecessor, which, as Garfield is wont to say, are "mine, all mine."

* * *

My gratitude to the National Endowment for the Humanities and the National Humanities Center at Research Triangle Park, whose generous grant for an unrelated project during the academic year 1990-91 aided in the completion of *The Wild Beach*. A more personal word of thanks to our translators—who in the last two years must have acquired an involuntary empathetic understanding of *Waiting for Godot*—for their tolerant patience; to Byron, for all the things debated, disputed, and shared in the course of our work together; and to Volodia Padunov and Nancy Condee, not only for the untold delight that is Kolia, but also for that steady flow of uninhibited exchange that makes it impossible to pinpoint all the intellectual gifts for which I remain happily in their debt.

Helena Goscilo
Pittsburgh, Pennsylvania
November 1991

Byron Lindsey

Introduction

*Our life is marked by a con-
flict between ethics and aesthetics.*
—*Andrei Bitov (1989)*

Whether rightly or wrongly, many experienced Russia-watchers perceived Gorbachev's call for "glasnost" in 1985 as just another party slogan. By 1987, however, glasnost had started to take on a life of its own, and the spontaneous audacity of all kinds of publications took us by surprise—from the leading literary journals, which for some time had printed little of literary value, to newspapers and popular magazines, which almost without exception had seemed determined to deceive their readers. The radical changes in the printed word were just short of incredible to those of us who believed change in Russia had been condemned to an eternally slow, birch-like growth. Even specialized pulp periodicals, toss-aways subsidized by faceless ministries, became not only readable, but hard to come by, their readers were so many. The new editors appointed under Gorbachev breathed unexpected life into the term "glasnost." Real life and fresh language made their way into the media; crimes and catastrophes were reported; fundamental issues were debated in print and on television; and totally forbidden literary works began being published in the journals—from Evgeny Zamyatin's anti-utopian novel of the 1920s *We* to Alexander Solzhenitsyn's polemical work.

Glasnost had become much more than the half-loaf of freedom offered by Khrushchev during the Thaw. Still, the phenomenon was hard to assess. Would it lead to a totally new political and cultural landscape or was it a rearrangement of the old one? One Russian historian, James Billington, put it this way: "We are living in the midst of a great historical drama which we did not expect, do not understand, and cannot even name." If "thaw" was not its name, so did "glasnost" seem a misnomer. Were there signs of genuine change in the Soviet Union, the empire that for so long had presented itself as impervious to change?

The present collection of prose reflects this period of disruption and uncertainty. The immediate freshness and vitality of new works stood out from the tedious potboilers of the 1970s and most of the '80s—dismal years during which Russian literature stagnated every bit as much as other sectors. Short fiction proved to be glasnost's most exciting literary genre; and these works, some written earlier and published only now, were diverse and dissonant.

The radical changes were reflected most sharply in the "thick" journals, where literature that had been prohibited for decades now started to appear. In a short span of time the journals and their counterparts in all areas of cultural and intellectual life gave free access to the best of twentieth-century art and literature, both foreign and Russian. Beginning with the Thaw in the 1950s and continuing in the underground culture, there had been an occasional display of Kandinsky, publication of Kafka, or reference to Joyce, but now all at once virtually everybody and everything appeared—the modern and post-modern, structuralism and deconstruction. Only the process of translation into Russian delayed the transfer into literature and that, even now, continues apace. The return of Russia's own banned literary patrimony, both emigré works and others, written in the Soviet Union but published abroad, was a dramatic aspect of this cultural deliverance. Many of these works had long been recognized as classics in the West. As they began to flood the publishing market, however, they obscured another important development: the first publication of works that had been "delayed" by the censors and never published anywhere.

Four texts delayed by the censors and printed only recently form the nucleus of this collection. Yury Trifonov's "A Short Stay in the Torture Chamber" is for several reasons the first among equals: a miniature masterpiece that bears the stamp of his subtle fictional craft. Trifonov portrays the persistent struggle between a moral need for memory and the force of an official history that would erase the truth over time. In its meditative but persistently analytical structure, the story represents one of the major thrusts of the glasnost phenomenon—a retrieval and reconstruction of the long-buried, fragmented, and frequently distorted Stalinist past. Trifonov suggests that this voyage to the past is a necessity for the present. His narrator understands there can be no authenticity to his present relationship with his old rival N. without a confrontation that would examine N.'s behavior in speaking out against him years earlier. At the same time, the narrator also comes to realize the absurdity of his fantasy of retribution. The exercise in righteous memory has its own inherent value and cannot undo past cowardice or change old betrayals.

Yet perhaps the cleared record will place the future on genuine ground, freed of falsification.

Vladimir Tendryakov's "Donna Anna" is one of a series of his posthumous autobiographical works published during glasnost, and reflects his opposition to Communist rule. He portrayed its injustices by writing "for the drawer." In "Donna Anna," writing against the grain of Soviet war fiction—a sacrosanct genre of socialist realism—Tendryakov depicts "the great patriotic war" in quite a different light, generally akin to Leo Tolstoy's vision of it: the war is shown as chaos and chance, mitigated by brief moments of individual courage, charged not by patriotism but by individual human loyalties. Tendryakov's story shows the human ties that bind Soviet soldiers to one another as they become debased and devastated by a second, silent enemy—the Stalinist machine's quest for "traitors within" and the blood of false retribution.

Vyacheslav Kondratiev's "At Freedom Station" also has affinities with Tolstoy's depiction of war through the consciousness of an individual. Kondratiev's young "hero" indulges in the lonely and romantic fantasies of his situation in a rear-guard reserve until, by chance, he encounters a shocking reality: as his fellow soldiers are shipped westward, other trains carry quite another human cargo to the east—ordinary citizens on their way to the Stalinist Gulag. Although Kondratiev's humanized treatment of the war made him a popular writer during the early '80s, this story's portrayal of the mass arrests and deportations that continued even during wartime prevented its publication until glasnost.

A prolific novelist throughout the post-thaw years and a liberal doyen of the Leningrad literary establishment, Daniil Granin also had to wait to see "The Forbidden Chapter" published. Subtitled a short story, it is actually a factual memoir in narrative form—a chilling account of a literal quest for memory. Granin's journalistic effort to record the complete story of the siege of Leningrad leads him through the corridors of power to Stalin's old office in the Kremlin to an interview with its then present occupant, Alexei Kosygin, Chairman of the Council of Ministers during the Brezhnev regime. Granin's portrait of Kosygin is a haunting study of the dehumanizing and crippling effects of a political power network. The fear, compromise, and partial truth that govern the structure deform the individual, even in old age. Granin's story is also a candid and critical self-portrait of a Soviet writer trapped in the relationships of power by force of his own professional trade.

Another aspect of the new writing was its frank exploration of long-censored, contemporary problems in the USSR—ethnic and national repressions, environmental catastrophes, and massive political and social failures. The title of Vitaly Moskalenko's story "The Wild Beach" is a metaphor that sums up much about the late Soviet landscape. The story belongs to *County Seat (Raitsentr)*, Moskalenko's novelistic collection of short works set somewhere in southern, Asiatic Russia. Social tensions ripple beneath the satirical narrative, and Moskalenko hints at racial conflicts there. Life in this small town with its market, bar, beach, and military base has become fragmented, and the isolation is felt everywhere. The places where people meet reflect the cruelty and emptiness—it is a community where even dogs get drunk. Society, human relations, nature—all emerge in the narration in bits and pieces. But the individual human spirit dwells here as well. Moskalenko's innocent bum Filipych is a contemporary incarnation of the Holy Fool, a perennial figure of the Russian cultural imagination. Or he could pass for a disinherited, seemingly demented Ivan the Fool from a Russian fairy tale. Moskalenko plants his version of this stock Russian figure in the midst of a young generation destitute in spiritual values and personal loyalties. With the technique of a well-equipped cameraman, he makes frequent optical shifts and takes the reader into his characters' anxious world of failing relationships. These are juxtaposed with Filipych's "crazy" self-sufficiency and sense of inner worth.

Other writers also explore previously forbidden areas on the Soviet social map. Leonid Shorokhov, a Russian writer living in Uzbekistan, is a representative of the current reformist realism. His "The Lifeguard" mixes elements of exposé reporting, detective novel, and social satire to create a powerful study of greed, political corruption, and catastrophic environmental destruction along the Central Asian Amu Darya River delta (modified slightly in the novella to Ak-Darya). The ill-conceived, gargantuan canal project begun in the 1950s to divert the waters of the Amu Darya and the Syr Darya, the ancient lifelines of Central Asian civilization, for irrigation and extension of the quickly lucrative cotton industry has devastated the human and natural habitat. Shorokhov's eclectic but energetic and passionate narrative uses the ecological tragedy as background material, and the author explicitly ties crime to politics.

The writer Nikolai Shmelyov, an economist by profession, has been an important advocate for reform during glasnost. He links his characters' personal moral compromises to Soviet social and economic conditions: politics required them to adapt or perish. Viktor Ivanovich in "The Fur Coat Incident" is naive in his understanding of the crooked rules of his world, despite his being a Muscovite. Although his survival is marked by only brief episodes of happiness, he at least manages to wrench a little wisdom and self-respect from the very experience of social and emotional captivity. If Shmelyov's fictional world is a dismal one, it probably reflects his profession of economist and forms a literary extension to his proposals for economic reform. Also "delayed" until the advent of glasnost, this story focuses on those abuses of state power that restrict and reduce the individual's capacity for creativity and self-fulfillment.

A short story writer of impressive technical skills and stylistic polish, by contrast, Boris Ekimov is no reformer, but rather a preserver of the past. His is a markedly different, conservative vision. His native Don River habitat, painted in primary, primitivistic colors and fine narrow strokes, is disrupted in "The Chelyadins' Son-in-Law" by interlopers who bring envy, greed, and violence from the distant urban demimonde. He is one of the few talented Russian writers still writing "village prose"—the dominant school of the '70s and '80s.

Also from the Don region, Natalya Sukhanova was known as a writer of children's stories until the appearance of "Delos." This story ventures into another painful spot long screened from public scrutiny in Russia—the maternity hospital, a notorious place where most Soviet women have faced primitive conditions and callous treatment. Having no other reliable means of contraception, they have had to resort to abortions, which they accept as virtually a routine necessity. Sukhanova's traditional and largely uncritical point of view bathes the experience of the hospital in an unconvincingly warm, optimistic light. By choosing to make her central character a male doctor, she perhaps misses an opportunity to explore fully the woman's point of view on birth and abortion, but her story makes a thoughtful entry onto these controversial grounds.

In the cycle of stories to which "Lucky" belongs, Lyudmila Ulitskaya turns to a fictional milieu—Jewish family life—that has been discountenanced in Soviet fiction, at least since the '30s; here she returns it as a rich resource for Russian literature. Her stylized, almost abstract technique endows her otherwise ordinary characters with a mythic dimension, and her matter-of-fact portrayal of human relations, unpredictable except in the stoic performance of responsibilities, gives her work an understated poignancy and spirituality.

Two writers in this collection, Vyacheslav Pyetsukh and Alexander Ivanchenko, place a high value on fictional structure and linguistic artifice, allying them with Tatyana Tolstaya, Mikhail Kuraev, Viktor Erofeyev, Lyudmila Petrushevskaya, and Gennady Golovin, whose stories appeared in our earlier volume, *Glasnost*. The telling is as important as the tale itself for Pyetsukh; his narrative fabric blends irony, parody, and philosophical discourse, and recalls Gogol in its taste for the grotesque and fantastic. In "Novy Zavod" Pyetsukh's prosaic protagonist, seeking escape from an oppressive humdrum existence, travels magically, perhaps in a dream, through an invisible looking glass to a utopian town outside of time. This encounter with a reverse mirror image of everything Moscow is not—a bountiful place where people are productive and happy with their lives—provides a witty satire on contemporary society and its empty slogans. "The Ticket" takes up a question straight from the Russian classics: how should a righteous man live? In addressing the question Pyetsukh keeps his propensity to philosophize in check, creating instead a rich gallery of lost souls and greedy gold miners in remote Siberia. Pyetsukh's playful language lightens his characterizations, which would otherwise be dark and bleakly grotesque. Alexander Ivanchenko, one of the most innovative new talents to appear during glasnost, uses fiction to explore the complex processes of consciousness and perception. His "Safety Procedure I" exploits modernistic narrative techniques of retardation and microscopic close-ups to take the reader into his protagonist's inner world of alienation, anxiety, and sexual fantasy.

The voices of glasnost are dissonant, eclectic, often strained, and, mainly, diverse. Each writer sets off, naturally enough it seems to me, in his or her own direction to explore what was forbidden until now and to create as an artist. But the journalistic and editorial achievements in breaking down the barriers of censorship have paradoxically created special problems for fiction, which, despite censorship, was for so long virtually the only vehicle for social and political debate and a primary source for reliable sociological information. Glasnost's journalistic explosion suddenly made everything possible, and there was an intense public hunger for access to fundamental facts about Russia and the outside world. Fiction has had to compete with freely expressed opinions and facts reported in detail by journalists and statisticians; and the new literature of civic exploration, with reformist, sometimes moralistic tones, is a reasonable artistic parallel to the other channels for change.

The return of the twentieth-century Russian patrimony in literature has been a sudden event in the life of the country, epic both in historical importance and cultural promise for the future. But it has also created immediate problems for contemporary writers. Critics and general readers alike have been slow to appreciate the validity of the new as compatible with the restored value of the old: Nabokov's fiction is published next to Pyetsukh's, Tatyana Tolstaya is compared out of context to Andrei Platonov. How to compare fresh innovation with suppressed, finely aged achievement? Contemporary writers are put at an artificial disadvantage, one that time itself will probably adjust. But more consistent critical attention would surely ease their difficult task of developing their own voices.

This anthology, like its companion volume, *Glasnost*, represents writers diverse in approach and literary priorities who share the fate of having been published in the late 1980s. Some are especially good as "exposé" reporters, others make voyages to those dark places of the soul that were off limits under socialist realism. While occasionally they may depict heroic women, the hollow positive hero has gone almost without a trace, and so has the staunch survivor of Thaw literature, epitomized by Solzhenitsyn's Ivan Denisovich. We find antiheroes now, kith and kin to the characters of modern Western authors. A favorite protagonist is the transient or drifter (*bich*), an occasional worker without family or social ties, who lives without clear goals and speaks with a certain naivete. Pyetsukh's Pasha and Moskalenko's Filipych are examples. But as Andrei Sinyavsky has pointed out, Pasha's nickname "the saintly" is a pun on "the name given to poverty, a divine scourge that struck the country or a village."

True to the acute spirit of inquiry characteristic of the times, these writers ask questions more than they give answers. In this propensity they belong to the Chekhovian tradition of skeptical examination. Rather than offer final answers to the national crises, numerous and profound as they are, they make short investigations into individual states of mind and look for interconnections between myth, social memory, contemporary technology, and an endangered or ruined natural environment. The dispassionate images of ruin in their fiction make for an ultimately tragic vision, yet an unmistakably Russian black humor emerges through the gloom. Maybe it is that ironic vein of slightly outrageous, self-mocking humor in their characters that unites such otherwise disparate writers as Pyetsukh and Trifonov, Shmelyov and Shorokhov, Moskalenko and Tendryakov; and in the previous volume, Petrushevskaya and Tolstaya, Valery Popov and Viktor Erofeyev, Gennady Golovin and Mikhail Kuraev.

Some have reported the demise of contemporary Russian literature: Viktor Erofeyev's *In Memoriam* essay is one of the wittiest and most controversial. But this collection and other vital signs surely indicate that such reports are highly premature. Whatever the future holds for the Russian world, its literature will likely be imaginative, articulately individualistic, and passionately concerned about its own provinces, whether they be the urban spiral of dark staircases, the remote field circled by dark forest, or the inner recesses of the lonely imagination. The tradition itself constitutes a special natural resource.

Byron Lindsey
Albuquerque, New Mexico

The Wild Beach
& Other Stories

Yury Trifonov

A Short Stay in the Torture Chamber

In the early spring of 1964, when I was still suffering from an insatiable love of sports, when I kept charts on the champions, knew by heart the best players of the Fiorentina and the Manchester United, when I believed that you could write as seriously about sports as, say, about the tomb of Lorenzo di Medici in Florence, when I had just released my legendary film about hockey and didn't feel at all embarrassed by it, I arrived in the Tyrol with a group of sports writers, lived in a mountain village not far from Innsbruck, and each morning took the bus to the games. The Olympics were being held in Innsbruck. Who won there, who lost, I don't remember. All that nonsense has been forgotten. I don't remember the name of a single athlete from that time—what I remember is the blinding snow on the slopes, the sharp blue of the sky, the freshness in the air, the smell of coffee, and my landlord, who would squint and squeeze out, *"Morgen,"* through his dry lips.

Sometimes when I didn't feel like going to town I would stay in the hotel and watch the games on television. On a table in the empty hall lay thick books in antique-looking leather bindings: *Gästebücher.* Guest books. Having nothing to do, I leafed through them, relishing the examples of German ingenuousness. The books had been kept since 1929, when the hotel first started up in the village of Stubental. All of the comments were the same: gratitude to the proprietor, praise for the mountains, the snow, the view, the girls, the selection of records on the jukebox. I reached the Anschluss: nothing was changed, the same delight about the snow, the air, the girls. And then the war: judging from the comments, wounded German officers took time off here, but it was impossible to find out anything from them, either, except raptures over nature, girls, Italian wine, Spanish oranges. Once there flashed a patriotic entry: *"Alles wagen, England schlagen!"* that is, "Give it your all— beat England." Someone had written above in pencil in small letters, "But

England really trounced you." And then still later, with a green felt-tip, "*O Sie gute arme Idioten!*" But it was unclear to whom this was addressed: to the beaten Germans or to those who rejoiced in the victory. And that was all about the war. The same comments continued: skis, sun, happiness, *Erlebnis*. The proprietor didn't care for us. We paid him money; he tolerated us. He did not enter into conversation. The only thing we heard from him through his clenched teeth was: "*Morgen!*"

But still, I liked the snowy mountains, the valley, the huge bridge across the gorge, the smell of coffee in the morning, and I liked what I was so madly and senselessly carried away with then, what filled the newspapers, what I wrote about at night, and at noon shouted by telephone to Moscow, and only one thing spoiled my mood: the presence of N. in our group. He had emerged from my distant past. Of course, I knew that he existed and I would come across his name in the newspapers, and from time to time would run into him one place or another. We both would act as if we were scarcely acquainted or, indeed, if we did bump into each other head-on, we would barely nod and would pass on by, although at one time we had been on friendly terms and had liked the same girl. But she was incidental. The girl had nothing whatever to do with the whole matter, which took place fourteen years ago—the point was this: we had lived separate lives all those years. He worked for the radio; I sat working at home. I thought I was done with him. And suddenly, he turned up in Innsbruck. N. was always far removed from sports. How the hell did he turn up in our group? The first minute we saw each other in the group gathering in Moscow, I noticed something waver in his face, like a momentarily repressed impulse to be glad, or, maybe, to nod in a friendly way, but he couldn't read this weakness in my face. I met him with a cold look and barely discernible nod which signified nothing on my part but an icy memory. That kind of relationship, I assumed, would become established between us, and somehow I would get through the twelve days.

Sometimes, when my friends would go to town and I would stay at the hotel, it would be partly because I didn't want to see the rosy-cheeked, dried-up, old-mannish N. There had been a time, I remembered, when he wore an army jacket and boots, smoked a handmade pipe and looked like a staid, patrician youth, deeply absorbed in something. Later, I found out in what. But at the time it seemed to me that his unhurriedness, his quiet, indistinct voice, and his gloomy look concealed something significant. I was engrossed in reading Blok* then, and it seemed to me that this line was about him: "Let us forgive the gloomy look,/For not here lies the hidden moving force." True, he did not resemble the lines that followed: "He was all a child of love and

---

*The Russian Symbolist poet, Alexander Blok (1880-1921).

light,/He was all a celebration of freedom." N.'s moving force had to do with
something else: N. himself alone.

But when we arrived in the Tyrol and settled in the hotel, something
strange began: he behaved as if nothing had ever happened. In the morning
he would greet me from afar with happy smiles, raise his hand in greeting
and nod earnestly, and the nods conveyed not only the old amiability, but also
a genuine esteem, the kind expressed to people you sincerely respect. I tried
not to pay attention. Then it started to annoy me. Once we ran into each
other in the pressbox at the stadium, face to face, and in passing he grabbed
my arm above the elbow, squeezed it rather familiarly, and said, "Hi!" I pulled
my arm away and muttered, "What is it?" But my mutter sounded more
frightened than hostile. He winked at me and passed by without saying anything else. Another time in the presence of two journalists, an Italian and a
German, he launched into a conversation with me about hockey, after introducing me as an expert, the author of an excellent film, *The Hockey Players*.
That's the way he said it—"excellent," and his voice sounded honest and simple, without the slightest touch of envy or irony, and, like it or not, I had to
respond and talk with him. But I cut the conversation short and left.

Later, the German found me and asked me to give an interview about how
the games were going, observing, "Mr. N. reads all your dispatches with delight. He said that they are genuinely *Spitze!*" I didn't know how to take this. I
didn't understand him and I didn't understand myself. Can it be, I thought,
that a person has completely forgotten *how he behaved fourteen years ago?* But
that's impossible. It doesn't happen. He didn't forget, probably, but looks at
his own past cold-bloodedly, as something natural, trivial, and worthy of
oblivion. If he had acted differently—had not greeted me, had scowled, passing by without a glance and wearing a haughty look—this would not have
bothered me. I would have accepted it as the way things should be. A person
who has done something evil to someone else always looks at his victim with
a scowl or passes him by with a haughty look. That is the nature of things.
But here he was pretending *that nothing bad had ever happened!*

And the more I thought about it the more I boiled with rage and just
waited for the opportunity to vent my rage on N. A fuss started about award-
ing the Rolex Company's "Golden Pen" award to the best journalist from each
national group, and N. nominated me. This was ridiculous. I am not a professional journalist and had not earned the "Golden Pen." Someone else was
nominated, and N. began to insist on me. It became so intolerable that I left
the room. Our meeting was taking place in the restaurant. I was beside myself
with anger. I waited for him in the hall. As soon as he appeared, I went up to
him and said: "What the hell makes you keep hanging on to me? I'm not
bothering you!" I probably had a malicious look on my face, for he was silent

for a second, looking at me in bewilderment, and then, seemingly flustered, shrugged his shoulders and said, "Me, hanging on to you? You're off your rocker. You've lost your mind, buddy."

"I'm asking you to stop bugging me."

"You're sick," he said. "You should get help."

It was a starry night. I walked along the asphalt road in front of the hotel, breathing in the warm night air of the mountain valley, now empty and silent, and thought: is it true that I'm sick? Occasionally the headlights from cars rushing past would flash over me. I reached the turn onto the bridge and looked at the range of darkening slopes; there, far in the depths, where the now-invisible road led, Innsbruck shone weakly with a handful of lights. It flickered below like a small forest campfire that hadn't been doused. I am sick, I thought, like a person who hasn't shunted his memory aside. I remember too well: the May evening before the meeting when he came without calling, on the pretext of returning some books because he was leaving for Berdyansk. He went to Berdyansk every summer to see his relatives. But I felt that something else had caused him to come. From the start his actions were unnatural: he didn't put the books on the table, he didn't say "Thank you," or "I'm returning these," or "Here are your books," but from a distance threw them on the bed without a word. There was nervousness, a lack of decorum, and decisiveness in this gesture. He was tossing aside not books, but something which had burdened his life. As soon as the two of us were left alone, he said, breaking into a little laugh, "Want to hear a joke? Tomorrow I'm going to speak out against you!"

"Against what?" I asked stupidly, not understanding a damn thing.

"Against you. You, you!" he smiled and poked a finger at me. I thought he was drunk. Something like that could happen, I supposed, but why come and warn me? I said people play dirty tricks without giving warnings. He mumbled something about having understood the "conscious necessity" of it. And I mumbled something meaningless. Suddenly I shouted, "Why did you come here?" He said he came not of his own accord. So Nadya had made him come. She demanded that either he not speak at all, or that he go to the person and honestly warn him. "You don't know what she's like. She actually went into hysterics on me."

I had forgotten about Nadya. Nadya was the girl we both had liked earlier. She had survived the Leningrad blockade; she was pale, fragile, and anemic, with straw-colored braids and a thoughtful look; she was soft-spoken, wrote poetry, and to me as an admirer of Blok, she seemed like the mysterious stranger in Blok's poem. Her whole family had perished in the blockade. Nadya lived in a domitory. Once I had dreamed passionately of her. The summer of '47, when we moved up into the third-year class, the three of us—

Nadya, N. and I—went on summer assignment to write articles about the hydroelectric stations at Lake Sevan. This was arranged through the Komsomol organization. We set out in July. At first everything was fun, poignant, intriguing, enveloped in the opiate of uncertainty and love. We had the girl right there beside us and we expected a struggle for her. We kidded around, sang songs, didn't sleep at night, and endlessly recited poetry. We had to transfer four times to get to Yerevan. In Sochi, I swam in the sea for the first time in my life. I remember how N. and I swam far out, while Nadya stayed on the shore and N. asked, "Shall we cast lots for Nadya?" That caught me off guard, and I almost choked on the salt water and blurted out, "No!"

He said, "Watch out, then, you'll have yourself to blame." This threat seemed absurd to me. I had blurted out, "No!" precisely because deep down I thought that if she had to choose between us, Nadya would choose me. I, too, wrote poetry, but N. composed articles for the Sovinform Bureau.

Our journey was becoming more and more tiring. From Sochi to Samtredia we traveled by a local train that was stifling and cramped, where all around people were shouting in a strange language. Some men made passes at Nadya. N. and I defended her, and the matter almost ended in a fight. Because of the closeness and heat everyone stripped down to his undershirt. We sat Nadya in the corner and blocked her from view with our backs. Samtredia seemed to us the Promised Land—it was quiet, peaceful, and people were selling pears and corn flat bread. But later we came to hate Samtredia: we couldn't get out of there.

As soon as the ticket counter opened, a bellowing crowd rushed over, and while were were making our way to our goal, using our elbows to help, the cashier said, *"No teekeets!"* and slammed the window shut. We went to the station guard on duty. He ignored us. N. got into an argument with him and threatened to write about him to the newspaper. He waved our assignment orders, which, signed by the provost of the institute, looked impressive, though they actually didn't mean a thing.

"Your papers mean zilch to me!" the guard said and swept them onto the floor without reading them. Then he said, "You won't get out of here alive!" We had to spend the night in Samtredia. We were afraid to spend the night in the station: that was the guard's territory and he could harass us there. N. proposed that we sleep in the square at the base of the Lenin monument, which was illuminated all night.

"Here they won't dare touch us," N. said. We were afraid that they would attack us and abduct Nadya. All this time N. kept quietly humming, "Enemy whirlwinds swirl above us . . ." He had begun to annoy me. Nadya calmly lay down on my raincoat, covered up with his jacket, and went to sleep, and we

guarded her, and grumbled and argued all night. I remember we swore at
each other over Akhmatova. But no one attacked us.

The next day we managed to get on a train by evening and we left for
Tbilisi. There our quarrels grew bitter: our money had melted away catastrophically, and I thought that we simply had to go on without delay, but he
took it into his head to stay a few days in Tbilisi. He had a friend there who
had served with him at the front. I objected strenuously. Suddenly, he said
that if I was going to be stubborn I could go on ahead, and they would catch
up with me at Lake Sevan. Something stirred up inside me and burst. As if a
trench had been dug out, a mine laid, and now it exploded.

I asked Nadya, "Do you really want to stay with him in Tbilisi?"

"I don't care," she said. "I'm not rushing anywhere."

An unusual honesty set her apart. But for some reason, her honesty burst
like a bomb and inflicted contusions on people. The friend from the front
couldn't be located, and we went on together. In Yerevan a hundred-degree
heat wave was raging—we just had to dream up a trip to Armenia in July!
The heat turned us into half-corpses: our energy sapped, we lay around in a
room that an old woman had offered us at the station. On the third day N.
advised me to look for a room for myself.

"Somewhere nearby," he said. "Not far from us." And I left them that very
evening. Just that suddenly everything ended. It was my first disappointment:
in friendship, in women, and mainly, in myself. To be so self-confident and
blind! But I didn't suffer for long. I was twenty-one.

Later, my relations with N. recovered, although our previous friendship
was no longer possible. We became distant, but not hostile to each other.
Without half-trying, I noticed that he and Nadya were going together, then
they split up, and about the time we finished the institute they got back together, and for good it seemed. But this didn't affect me. I was busy with
something else. I was writing a book. Other women with straw-colored
braids came and went. Suddenly, I got married. Life flew by in youthful impatience. My second-rate book became famous, a fog obscured my vision, and
then a mountain collapsed on me.

For four years N. had not once come to see me, and suddenly he turned
up. This didn't scare me: he was only a small part of the mountain. But what
was puzzling and what I cannot understand was why did he come and warn
me? Although I cannot understand it now, at the time, suprisingly enough,
when I heard that Nadya had made him come, for some reason I _understood_
and _agreed_. The matter involved a threat of expulsion. I had finished the institute, but had remained a member of the institute Komsomol. The second-rate
book suddenly received a prize. Therefore, it was sweet to expel me. And
there was a reason: in my entrance application I had concealed that my father

was an enemy of the people, which I had never believed. What N. had said when he came to see me at night was sheer madness. And what Nadya had demanded from him, which implied honesty and openness, was also sheer madness. Everything was sheer madness; the month of May, the prize, the expulsion, the applause, and the animosity. And perhaps the plea for remission of sins was also madness. They would have liked for me to say to them, "Go ahead!" and maybe they heard the words "Go ahead!" for I muttered something incoherent, as in a dream, yawned, and shook hands on parting. Sometimes dreams such as these do occur. All the absurd things that happen during the dream seem incredibly logical and perfectly reasonable, but when you wake up, you can't for the life of you figure out why all that hocus-pocus seemed so clear to you. So, all the speakers talked only about the entrance application. They needed more, something concrete that would confirm that I was *rotten inside,* that the case of the application was merely evidence of a general *rottenness,* the way feverish lips are evidence of a breakdown of the whole organism with a cold. N. spoke with difficulty, as if it was painful. It was hard for him. After all, he had been on friendly terms with me. He could barely put words together. He said that he had a torturously dual relationship with me: on the one hand this, on the other hand, unquestionably, that. Details are important in such things: well, for example, what I once said about Akhmatova. This was long ago, but so much the worse for me. That is, already at that time I had some faulty ideas. Once I praised so-and-so. Another time I was all upset about something. Once I teased him when he wanted to sing revolutionary songs. But I was not a hopeless case, however. Therefore he was against expulsion, and for a severe reprimand and warning. After long arguments the meeting decided just that way. But the Regional Committee expelled me; the minor details of N.'s testimony were good enough for that. Later, the City Committee reinstated me with a stiff rebuke, or as people used to say then, half-lovingly—a "stiffy."

In the Tyrol all of this seemed ancient; by now it had receded into such a biblical antiquity that you suddenly thought: did all this happen to me? Maybe I dreamed it. Maybe someone told me a pack of tall tales, and in my mind everything got turned around and upside down? Someone said that in Russia a writer has to live a long time: and it is true, you can come upon many surprises and marvels. Time darkens the past with an ever-thickening veil, and you won't see through it, for it's pitch-dark. Because the veil is in us. And the surprises also disappear behind the same veil. Chekhov could have lived to see the war. As an old man, he could have sat as an evacuee in Chistopol, have somehow lived on ration cards, read the newspapers, and listened to the radio. With a hand growing weak, he could have written something important and necessary for that moment. He could have reacted to the liberation of Taganrog, but how would he have viewed his own past, remaining behind the dusk of days? His own *Uncle Vanya*? His own chopped-down orchard? How would he have viewed Olga, who dreamed, "If only we could know! If only we could know!" As soon as we find something out, it vanishes into a fog. Indeed, Anton Pavlovich would have been able to find out before Chistopol about things that poor Olga wouldn't have dared to dream of. So, he found out—and so what? He couldn't find out the main thing—how the war would end. But we know this.

Strolling at night along the highway in front of the Stubental Hotel, I suddenly decided: I have to have it out with N. Why I had to was unclear. But I was possessed by the idea. Now, when it's all stopped hurting, and we're both free of those days, and the waves are rolling us in different directions, it's easy to ask: why did you do it? I began to wait for a convenient time. While the games were going on, we rarely met: I was watching hockey; he, figure skating. And then it was all over. The hotel proprietor smiled for the first time as he said good-bye to us, and we left by bus for Vienna, stopping along the way to have a look at this and that. The weather was warm. We were tanned, as if we had been in the south. In the bus he looked friendly and again nodded amiably, as though nothing had happened. Sometimes he would ask me something insignificant in passing: "Do you know what the next stop will be?" or, "Did you happen to notice where the bathroom is?" I always answered dryly. I thought: "Just wait, I'll ask you something altogether different. You'll stop smiling!" On the second day after lunch in Salzburg, we went on an excursion to a castle which housed a medieval torture chamber. I thought: "Here's the very place!"

Everyone was feeling a little high after lunch—we wandered through the huge castle laughing and joking, and lingered in the passages and halls of the dungeon, where in the semi-darkness, as luck would have it, instruments of torture stood on end and the two of us turned up alone in one of the rooms. I asked him, "Listen, I've been waiting a long time to ask you, just out of curiosity, why did you try to do me in then?"

He didn't understand. "When?"

"You know, during those years, the devil knows when. They were expelling me. Remember?" We were standing in front of a huge tub into which they used to place a criminal and then, with a windlass, lower him into a well of putrid water with snakes and toads. There the victim was either drowned and his corpse dragged out, or he was kept half-drowned, then tortured and forced to tell his secrets. This information was conveyed on a plaque inscribed in beautiful Gothic letters. This occurred in the sixteenth century. We looked into the depths of the well. It was now dry, but had no bottom. Our voices disappeared in a rumble below.

I knew what he would say. "I swear to you, old man, I acted sincerely! We were fools. I believed that you needed to be punished, that your father was an enemy, and that mercy shows weakness. If you like, one should feel sorry not for you, but for us sincere fools."

I would answer: "But the difference is that you fools weren't threatened by anything, but I was, of being without work, without money, and maybe, without a home, without a family. Times were grim, but that didn't trouble you fools. What could one expect from you? You acted sincerely. There's nothing nobler and more remarkable than sincerity!"

"Are you calling that into question?"

"If it means sincerely forgetting about conscience, about other people's suffering—then to hell with sincerity! You didn't give a thought to what your sincerity was turning into. You didn't give a damn what was happening to the people who ran up against your sincerity, shining with its satanic light! And you know on the day of the damned meeting, my mother..." All of a sudden a crimson cloud of rage sailed into me.

"Your sincerity is villainy." And grabbing the puny N. below his knees, I lightly lift him over the well and throw him across the barrier. He plops into the tub. There's a inhuman scream, the windlass crank begins to turn, faster and faster, the tub crashes below, the scream dies out, the crank turns on and out of control, and I run up the stone stairway. In the bus no one notices that N. is not there. It only dawns on them two hours later. They turn back. Everyone has suddenly sobered up. They run through the castle looking for him, wailing, calling, while I sit on the porch and smoke. Gradually, the terrible truth becomes clear. "Well?" they ask each other with terrified eyes. And someone says, *"But you know, there was something out of kilter with him."*

"Where?"

"In Innsbruck."

"What was it?"

"He stood around a lot on the street reading notices..."

N. looked at me in fright and, shaking his head, whispered, "You've forgotten everything, old man. I didn't try to do you in. I tried to save you."

"Save me?"

"Of course, I shifted the course of the meeting. They wanted to expel you, but after my speech they gave you a 'stiffy.' You thanked me. Don't you remember?"

"I remember something else: you said something about Akhmatova, about my being two-faced."

He stared at me with wide eyes, as if I were a madman, and then grabbed me by the shoulders and shook me. "No way! I saved you! I dragged you out of the fire! Later, I caught it: why, they said, did you go out of your way to defend him? He's scum. I quarreled because of you. How strange that you've forgotten everything."

Yes, I did forget, I didn't remember, I mixed it up, everything disappeared into a fog. He stretched a tentative hand out to me, and I shook it tentatively. We climbed up out of the dungeon into the open air. The snowy white backbone of the mountain flashed in the blue sky. The alpine spring was in full swing. Music floated over from the bus—our driver had turned on Mozart. He liked to doze to music.

I thought about the thick books at the Stubental Hotel: in fact, there really is nothing else in the world but snow, sun, music, girls, and the fog which comes with time.

Fifteen years have passed since our visit to the torture chamber, and it is also covered in fog. N. died of heart disease eight years ago. I don't know what became of Nadya. I haven't been to the stadium for a long time now, and I watch hockey on television.

1986

Translated by Byron Lindsey

Vitaly Moskalenko

The Wild Beach

"Okay, come on out!" shouts the watchman. He's standing by a mountain of empty crates in a corner of the market. "Come on out! I'm talking to you, dammit all!"

Not a sound from under the crates.

"Filya, you hear me? Don't try any monkey business. Come on like a good boy, or else I'll call a cop. You hear me?"

Sunlight floods the market and splinters in fragments on the leaves of the maple tree growing between the stacks of empty crates.

"Say something, you fool! I've caught you, understand? I heard you singing."

Silence.

"You want me to come in and drag you out of there? Then for sure... Then I promise you... What's that?"

A mutter is heard from under the crates.

"I can't hear you. Louder!" shouts the guard and stretches his neck toward the sound.

"Move away from the crates," a voice calls out.

"What for?"

"Move away..."

"Why move away? I don't get it... Ah-hah! You're afraid I'll start hitting you. No, I won't... Come on out!"

Silence.

"Okay, okay. I'm moving to the side. I've moved off."

The guard moves about thirty feet away and turns around.

"Come on out!" he shouts.

A head appears beside the maple trunk.

"Move off further," says the head.

"Further where? This is already far away."

The head makes no response and just looks at the watchman.

"Well, all right. That's enough of your games," says the watchman. "Come on out! I won't touch you."

The head doesn't move. They look at each other for a long time.

"So what's the silence all about? Feeling guilty, huh? Well, all right, I'll move back further..." The watchman moves off a bit, then shouts in a bossy tone, "Come out, Filipych, I'm not kidding. I've got a dozen things to do in the market. I don't have time to fool around with you!"

The head disappears and reappears in a straw hat. Then it raises its eyes upwards.

"Tweet, tweet, tweet!" The head chirps like a sparrow.

"You think you can kid around, you scum!" the guard yells out. "I'll turn you over to the militia!"

Some hands appear above the head, and clutching at a branch, a man of forty or fifty climbs out onto the crates. His pants and shirt are all rumpled, and, standing on the top, he stares at the watchman.

"Come on, come on..." the watchman says softly, sucking in his breath. "Come on down."

"But what's that you got behind your back?" asks the man.

"Where?" the watchman asks in surprise.

"Behind your back there..."

"There's nothing there. What's wrong with you?"

The man carefully begins to descend, without taking his eyes off the watchman. Suddenly he stops.

"What's wrong?" asks the guard.

"Whatta you mean, what's wrong! You're coming too close!"

"Me? What are you talking about! I'm standing still... Don't be afraid, come on—I won't touch you."

The man sees the watchman awkwardly hide something behind his back and looks up skyward again.

"Tweet, tweet, tweet," go his lips, but more softly than before. His head, tilted upward, is frozen in place, but his eyes look down at the watchman. "How come you're all tensed up like an old hound dog?" the man adds.

"Who's tensed up?" the watchman says, flustered. "Who's an old hound dog?"

"You're all tensed up. You're buzzing like a telegraph pole. Take it easy now. You won't catch me!"

"Filipych, Filipych! Don't you argue with me, you scum. I'm gonna give you hell! Come on down this minute! Come on, move it!"

The man climbs down a little lower. As soon as his leg touches the ground, the watchman is off and running, grabbing a stick from behind his back as he shouts, "Okay, you bum, hold it. I'll teach you to play tricks on an old man!"

The man dodges the blow, but it's too late for the watchman to stop: even as he flies past, he manages to land a blow with the stick on the man's back. He misses with his second blow and almost falls. The man runs off to the side, and prancing around, yells some gibberish. "Karri-marri-darri-farri! One fool beats another fool! One fool beats another fool!"

"You watch out!" Chuckling with pleasure, the watchman threatens him again with the stick. "By God, you're asking for it!" He flings the stick aside and shouts to the man in the straw hat, who's walking away. "Where are you off to? There's the gate over there. Over there!"

"I know!" the fellow says without turning around and goes toward the exit.

That's Filipych. A Holy Fool. He's part and parcel of County Seat*—like the train station, the market, the courthouse, and the beer stand near the movie theater. Tall and thin, with a large head and a high forehead. His hair—flaxen, sun-bleached and dirty—hangs in curls around his forehead. Only his eyes give him away: helpless, kind, frightened eyes—round and blue, with enlarged pupils. Prancing and skipping along, Filipych comes to the square in front of the market.

"Karri-marri-darri-farri!" he shouts in a nasty tone. He wants to be on the safe side—in case the day turns out to be the way he senses it will—a rough one. People were milling about and cars passing: at the center stood a militiaman with his back to Filipych.

"Hey, you!" he says to the militiaman. "You diddler! Whatta you standing around here for like a prick, huh?"

The militiaman turns around with a yawn. "I'm gonna catch you now and work you over..." he says indifferently and looks down at his polished boots. "Where'd you spend the night? Inside the market?"

"'Work you over...'" Filipych repeats and looks back. His conversation with the militiaman is short and simple. "I spent the night where I wanted to."

"If you sleep inside the market one more time, I'm gonna turn you over to the nut hospital. Keep it in mind! You've got a home, and there's no reason for you to be bumming around. Get out and look for a job..." The militiaman doesn't finish his sentence, as if suddenly recalling who it is.

"Ha-ha-ha!" Filipych laughs. "But I don't have a passport!"

Raitsentr, literally, district center.

"And just where is your passport?"

"I lost it. About ten years ago. Ha-ha-ha!"

"Okay, okay... I've told you! Why don't you just bug off?" The militiaman carefully examines his polished boots, especially the back of the tops and the heels.

Sunday's a big market day. Kolkhoz trucks and private cars drive up to the market square.

Filipych stands at the gate and sets up a checkpoint. He bows to the left and to the right, takes off his hat, sticks out his tongue, dances and sings. The cars drive through the gate, and the drivers laugh soundlessly behind their windows while Filipych laughs in reply. He's happy that the day's started, that all around there's a lively hustle and bustle, and people are looking and pointing their fingers at him.

The market's going full swing, people buying and selling. Filipych sits on the same huge pile of tomato crates as before, at the very top, beside the maple branches. You can see his gray head from far away. The watchman has left, so now he can have a peaceful breakfast. Tomatoes, green onions, and boiled potatoes are laid out on a newspaper in front of him. In the market down below a huge crowd swarms and snakes its way around the stalls: the play of colors in the sun—blues, reds, greens on sateen or homespun cloth— is like a magnificent scarf held and shaken lightly by the corners. A steady, ceaseless din hovers over the market. Sometimes a car makes its way slowly through the crowd and apparently honks: people jump aside like bees. From time to time lines form at different ends of the market, but just as quickly disappear. Dust hangs over the throng of people, colors, and sounds. It's County Seat brown dust that seems to have come out of nowhere—not from the market, which is paved.

Filipych eats everything to the last crumb, rolls up the newspaper and hides it between the crates. Then he looks at the sun, picks his teeth with his tongue, straightens his hat, and for several minutes whistles, "Tweet, tweet, tweet!" Finally he makes his way down and walks through the market, looking around in case something good turns up.

"How much?" he asks and points at a stack of apples.

"Get away from here, you dummy!" the plump woman selling the apples answers with a laugh. "Don't start begging. There's no way I'm gonna give you any."

"But can I just try one? Maybe I'll want to buy a whole sack—who knows?" Filipych cocks his hat over his eyes and examines her hips and bust. Her body bulges out in soft contours from under a thin cotton dress, like dough spilling out from a baked crust of a loaf of bread—fragrant and hot—

too hot to touch. Filipych moves a step closer. "I can buy some apples and whatever else I want!"

"Yeah, you won't buy 'em!" the plump woman says and turns red. "You haven't got any money."

Filipych rummages in his pocket and draws out a dirty ruble. "Look!" he says and suddenly starts to laugh. He laughs in little spurts, as if hiccuping. A minute earlier an onlooker might have thought that from beneath his cocked hat some town stud and loafer was sizing up the apples and the plump woman's hips at the same time. But now it's obvious that the man who was dancing barefoot along the town pavement is sick, that he's what old women call a Holy Fool. He's one of those guys who, even now in places like County Seat, get chased and teased without mercy by boys who shout: "Two-four-six-eight! Let's give your head a break!"

"What you talkin' about, huh?" Filipych says and conspicuously puts the ruble back in his pocket, then chooses the biggest apple in the bunch and takes a bite out of it.

"So now, whatta you say? You're not gonna buy a single one, are ya?" cries the apple woman, swinging her hips and laughing heartily.

"No, they're sour. They were okay last Sunday, but now they're sour."

"Well, you polished one off then and didn't pay either."

"When do you mean? Whatta you talking about?"

"Me?!" says the plump woman, and looking around, blushes and walks up to Filipych. "Okay, give me your ruble! Get it out of your pocket, come on, or I'll get it out myself!"

"He's got a hole in his pocket!" someone in the crowd says. "Maybe you'll grab something else out of there along with the ruble. You might get hold of something you didn't count on!"

People laugh and a crowd gathers around Filipych and the plump woman, as the two of them face each other down.

"Hey, Filya, show her where to get off!" someone shouts from the crowd.

Filipych provides entertainment on market days, but on this day when the curious get to be too many, a militiaman's cap appears above the heads of the crowd and a pair of polished boots make their way through the throng. Right away the circle of onlookers breaks apart at the other side, and Filipych quickly vanishes into thin air.

"There he is! Over there! Catch him!" someone shouts weakly, just to be on the safe side.

The crowd disperses, and suddenly there's not a soul to be seen hanging around where the plump woman and the militiaman stand.

"What happened?" asks the militiaman, holding himself erect. His sparkling boots blind everyone. The plump woman gets flustered.

"What's the problem, lady?" he asks again. "What kind of fuss is going on here? You were yelling loud enough to drown out all the buses and trucks! I could hear you screaming clear from the square!"

"Well, I was just selling my apples, and he started hassling me," the woman says.

"Who's 'he?'"

"Him—the crazy guy."

"Now it's beginning to make sense! And just how did he hassle you?"

"How? Oh, the same old way. He ate one of my apples."

"Just one?" he asks, shifting his feet importantly.

"What?" the fat woman asks in turn.

"You mean he ate one apple, not several?"

"One."

"Are we going to make a complaint?"

"What?"

"A complaint. Are we gonna file?"

"What for? To heck with it! It's only an apple."

"So that's your attitude? To heck with him, then?"

"Yeah, it wasn't really out of spite... He was hungry..."

"But it's a case of theft! What do you mean it wasn't 'out of spite'? What do you mean, 'he was hungry'? Are you kidding me? After all, he stole something from you, and here you are, defending him."

"Who, me?! Defending him?!"

"Who else?! I'll make out a complaint right now and arrest him! Later we'll put him in jail. So, are ya coming?"

"Where to?" she says in alarm. "Coming where?"

"To the police station."

"Are you crazy?! I'm not going anywhere. I'm supposed to be selling apples!"

"You won't go?" asks the militiaman.

"No way!"

"Well, okay... How much are your apples? Can I try one?"

"Go ahead."

Then the militiaman, squinting down at the reflection of sunlight on the tops of his boots, eats an apple.

"Sort of sour, but not too bad, really. How much are you asking for them?"

"Forty kopecks a pound, three pounds for a ruble."

"Pretty high." The militiaman turns on his heel and strides to the exit.

———

Around noontime a rosy haze settles over the town. People walk slowly and lazily along the streets. Dust and heat envelop the streets and houses like a cocoon. Life has come to a standstill and must wait five more hours until it can reappear from the nooks and crannies and assert itself again. Once in a long while, trucks whiz through the streets—as if frightened by something. Then again there's silence. No dogs, no birds—nothing makes a sound. There's not even a sigh to be heard...

Only one place shows a sign of life—like the pulse of someone sleeping... There, slowly and languidly, tongues wag and feet keep time—along with hands and beer mugs. That's at the beer stand.

About thirty men are standing or sitting or lying around the place. The serving counter—set up beside a movie billboard—has collapsed on one end, and there's no room for all the drinkers. So, with their beer mugs and little spread of kippers, they sit on newspapers or simply on the grass under a mulberry tree—and talk. Here they rake over all the latest in the family, the town, the county, the area, and the whole wide world.

And this is where Filipych heads. He starts even from a distance. "Karri, marri, darri, farri!" he shouts and does a jig. "Hi, guys! I'm on my way! I'll show you everything you want to see! Just give me a minute!"

But nobody pays any attention except one guy. Misha Zemleroi has staked out a place for himself near the billboard at the end of the counter. Zemleroi is actually a nickname. Nobody remembers his real name. The billboard is a piece of white paper with large, crude lettering in an ink marker announcing *Phantomas on a Rampage*.

Misha hasn't been able to find a place in the shade, so he sits broiling in the sun... His face is bruised from last night's brawl. With legs spread wide for balance, he sways like a sailor wobbling through a storm and watches Filipych run.

"God, it's hot," Misha says and stares at Filipych running. "A real scorcher," he repeats as he looks down at the empty beer mugs. "Look! Look! Look over there! Hey, he sure knows how to run!" He nods in Filipych's direction. "He's runnin' for a swig of beer. He may be a Holy Fool, but he likes a taste of beer! How about another round or two?" Zemleroi asks the guy beside him.

But his friend just nods and sets his gaze far, far away into the clouds. Even when his hair falls over his eyes, he doesn't brush it aside. So Misha takes the mug out of his hands and, as if staggering along a ship deck in heavy seas, goes up to the bar.

"Varya, gimme another round," he says, his head drooping.

"Where'll you put it?" Varya answers lazily. "You're already up to the gills!"

"Shh!" Misha says as he grabs an armful of mugs on the sly, turns around and moves off, swaying like a boat sailing away from a wharf. "Ya hear,

Seryozha?" He shoves his friend on the shoulder. "Wake up, Seryozha. Your old mom's come and brought some fresh milk for her sonny boy. Ya hear?"

Seryozha grabs the wet mug with two hands.

"He-e-y, guys, hey, kids!" he jokes back with half-numb lips. His hair has fallen in his eyes, but he looks doggedly straight ahead, beyond the horizon.

"I wa-a-a-nna swig a beer," Misha says with a grimace. "I waaa-a-a-nna swig!"

Filipych, meanwhile, doing his jig, goes up to the stand and grins as if he's about to say something weighty for everyone concerned. He waits wide-eyed for some response and, beaming, looks first at Misha Zemleroi and then at Varya, who, in her greasy smock, keeps on shoving out mugs of beer.

"Hey, you guys!" he yells. "I'm here—come to drink beer with ya."

"But we weren't really waiting for you," says Misha quietly and with a scowl.

"Yeah, like we really missed you a lot," Varya drawls out with a yawn big enough to fill the window of her beer stand. "We just couldn't wait!"

"But I just thought I'd drop in and see you," Filipych says and swirls around.

"Come on, do the goose step—like the soldiers in a parade," somebody shouts from under the mulberry tree.

Filipych does his goose step and everybody laughs.

"And how do dogs scratch themselves? Come on, show us!"

Filipych squats, goes down on all fours and scratches his side with his right foot. They all laugh even harder.

"And how does a woman piss? Show us that one, Filipych."

"No, no! A militiaman will cart me off. I know that for sure!" Filipych laughs.

"But they're not around! Come on, show us!"

"Aw, I'd have to take off my pants. No, not a chance!"

"Okay, come on, show us. Don't be coy!" Misha Zemleroi says, moving over to Filipych. "Come on, come on. You didn't earn your mug of beer last time!"

"When do ya mean 'didn't earn it?!'" Filipych yells. "I sure did. I did every-thing. Don't give me a hard time!"

"No, you promised to do a Polish jig, but didn't deliver, and then you moved in on my beer!"

"I didn't drink a drop of your beer. I didn't!"

"Come on, come on..." Misha grabs Filipych by the arms and, hunching down, gets ready to dance.

"Let go, you creep!" Filipych screams. "Karri-marri-darri-farri! Let go!"

"Don't give me your 'karri' routine. We've heard it before. Come on, dance! Earn your mug of beer fair and square."

"He cheated us, he cheated..." Seryozha softly repeats to himself. "I remember..." and almost drops his mug. "I see it a-a-all. You can't fool me."

"Come on, dance, dance, you fool!" Misha squats down, pulling Filipych along. He presses him down to the ground, and at first Filipych resists a little, but then bends double like a finger joint.

"Come on, come on. You didn't earn that mug, you conned us! Vovka's not here today. Nobody's gonna stick up for you. I'm gonna skin you alive for that mug! Come on!"

The laughing stops.

"Leave him alone, Zemleroi, leave the poor fool alone," someone calls out to say from under the mulberry tree.

"Whatta you mean 'leave him alone?!' He's swigging my beer, and you want me to leave him alone?! Hey, you gonna dance or not? Dance, I tell you! Fool or no fool, he's not above snitching a free beer!"

"Hey! Hey! Hey! Stop it!" someone shouts in a threatening voice from the other side of the yard. "Let him go! You'll break his bones, you bully!"

Misha lets him go and looks around.

"What'd you say?" asks Misha, jutting out his jaw. "Whatta you blabbering about?"

"Clean your ears out!"

"Who's the bug—uh, big—mouth over there?"

"Who're you calling big mouth?" somebody answers from under the mulberry tree.

"Ah-ha! So it's you, Volodya!" says Misha, backing down with a little smile.

"What! Don't you recognize me?"

"I didn't guess it was you."

"About time you started guessing. Come on, beat it, you jerk!"

"Yes, sir!" Misha salutes and, with a little show no worse than one of Filipych's, sets off in goose step toward his buddy Seryozha, who is holding a mug of beer and looking off somewhere beyond the horizon. "And what are you gawking at?" Misha says, as if taking his humiliation out on Seryozha. "What the hell are you staring at over there day after day?"

"I see something..."

"Whatta you see?"

"I see... I see it all, Misha..."

"Yeah? Tell me about it."

"Easy, easy, now don't touch me or I'll lose it. I see some clouds. And far, fa-ar away—a bird! It's flying away into the sky and doesn't give a damn... It's got no problems..."

"And do you have any problems?!" Misha Zemleroi asks angrily.

"I don't know... But it's there far-fa-a-r away, and I'm here. The bird will fly away, and I'll stay here."

"But where the hell could you go?" With lips swollen from last night's fight, Misha blows the head of foam off the rim of his mug, and, silently and solemnly, the two friends go on sipping their beers.

Half an hour later Filipych is sitting in the heat of the sun, leaning against the beer stand. His hat is lying beside him on the pavement and he has the same befuddled, bleary-eyed look as all the others. A stray dog has curled up at his feet: it's the dog that eats the scraps of fish and food found around the beer stand and then gets sick for a long time and coughs up the bones. The dog has put his head on his front paws and is staring at Filipych, and he stares back.

"You're lying here... And I'm sitting... That's it..." Filipych says, taking a sip of beer. "You want a piece of fish and I want a mug of beer... See..."

The dog looks at him without blinking, his tail beating on the pavement. His eyes are listless and sick.

"Everyone wants some beer around here. Me—and him—and him!" Filipych says and points around. "But you want some fish... And I don't have any fish. I've got some beer. But you don't want any beer..."

"Yes, he does," somebody said from above.

Filipych raises his head. Varya's eyes are shining through the stand's little window.

"It drinks beer..."

"The dog?"

"Who else? You think I'm talking about myself? I can't bear to look at beer..."

"There... Karri-marri... Have some..." Filipych says and splashes a little beer on the pavement. "There, have some..."

The dog looks at Filipych, then at the puddle of beer flowing out in front of its nose.

"There, there... drink..." Filipych says. "Both of us will have a drink... Who else are we gonna drink with, huh? There, there, drink!"

The stream of beer foam spreads, but the dog waits until the puddle reaches his front paws. Only then does he bend his head and, without getting up, lap at the beer. He licks up a bit, looks at Filipych and occasionally beats his tail heartily against the pavement. When the dog has lapped up the beer and even licked off the spot where it spilled, he rests his head on his front paws and stares at Filipych again. The dog gets high very fast. His eyelids begin to quiver, he stops beating his tail, but goes on looking at the place where Filipych's eyes should be. And he gazes back at the dog. So they sit, silently fixated on each other. All at once the dog yelps and, reeling a bit, runs off to the side. Filipych looks at the dog without understanding what's happened. Still yelping, the dog runs over to the beer stand and starts howling softly, his tail hanging between his legs.

"And that's what that dog does all day long!" Varya says from behind the window. "Chase it away—the pest—it's crazy! You alcoholic bastards have turned a miserable dog into a drunk." Varya pronounces "alcoholic bastards" as lightly as if she were saying "sewing machine operators." "Hey, ya hear me?" Varya shouts. "Chase that dog outta here. I'm sick of it, more than I'm sick of you—you alcoholic bastards, ya hear!"

"Now whatta you want?" somebody asks from under the mulberry tree and a tanned face peers out. "Whatta you fussing about?"

"Come on, chase the dog outta here!"

"Chase who out?"

"This damn... dog!" Varya points down at something beneath her window, and it looks as if Filipych is the one who's supposed to be chased off.

"Oh, let him be! What's wrong, is he buggin' ya?"

"Yeah, he's buggin' me!" Varya shouts and her pale nose and painted lips protrude noticeably as she sticks half of her face out the little window. "It doesn't bother you at all, but it bothers me. You get the dog drunk, then it fouls the place up, but none of you would pick up a shovel and clean up after it!"

"Clean what up?" asks the voice from under the mulberry. "Var, what's got into you? Cut out the bullshit! Hey, look, guys! It's time to get ole Varka off to a doctor..."

"I'll shut this place down in a minute and you can all go to hell. You'll get diddly squat from me... You big blabbermouths!"

The dog, meanwhile, runs over to a place midway between the beer stand, the counter for the mugs, and the mulberry tree, raises his head, and starts howling.

"So, you like its howling, right?" Varya says in the same fussy tone. "Get away from here, you pest! Get away!"

"The dog senses something," says a tall, well-built, muscular, and curly-haired guy who walks out from under the mulberry tree. "It's not howling for nothing..."

He looks at the dog, but the dog runs off to the side and, with his tail tucked between his legs, barks in one direction and then the other.

"Chase him off, Volodya. I can't take it any longer," Varya goes on complaining. A man the spitting image of Volodya, only smaller, appears from under the mulberry.

"They sense all kinds of things—dogs do," he says, stretching himself. "Earthquakes... and stuff."

"This is my brother, Timur," Volodya proudly tells Varya and points to his brother. "My older brother. He's a scientist and all that stuff. He's studying in Moscow."

They go up to Filipych.

"Get up," Volodya tells him. "Wanna go with us to the river?"

"I want a beer... Buy me one, okay?"

"Forget the beer... We've got some vodka. Wanna go?"

"*Vodochka?*" Filipych says with a smile? "I'll go, but buy me another beer anyway..."

"Buy him one," says Timur, examining Filipych's clothes with revulsion. "Is he the one?"

"That's him! Sure is!"

"Oh, man! Volod! I thought this was going to be something worth the effort!"

"It's worth it all right—you'll see. But we better go or we'll get caught in the rain," he says, looking at the sky. "And we have to bring her back..."

"You think she'll be there?"

"You bet. We agreed on it."

Timur looks at Filipych again. "Hi! I'm Timur. Let's get acquainted," he says and extends his hand.

"Buy me a beer, dog," Filipych says with a laugh. "Ha-ha-ha!"

"What's his problem?" Timur asks in surprise.

"Don't pay any attention. He has these spells."

Volodya grabs a mug of beer and gives it to Filipych, who starts downing it as he looks closely at Timur.

"Dog, dog, dog!" he says, choking on his beer. "I can see that he's a dog. There's his tail! There, I see it!"

"God," Timur says softly. "Volod, he's nuts!"

"Shut up, Filya!" Volodya hushes him up and takes the empty mug out of Filipych's hands and nudges him toward the mulberry tree.

"Fangs, fangs, dog hair, dog hair!" Filipych is shouting now. "He's a dog!"

"Okay, that's enough outta you," says Timur, shaking his finger at Filipych, and he puts on his helmet.

"Get the bikes going!" Volodya yells from under the mulberry tree. "It's gonna rain."

With a roar of engines, four motorcycles soon roll out onto the lot in front of the beer stand. The drivers raise a howl as they gun the engines. The mufflers have been removed, and in their painted helmets and visors the bikers look like medieval knights, only with puny little bodies and without chain and spears. Volodya is the only one who sits astride his bike like a giant. His hair sticks out in curls from under his helmet; his muscles bulge at the seams of his tee shirt. He nods toward the back seat of his motorcycle: "Come on, Filipych! Get on!"

The motorcycles blast off, raising dust and scaring the sparrows out of the mulberry tree. The whole line of beer drinkers watches the cavalcade of puny, twentieth-century knights in their big plexiglas helmets. And through the dust from his back seat Filipych yells, "Karri-marri-darri-farri!"

He sticks out his tongue, twists in his seat, and grins.

As everyone watches silently, out of nowhere the dog appears and chases the last motorcycle from all sides. The dog runs after them for a long time, barking and barking until, finally exhausted, he raises his head and howls.

A bridge stands high above the water, and the dappled sunshine reflected on the rushing water illuminates the bridge from below. Sandy beaches extend along both sides of the bridge. About a hundred yards from the railroad, barbed wire fences close off the beaches. This is a zone guarded by soldiers—a place forbidden to outsiders. A forest stretches out beyond the river and its beaches. A soldier stands in faded fatigues on the bridge. He has a rifle on his back and binoculars in his hands. Supporting himself on the bridge rail, the soldier trains his binoculars on a spot below. But on that side, where he's looking, a concrete piling juts out from the old bridge—a kind of pier, which hinders the soldier's view. He's fidgets about, moves from place to place, but clearly nothing works out. The soldier wipes the sweat from his brow and shifts his rifle from one shoulder to another.

It's sultry. Swallows fly low over the sand, and beneath them a woman is lying on the beach. She's sunning herself without a bra, and her daughter Olenka is nestled on the white quartz sand beside her. The mother has stuck a plantain leaf on her nose and a copy of *Woman Worker* under her head.

Olenka can't lie still like her mother any longer. With short little steps she gets up and then sits down every other minute, blocking the soldier's view. He's gotten all worked up, he wipes the sweat off his face and quietly curses.

Olenka doesn't want to lie down. She wants to run and jump in the water. From behind her hand she looks at her mother and sticks out her lower lip.

"Mama, hey, Mama, I think I'll run around a little..."

"No, lie down and keep still."

Olenka watches the swifts diving at the water. It looks as if they're certain to hit the water one after another, but at the last minute they soar upward in black, curving, spiral lines. They wind into the heavy, midday air and disintegrate into the sky like petals of an instantly fading flower.

"Mama, hey, Mama. Just a little bit, please, huh?"

"Lie still."

Olenka digs a little hole in the sand and sticks her tiny finger in it.

"But later maybe, when Uncle Volodya comes. Can I then?"

"And how do you know he'll come?" The mother's voice sounds cross.

"Whenever we come to the wild beach, he always comes, doesn't he?"

"I don't know what you're talking about. How'd that get into your head?" the mother asks with a sudden interest.

"How? Just whenever we..."

"Okay, that's enough!" The mother hushes her up. "You're a little smarty pants."

In the spring Olenka had pneumonia, and all summer her mother has been bringing her to this wild, undeveloped beach: she thought the warm sun and sand would help her recover and she often sunbathes herself here in the nude. The soldier on the day shift has been watching through his binoculars all summer.

Olenka sees a horsefly light on her mother and thinks it will sting her. Just as she tries to grab it, her mother swats her thigh and the fly falls from her hand onto her bare breast. Regally swaying her full, white breasts, the mother shakes the fly off onto the sand and turns over on her stomach. Olenka picks up the dead horsefly and examines it. Smashed by what must seem a monstrous force, its wings shake slightly, its legs claw spasmodically at a space through which it will fly no more. The soldier trains his binoculars, but immediately lowers them, and, propping his head on his hand, takes a break from watching. He grimaces and teeth show through his thin lips as he gazes gloomily down at the water. From his perch he can see big fish swimming in the depths. In the evening they swim closer to the surface. It's in the evening that they cross the current, thrashing through the swell of water and twisting their powerful, slick bodies as they slowly plunge back down. This is when they seem like mermaids to the soldier.

Olenka sits down, makes a little grave, drops the horsefly into it, and sticks a twig on top. Then she destroys the mound, gets the fly out again and tosses it around.

"Mama, somebody's coming," she says.

Her mother gets up and listens. She can clearly hear a growing sputter of motors. There's a bang like the pop of a balloon and the sounds get louder, and voices yell over the din. Olenka's mother fastens her bra.

Volodya rides onto the beach with a roar, tearing up the sand. Timur follows and two other motorcycles are close behind.

"Water, water, water!" Filipych jumps off the motorcycle and runs toward the water ahead of all the others.

With a flying leap he flops into the water with his clothes on, turns over on his back, then again onto his stomach, then dives. His hat floats downstream, but he catches up with it, grabs it, and raising it high above the water, shouts, "Karri-marri-darri-farri!"

"Filya, Filya, show us a trick, show us something!" With a pleading glance at her mother, Olenka runs toward the water.

Filya stands on all fours in the water, breaks into a protracted bark, then wades onto the sand. He sprinkles Olenka with water, smiling and chuckling with pleasure. She screams in delight, pressing her arms to her chest, and glances back at her mother, who, arching her back and rubbing herself with suntan lotion, pretends not to see the motorcyclists.

Volodya turns off the engine, puts his motorcycle on its stand, and walks over to to her.

"Hi!" he says as he takes off his helmet and shakes his hair.

"Hello, Volodya."

"Like we agreed... Three o'clock. No, I'm twenty minutes late."

She rubs the lotion into her stomach and hips.

"Is something wrong?" he asks.

"What should be wrong?"

"I don't know... You sound funny?"

"What do you mean 'funny'?"

"Len, what's the matter?"

Lena doesn't answer. Volodya purses his thin lips and looks her straight in the eyes. Lena looks up at him and suddenly smiles.

"Volodya, hon, couldn't you have come alone? Why'd you drag all of them here? Who needs them here? Do you want them here? Do I? I don't understand..."

The last motorcycle engine shuts off. There's silence. A stifling haze hangs over the wild beach. There's not a sound—except in Volodya's head, where he either still hears the banging drone of their frantic ride or the words he wants to say to her now. Volodya looks at his girl friend and drums his knuckles on his helmet.

"Yeah, it's time to drop her..." he thinks to himself as, with a wave of the hand, he announces: "Meet my brother. He's just arrived from Moscow this morning. Timur—Elena... She's a good friend of mine."

"Nice to meet you."

"Me, too." Lena takes a long time screwing the cap on the lotion tube, rises and walks out to the water without a word.

"You want us to stay or go?" Volodya yells at her as she leaves.

"No, stay," Lena says without turning around.

"So you don't mind?" He drums his knuckles again on the helmet.

"No, I don't mind." Lena stops and gives him a look that makes all the other guys flustered, and they start taking off their helmets and quietly making small talk. "Maybe it's better that he find out, huh?.. Whatta you think?.."

"Maybe so."

"That's just what I say." Lena moves away, stepping gingerly with her long legs on the blistering sand. Her hips sway, her body is tinged bronze: she has a beautiful back, beautiful legs, a beautiful body.

Something worth seeing is going on at the water's edge! Filipych is standing on his hands, waving his legs in the air, and crowing.

"Rooster, rooster, why are you standing upside down?" Olenka yells.

"I'm a rooster in reverse!" Filipych hops about on his hands and falls onto the sand. "Cockle-doodle-do!"

"Cluck, cluck, cluck!" Olenka imitates a hen and rolls with laughter.

Her mother jerks her up and tells her quietly, "Go lie down on the sand... Don't get up and don't go near the water!"

"Karri-marri-darri-farri!" Filipych shouts and grins at Elena.

"You're the same as always. You never change. All you need is your 'darri-marri' and so on..."

"Ha-ha-ha-ha!" Filipych laughs in her face. "I'm better off than you! You've got LOTS to deal with!"

A few tomatoes, eggs, a little bacon and some bread are spread out on newspapers, and a bottle of vodka stands in the middle of the circle. Everyone is sitting on the sand and eating at leisure.

"Try to put it away," Volodya says and holds out a glass to Timur.

"Naw, I don't want any," Timur answers and passes the glass on around the circle. "Here, you help out."

"Yeah, I'll help," the guy next to him says and drinks it down.

On the opposite shore there is a cliff with a multitude of nests in holes which swifts fly in and out of, dropping to the water like rocks.

Olenka munches her hard-boiled egg and looks across at the cliff. The soldier watches them through his binoculars as they eat and drink. He's got four more months to serve. Yesterday on the railings of the bridge he carved out the words "YURA LIKHACHYOV DISCHARGED NOVEMBER 19. GOOD-BYE BRIDGE. I'M NOT COMING BACK NEVER."

Timur makes a sandwich and offers it to Lena. "Let me take care of you. You want something to drink?"

"No," Lena says as she looks at Volodya. "I don't drink."

"That's good. It's a form of suicide to drink in this kind of heat."

"But we're drinking!" Volodya smiles at Timur. "And we're doing fine!"

"So far!" Timur moving over closer to Lena. "Do you smoke?"

"No."

"Here, can I peel a cucumber for you?"

"Usually we eat them unpeeled."

"Pour us a round, Volodya."

"You said something about suicide."

"There's no harm in having a drink with such a gorgeous girl." Lena looks flattered, Volodya smiles, and the three of them clink glasses and drink up.

"Are you really a scientist?" Lena asks.

"In a sense—a graduate student."

"This is his fifth year at being a grad student!" Volodya laughs. "Tim, where's the rest of the vodka?"

"Under the seat of the motorcycle. Hey, come to think of it, cool it off in the water!"

"And why haven't I heard anything about you before? Volodya didn't tell me a thing about you."

"I've been away from here so long that everybody just forgot about me."

"Probably you forgot about them."

"Oho! What a dig! Maybe it's true, at that. But, seriously speaking... I don't see any point in wasting my life away in County Seat."

"And what about there—in Moscow?"

"There, too, it's not all sugar and honey."

"It's not a bed of roses here either."

"You've got a sharp little tongue."

"I'm just myself."

"Yeah, it's always greener on the other side, as they say. But I remember you. You're the Lepilins' daughter. You used to live on Komsomolskaya Street, right?"

"Yes."

"Now I remember. I remember. You people had a motorcycle with a side-car."

"We sure did."

"Your older sister was good-looking."

"She sure was. And like you, she left for Moscow. Now she writes heart-breaking letters about how bad it is. She wants to come back home."

"You mean Lyuba's in Moscow! Give me her number. Maybe I'll call her sometime."

"She's got a jealous husband. Really jealous!"

"And you?"

"Don't come on so fast. Don't! I mean it."

"You're right. I got a little carried away. Sorry."

"No need to apologize. It's cool. Life's no snap for any of us... Olenka, put your hat on! It's scorching out here!"

"Yeah, you said it. Life's no snap anywhere. Lots of people got it tough. It's only his kind," Timur points at Filipych, "that couldn't care less."

"You think so? But maybe not."

"Him? Come on, you're kidding! He's got a set of unconditioned reflexes. He's an animal. I remember how, when I was a kid, he used to put frogs in his mouth. Just remembering it makes me sick to my stomach."

"But why are you so mad at the world?"

"Me? I've never thought that."

"You should have. I told you once, Olenka—put on your hat!"

"Really? Why do you say I'm mad at the world? No. I just hate sick people—cripples, weaklings. I hate them."

"See, you said it! 'Hate'—it's your word."

"And what's yours?"

"Mine is—love!"

"Tim!" Volodya shouts. "Come here! I can't open the storage box."

"Okay, I'm coming! You say 'love.' Okay, I understand. But do you love your husband?"

"Tell me—is everybody in Moscow like you?"

"Like what?"

"I don't know... Like you... so sharp."

There's a long silence. Timur and Lena watch Volodya squatting and trying to unlock the storage compartment of his motorcycle. The two other guys, sitting on the other side of the little circle and already tipsy, carry on a conversation. The tall one's name is Dryn, the short one's, Lelik.

"Your chain's loose," Lelik says, "You should tighten it up."

"I should," Dryn answers. He is tall, bony, and freckled.

"I've been hearin' it jump around." Lelik says.

"Yeah, it's jumpin'," Dryn replies.

"Clean it off with some gas... Or take a link off. The chain's got stretched."

"Yeah, I oughtta put a whole new one on."

"Sure, that's a good idea—put a new one on!"

"I don't love my husband," Lena says suddenly in a low voice. "I love Volodya, but he doesn't love me."

"Maybe I shouldn't change 'er?" Dryn says.

"Who?"

"This... chain..."

"Well, maybe not."

"Timur! Come here! I can't unlock it!"

Timur gets up and goes over to Volodya.

"What's the problem?" he asks angrily.

"Look—it's stuck again. I've been wanting to break the damn thing for quite a while!"

"Okay, let's break it open then!"

"I kinda hate to..."

"Why do you hate to?" Timur shoves Volodya aside, grabs the seat with two hands and jerks it off by force. Something rips inside and Timur stumbles on to the sand with the seat in his arms. "That's all it takes!"

"That's the simplest way."

"It's sure the fastest way. Change the lock and your problem's solved. But now how are we gonna divvy up?"

"Divvy up what?"

"Not what, but who! She's a classy piece."

"No way, Tim! It's won't work. Not with her."

"Come on! Everything'll work out fine."

"No, Tim. She's gotta be home in an hour. And for lots of reasons... Tomorrow, we'll do it all tomorrow. Just like we planned: we'll get a tent, a couple of chicks... I've already promised..."

"But that's tomorrow. I want it today."

Volodya doesn't answer. He sticks the bottle of vodka in the water. Timur gazes dully in the direction of the bridge.

"Then let's take turns!" He wrinkles his nose mischievously.

"What?" Volodya raises his head.

With a look of pity Timur takes measure of his brother, who returns his gaze, and Timur ruffles up Volodya's hair with the palm of his hand.

"Okay, okay, little Pioneer. How old are you?"

"Twenty-one."

"Twenty-one," Timur repeats. "Fine... Then, tomorrow?"

"Tomorrow, Timur."

"Okay, then, tomorrow." Timur looks across at the bridge and changes the subject. "Does he jump from here?"

"Who? Filipych?"

"Yeah."

"No, from that pier."

"That's high..."

"Well, what'd you think? About 100 feet."

"He won't crack his skull?"

"Him? Never."

Timur turns away and starts toward their improvised table, then stops.

"But maybe you'll change your mind?" he asks, wrinkling up his nose mischievously again.

"No, no, no... Ya see... She's all hung up on me... She treats me real good. This means something, ya know! Besides, we're friends. And things haven't worked out for her... She rushed into marriage, and now see..."

"Rushed into it..."

"No, Tim, ya see..."

"Yeah, I see everything! What're you blushing for? I was kidding. Just kidding! Where's your sense of humor?"

"I just misunderstood."

"You gotta understand such things. You're not even a Pioneer! You're still a Cub! So this is what I'm gonna do. I'm gonna lie down and take a little snooze... then that fool'll do his jumping stunt, and we'll all go home. That's it! I'm still tired from the train... And in general... I'm tired!" Timur breaks off and stares at the bridge, at the soldier on the bridge, and at the sun.

It becomes stifling hot. Sounds echo in the air as in a steam bath—distinctly and too clearly. Words seem to take on weight and hang fluttering in the air. Dressed in his black sateen shorts, Filipych is sitting beside the water, where he's been for about an hour. He's constructed a sand city around himself, complete with streets and squares, and this city looks like the one he has just come from. Filipych takes wet sand in his hand and sprinkles it around. The water instantly disappears and the sand hardens. Again and again Filipych dribbles the sand down in total concentration and detachment from the world around him.

Timur is lying beside the table where everyone except Filipych is sitting. They had been tossing pieces of bacon and bread to the latter, and he would down them at once.

"Catch!" Dryn had yelled and had thrown the bacon and then the bread.

Filipych caught it, ate it up, and now sits digging in the sand. Lena's putting Olenka down for a nap. Volodya, Lelik, and Dryn pour a round of the vodka. Volodya's not drinking, watching out of the corner of his eye as Lena puts her daughter to bed. He still can't get over the talk with his brother; he pours the vodka and passes it to his friends.

"See if you can lift this—it's heavy stuff," he says to his friend.

"An interesting offer... I accept."

"Well?" the tall one says, frowning.

"It's a little on the warm side."

"Drink it while you've got it."

"I'm not turning it down."

Timur is lying on his stomach, with his head on Lena's magazine. From time to time he opens his eyes, looks above the sand in the direction of the woods. The upper half of the trees looks greenish blue and isn't stirring. The lower half slowly swings rhythmically, melting in the hot sand. And swallows are flying overhead, flying over the sand, but to him, lying down, it looks as if they're flying over the woods.

"It's gonna rain," Timur thinks. "Rain cats and dogs."

"The right plug is always sputterin' on me. What do you think I oughtta do?" he hears somebody say.

"Don't do anything. Toss it out and cut down on the throttle."

"Cut down on what?"

"On the throttle. Give it less gas."

"But maybe the oil's leaking. Then what?"

"You've gotta check. Maybe it's time to change the gasket. Here, put this one away."

"Good deal!"

"Can you handle it?"

"I've already handled it!"

"You gotta check how much oil you're pouring in the tank... What's the proportion?"

"What?"

"What kinda proportion you usin'?"

"Where've I got a proportion?"

"In the tank."

"In the motorcycle or what?"

"What're we talking about anyway? A cablecar?"

"What cablecar?"

"You dummy! I'm talkin' about the proportion... How much oil there is to how much gas! In the tank!"

Timur closes his eyes. He's sleepy.

"Yeah, I've got to do something..." he thinks. "How long can you go on just talking, drinking, roaming about, sitting around! It's the same thing here—sit around, roam about, drink... I've gotta do something... It's all so empty... God, how empty..."

Without opening his eyes Timur reaches for a tomato from the table, takes a bite and sucks out the cold, sour juice.

"The strangest thing is that I don't have any desires—none at all..."

He feels the cold juice trickling into his stomach. When he has sucked it dry, he tosses the wrinkled peeling away.

"It's gonna rain..." he thinks.

"Did you get her to sleep?" he hears Volodya ask cautiously. "Let's go!"

"She's still awake," Lena answers. "And we're not going anywhere any-more."

"Whatta you mean?"

"I've had enough."

"I don't get it."

"You get it fine."

"And he'd already started to pass..." Dryn's drunken voice intrudes. "He swerved out into the left lane and smashed head-on into a dump truck. Smashed to bits. It took them three hours to pick all of him up. His arms were on one side of the right of way, his legs on the other..."

"I just can't figure you out recently." Volodya's getting riled up. "I don't understand a damn thing!"

"What's there to figure out? What?! How come you brought him here?"

"He's gonna jump off the pier."

"Who?"

"Filipych."

"I'm not talking about him! I'm talking about your brother. What'd you bring him here for? What were the two of you talking about so long standing over by the motorcycle?"

"Nothing much. Just shooting the breeze..."

"Shooting the breeze? I saw what kind of face you were making when you walked off! Olenka, close those eyes! Take a little nap and we'll go home! I'm telling you for the last time—shut your eyes! Do you hear me?!.."

"We also had a case," Lelik chimes in. "A guy was taking people home from a wedding—the back of his truck was packed. He was drunk and turned over and crushed them all. But he came out of it alive. At the trial they tell him: the max—the firing squad. You see, you've got so much coming for the people you killed, so much for the ones you crippled... But *he* says..."

"Okay, okay, don't get all worked up..." Volodya says coaxingly. "Let's take a stroll in the woods. We'll take a walk, pick some flowers for Olenka. Come on, let's have a quiet talk."

"I know you and your quiet talks. Olenka, are you going to go to sleep or not?"

"No," Olenka says. "Mama, I wanna go home. It's gonna rain soon."

"Stop worrying, shut your eyes, and take a little nap like a good girl... And I'll bring you some pretty little flowers from the woods."

"Lilies of the valley?"

"Lilies of the valley were in the spring... I'll bring you whatever kind of corn flowers I find. Now go to sleep..."

"So what of it—you and your guy! A wedding! That's piddling!" says Dryn. "I'll tell you what I heard happened in America!.. Two of the BIGGEST cargo planes collided over some city! There was a load of gunpowder in one of them, and in the other... Well, I don't remember what was in the other one..."

"Also gunpowder?"

"Naw... It'll come to me in a second."

"Nitroglycerin, maybe?"

"No, no! Just a second, just a second..."

"Trinitrotoluene?"

"Naw. What is that, anyway?"

"Well, it's also something for killing..."

"No. But the other plane was carrying heavy water!"

"Water?! Heavy water? What in the hell is that?"

"It's... Listen... And such a reaction occurred... And this of course was at such a HUGE altitude! So there was such a strange reaction that everything was destroyed!"

"Really everything?"

"Yeah, everything! All blown to hell!"

"And nothing was left?"

"Nothing."

"What about the air?"

"That's the whole point—not even the air was left. The airlines made it forbidden for their pilots to fly over that place, because one day, okay, two days, a whole month, okay. And then K-BOOM! That's how water sometimes acts on gunpowder..."

"Heavy water..."

"Yeah, exactly, heavy water."

Timur is falling asleep. His thoughts intermingle, get mixed up and turn into a mush of memories, gestures, and exclamations. He tosses off this burden as if freeing himself of ballast, but a final obsessive thought pervades his sleep nonetheless and becomes the basis of his dream. It's the thought: "Still, they did go off! And she didn't even wait 'til her daughter fell asleep! EMPTINESS..."

———

Olenka is sitting on the sand looking in the direction of the woods where her mother went with Volodya. A few feet away Timur is sleeping, his face covered by the copy of *Woman Worker*. Dryn and Lelik have gone for a swim. The soldier on the bridge, having nothing better to do, takes his rifle from his shoulder and aims at the birds flying past. Filipych is sitting near the water. His city has mushroomed and now he has to crawl carefully between the houses to keep from accidentally wrecking a house or a street where he had walked earlier in the day. Olenka gets up and goes over to Filipych. His hat, pants, and shirt lie in a heap on the outskirts of his city. Olenka squats down and with wonder inspects the market place, the movie theater, and the streets.

"Did you do all of this?"

"Um." Filipych doesn't turn around.

"And can somebody live here?"

"Um-m."

"But who's gonna live here?"

Filipych doesn't answer.

"Swifts are gonna live here, right?"

"Huh?" Filipych asks and turns around. "Swifts?"

"Well, why not! Swifts..."

Filipych gives a laugh and starts repeating the word "swifts": "Swifts-swifts-swifts swifts swifts swifts so-wiftsy-wiftsy-wifts! Ha-ha-ha! Wifts-wiftsy."

Olenka also laughs and repeats "Wiftsy-wiftsy-wiftsy!"

"Here," Filipych says to Olenka and passes her a handful of sand. "Come on!"

"What?"

"Come on... Help me!"

"Help you build the town, huh?" Olenka carefully steps closer to the water and scoops up a handful of wet sand. "Where should I start, Filya?"

"Here!" he points. "This will be your house."

"And where's yours?"

"Right here. I'll come visit you. Hi-ho, hi-ho! Off to visit you I go!.. But where's your house?"

"I'll build it right away!" And Olenka starts building her own house in the sand.

———

The soldier looks along the railroad tracks to that horizon for which he will depart in late fall. He feels like smiling, but the smile turns into a yawn. "Must be the weather," he thinks and begins to count the railroad ties aloud. "One—two—three—four... twenty-one—twenty-two—twenty-three..." He can't make out the last two, but he wants to count as high as possible. "Twenty-four—twenty-five..." Farther than that, the ties blend into one big gray strip and his thoughts also come to an end. It's stifling hot. And his mind grows blank.

"It's hard when there's nothing to think about," the soldier says aloud, listening to his own voice. He doesn't like the sound of it—a harsh, obnoxious voice.

"You can actually forget how to talk out here!" the soldier thinks and repeats aloud. "You can lose your... lose your voice... lose your voice."

Now he stands looking straight ahead, amazed at how long a person can stand and just look straight ahead. One minute passes, a second, a third. He gets fed up with just standing there. He shuts one eye, stands for a few more minutes, then shuts the other. "This is just like death," he thinks.

"Death!" the soldier says aloud and quickly opens his eyes. He sees a train approaching in the distance. "I'll stand here until the train hits me," he thinks. "I'll go home four months earlier—only in a coffin. Still, it'll be earlier. And without a head. My head will be lying there under the bridge. Those big fish'll eat it, and they'll get even fatter and longer."

The train comes to a stop and the engine lets out a warning whistle.

"No, I'm gonna stand here. I wanna go home."

The engine is already so close that you can see the engineer. He lets out a deafening whistle, and the soldier's legs, as if of their own accord, carry him away from the ties to the bridge railing.

"But I didn't want to move out of the way..." the soldier has time to think. The train wheels rush past with a rumble and something hits him painfully on the shoulder. Growing smaller and smaller in the distance, the engineer shouts something and waves his arm. A glass he has thrown at the soldier shatters on a girder of the bridge and the fragments fall slowly into the water. The engineer taps his head with a finger as if to say, "Are you crazy?" Swaying as they fall, the pieces of glass sink in the water. A large fish swims over to one of them, sucks it into its mouth, immediately spits it out, then swirls around and drops to the bottom. That's where the soldier's head could have been lying now. But he, as if nothing had happened, turns his head from one side to side, walks out onto the ties, and watches the train disappear into the distance. The last car is empty and wobbles away into the distance. The soldier rubs his sore shoulder and watches until the train, as if kicking up its heels with the swaying caboose, disappears around the bend. Then he goes over to the rail and focuses his binoculars. A lump rises to his throat. A man and a woman have emerged from the woods. Slowly they walk across the sand toward the rest of the company. The woman is carrying a bunch of wild flowers and her gait is graceful and dreamy.

"The bitch," the soldier says aloud. "Damn bitch! I could just shoot you for that!"

He jerks his rifle off his shoulder, inserts a cartridge and aims, then thinks better of it and takes the cartridge out. But he doesn't deny himself the fun of aiming at her. Lena skips her way into his sight aperture. She fits neatly in his gunsight except for the hand with the flowers, which remains outside.

"Cli-ick!" says the soldier. "And there's one bitch less!"

Now it's Volodya's turn. His curly head doesn't fit in the sight, but sticks out.

"Cli-ick!" the soldier says again and lowers his head. "Okay, go on living..." he whispers and spits into the water. "For now."

"Well, and now for the last act on our program!" Volodya shouts from a distance. "Wake up, Timur!"

"Huh?" Timur jumps up, and it's obvious that he's had a bad dream. His face is creased and pale. "A-a-ah... It's you guys... You're back." He lies down again wearily on the sand. "God, what a crazy dream I had!.. Never sleep in the hot sun and drink vodka... Never."

"Well, so how about having the last act on our program, okay?" Volodya repeats and sits down by the table on the sand. "Where are our eagles?"

"Who?" Timur asks, closing his eyes. "What eagles?"

"Where are the guys?"

"How should I know?.. Hey, let's go home. I'm too tired. I think I got sun-burned, didn't I?"

"Yeah, a little bit."

"And here we are!" Lena says loudly, playing at being the Russian Snow Maiden as she jumps out from behind a fir tree. "Here we are back again! Olenka! What are you doing over there?!" Her voice is soft, velvety. "Hey, you little rascal, you've got into the water again. You're gonna be coughing again. Ugh, you're as filthy as a tar baby!"

Waving her arms covered with sand up to the elbows, Olenka runs to her mother.

"Mama, Mama, we built a whole city—can you believe it? We built a city and we're gonna live in it! Really!"

"If you could just see yourself!" Lena says. "No, just look!"

"We built a..."

"What did you build?"

"A city, Mama! A whole city with streets and parks! A real city!"

"Now I have to wash you off. Get the soap and let's go! It's time to go home."

Lena and Olenka head for the water. Meanwhile, Dryn and Lelik come back over the shoal from the direction of the pier.

"We were over there," Lelik says. "You can't dive from there. The river's gotten shallow."

"Yeah, we checked it out," Dryn says, sitting down on the sand. "You can't dive."

"Which side did you look from?" Volodya asks.

"The bridge side."

"Oh, wake up! He jumps from the other side. That's the whole idea. That redheaded guy busted his head on a beer crate by diving down from the bridge side, but Filipych is gonna jump over here on our side."

"Oh, yeah?" Lelik says and looks at the pier. "Still, there's nothing but rocks sticking up over there. It's a long drop down to the water. To make the jump you've got to have some running space. Where on the pier is there to start running?"

"That's the whole point—this guy jumps on the opposite side!" Volodya repeats, glancing at the pier. "I'm gonna go ask him. Filipych!"

Volodya walks out to the water's edge.

"I hate to get mixed up in something like this," says Dryn, tossing a rock up and down in the air. "He'll bust his ass, then we'll have to answer for it."

"Answer to who?" Timur asks without raising his head.

"What?"

"Who are you planning to answer to?" Timur repeats.

Dryn turns away and falls silent.

"They'll find somebody for you to answer to," Lelik says brusquely to Timur. "They'll say you made him do it. That redheaded guy was normal. He was responsible for himself. He jumped just for a pack of cigarettes."

"Sure, he was okay—just a regular guy!" Dryn says, turning back around and continuing to toss the rock up and down. "He answered for himself! But this guy can't for sure... They can send you up for it."

"Whether they send you up or not," Lelik says quietly, "I feel sorry for him. That's it. No, he shouldn't jump," Lelik says, waits a minute, then adds: "You guys do what you like, but I'm gonna get hold of him and take him with me. I'll step on the gas and we'll head out of here for home."

Timur goes on lying there motionlessly. Lelik watches Volodya as he tries to talk Filipych into making the dive. Dryn looks at Lelik.

"What's wrong, Dryn, whatta you staring at me like that for? Let's get dressed and get the hell out of here."

"Hold on... Maybe nothing'll happen."

"How the hell won't it? Once Volodya wants to do something, he'll raise the dead to bring it off. Just look!"

Bobbing his head, Filipych grabs a bottle of vodka, looks up at the sun, squints, and does his little jig. Volodya takes the vodka out of his hands and points at the pier. Filipych guffaws, jumps around imitating a warm-up, again grabs the vodka bottle and kisses it. Then he puts it beside his clothes, turns round to the others, and shakes his finger, warning them not to touch it.

"Like we really need the stuff!" Lelik says softly. "Dryn, let's take off. I'm telling you, you dummy."

Glancing all around and raising his arms in the air, Filipych heads for the pier.

"Okay, that's it!" Volodya says as he walks up. "It's all set."

"He agreed?" Timur asks and get up off the sand.

"Of course, he's already gone. Why shouldn't he? What difference does it make to him, anyway?"

"Yeah," Lelik says, "what's it to him! He'd dive into ice, much less water. Dryn, you do what you wanna do, but I'm stepping on the gas outa here."

"Well, go on then, get going!" Volodya swings around and faces him. "What're you moaning about—get on your way!"

"Don't you yell at me! Ya hear? Don't screech at me. You should've gone down and taken a look at the water first. It'd been better if you'd gone down there instead of off to the woods!"

"What'd you say?" Volodya raises his fists at Lelik.

"Nothing. Never mind!" he says and jumps aside. "That time the water was way high, and even then Red busted his head. They looked all over for him and then barely pumped all the water out of him and saved him. You didn't see it, did you? But I did!"

"Okay, okay, you guys, stop acting like fighting cocks!" Timur moves in between them. "Maybe it's really not a good idea, Volodya."

"You mean you think I don't know what I'm talking about?" Volodya says, flaring up. "He's like a cat. In the winter he goes around without a coat! When it's thirty below he wears hightops without socks! Cut it out! Let him jump! I'll answer for it, okay?"

"Okay!" Lelik yells. "Only I'm not taking part in this! Maybe I'm just sorry for him. Simply sorry, understand! Filipych! Filipych!" he suddenly yells and runs in the direction of the pier.

"Stop, I'll kill you!" Volodya shouts and takes off after him, catches up with him and knocks him down. He pins him to the sand and holds him down.

"Filipych! Don't jump, don't jum..."

Volodya presses Lelik's face down into the sand.

"Shut up, you creep, I'll cream you!"

Filipych doesn't hear anything. He gets into the water, crosses the current diagonally, and paddles toward the pier.

Timur comes up. "Let him up. He's not gonna turn back now anyway."

Volodya lets him go and Timur looks at Lelik, who without getting up squints as he takes the measure of both of them from head to foot.

"I hate you both!" he says. "I hate your whole brood! And I hate you, understand? You arrived and they've gotta organize a show for you!"

"What in the world do you hate me for, kiddo?" asks Timur with a smile. "If he busts himself up you'll be in the same situation as me and him." Timur points at everyone. "This is being a party to a deed, kiddo, get it? Now get up and stop looking at me like that. Anyway, you were seen leaving the beer stand with us. So don't try to weasel out of it!"

Lelik gets up, then sits down on the sand and suddenly starts crying.

"Dryn, what're you just standing there for? You yourself saw... How Red... You saw it—the water just comes up to your waist. He's gonna break his neck."

Lena walks up.

"What's going on?" she asks with a frightened look. "What happened?"

Lelik rushes over to her. "Len, at least you tell them..."

He waves his hand in despair, walks off, and sits down on the sand.

"What happened, Volodya?" Lena asks.

"Nothing! We're gonna go now!"

"What happened? I'm asking you!"

"Oh, Filipych is gonna dive—dive!" Lelik yells to her and points to the pier. "He'll break his neck! There's no water five yards from the pier! And they sent him to do it! It's a show for this guy."

There's a heavy silence.

"Dryn!" Lelik suddenly yells and rushes over to his friend. "Why don't you say something? Tell them! You're strong, you jerk!"

"Yeah, okay, what're you so hot about..." Dryn mutters. "He's not gonna hurt himself. What're you..."

"But if he does?! If he does?!"

"Well, we'll say he did it himself—he just fell off!"

Lelik stands in front of Dryn and stares him in the eye.

"Yeah?" he says and wallops him in the face. "There!"

Dryn grabs Lelik by the arms and twists them like willow twigs behind his back.

"Go ahead and let him have it—he's been asking for it!" Volodya says with a laugh. "You got it good right in the mug from your best friend, didn't you?"

Dryn hits Lelik lightly on the neck and he falls down on the sand.

"Cut it out!" he says to his friend's back. "I hit you about like I would a mosquito. But if I really let you have it—then I'll make sure you feel it..."

"Stop this right now, do you hear?!" Lena says as she goes up to Volodya. "What're you thinking of—you want to get locked up?"

"Okay, okay, okay!.. Hold on! Soon as he jumps we'll go!" Volodya says without turning around.

"Mommy, what's going to happen?" Olenka asks, pressing up against Lena, who's wearing a bright summer shift.

"Stop it right now, you hear?"

"Yeah, I hear. You think I'm deaf or what?"

"What kind of people are you, anyway?!" Lena says louder. "Don't you feel sorry for him at all?"

"Who—them? Sorry?" Lelik shouts. "Sari—that's what Indians wear!"

Lena cups her hands to her mouth and yells, "Fil-lya-a-a! Don't jump! Don't jump!"

"Ump-ump-ump." An echo bounces back over the sand, the river and the bridge.

"Well then, I'm going over there and drag him away!" Lena says.

Volodya takes her by the hand and stops her.

"Let me go," Lena says. Volodya holds her.

"Let me go, I said!"

Without releasing her hand, Volodya squints against the sun in the direction of the pier.

"What are you doing? I told you—let me go! You hear!"

"I hear you. We'll go any minute now. As soon as he jumps we'll go. That's what I want to do."

"And what else do you want? Huh?"

"I want you to shut up."

Volodya is holding her by the wrist, and Lena's hand has turned blue.

"Let me go, you're hurting me!" Lena says, trying to twist away. "Let me go!"

Filipych has already appeared on the top platform of the pier.

"Don't jump!" Lena yells.

"Ump-ump-ump!" resounds the echo over the beach and the woods, and only the startled swifts stir in the still air.

"Mama, Mama!" Olenka whines, pressing against her.

"What the hell are you doing?! What's there to get hysterical about?" Timur says impatiently. "You'd do better to look at the beautiful view! The sun! His figure in the background. You may not see the likes of it again! By the way, people usually have to pay money for a show like this. And we're getting it free, you might say—for a bottle of vodka."

"That's it. I'm going." Wiping the tears on his face, Lelik gets up from the sand. "You can kill me if you like, but I'm not watching it."

"Wait a second, Lelik," Dryn says and stops him. "We'll go together. What's got into you?"

"Take your hand off me, you shit!" Lelik wails painfully. "I can't stand the sight of you, you ass-kisser."

He turns away and quickly goes toward his motorcycle. On his way he grabs his shirt off the sand, slips it on as he's walking, and without stopping, tucks it into his pants. He tries to start the motorcycle, but he can't get it started. The motor dies.

"The right plug's worn out..." Dryn says as he watches from afar. "The spark plug needs cleaning... or changing..."

"I wonder, can he do it or not?" thinks the soldier. Through his binoculars he watches Filipych, who's standing right nearby on the platform of the old pier. "Can he or not? I wonder... Two years of standing around on this bridge and..."

"Go for it! Go-o-o!" He hears Volodya's voice.

"Go-ho-go-ho-go-ho." The echo hits the steel girders of the bridge and bounces back.

"And not to fire a single shot," thinks the soldier. "It's nothing but a joke! I won't have anything to tell at home!"

The soldier inserts a small bullet tentatively into the cartridge. The bolt snaps. The soldier aims. At Filipych.

"The sun—the sun—the sun—the sun!" Filipych shouts, throwing back his head.

"Un-un-un-un!" The echo flies over the wild beach.

The soldier playfully aims at Filipych, then at the sun, then at Filipych and again at the sun.

A dark storm cloud falls across the fiery sun. Gloom and silence descend upon the beach. The swifts have flown away. Everything has taken cover. The rain will come any minute now. The soldier pulls his trigger several times, but there still is no shot. He has put the safety on.

"P-ee-yu!" he goes with his lips and grins.

Filipych jumps.

The soldier takes out the cartridge, slips it into his bandoleer, and smiles. "I wonder, can he do it or not?"

About a minute passes. The seconds seem like years.

On the beach they are all standing and shading their eyes with their hands. Lelik with his motorcycle is at the water's edge, the others are a little farther off. A cold wind starts to blow. The newspapers which had formed their table flutter off toward the water, where they alight and sink.

"So what's happened? Is he gone?" Volodya yells, unable to contain himself any longer.

Lelik dashes off fully dressed toward the pier. His motorcycle stand sinks into the sand and the motorcycle falls. Dryn dashes off after Lelik, and Volodya follows.

"I don't know how to swim..." Timur says lamely to Lena and jogs toward the water. Then he suddenly stops and goes over to Lena. "You understood, right?" he says, the dark holes of his pupils peering into her eyes. "You did understand, didn't you?"

"What?" Lena answers him.

"Don't go blabbing anything unnecessary... You got me?"

"No."

"You'll say what I tell you to say, get it?"

"No."

"Whatta you mean 'no'?! What?!"

"I said—no!"

Tossing her head back, Lena furiously looks Timur up and down.

The others have been diving around the pier now for about five minutes. Volodya, the strongest of them, dives most often. He stays only briefly on the surface: as soon as he catches his breath, with a powerful thrust he disappears beneath the water again. Dryn dives less frequently—he's "handled the hard stuff" too much today, and after a few dives, Lelik crouches on all fours by the water. He feels sick.

The soldier is having fun watching them dive. He can see everything and understands exactly what's going on. Several times he feels the urge to yell something to them, but he holds back. A light rain begins to fall.

Timur is outwardly calm. He walks back and forth glancing in the direction of the pier. He's whistling.

"Okay, then," he says and heads decisively for his motorcycle. "We've got to be the first to report it."

With a half-spin of the pedal, he starts the motor and drives over to Lena. He slowly steps on the gas. Pressing Olenka close, Lena moves aside.

"You remember what I told you?" Timur says and puts on his helmet. "Repeat it."

Lena doesn't answer.

"Repeat it, or else... I'll smear you so bad that you won't be able to wash the dirt off as long as you live."

The motorcycle is roaring and his words are inaudible, but his thin lips spit something contemptuous and spiteful from his mouth. A white foam has formed around the edge of his lips.

Lena holds her hands over Olenka's ears and presses her face to her. Olenka is sobbing.

"You're a fool..." Timur says threateningly. "Nobody will believe you anyway..."

Over on the bridge the soldier is just dying with laughter. He can see that the man who jumped has hidden between the rocks on the other side of the pier.

That's right, Filipych decided to play a joke. He thought he'd hide and wait to see what happened. Now he has to climb out. It's starting to rain.

Filipych dives into the water. The current quickly carries him far from the divers. Before they have time to notice him, he gets out, laughing, on the shore and walks over to Timur.

"Ha-ha-ha-ha! One fool tricked another! One fool tricked another!" he laughs as he spits out water and pokes his finger at Timur.

"We're late going home," Lena says quietly, squeezing her daughter's slim little shoulders.

"I'm cold, Mama, I'm cold..." whispers Olenka, glancing at Timur. He shuts off the motor, carefully puts the motorcycle on its stand, takes off his helmet, and straightens his hair. Only then does he go up to Filipych.

He hits him on the face with a powerful, direct blow. Filipych falls backward into the water. Timur catches him by the hair in the water, turns him around and drags him out on the bank. He pulls him up and hits him again. Now he aims his blows more precisely. At first Filipych falls on all fours, then collapses on his stomach. Timur steps back, then bends over and kicks him in the stomach. A pink foam streams out of Filipych's mouth. Dryn and Volodya swim over and get out of the water, staggering slightly.

"Cool off!" Volodya says, grabbing Timur by the arms.

Dryn turns around and looks toward the spot where Lelik is lying on the sand. "Should I go over to him or not?" he's thinking.

"Hey!" Dryn shouts to his friend. "We're leaving! Lelik!"

"That's enough, enough," Volodya says, clasping Timur tightly and raising him off the ground. "If he didn't drown, then you'll kill him. Cool it!"

Filipych leaps up, runs toward the water and his clothes, which are lying on the outskirts of the sand city.

"Ah-h-h-h!" cries Filipych, his eyes bugging. "Help!"

"Hey, you! Down there on the beach!" the soldier shouts. "You, stop it!"

Timur twists out of his brother's hold, catches up with Filipych, and trips him face down onto the sand city.

"Ah-h-h-h!" Filipych cries, but Timur cuts off the cry with a skillful blow.

Filipych makes no sound. Volodya runs up and pulls Timur away, but he tries to slip out of his brother's tight arms. Volodya holds him forcefully, but his brother is writhing in a rage, and they fall together onto the sand.

"You, down there, stop it!!" the soldier now yells louder through his cupped hands and in a threatening tone. But, just as before, no one hears him. He's too far away. "He-e-y! I'm fixin' to shoot!"

"Lelik! We're going!" Dryn yells. "What are you sprawled out over there for? It's no time to be sunning when the clouds have moved in!" He goes over to Filipych, Volodya and Timur—all thrashing around in the sand, hesitates, peers down at them, and turns again in his friend's direction. "Come on, enough sunbathing, I said!"

It starts pouring. Lena scoops Olenka up in her arms and runs with her toward the woods.

"Fiends, monsters! Fiends, monsters!" she mutters, hugging her daughter to her.

"They don't hear me," the soldier says aloud and for a while longer without his binoculars watches the dots of people scrambling about on the beach. "Nobody hears me. Nobody. You stand here..." he reflects, propping his elbow against the railing and his cheek on his hand. "You just stand here. You can't even fire into the air. You'll get asked, 'How come you fired?' 'A fight was going on.' 'In the area of the bridge? Inside the barrier? Or beyond?' 'Beyond.' 'You know the regulations?' 'I do.' 'To the guardhouse. Abo-o-ut face! March!' The army's the army. You take an oath. Yea-ah... Duty's about over, my relief'll be here soon."

The soldier goes into his booth at the edge of the bridge and closes the door fast behind him. "My relief's on his way, stomping through the rain, ha-ha..." He stands his rifle in the corner, and, stroking the steel, looks at it raptly for a long time, as if he'd just seen it for the first time.

"We're out of here!" Volodya starts up his motorcycle on the beach. "Timur, get a move on!"

Timur has a hard time putting on his wet shirt, tries to button the ripped off buttons, but can't. Then he tries to put on his pants, but gives up and tosses them into the motorcycle storage box.

"Leli-i-ik!" Dryn calls, starts his motorcycle and rides over to his friend. "Let's go! What're you sprawled out like this for?"

He is lying down with his head on his hands.

"Lelik," Dryn says. "Stop sulking and let's go! Hey, okay, I'm sorry!"

Lelik doesn't move. The beach is becoming wet, soon the water starts running down onto it from the forest above.

"Okay, I'm sorry, ya hear? Let's go... Or else we won't be able to make it through the woods. The low places will be flooded, ya hear? Well, you do as you like, but I'm leaving... with the guys..."

"Come on, come on!" Volodya is yelling, waving his arm and driving off toward the woods. Timur is following him.

Dryn bends down from his motorcycle, stretches his hand out to touch his friend, but reconsiders, puts his hand down and looks dully at his back.

"Well, okay... Have it your way... Go on laying there... Wimp!"

The skies open! A genuine summer downpour with thunder and lightning begins! It gets dark as night. Waves roll in on the beach, raising whirls of yellow sand. Thunder crashes and a flash of lightning momentarily illuminates the bridge and a huge fish leaping up in its stream. As the tail of lightning strikes again and again, it seems to spotlight the foam seething on the water, the pier in the middle of the river, Lelik lying in the sand, and Filipych, who has fallen at the edge of his sand city. The city is ruined. The water washes away its remains, sucking it under Filipych's body, and washing up onto his house as well as Olenka's, which his body shields from the waves. They lap at the street down which the two of them imagined walking to visit each other. Rain pours down on the beach, the water, the woods—and moves farther and farther toward the city. Then, from around the bend in the river something like an enormous finger appears, prying along the water and sand. It's a tornado! It sucks up leaves, sand, sticks, all sorts of rubbish, and whirls all the dregs and dirt up above the bridge into the violet sky. A tornado! With a howl it hits the bridge and the soldier's booth, where he huddles in fright, and plunges along the railroad embankment toward the city. Before long it overtakes the woman in the woods, who, clinging to the trunk of a huge elm, presses her little girl to her breast and weeps. It overtakes the three motorcyclists, who, skidding over the low spots, race through the dirt. It overtakes everything along the river, on the beach, in the forest, and in the city. And it pushes threateningly at the city. Like a huge snake standing on its tail, it whistles and hisses as it pokes menacingly at the city.

The thunder crashes, rolling for dozens of miles into the distance, as if reminding and warning people of something serious and important.

"Get up," says Lelik, standing over Filipych. "Let's go."

His motorcycle is lying half in the water, half on the bank. Filipych lies motionless, then sits up and looks at the turbid water rushing down past him and under the bridge. Lelik sits down beside him and also looks at the water and its racing flotsam of leaves, grass and foam. A huge log swirls in an eddy beside the steep shore opposite them, and they look at this log.

Swifts are flying over the water and far in the forest a woodpecker is tapping away. The soldier steps out of his booth. He had dozed off to the patter of the rain. His body's gone numb, and he does a knee bend, shakes his arms, and stretches his limbs.

"Good!" thinks the soldier, gazing at the freshly washed earth.

"Go-o-o-ood!" he yells, throwing out his chest and shouting with the full force of his lungs.

"O-o-oo-oo-ood!" the echo resounds between the wet girders of the bridge.

Translated by Byron Lindsey and Vyacheslav Davidenko

Originally published in *Znamia,* July 1987

Leonid Shorokhov

The Lifeguard

1

On the bank of the Akdarya River, a quiet, inconspicuous little dive known only to a small circle of the initiated was flourishing for the fifth year now.

About eight years ago, out of concern for broad masses of drowning people, the OSVOD (Aquatic Lifesaving Society) organized a post on the bank of the then still mighty river. Three kilometers down the Akdarya from the town a modest wooden booth was erected with a deep blue lifesaving ring painted on it, resembling a melon more than a circle, and a seventy-ruble personnel budget was allotted for some kind of guard at the unimposing booth or a sentry for the powerful river. Incidentally, the ill-defined position carried a rather weighty title: sailor-lifeguard second-class.

An uninformed person would have found it hard to imagine anyone in the said position besides a little old decrepit granddad who had begun his naval stint during the time of Ochakov and the Crimean conquest, someone with a light blue anchor, faded with age, tattooed on his shrunken, birdlike arm. But life is more cunning than our conception of it. And the person doing the guessing would have erred greatly in this case. The booth looked sleepy and run-down amidst the unruly expanse of woods on the banks—the *tugai*, but the man who stood on the threshold of the booth wasn't sleepy or run-down. Lumps of steel muscle rippled under his smooth skin; his chest stretched his sailor's shirt until it was ready to split; his hairy legs planted firmly on the ground, his small sharp eyes scanned the Akdarya for many kilometers in both directions at once.

Doubtless, if the days of sailing ships were to return, the sailor-lifeguard second-class depicted here wouldn't have hesitated for a moment to trim the angle sail on the bowsprit of a three-hundred-ton schooner all by himself. But, alas, those golden days of yore are past.

Vladimir Vasilievich Sagin—the sailor-lifeguard usually signed in next to this name in the payroll office's register—or, plainly speaking, Volodka the Lifeguard, had only the foggiest notion of sails. But then the fog of ignorance in his head extended over other fields as well. It was much easier to list what Volodka knew than what he didn't know. It turned out that to get on in life no knowledge was necessary, with the possible exceptions of the counting rules and the ability to write clearly the five letters composing the modest surname Sagin. All the rest just needlessly jaded the mind.

And how surprised his school teachers would have been at Volodka's accomplishments now, when they once foresaw a hungry death for their certified mediocrity of a student due to his lack of abilities in all fields of learning. Now Volodka simply chuckled recalling their gloomy predictions—how many of his teachers themselves had attained in this life what for the sailor-lifeguard second-class had been a cinch? If you judged by salary, then the difference wasn't great; comparing the volume of useless knowledge with which the teachers' all-wise heads were chock full, then, it's true, the pedagogues flashed far ahead; but if one started to reckon according to the real yardstick of existence, it turned out that not one of Volodka's former mentors could hold a candle to him!

Spending their entire lives teaching others, they managed not to amass any brains of their own: for years they suffered, trekking from nook to nook in other people's houses, not knowing how to get their own; they miserably hoofed it, stamping about the streets of their small hometown, where every second inhabitant was a former pupil of theirs. All of their pauper's bank savings didn't surpass the amount without which Volodka would disdain to go out for cigarettes, and it was questionable whether all of them even had a passbook! No, one doesn't get fat on learning—Volodka was convinced of that at a very innocent age.

2

Sagin had departed the temple of learning fifteen years earlier. By the way, the word "departed," it seems, didn't really fit his case. It wasn't so much that he left the school as that the abode of knowledge finally severed its long-standing relationship of petty and tiresome warfare with Volodka. Be that as it may, the time to part nonetheless arrived, the school breathed a sigh of relief, and its graduate sighed with even greater relief.

The ever so sweet pie of life beckoned to his imagination with stupefying aromas. Volodka belched from craving and hurled himself full tilt at the coveted plunder. A most favorable climate set in. The jeans craze was licking at the whole country like a blue flame. It attacked not just individuals who were hypersensitive to the blue epidemic—collectives and entire social strata fell victim. Housewives and academics, construction workers and ministers, musicians and janitors—they all craved to clothe their buns, varying in fat content, in the foreign denim. Back-alley goons were motivated by the mania of herd symbolism; Ph.D.s in science—by practicality. Both agreed on one thing: not just any kind of foreign stuff was suitable and saleable, but only that which had been maximally smitten with the decay of imperialism. Only its system of stitching seams and its label design equally satisfied both the happy hippy types and sullen deputy procurators.

Sagin's first real profession was black marketeering. But his craving tripped Volodka up. He badly wanted to have everything, and right away. An unpleasant meeting with the organs of justice took place, after which Volodka cooled to open crime. It wasn't worth the trouble. The year spent behind barbed wire proved to Sagin in a most convincing manner the depravity of his rush to stick both hands into his mouth at once. Moreover, the food in the minimum security camp was unbearably bad. And if he were to persist in black-market carousing, he'd inevitably be in danger of getting the "max." How can you put meat on your bones there? No, the calorie count of camp fare in no way corresponded to the needs of Volodka's stomach. He had to search out new ways and means of living.

3

Sagin's casual gaze skimmed the area and halted on the murky, yellow stream of the Akdarya.

The river's heavy body was barely stirring. The far shore was lost in a foggy smoke. The low evening sun played in wet patches of light on the young reeds bending to the breeze. The stability of life, unexplored by Volodka, reigned in age-old, natural balance. Sagin felt as if something jolted him below the heart. Stunned, Volodka stared into the water.

"Why, here it is!" came out of its own accord.

The Akdarya was roiling with fish. You had to stand but ten minutes on the bank, taking in the limitless light-brown smoothness, and your heart began to quiver like a burbot liver—to the left, to the right, and right there in front of you as you watched, smacking, sonorous slaps resounded: churbaks two feet long and sparkling gold—the famous Akdarya carp flew out of the water in a haze of spray, turned over awkwardly in the air, displaying their shiny fat sides, and loudly flopped back in. The resounding slap carried far across the smooth surface of the river, and right away another golden beauty soared up nearby, and, so it seemed, there would be no end to it.

Sagin's fate was decided in the blink of an eye. Volodka grunted with relief: apparently there was a reason why the swampy, reedy banks and wide riparian expanses had lured his imagination from his earliest, snively childhood. It would have been inconceivable not to fatten himself on such a rich treasure chest of nature.

Volodka would go out to the wet bank early in the morning; the endless ribbon of river swayed murkily in front of him; the frolicking and the heavy slaps of the carp on the water would begin before the sun's first rays.

Sagin did some figuring: an 18-pound churbak, take, say, a hundred of them, cover them over with wet grass (it's a trifling task to cut *kuga* and young reeds in growths like this), pack them into the back of a GAZ truck, and then everyone knows where to go—straight to the mountains, to the mine. The mining settlement's big. It has at least some five thousand people. The ride is about three to five hours, and they'd snap them up, as sure as God's in heaven, they'd snap up all the goods in half an hour—those people are really loaded. Three rubles apiece, what do you mean, three—lay down a fiver! After all, in their caves they don't even see a dead sprat for months, much less a live carp. You could make the trip there and back in one day—before you know it it's evening and you're home. Half a hundred to the driver (well, at most a hundred, if a really daring one turns up), and the rest you skim off—three-four hundred—that's it! Money galore in your pocket, and in your hand, and under your belt—rubles, threes, fives—wow!

Volodka surveyed the Akdarya with wild eyes. The water surged and receded beneath his gaze.

"Life," Volodka sighed hoarsely, "is given to us only once!"

4

A year later Sagin came into an IZH motorcycle with a sidecar. And the next year he took a plot of land and began to build a house for himself.

Hundred-meter dragnets made of nylon towline were piled in taut rolls on the uneven floor of the little barn-shelter; on the roughsided planks of shelving were hidden the rolls of new nets not yet mounted on parachute cord—the strongest there is; about them lay commercial nets, already stained brown by the Akdarya's corrosive silt. Volodka kept nets for every sort of fish habit and size: there were three-strand, and four-strand, and six-strand, and eight-strand nets; with gill traps and without; with cork floats and styrofoam ones; with lead and ceramic weights; in fifty-, one hundred-, and two-hundred meter lengths, made according to Volodka's orders by local craftsmen, as well as imported from Astrakhan (from the old-time sturgeon works that were now short on sturgeon); there were purchased nets, stolen nets, nets won at gambling, in bets, and given in return for favors.

In an inlet of the Akdarya alongside the reed, clay-walled hut, a nice new motorboat rocked slightly on the Akdarya's yellow waves: and not just a boat with a motor, like the ones all of Volodka's competitors in the black market carp trade had, not a tarred trow with a chopped off stern, knocked together willy-nilly out of rough boards—no, in the inlet, awaiting daring nocturnal raids on the carp holes, was a genuine sea sloop, put together out of very narrow pine strips drawn tightly, with an overlay, one on top of the other, on the expansive oak ribs.

The plans for this vessel possessed of enviable nautical qualities were torn out of the magazine *Technology for Young People*, and were third- or maybe fifth-hand when they made their way to Volodka, to find material embodiment in his commercial fishing boat.

The Asian, roasting sun bestowed brown burn spots on Volodka's sloping shoulders; only the straps of his undershirt left white stripes. Brown bordered on red, pink on brown. Volodka had gotten tough and stocky. Deep creases cut his tanned forehead and in the sun sparks flew from the red scruff on his neck and chin. Life for Sagin was like a defiant girl taken crudely, against her will—in torment and unbelievable delight. That's how he tasted the painful, bitter flavor of someone else's blood on his chapped lips.

5

Sagin married as quickly ar.d unthinkingly as he did everything: a fortuitous occurrence sought him out and made a gift of solid family happiness.

Six years have passed since that Sunday when Volodka was standing at the entrance of the bazaar, wondering whether or not to down a couple of tankards of beer on the occasion of his day off. Then up rolled a buddy whom he knew from the nighttime fish business. The conversation spurted in a small stream in the direction of the Akdarya. The buddy was trying to force his way into a commercial association. Volodka was plainly turning him down.

A young woman who was passing by exchanged greetings with the buddy. A girlfriend was clinging to her side. The ladies lingered a moment and swapped tidbits.

"Well, so long."

"So long."

The chance acquaintances set off about their business. Volodka let his indifferent gaze follow the hen party. His eyes sleepily moved from the shoes to the ankles, the calves, went up a little higher... Here Volodka's pupils suddenly widened and gleamed: "Wow, your girlfriend's girlfriend!" He grabbed his friend's arm tightly.

"Who is she?"

"Oh," the good friend let drop indifferently, "some single babe."

"Does she put out?" Volodka sighed.

The friend waved his hand: "No way. They say she's still a virgin. Saving herself. Looking to get married."

"A vi-i-i-rgin!" Volodka froze, not breathing. With an ass like that she sure won't be a virgin for long. His gaze just couldn't peel itself from the torrid curves of the girlfriend's figure.

As if sensing that gaze on her, the girlfriend's girlfriend slowed her steps. Her hips started a slow rocking motion. Volodka's palms started to sweat and his lips grew dry.

"Somebody'll snatch her up," he thought in fear, "sure as God's in heaven, they'll snatch her up."

The unknown woman turned the corner.

"A virgin," muttered Volodka, "No way, you won't go to someone else!"

He licked his lips. He must get married right away. The silver trumpets of fate had summoned to action.

"As soon as its evening we'll go courting," he announced decisively to his friend.

The very same day he and his buddy, a little befuddled on account of Volodka's passion, were already putting away vodka with the future father-in-law. The next morning Volodka greased a palm at the wedding bureau so they wouldn't keep him hanging longer than need be, and already by evening, at last, he had clawed his way to what he so furiously and irrepressibly coveted.

Lyusya, it turned out, wasn't exactly a virgin. All the same, she compensated for what was missing with something extra—her undeniable female attributes were even greater than Volodka had imagined at first glance.

In addition, her character suited Volodka—the house sparkled with cleanliness, the bed occupied half of the bedroom, little pleasures were never refused at any time of the day or night, and Volodka's appetite was sated in "five seconds" (as the amenable young bride liked to joke playfully). All the meals she prepared consisted three-quarters of meat. So, what else could he have demanded from his beloved wife?

Volodka didn't care for the intricacies of love or anything out of the ordinary. Plain food, in his opinion, was better for one's health than any pickled concoctions. He was satisfied with his wife.

6

In the third year of his unfettered pursuit of rubles, Volodka came up against the fisheries bureau. It got so tough that he would soon have had to pay with his own hide, for grease wouldn't help any more.

At that time Volodka was listed as a watchman on a construction project. His pay was obviously nothing, crumbs instead of pay, and he didn't even bother to pick it up; all he did was sign for it. Time was more valuable to him than any pay. If the matter came up, he would have paid a little himself just so as not to be bothered in what mattered most, his chief occupation. All of his pay could be contained in one lucky cast of the float net. So let those who need them make use of those kopecks from now on; it sometimes happened that in one night Volodka made the equivalent of his entire annual salary. For the sake of seniority and appearances, Sagin kept an employment book at the personnel office.

Everything would've been fine if things had kept on as they were, but then a new misfortune struck Volodka. Fish inspectors, the bastards!

As long as there was plenty of carp in the Akdarya, no one cared to eat it, as long as anyone and everyone could catch them without the slightest effort, to his heart's content, the fisheries officer didn't even look Volodka's way. Well, maybe sometimes he put the squeeze on Sagin but he didn't go too far.

"Look how many of these Volodkas are hanging around the Darya carp. What am I going to do, tear all of their heads off?" the protector of the people's wealth reasoned practically. "What's more, they won't haul those carp out of the country; it's our own people that'll buy them, and our own that'll eat them. There's enough of this wealth to last our lifetime. Let them take advantage of it for now."

The train of the officer's thoughts suited Volodka just fine.

But then there started to be less fish; fish became expensive, and it immediately became clear what jealous eyes were concealed beneath the shiny little visor of the uniform's black cap. Volodka's every step became a problem. The inspector began to milk Sagin beyond the norm for his rank. Volodka was forced to divide a float cast almost in half. He just ground his teeth at the unprecedented robbery. In the dead of night the propeller of the fish inspector's motorboat would clatter along on the trail of watery whiskers from Volodka's fishing boat. The clinging snake practically poked out of the water along with

Volodka's net. Sagin wouldn't have been at all surprised to unexpectedly discover him (may he drop dead!) as a third person in his own bed!

Finally it got so bad he couldn't breathe. Volodka started trying to reason with the rapacious guardian of riparian wealth, heart to heart. But no! The inspector puffed himself up like a fine turkey.

"Who's master here on the Darya?" he hissed with contempt between his teeth. "I'm master here. And what are you? You're a cheap wheeler-dealer. You live at my mercy. Look how you've fed yourself on fish for two years. You have a nice IZH motorcycle with a sidecar and you have whatever kind of nets you want, and a big fishing boat, a real beauty, and you've already started building a huge house for yourself—and all of this on what? You think I don't remember how you turned up on this river? Bare-assed and your teeth chattering, that's how you came. And now you're a lord. But somebody might ask who are you, anyway, to play fast, let's put it like that, with the people's wealth? You're just a mean poacher and speculator, and your place isn't by the river, but you know where! And you can hush up, like a mouse, so I don't have to hear any more of your crap! You live as long as I say; and if I want, you'll disappear for good. Know your place. If I cut you down, that means the time has come to do some cutting. By God!" it was as if the fisheries officer had pounded a sharpened oak stake into Volodka's head.

Volodka was going to hint to the brazen snake that more than one smart guy had already taken a swim down to the first big hole as a snack for the catfish, but he held his tongue. It's not the dog that barks you should fear, but the one that's silent. He couldn't hide the fishing boat and the nets—there they all were, all of Volodka's fishing spots down to the last one were familiar to the inspector. If he wanted to stir things up, it'd be a cinch to snare him in the heat of his work, then there'd be a search and you'd be left in your birthday suit, if you'd be left at all. The second conviction isn't like the first— they'll stick you with a sentence, give it to you with both barrels—Moscow doesn't much believe in tears.

He was forced to keep quiet.

The sheepskin coat was no longer worth repairing, and Volodka's nimble noggin began to stretch out a tentacle of short thoughts.

What now? Fix the snake on the quiet, sink him somewhere in a deep, out-of-the-way pool with a couple of boulders under his clothes? Volodka knew a great many such spots along the Akdarya, and then, give it a month, and the famous Akdarya catfish would've picked his bones clean. Or maybe the time had come once again to switch to a new field of activity? But what about the money spent on the boat, the dynamo motor, or the nets, and the chain of buyers that was worked out, and the habit of living just as you saw fit and as you pleased? And to throw all of this to the dogs because of some water snake? And to begin again from the beginning, from a paltry, insignificant nothing; to kowtow and mess around until you barely get on your feet once again? Of course not, neither age nor character would allow such a thing.

Volodka did some hard thinking. And at this, his most difficult moment, he discovered how well he'd chosen his companion for life. That Lyuska, what a head she had on her! She put it short and sweet. Of course, they had to look for protection behind the cover of some state office. Just try to touch someone then!

Volodka jumped up.

"R-r-right!"

He ran to see some old acquaintances, prowled the banks of the river, and stumbled upon the recently opened station to save drowning people. It was manna from heaven. Just as if God's own finger had pointed at Sagin—henceforth, pal, you'll be a man with a special fate and a special destiny. So Volodka became the sailor-lifeguard second-class for the local division of the OSVOD, or simply Volodka the Lifeguard.

Oh, mama, now he could hang about the river round the clock, both day and night, and on the most lawful of all lawful bases. When and where a drowning person would go under—the date and place—no one could determine: that's what the OSVOD was for, to come to people's aid at a whisper!

Volodka and the Akdarya became as one.

Before, the fishes' patron could always shoo Sagin away from the river. What, he'd say, is a construction warehouse watchman supposed to be doing in the middle of the river at two in the morning? Get on out of here, hurry, guard what you're supposed to!

But not now, no way, brother, the deep stretches are Volodka's proper concern, a drowning person won't turn up on a shoal! And as to the dead of night, we're watchful: what if his best buddy—the fish inspector—capsizes at his battle post and starts sending up bubbles? Who'll save him then? There's a man placed there by the state for that, the sailor-lifeguard second-class, Volodka Sagin—he'll save him! By God! And if you don't want to capsize, dear friend, shoo. Now not only you, but I too, Volodka, have a job that demands courage and vigilance. Keep your distance!

7

Three years ago they built a canal from the Akdarya to the Solyonaya steppe. Several tens of thousands of acres of most fertile virgin land, dessicated to whiteness, lay useless within two hundred kilometers of the river.

About ten years before Volodka's carp business got started, a firm decision
was made in high state circles: to take half of the river and send it along a perfectly straight, narrow thread of a canal, like the blade of a bayonet, into the
very middle of the unproductive loess plain. Fantastic cotton harvests were
expected. None of the decision makers gave a thought to the future of the
Akdarya. But then there were tasks more important than the preservation of
old river beds on the flood plain and the Akdarya's meandering channels.

A year later scores of mobile mechanized columns moved into the corridor
of the future canal. An incredibly intensive, ruthless battle with nature went
on for twelve years. A cursed ridge was in the way, its marl knolls, measuring
a hundred meters thick, blocking the future water artery.

In the year that Volodka faced the walls of his future palace built of baked,
solid brick with inexpensive hollow reject brick (he, for one, was well aware
what sort of rejects they were—the real rejects went into the state's four-story
apartments), in that year, which was so fortunate for Sagin, the ridge finally
yielded to the persistence of unrelenting human will and the power of machinery. Water flowed into the canal. The Akdarya suddenly grew shallow.
Islands appeared where formerly there had been spits of sand. The spawning
grounds and young carp's massing places were left above water. The largest
body of fish slipped into the holes. Dozens of shoals cropped up on the previously navigable river. All at once the water became clear. The Akdarya began
to wane and fade.

That year Volodka was blissful. It was possible to scoop the befuddled carp
out of the holes with dragnets, as if out of an ordinary hatchery. There was
only one thing—carp fell in price. But Volodka compensated for his losses by
the amount of fish he caught.

The abundance lasted a year, then two, and Sagin blithely believed that
such a paradisiacal life would go on forever. The magical fairy tale came to an
end in the third year. After two years of merciless fishing the carp were almost
entirely wiped out. The stock of fish wasn't replenished—there was no longer
anywhere to spawn. Moreover, yet another misfortune befell the carp folk.
Into the lakes and headwaters of the Akdarya were introduced fingerlings of
an amazing fish that only inhabits the heavy, muddy waters of rivers on the
Great China plain. Transplanted into Central Asia, it was marvelously hardy
(it could do without water for days), uncommonly tolerant, and wonderfully
adapted to all evils in the whirlpool of existence.

The foreign fish could crawl on its belly over the silt and wet grass like a
real snake. In fact, in appearance it resembled a genuine reptile. Its narrow,
pike-like snout poked out just as if it were sniffing, its beady eyes instantly
caught the slightest quiver of a reed. The elongated black body seemed to
consist only of muscles, and a wide fin ran around the back and belly of the

bizarre fish. The beast could hop and bite like a wildcat, its pointy shark-like fangs jutting in different directions from its voracious mouth. Behind the fangs was another row of teeth, their setting resembling a boot brush.

Having studied the beast, local scientists conclusively stated that this underwater, above-water and marsh tiger was at heart a vegetarian. After all, in the rivers of China it chiefly devoured all sorts of water plants—seaweed, *kuga,* young reeds—and it didn't even disdain slime. But wiseguys were disposed to think that the beast had been on a diet of greens simply for a lack of counterparts, the latter having been eaten up beforehand by the Chinese themselves. But what don't they say in scientific circles.

As for science, it assumed that, once introduced in the proper quantity and released into the canal, the beast would make good on the costs of its introduction by plying its trade as an aquatic janitor. The Ph.D.s of fish science expected the transplant to clean up almost completely all the unwanted aquatic growth that in a single year could turn a water route of any width into a brown swamp.

Several tens of thousands of the fingerlings bought with foreign currency innocently rollicked a couple of years in the peaceful, musty reservoir waters. But before the exit canal began to operate, the river had a raucous, unbridled character. In one of those years, when the sun was warming the earth a thousandth of a percent more than usual, spring came to the valley a month ahead of schedule. The ice fields suddenly thinned and the Akdarya, taking in a huge volume of icy water, reared up and left its banks.

The dam around the lakes was broken. The toothy alien, now a fanged youngster, escaped into the river. For three years there was no news of him. The year that the new canal divided the Akdarya into two rivers (one flowing to the sea, as it was supposed to, and the other into the steppe), fishermen began to hook an unusual fish. It was amazingly uniform and awesomely gluttonous. Science, having lost the object of its research in the washed-out lakes, immediately recognized its runaway in the black horror. It was the hydrahead that later became famous.

Somewhere over there beyond the frontier, in the meager river pastures of China, perhaps it did feed on slime borscht and duckweed stew, but in the Akdarya, unfortunately, there were still fish. The immigrant set about correcting this mistake of nature with all the passion of a confirmed Maoist Red Guard. It proceeded to eat everything and everyone. In a year almost all of the young fish had disappeared from the river. The carp tribe, shaken and diminished in its merciless contest for water with king cotton, lost the fight out and out this time. The hydrahead started a campaign for the carp's total elimination. How could the soft Akdarya sybarite vie with the toothy Maoist offspring?

The carp's former renown dissipated like smoke. In the gloomy, hidden creeks and the depths of the branch-littered holes there were still 18-pound fortunates that miraculously survived, no longer daring to sally forth onto the free expanse of the river for merry carp play. They were saved from the shark-like fangs of the hydrahead only by virtue of their size. Incidentally, having wiped out everything around it that could be wiped out, the hydrahead resorted to cannibalism. Apparently this merry pastime was more suited to the demands of its nature than was tiresome munching on grass.

The carp was almost gone. Prices for it jumped sharply. They almost matched the prices on meat. People paid a ten-spot for a large, ten-pound fish. The deficit quickly elicited increased demand. Those who had disdained fish all their lives began to eat carp. On a festive table, the smoked celebrity from the Endangered Species List became an essential sign of the diner's membership in the establishment.

Volodka had appreciably more work.

8

Sagin's life was made much easier when he received a uniform cap. His snake-in-the-grass pal of a fisheries officer could only grind his teeth at the sight of Volodka's official speedboat, but he couldn't do a thing (crows don't pick crows' eyes, one office doesn't feed off another); he was forced to divide the Akdarya in half.

Sagin did indeed acquire an impressive motorboat. When they hauled the patrol boat, which had been decommissioned because of unfitness by the DOSAAF (Voluntary Society for Cooperation with the Army, Air Force and Navy), to the lifeguard's post, Volodka could only gasp quietly. The sturdy aluminum trow that had served the military organization faithfully and truly for a good ten years instilled terror. It was extremely worn. Half of the rivets had fallen out, the sides were so covered with dents that it was as if the patrol boat had come under heavy fire from a large caliber machine gun, the windshield was missing, the thwarts were smeared with grease, the suspended "Vikhoryok" consisted of a punctured gas tank and rusty reinforcing brackets, and everything else had been "liberated."

Volodka scratched his neck: he would have to assemble a living being out of these unearthed bones. He rolled up his sleeves. A wolf's legs are what feeds him, and the patrol boat was set to become Volodka's new legs.

A day later the patrol boat migrated from the dock to the local garage. Sagin counted the director in as a future fisherman, gave the foreman in the main shop a small advance, and guaranteed the metalworkers an uninterrupted supply of a name brand fuel marketed in half-liter quantities.

The planned prize trotter would have to acquire a dependable heart. Volodka rushed off to his pals at the taxi park. A rejected uninventoried Volga motor was taken apart down to the last bolt and put together with the newest parts (still in factory grease). The kopecks didn't go to waste—the taxi park handyman honed the engine block head to the nth millimeter, sharply increasing the compression, and the motor acquired extra muscle.

"No one will catch you even on dry land with a motor like this!" the engine repairman merrily winked at Volodka.

Volodka winked back:

"That's the idea!"

The winking cost the repairman three weeks of regular and overtime work, and Sagin five hundred smackers. Both sides were satisfied with one another. The motor left the garage and took its place in the nose of the lifeguard's patrol boat. The drive shaft ran under the boarding ramp planking and dove into the aluminum hull.

The propeller called for Volodka's special care. The motor was good, and the propeller had to be just as good. Volodka weighed a store propeller in his hands and threw it down.

"That's not it," he pronounced thoughtfully. "We need something else here."

Thank God the garage had its own casting plant. Sagin came to pay his respects to the spirits of the hearth. The most difficult thing turned out to be explaining exactly what it was he wanted. It turned out that Sagin himself didn't know exactly what he had in mind. However, these ingenious fellows of fiery labor in their dirty work suits easily cracked the tough nut.

Ten brass castings brought to a mirror-like brilliance with emery and a sandblaster won Volodka's heart. Twin-bladed, bright yellow, and twice as fast as standard ones, they matched Volodka's dreams to a tee.

"Just the thing!" the enchanted Sagin sighed, looking at the brilliant metal.

True, it was still necessary to struggle some with the mounting. The draw of the keel passed above the drive shaft, and the propeller's knife blades protruded threateningly beyond the cut plate.

"You'll bust a blade in the shallows," the craftsman warned Sagin. "And there's no sense in putting on a shield—the boat will crush it with its weight anyway, if you find yourself on a sandbank, say; or if you don't watch out, the hull will get ripped."

"To hell with the shield," Volodka waved his hand. "As long as the drive puts out like it's supposed to. And if it busts, that's not such a big deal. It can be replaced."

"It'll put out," agreed the craftsman. "Look what a propeller it's grown into. Watch so you don't take off."

Volodka burst out laughing.

Now, flying by the slow-moving fish inspector in his glittering aluminum racer, Volodka jauntily put two fingers to the visor of his uniform cap, and in response the inspector nodded with tender hatred.

"So near and yet so far," Volodka grinned.

"A horse has four legs, but it still stumbles. You'll stumble too," the fisheries officer gazed after him in silence.

Sagin finished his house. He bought a Yugoslav dining-room set, Finnish bedroom furniture (Lyuska wouldn't let him out of bed for a week, thanking him all that while), and finally, Sagin had his own little Zhiguli.

It seemed as if the cup of his life was beginning to overflow for Sagin.

9

Surfeit transformed him. His gait became measured, an egg-shaped stomach became clearly noticeable. Yet the prison camp tattoo on Volodka's forearm turned out to be more prophetic—the memory of his misguided first steps towards riches. "There is no happiness in life," affirmed the dark-blue needlework, the wisdom of existence behind bars.

Life's happiness was indeed incomplete, as if it had been amputated. Volodka discovered that no one esteemed him. The friendly smiles of bosom buddies and fishing companions didn't count. Volodka realized that their amiableness was all for show. Every carp Sagin caught was in effect the loss of a red-colored note from their pockets. There was no longer enough booty for everyone, and any chance night meeting at one of the Akdarya's bountiful holes could easily be bathed in blood. No, Volodka didn't put trust in his buddies' respect, and he kept some distance from his colleagues. And yesterday's classmates? What about them? After all, none of them, note, had become a bigwig. Petro was a metalworker, Kostya was at the wheel of a MAZ, and Alik filed some sort of papers in an office. You'd think they could treat Volodka with respect. But they even greeted him reluctantly, through their teeth, obviously looking down on their successful classmate. The paltry metalworker, too, stuck up his nose. You couldn't imagine how offensive that was.

"They're jealous," Lyuska snorted. "How can they compare to you? They'll just slog away all their lives on only their pay."

Volodka shrugged a shoulder. Something was wrong in his life; certain ends weren't coming together. He felt something was missing.

Sure, the carp, sure, the house, and the car. Fine, of course! Fine! Did he have money? Yes. A position? Yes. A uniform? Yes. He had everything. Where was the respect? If he had everything, then he should have respect too! After all, nothing in Sagin's pocket fell from the heavens, he had achieved everything himself. So where was the respect?

There wasn't an ounce of respect. Perhaps the problem was that the position was too low?

For the second time in his life Volodka thought hard. What should he do? Of course, to wangle his way in among the big bosses would have been the ultimate stupidity. And the reason for that wasn't his lack of abilities. Volodka's intelligence would have sufficed for three bosses plus half a dozen assistants. But to throw fate to the wind, to give up the sort of lucrative spot he commanded to whomever—one would have to be completely loony. No position in the world, not even a minister's, offered Volodka such earnings. What's more, was he to expose himself, with the gap he had in his biography? If sometime he got to blabbing, they would recall his dubious past right off. Can you clamber up a mountain with a cannon ball on your leg? Save us sinners.

A different path glimmered faintly ahead. To get respect, it wasn't at all necessary to be among the aces yourself, it was plenty to strike up friendships with bigwigs, get close to them. And then, who cares what rank you have, should one of the town bosses greet you by shaking your hand in front of everyone, in the middle of the street!? He must have earned it, since they don't shun him! Then it would become clear to anyone who walked or drove by that Volodka was no ordinary person. Now that's real respect—greetings, sir. But how to get it?

Sagin kept mulling it over and mulling it over, and smacked the meaty nape of his neck with his palm:

"Hey, musclehead! It's a pushover!"

Incidentally, in fairness it should be noted that Lyusya whispered a thing or two. There's a woman for you! God didn't short her on the bottom or on the top. She was his right hand.

Volodka loaded a dozen smoked carp into the trunk of his Zhiguli, stuffed his wallet with dough, and took off for the regional center as the day dawned. There, thank God, his immediate boss could be found, within two hundred kilometers of the Akdarya. The remoteness of Volodka's place of service from operational headquarters benefited his work.

Volodka returned from the regional capital late at night, emitting the pleasant aromas of shashlyk and cognac. In his inside pocket, neatly folded in four, nestled a paper with an official number and stamp. The OSVOD regional council requested of the appropriate authorities the allotment of a modest piece of worthless land on the banks of the Akdarya in order to organize not simply a post, as before, but a permanent OSVOD station with an appropriate facility and inventory. The OSVOD obligated itself to thoroughly equip the allotted territory and decorate it with instructional lifesaving posters.

Next to the letter lay an excerpt from the order appointing Volodka director of the newly formed OSVOD permanent station with a guaranteed wage of ninety rubles. The order vaguely promised to appoint additional personnel.

How the said excerpt appeared and what it cost Volodka was Shhh, hush-hush! Mum's the word. Mum!

10

Two months after this historic event, in place of the insignificant old booth, on the banks of the Akdarya there stood a splendorous structure, half-barn, half-palace, beneath a glittering zinc roof.

A piece of the huge sandy cape set aside by the local authorities for saving drowning people was enclosed by a high link fence.

Volodka grew his sideburns. His grandeur increased with each day. The fence had cost some money after all. Each linear meter of metal posts was paid for, and the Akdarya's carp had sacrificed their short lives for every square meter of link.

An unassembled Finnish cottage for two families arrived in Bayabad from the regional center. Volodka didn't spare costs for wining and dining the suppliers. The assistant director of the regional administration lived it up with Volodka in his lair for a week, and the object of envy for many—the luxurious frame house from the land of Suoumi, having lain in the OSVOD warehouse for four years without going anywhere because of the heated arguments over who should have it—arrived safely by barge at the Bayabad station on two MAZ trucks. Nor would the MAZ wheels turn when dry, and those wheels had to be greased too.

The assembly took two weeks. Volodka acquired a passionate taste for the life of a boss. How sweet it seemed to yell sternly at the workers laying the concrete foundation beneath his future office. Oh, mama mia, does power taste good!

Once he'd poisoned himself on the first drop of it, Volodka grew frantic. They'd finish their work and leave. Then what? What the hell kind of director was he if there was no one to whom he could give a good dressing down to clear his brains? Where were the subordinates? How can a director exist without people to execute his orders?

Once again he was forced to drive to the regional center. This time he wasn't able to get away with cognac and smoked fish. The question was reviewed so laboriously that Volodka even became thinner. Actually, it wasn't so much Volodka but his wallet that grew thin—Volodka actually shriveled up in the face of the extraordinary demands and pretensions.

"The capital," he sighed mournfully while driving home. "No one even wants to sneeze for free. They think that out here money falls from the sky."

However, the deed was done. The personnel were approved. A sailor-lifeguard second-class and an instructor on lifesaving technique came under Volodka's supervision.

In spite of the ghastly dent in his wallet, Sagin was satisfied; life was shaping up along the lines that he had plotted. As for financial losses, well, the Akdarya's round-sided aborigine would have to answer for them.

Volodka picked the lifesaving instructor right away. His brother-in-law Sashka, loyal companion of his nocturnal carp exploits, with a Master's degree in dragnets and a Doctor of floating nets, was perfectly suited to Volodka's new plans. The guy was easy to get on with, reliably tested in the deep, dark nights above the bottomless Akdarya holes, involved for the second year in both the catching and the sale of fish. No two ways about it— Volodka wouldn't let any stranger within a mile of his new office's dock. Sashka fit the instructor's chair to a tee.

It was more complicated with the sailor-lifeguard. Volodka was a little jealous of his former position. He was tormented by doubt about whether he could find a candidate who was really worthy to follow in his footsteps. After all, he had spent five years in the striped overalls of a sailor-lifeguard—a chunk of life, a good chunk. It would have been unpleasant to see an unworthy person in the familiar position. For the time being this question remained open.

In addition to the link fence, the panels of posters, ablaze with bright colors, formed a second belt around Volodka's little manor. Again he had been forced to dig deep into his wallet. Volodka had never imagined that people in art would be such blusterers and cutthroats. However, after driving all over town and sounding out all of the town's decorators, Volodka became convinced, to his chagrin, that they knew the value of a kopeck. Moreover, it looked as if the masters of brush and paint were in collusion; the honoraria they set coincided within ten rubles. Such barefaced mercenariness on the part of creative workers came as an unpleasant surprise to the dismayed Volodka. "Nothing in this world is sacred anymore!" he complained.

But his plans were too far-reaching for him to sacrifice the slightest thing in order to save another fifty. He was forced to dig deep and pay. Furthermore, in the town's higher echelons, where questions of land allotments were decided, the promised instructional posters was what decided the matter in Volodka's favor, so there was no turning back. Maybe Volodka's entire future rested on the lifesaving watercolors. It was impossible to it let slip out of his hands. And apart from everything else, the florid panels would create an impenetrable barrier around Volodka's estate, and that alone was enough to cover all of the art expenses.

"Whew, what haven't I spent money on," Volodka waved his hand, opening his long-suffering wallet. "Smear it on life-size!"

A month later Sagin loudly proclaimed to the whole wide world in red, white, and blue the truly far-reaching goals and responsible duties that he had taken upon himself, and at the top of his voice threatened not only to carry out, but also to overachieve by a huge percentage, the incredibly difficult task of saving drowning people.

11

Time raced like mad. Volodka's life on the manured field of the dear OSVOD bloomed a raspberry color. True, not a little manure had been required.

The bigwigs turned out to be not as unapproachable as they appeared in the stern silence of their offices. In fact, out in nature, in a close, intimate circle, many of them turned out to be likable fellows. And the ones who didn't were the ones who hadn't a clue about Volodka's merry office.

At first he was somewhat hesitant to take part in their conversations, wary of shaming himself because of his limited learning (he still thought that the big directors' subjects of interest must be extremely important, terribly intellectual, and utterly inaccessible to his simple understanding), but after listening in a bit, Volodka gave a sigh of relief and cheered up. The conversations of the imposing dignitaries turned out to be of the simplest kind. The talk was mostly about women, drinking, and parties. True, sometimes squabbles arose as to who had tricked whom more and when.

This was Volodka's special subject. He took to it like a yearling carp to the Akdarya shallows. Soon he noticed with secret glee that they didn't put him off in the general chatter, as had happened quite often before, when Volodka was quieter and only rarely ventured to offer a trifling remark.

No, now they listened to him and paid special attention when Volodka, getting impassioned, would tell about his numerous conquests of the weaker sex. And the more he went into detail, the more attentive his listeners became. The eyes of the men in the group would begin to glow warmly and their faces flush, and Volodka sure knew how to lay it on, embroidering and embellishing, laying out the finest nuances of his refined sexual technique to the necessary people.

Nowadays he expected important guests in the evenings. Saturday would come, and every Saturday Volodka Sagin received indulgent dignitaries according to all the written and unwritten rules of Eastern hospitality. Of course, it cost a few kopecks. But how can you avoid that? Without these constant receptions in nature Sagin's success would never survive.

His brother-in-law was dispatched to town for cognac and smoked sausage (happily, they knew all too well at the meat processing plant just who Volodka was hanging out with). Sagin didn't even consider vodka as something drinkable.

Sashka was a simple fellow, and therefore he had to be thoroughly instructed! Sagin took a terrible liking to various terms for giving orders.

"You're not to take any local slop!" Volodka explained. "Or Georgian *chacha,** but get five-star Armenian cognac, even if you have to dig it out of the ground."

Sashka shrugged his thin shoulders, surprised. For his brother-in-law's very simple taste all of these cognac-shmognacs were good only for killing bedbugs. You couldn't compare it to good ole pure vodka, tested by many years of uninterrupted abuse! But the bosses, as you'd expect, wanted to show off. Something that pleases everyone else always displeases their sensitive nostrils. His brother-in-law disapprovingly shook his tiny birdlike head and spat juicily on the floor of Volodka's office.

"You know best."

Volodka turned scarlet and hissed like an enraged lizard:

"Wipe it up!"

Sashka didn't understand.

"What's the matter?" he stared uncomprehendingly at the floor.

"Wipe it up!" Volodka choked, turning blue in the face and rising from his chair.

Sashka still didn't understand. His unclouded eyes roamed the gleaming floor and he raised them to Volodka.

"Whad'ya mean?"

Drained, Volodka plopped weakly into his chair and exhaled, as if expelling all the air inside him in one breath.

"Get going."

Sashka jerked his shoulders in wonder at Volodka's puzzling behavior and headed for the door.

"And you, you better be straight as an arrow!" the lifesaving station boss yelled at Sashka's ramrod back.

*Grape vodka.

Volodka sat a few minutes, sorrowfully pursing his lips. "You take him in and feed him, keep him at your side, go easy on him, like he's one of the family," he thought resentfully, "and that's charity for you, and then it's you who gets it back in the face. Was it so long ago my brother-in-law was tossing away ten-kopeck pieces in the beer halls and poaching small fry on the river? And he wasn't poaching with his own equipment but using his boss's. And now, after he's been raised out of the filthiest mud, has received from Sagin a striped sailor's shirt and a uniform cap with a crab on it, and has thus joined the ranks of respectable people in good standing—how does he respond to the incredible goodness of his benefactor? With what sort of services and favors?" Volodka even gave a moan at the injustice. "He doesn't even talk to me respectfully; he doesn't call me by name and patronymic or even address me as comrade boss (well all right, not at night, of course, not under wet sacks of fish), but in front of other people, right in the open! You'd think he could figure out that it was uncalled for to have the boss of the lifesaving station for the entire district get slapped on the back by his subordinate, some insignificant instructor of lifesaving methods, and to be loudly called 'Lifeguard'! After all, that's uncalled for! I'll drive him the hell out if he keeps being so familiar!" Volodka decided as he suddenly felt enraged at his brother-in-law. "I don't care if he's a relative. It looks as if a stranger's better than one of your own."

Squinting with pleasure, Volodka whispered the form of address appropriate to his position, "Greetings, Vladimir Vasilievich."

"Hello, Comrade Sailor-Lifeguard Second-class!"

"Y-a-a-a-h-h!" sighed Volodka. "It's a lotta work, real work, to get them to understand."

First thing in the morning Sagin took off for the foothills in his Zhiguli to see his shepherd friends, and he brought back a pitifully bleating small ram. Guests were expected by evening. For the pilaf to thicken in time he had to begin the preparations no later than noon. All of the fish was his own. He didn't expect any trouble there—ever since yesterday he'd had catfish meat, and carp, and bream, and small fry like roach as fillers waiting for the guests.

By four-thirty the fire beneath the three-bucket cauldron was put out. The pilaf began to steam. A fantastic aroma wafted from the fish soup. Volodka began to agonize over the wait.

At five-fifteen a dusty white Volga drove up. A tall, imposing man unhurriedly got out. His handsome face wore a peeved frown, and his large drooping nose looked as if it was sniffing. This was the assistant director of the town administration.

Sagin fawned upon his benefactor like a petty demon. The latter passed through the yard to the office, stretching his fat legs. Volodka ingratiatingly supported his teacher in life by the elbow.

The assistant director ran his agate eye over the posters with cheerful life-saving slogans and gave Volodka a satisfied nod.

"I see, I see. Well done. Turns out you're smart. You're coming along. We weren't wrong about you, it's obvious."

Volodka bloomed like a peony. His round visage shone unctuously at the boss's kindness.

"We try," he took up with bravado. "This quarter we're proceeding to over-fulfill the plan for saving drowning people!"

The assistant director grinned: "Where the heck do you get them, these rescued ones? Do you sink them yourself or what?" He poked Volodka in the ribs with his elbow. Volodka tittered playfully.

"We find ways to cope. Some of them, of course, we provide ourselves. The plan is something sacred."

Volodka had sunk and saved all of his close and distant acquaintances in paper water and had begun checking each of them off a second time; so indeed all was really in order as far as the plan went.

"Well, keep it up, keep it up. Just watch you don't overdo it." Setting his face sternly, he turned to Sagin. "Who else is expected here today?"

Volodka drew close to the director's ear and, his hand over his mouth, quietly whispered a word.

"Ah-h-h," he grew animated. "I approve, I approve. Like I said, you're smart. Well done."

Obviously pleased by the information, he moved on.

"So, what have we here?"

Volodka briskly ran to his side.

"Come on, this way."

A high dais was set up over the water in a small inlet behind the pier. Four powerful I-beams of blue steel, two meters in length, extended into the gravel of the Akdarya's bank. A framework surrounded the columns and on it was set a spacious wooden dais with a lattice fence for about twenty people. It wasn't for nothing that Volodka had driven a bulldozer and a drilling rig onto the bank—this place of well-earned rest was made to last forever. The rough flooring of the dais was overlaid with plyboard.

The assistant director grinned again. He recognized the plyboard. Camel hides lay on top of the wood. Satin cushions lined the perimeter of the low table like a multicolored rainbow belt. In the middle stood several trays painted in the colorful Zhostovo style with apples, grapes, dried apricots and other gifts of the bountiful Eastern land. Off to the side you could see a separate tray with flatbread.

Another Volga drove into the yard. There wasn't a speck of dust on the car. Volodka dashed up to it as fast as he could. His hand pressed against his chest and, bending in a low half-bow, he opened the white door.

12

They partied a long time. The pilaf and fish soup were consumed, and in the course of things they had prepared and gobbled up the *domlama,** but there was still no end in sight to the merriment. Before eleven they were already getting stuffed, and drinking and sweating a lot. After eleven one of the bigwigs developed a certain appetite. Letting out a satisfied belch in Volodka's direction, he raised his mawkish eyes and beckoned to the director of the life-saving station.

"We have to talk."

Volodka crawled on his knees through the mess of plates, tea cups, gnawed bones and empty bottles. The bigwig, half embracing Sagin around the shoulders, fell upon Volodka with his huge stomach.

"I need a mama, Volodka," he said, enveloping Sagin with the satiated smells of mutton fat and cognac.

Being half drunk, Volodka didn't immediately catch on to what was being put to him.

"Huh, huh?" he asked stupidly. "Whose mama?"

The bigwig winced aggravatedly.

"Maruska, get Maruska! We'll have some white meat!"

The regional boss came up on one side.

"Yes," he purred. "Just the thing. Just the time for it. Only make sure, Sagin," the boss threatened Volodka with a chubby finger on which a signet was firmly dug into the flesh, "that everything's nice and clean. We wouldn't want to catch anything."

Now it got through to Volodka.

"So that's it. You should've said so. Else with this 'mama, mama,' how could I figure it out right away?"

The guests had to have dessert. Volodka, feeling lazy and full, started to try to get out of it.

"It's already late, where are you going to find that now? You should've ordered sooner."

*A rich Uzbek stew.

But the bigwig's little eyes had completely sunk into his lardy, puffy cheeks.

"E-e-e-h, Volodka, such a little thing, what'll it cost you?" he flattered him. "You mentioned it yourself," he poked Sagin. "Don't waste time. You know the custom? Don't offend the guests."

Volodka sighed and got up from the cushion. He glanced at the clock with annoyance. Eleven-thirty. No, really, whose door could you knock on at this time of night?

Sagin winked at his brother-in-law. Though stone drunk, he came over in a flash. Volodka had cooled off. There was proper training for you—it was already showing. Sagin tossed his relative a ring of keys. His drunk brother-in-law caught them on the fly.

"Take the jalopy," Volodka ordered sternly, "run to the restaurant. They'll just be closing up there now. Maybe some rats are still free. Hook 'em on the fly and drag 'em back here."

"And if it's bare?" squinted Sashka, who was very experienced in these matters. "Then what?"

"Then nab a couple of waitresses," Volodka explained with annoyance. "Say that Volodya the Lifeguard is asking and he'll answer for it. Say there are juicy pheasants, the girls won't be disappointed."

"So which of 'em exactly should I pick up?" the relative kept up the needless questions.

Volodka became rabid.

"What are you, some kind of innocent lamb?" he asked venomously. "Or did you forget everything you know? Or maybe you yourself never used these goods?"

Sashka began to rock with indignation.

"Bro, you've got a lot of... Bro, heck, I'm a married man, I, got it, never, never... I never set foot in there."

Volodka almost bit off his tongue at his brother-in-law's gall. For a few moments he was silent, unable to find expressions strong enough for an answer, then he laughed hoarsely:

"Well, aren't you something, Sashok. So you've hung one on."

Sashka continued to sway, but now in silence. He seemed to be sleeping.

"'Member last week," Volodka woke him, "you forget who you were posing with like in a museum picture, in this very place?"

"Picture. . ? Ahh, a picture," his brother-in-law appeared to remember.

Volodka shoved him towards the car.

"Get a move on before they all run off. If nothing else, you get Katya, the dining-room head, and maybe the little new girl, Nelka."

"That's the blondie?" Sashka smiled drunkenly.

"Yeah, yeah!" Volodka roared after him. "You finally remembered. That's not like doing Ivan the Terrible and His Son in the nude!"

Nelenka, the blonde, a new waitress from a big city restaurant, had come to town a couple of months before. Tall, buxom, and rosy-cheeked, and her hair, lightened with peroxide, was puffed up in front like a horse's bangs and grew to her waist in back. Nelka fit right in in this run-down provincial hole.

Volodka had faint hopes that perhaps she was not busy that day, though it was hard to hope for that. They were biting at Nelka like the hydrahead itself. Nelka was dazed by the nuts showering money on her. There, in the city, her price was a three on a good market day; here, far from the easily obtainable temptations of the big city, there was a host of enthusiasts for Nelka's pinkish-white charms.

The district aces were especially knocked out by this piece from the capital. Her first month's work at the restaurant was also the month of her biggest haul. She took up with the chairmen of remote kolkhozes and regional co-op supply big wheels. She had come to her sister in Bayabad for an orphan's dole, barefoot and naked, with a sad-looking little fiber suitcase, and she worked as a dishwasher at the Zeravshan, but in a month Nelka was dressed like a foreign movie star, decked out from head to foot with gold trinkets. If it were possible to wear rings on your toes, they, too, would have appeared on Nelka's feet. But now the third month of her service at the restaurant was running out. The initial appetite was satisfied, and the rich clientele noticeably cooled to her plentiful figure. Besides that, Nelka, stunned by the demand, came to believe in the endlessness of the crazy stallion feeding and she became more expensive. If for the managers of tens of thousands of acres of arable land no price seemed too high, for their assistants Nelka's new valuation was not affordable. Even though he wasn't at all involved, Volodka quietly swore through his teeth. Just to think how easily big money found its way to that rat. In the most literal meaning of the word, Nelka didn't even have to get out of bed, and to boot, now and then she probably even got a kick out of working at such a profitable occupation! Sagin got furious when he thought about it. True, he made a small correction here. What kind of kick could she get out of the big-bellied lard-assed runts who, to a man, filled the cushy slots at the top of the district management. All the same, how could you compare Nelka's easy work with Volodka's hard labor?

It's the middle of a pitch-black night, a cold gusty wind over the water, an angry wave beating at the speedboat's vibrating jaw; weighty, wet nets; slippery, strong fish writhing furiously in your hands; the lattice floor dancing under your feet—just watch you don't end up overboard, and then the boat will come keel around onto your noggin, and then you can remember Vladimir Vasilievich and his hard life in your prayers.

And all the while, and all about, just keep an eye peeled, just watch out, just keep your ears up lest somewhere (you guess behind the island, but it seems that it's next to the heart, which is panting in nervous palpitation) the ragged cough of the fisheries officer's patrol boat is heard, or the stabbing eye of the searchlight flares up in the middle of the foggy, night water, trained on the very center of Volodka's fear!

And then? No better. Leaden sacks of fish; gasping, Volodka loads them into the back of the old ZIL pickup truck, heaving them with a grunt over the towering side. His brother-in-law is off to the side, by the road, on guard: where might the OBKhSS* agents be—sleeping or not? And Volodka's trained ears are ever on guard for the drawn-out whistle—the signal for mortal danger.

And on the road? Each oncoming headlight scares you shitless—you can't put it any other way, by God—such an inhuman dread rises in your throat from the very bottom of your icy stomach. But what's a headlight? Every low star seems like the light of a militia motorcycle: now you've gone too far—now we've got you! Before you reach your destination, your mouth is full of sticky, salty saliva. You can wring your shirt out by the end of the trip. And the result of all these ghastly labors and fears?

Volodka spit bitterly. It's good if about three hundred is cleared in a night. That is, God willing, and a thank-you to fate, too, for a generous present, sometimes along the way more goes out than comes in. Give to one, and give to another, and a little grease here, a small share there—and anybody and everybody sticks his greedy paw straight into Volodka's pocket. As if to say, So what?, you can still get as much as you want out there. There are more carp in the Akdarya than you can see or count, all yours, enough for a hundred years, and our children will still have some! And what's left? What's left is what Volodka, today, right now, will take. And it's precisely from this, from what is hard-earned with heavy labor and risk, that everyone tries to skim the milk fat.

How could you compare Volodka's earnings with the lucky winnings of some red-headed slut? No fisheries officer, no GAI,† no OBKhSS would nick her in a thousand years—like, where was the thing obtained and for what kind of dough? How could they? If they got onto something, she would find a chance to rip them off. And what of it? They're men too, made from the same flesh, how can they resist? And if they got a free ride, why, you couldn't even pull them off by their ears!

Volodka chuckled. Not long before, he had gotten burned by this Nelka. He'd been really plastered, accidentally happened upon the bitch, well, and

*Department for Combating Theft of Socialist Property.
†State Auto Inspection.

his deep craving could not be held in check.

Volodka squinted with pleasure. How could Lyuska compare to her? His wife was a dead log compared to Nelka. To loll about in bed with Nelka was the same as a visit to paradise. There was a reason she raked in the dough.

It was a good thing that Volodka only had twenty-five with him then. After Nelka, everybody knows, there's no money left for the trolley. How the red-headed rat nagged him after that, did she roast him, she just couldn't believe that Volodka had dragged her to his OSVOD den for the whole night with such a pittance in his pocket. Was she ever angry! True, in the morning Volodka made it up to her with smoked fish, he packed up five amber carps, translucently fat. That is, figure it, a red ten-ruble bill apiece, which comes to half a hundred, but Nelka remained dissatisfied; she was used to real money, the damn woman, so she didn't consider any substitutes good enough.

Volodka grinned. Never mind, you'll get it back from the fish all the same; leave it there in your dive with Katka the headwaitress for twenty-five apiece. Or cut it up and it'll come to even more. Clients are fools—after half a liter they'll gobble herring and think it's sturgeon!

The car flew into the yard at breakneck speed.

"It's all set!" hollered his brother-in-law. "When I give my word, I give my word!"

And Sashka honked so the whole Akdarya could hear.

"Welcome the guests!"

Sashka's shouts were interrupted by women's laughter and squeals from the car.

Let's party! Let's get crazy!

13

That summer Ivan Sergeevich Nikitin turned twenty-three.

In Ivan's view, a respectable age. All sorts of things were already behind him. For instance, the army. The draft. He was sort of forced to put in his labor along with everyone else, and Ivan was discharged as a lieutenant. And not for some carefree civilian life but for a new service, almost the same as the military—preserving the people's wealth from all types of nighttime crooks as a fish inspector.

How had he served in his new position these one-and-a-half years? His epaulets told the story. To become an officer in fifteen months with a secondary education—that wasn't easy. Wits, and intelligence, and maneuvering, and much else besides played a part. Every last bit of his life had to be put into his work, and even that might not have helped if Ivan hadn't known a certain sacred word.

That word was the chief thing in Ivan's life and it sounded like this: "LAW!"

From the very first day of his service as a soldier, even before taking the oath, while sweating through the tough "young warrior" school, Ivan Sergeevich imbibed this wonderful, imposing word. It was precisely because it didn't admit of any isolated life, apart from other crucial words, that the word proved to be close to Ivan's heart. Submitting to a military routine, the word would only march through life in file. On all sides it had friendly support from other words with the same redoubtable strength.

One of them, CONSCIENCE, stood out in the same rank as LAW. And others marched right alongside; for example: LABOR, HONOR, and ORDER.

The words supported one another and Ivan himself, in turn, supported them. Generally speaking, it's hard to say whether Ivan supported them, or was himself dependent on them, but in any case these words became such a part of Ivan that should they have had to be ripped off—well, a lot of blood would have flowed.

And people tried to rip them off, more than once. Sometimes brazenly, sometimes subtly. What didn't they promise! He wouldn't give in. And each one of his years of not giving in he counted as three of giving in. So Ivan went on counting—a year for three, a year for three. As in combat.

And he adhered to his straight line without flinching. "You're not behaving according to the law. Not honestly. And consequently there will have to be an accounting." And when from out of the darkness he heard morose grumbling in retort, he would add for clarity's sake:

"The way they write about it in the papers, that's just how we're going to live and act. It's written for us, not for foreigners."

And seasoned, hounded beasts who had long ago misplaced their conscience, and truth, and the law retreated in the face of his naive, fearless belief in the power of the naked truth. It turned out that it wasn't so simple to handle a man who would fearlessly tell any thief to his face that he was a thief!

Among the protectors of nature, the Bayabad station of the fish conservation office was not considered a great find. It's a long way to the regional center, and, then, these places are isolated, a lot of things can happen in the woods. And so, when the old supervisor got into a fix and had to leave, there wasn't any great competition for the opening. In the higher conservation echelons it was decided to entrust the young lieutenant with shaping things up his way on the Akdarya, instead of at regional headquarters.

That's how young Ivan landed in the very middle of—shall we say—Volodka's realm.

In handing over his duties the old inspector didn't look anybody in the face and he spoke through his teeth. It seemed that he, for one, understood well why they had come down so hard on him. Of course, they had to come up with a cozy little spot for one of their own. And the newcomer even demanded that the position be turned over according to the book.

But what was there to hand over? The Akdarya—there it was. The woods—what wasn't burned out was there, and what was burned out would grow up again, God willing. All the carp were in the water and you couldn't count them; the poachers ... Ah, the poachers. Well, we'll hand them over with great pleasure.

The old inspector got worked up.

"There's a guy around here, called Volodka the Lifeguard; he's not subordinate to anyone or anything on the river..."

As soon as they got around to Volodka, who stuck in his throat crosswise like a bone, he immediately found his tongue.

The young inspector just shook his head disapprovingly.

"Why," he asked, "don't you observe the law?"

The old inspector silently directed his eyes upwards.

"His defenders. He feeds them like a fisherman feeds carp."

The junior lieutenant only pressed his weathered lips more tightly.

"You read the latest editorial in *Pravda*?" he asked quietly.

The old inspector nodded his head in understanding. "He won't last," he couldn't help but think... "Look what it's done to him. You can't shield yourself from death with *Pravda's* truth, you can't make a pillbox with newspaper. Life's got its own truth. With the naive eyes this guy's got, you can't last long in the world, you can't get by."

The old man felt an unpleasant stab in his heart. "So that's why they sent him here," he thought. "And I was about to get all mad. Well, so what—it's their decision. It's official, so that's how it has to be, and I'm out of here."

"So, right here, in the middle of the river, that's what kind of sore has sprung up," cautiously hinted the old inspector.

The young inspector grew stern.

"We'll wipe it out. We'll begin with him to establish order on the river. It's time."

The old inspector looked away, his eyes burning with triumphant joy. If this puppy gets his teeth into your thigh he won't let go!

War was declared, although for now only unilaterally. The conversation took place in the evening, and the next morning (both of them could hardly wait for sunrise) they set off to meet their enemy.

14

It was barely dawn when Volodka felt an urgent need to pee. Disheveled from sleep, half-drunk, still not having come to after the carousing of the day before, he made his way to the river bank and went down toward the water.

A milky light was emanating from the far bank, which undulated in the pre-dawn haze. Like a mirror, the night's dew had covered the planks on the pier. The river slept.

Having relieved himself and had a yawn, for a long while Volodka rubbed his sleepy eyes with his fists. Mother of God, did they ever go wild last night!

The bosses departed after two in the morning. The ladies were sleeping like logs. Let them rest up for now. In the morning they'd still have some little odd jobs.

Volodka was on the verge of going back to the office to finish his sleep when his attention was caught by the faraway clatter of an engine sailing off over the water. He stopped and listened closely. The sound grew. Now it became distinctly audible, and Volodka's experienced ear detected a familiar coughing in the even throb of the boat's engine. Sagin grinned—his old snake-in-the-grass buddy the inspector was riding his trow through the middle of the slumbering river.

"God, the snake can't get to sleep," Volodka surmised hostilely. "And where the devil is he taking off to on the water at such an hour? All decent folk are still sleeping, only that rot is out on the river amusing himself." Sagin waited a little more. "He isn't heading for my place, is he?"

Sure enough, the engine's knocking grew ever more distinct. In a couple of minutes a black tub poked out of the sultry shroud of fog. In the middle of the patrol boat two dim figures in uniform were frozen stockstill. The motorboat set a course for Volodka's pier. He was surprised. What was it that the fisheries officer suddenly needed at his homestead?

For the third year running, the inspector and Sagin had been studiously ignoring each other. Coming face to face on the river, they would turn away and drive off, resolutely contemplating opposite banks.

Volodka raised his guard.

Softly the motorboat came in at the OSVOD pier. A sloping wave ran onto the bank, licking it affectionately. The two dark figures lithely emerged onto the wide, board surface and set off toward him. Volodka recognized his mortal well-wisher the inspector at once (him, him, the nice guy, and his mug, unhappy with the whole world, it's his. My, how he pulls a face, darting his wolfish eyes around like that); Volodka didn't know the second one.

Keeping one step behind the old inspector, a light-haired young fellow of modest height, with a lieutenant's chevrons on his light-blue shoulder straps, planted each step energetically. Volodka, admiring this robust bearing, unconsciously pulled in his ample stomach too. However, he immediately came to his senses. Who was he standing tall for? Hadn't much more important men left there two hours ago? It still wasn't clear who should stand at attention before whom.

The inspectors came up to Sagin and simultaneously touched their visors. Volodka's chin dropped. What sort of wonder was this?

His old antagonist, grimacing and sour as a lemon, announced himself, fixing Volodka with hard eyes:

"So, you know, citizen Lifeguard, as part of my duty I'm introducing to you the conservation office's new officer for the Bayabad Station, Comrade Nikitin. From now on he's going to be protecting poaching on the river and its adjacent locales."

Here the young inspector jerked his shoulder and corrected the old man:

"Protecting against poaching. Against!"

The old one turned to him in puzzlement.

"That's what I'm saying. To rein in the operators." He shuffled awkwardly in place and added, "So that, you know, there's some order. Otherwise, it's outright stealing."

But, stepping forward, the young lieutenant himself was already announcing to Volodka that his name was Ivan Sergeevich and that the state had entrusted to him the vital task of preserving, in total and untouched, this twenty-five kilometer stretch of a great Asian river.

Somewhat stunned, Volodka finally came to himself.

"Why am I being so honored?" he asked venomously. "I don't see that I have anything in particular to do with your concerns. And how are the defenders of the people's wealth planning to save it from plunderers, individually or together?" viciously added Sagin, glancing in the direction of the old inspector. The other keenly detected the gibe in Volodka's question.

"They're takin' me out, takin' me out of service, you heard it right," he answered glumly. "This mare is old, I guess, old, all worn out, it's time for the glue factory. Only there's little profit in it for you." And wiping away the merry smile that had splashed up in Volodka's eyes, with morose determination he went on about how, according to his deep and longtime conviction, the first and meanest enemy of the Akdarya was the brazen, free-wheeling lifeguard Volodka. "And the enemy, you see, you have to know by sight so that when the opportunity arises, you won't make a mistake but will hit the bull's eye. That's why we came," he said, finishing with malicious glee.

Volodka cut his well-wisher's report short.

"But you're not a thief until you're caught! You heard of that? Everybody's great at shooting off their mouth but watch what you say, so you don't go too far. You're not dealing with some lousy drifter, damn it, but a director in the State Lifesaving Service. And bad words and false slander can be easily prosecuted, according to the appropriate statute," Volodka turned the screw.

The new inspector, batting his light eyelashes, silently listened to the fencing of the old acquaintances. And only at the end of the conversation, when Volodka, heated up on account of his lingering intoxication, announced with a mild threat that he who is master in town is master of the river, and that it wouldn't hurt certain people to be slower to show their teeth, lest by accident they fly out together with their head, only then did the reticent young lieutenant drop a quiet word that burned Volodka's loosened tongue like hot pitch.

"The law," he said, firmly pronouncing the letters. "Throughout our country the law is master, both on the river and off the river." The lieutenant once again put his fingers to his lustrous visor. "It was a pleasure to meet you. I hope you've understood that it's impermissible to break the law. We won't allow it." He lithely turned on his heels and as accurately as before he set off, measuredly planting each step.

Volodka followed him with a mocking look. A greenhorn. A raw recruit. A young carp. Look what young roosters are starting to crow. First get your voice, then sing. The law... the law is the taiga, Comrade Junior General. All last night your "law" partied on my good money. That's what the law's all about. Just let someone peep against Sagin now—in an instant a hand with five hairy fingers will pick up the phone and... Careful, young Ivan, or else in the very near future you'll be off to protect the natural wealth of the Karakum desert. After all, I dare say there's something to protect there too, in them there sands. Volodka broke into laughter. The old inspector seized Sagin by his vest.

"Baring your teeth, Lifeguard?" he hissed into Volodka's face. "And have you forgotten the saying, he who laughs last laughs the longest?!"

"Bug off," Volodka flung the grasping palm from his sailor's shirt. "Keep your paws to yourself! It's about time you saved your own throat instead of pawing at someone else's. Your arms are short nowadays. Got it?!"

The inspector turned from yellow to green.

"You think I don't know why you got so brave?" he hoarsely hissed. "Or I'm not wise to who you were partying with last night? I'm wise to it all. You think you fed the big shots, plied them with drink, bedded girls under them, and that's that? You're on top? That's all right, there's more than one way to skin a cat! I couldn't handle you, my fault, I'm to blame. Only you won't always be swimming in honey. The weather outside has turned lousy, I'm burning, but so are you, Lifeguard, the day will come when you'll go up in smoke!"

He threatened Volodka with a bent, shaking finger.

"Young Ivan is pure through and through. You won't be able to get at him by hook or by crook. Watch that your big-bellied buddies don't get a shaking up too! Then you'll remember how you were dancing while I was sinking. Life is long."

"Get out, get out of here," Volodka frowned. "I'm not at all interested in your misery now. You've sung your song and that's enough—we've listened to you a long time and don't want any more. You can finish singing to the prosecutor..."

The old inspector turned away and quickly went to the motorboat. At the very end of the pier he looked back at the broadly smiling Sagin and yelled, spitting it out:

"You'll understand, you scum, what it means to joke with the law!"

The motor began to rumble. Volodka shrugged his shoulders, spit boldly and went to catch up on his dreams.

And only somewhere on the very edge of his consciousness, wisened by life, gnawed a vague premonition of unpleasant changes in the offing. The eyes that had looked at him a minute ago from beneath auburn, sun-bleached brows were just too pure and bright.

"Ah, it doesn't matter," he reassured himself. "He'll get licked into shape. The Akdarya has washed the stupidity out of better than him." And yet, regardless of all the pleasure derived from the defeat of a longtime enemy, Volodka would have preferred to continue dealing with him. With one like that you knew where you stood. But the new one? He was young, hot, he might throw a wrench into things out of stupidity.

"Oh," sighed Sagin. "I wan-n-n-a sleep!"

15

Two days later Sagin was seized with his nets at the Kiyarskaya hole. And thank God that he hadn't yet managed to make even one cast. He got by with a slight scare. The nets were confiscated, a protocol drawn up, and Volodka was fined fifty.

Of course it was unpleasant for him but he just grinned: a new broom sweeps clean. What can you do about that? We'll wait, bide our time. A shower doesn't always wet the ground, nor does the sun forever bake it. He was certain that young Ivan's raids were temporary, just to instill fear. Volodka himself would have been just as smart-alecky were he in Ivan's place. After all, eventually he would get his fill of power and settle down. Then we'll have a heart-to-heart chat.

But he couldn't manage heart-to-heart contact. Shortly, there followed yet another nocturnal encounter at the hole, with evidence. This time there were a hundred kilograms of freshly caught carp in Volodka's speedboat. He was hooked yet again a few days later.

The very same morning a search was made at his station. Eighteen nets and four large dragnets were confiscated. Why he had been so absolutely certain of the detectives' total lack of access to the office warehouse—God knows, but anyway, he suffered a great loss. The only tackle Volodka had left were the two dragnets and four nets that were at home.

The OBKhSS instituted a case against him. All of the essential materials for it were supplied by the officer of the fish conservation bureau, Nikitin.

Volodka did not tell anyone what went on in his soul that terrible month when young Ivan, with an unflinching hand, destroyed his prosperity of many years and prison threatened him again. Now even Lyuska couldn't suggest anything helpful. The Akdarya turned into a virtual minefield, you might say he was forced to step with caution and furtiveness in his own garden.

Only towards the end of the month could Sashka, who had gone along as an accomplice but by now was scared to death, finally see Volodka's tiny eyes lose their ashen dullness and the back that had been bowed in the police corridors straighten up a bit.

The investigation was temporarily halted. Signed statements were taken from Volodka and Sashka saying they would not leave their home area. It was likewise mandated to present the investigation with utterly unimpeachable character references and a petition from the collective to release and place the accused under its supervision.

Volodka got a breather.

The first and hottest burst of flame Volodka put out himself; he didn't knock on any doors for a helping hand. More in the pit of his stomach than in his mind, he felt that the time for such knocking hadn't yet come.

Thank God a circuitous passage was found into that same inconspicuous office out of which at some fine moment Volodka Sagin could easily have been led in handcuffs.

"There, you see," his happy wife excitedly whispered into Volodka's ear in the quiet of the night, "they're all people, none of them is above it. Why is it you can't make it up with the inspector himself? Is it that something else came up between you, or is it that you're hiding something from me?"

Sagin just waved his wife off.

"What's there to hide? If there was something, I would have said so a long time ago!"

"Then what's the matter?" Lyuska wouldn't let it drop.

"You see, he's an honest man, and that's why he isn't on the take." Volodka pronounced these words, which for him were monstrous, with difficulty.

Lyuska hissed like spittle on a hot griddle.

"Why, you've gone completely nuts from fright, my dear little man," she burst out with gusto. "That's the truth, you've gone nuts. Who anywhere ever heard of such a thing, that a boss was offered something and he didn't take it? Ho-o-o-nest..." she drawled with indescribable contempt. "Just who is he, a government minister of some sort, maybe, to be honest like that? Or does he already have a hundred thousand tucked away, that he's gotten so proud? Small birds shouldn't fly in the clouds. Can he be honest on his salary? And people better than him don't disdain a kopeck. What a number, making out like a virgin. When he makes his way in the world, when he grows his feathers, then let him make a show of himself. Honest, ha!"

"There's no need to go into long explanations," Lyuska sternly told her husband. "You'd better buy him off right away with all the trimmings! Give as much as he asks. He drives up the price, plays stupid, just go along. Hey, it's simple. First thing in the morning go and grease his palm without worring about the cost. It doesn't matter, we'll still get ours, if only he lays off."

In despair Volodka struck his fist against the damp pillow.

"Didn't I promise him?! He won't even hear of it."

"See, see," Lyuska took up triumphantly, "You promised. You can't feed a nightingale on tales. You show him money, good money. Let him see it with his own eyes. There's no way he'll turn it down! You and your promises..."

Volodka thought, and thought, and that's what he did. What else was left?

The lieutenant took the money. And in half an hour the high-flying Volodka was nabbed right on the street. It was fortunate that at least no witnesses were found. Sagin denied everything and sat tight. The result of his daring act was an additional charge of fresh criminal activities, true, this time according to another article of the Criminal Code. An attempt to bribe an official in the performance of his duties. Plus three years.

Volodka almost turned gray. And the money went to waste. He flatly refused it and the one grand somehow evaporated unnoticed in the corridors of power, without ever reaching the state treasury, and the upshot of the whole deal turned out the opposite of what his wife had planned.

"Damn asshole!" Volodka growled, either at his dear better-half or at himself. "Who was I listening to!"

"Can it right now," the investigator told Sagin. "If you keep on screeching, I'll jail you. I gave you a little breathing room, so don't think you've crawled back on your horse again. Just watch it! And have the papers to clear you on my desk tomorrow. Public opinion had better stand behind you like a mountain, or else... And as far as Ivan Sergeevich is concerned, I'll put it to you this way, Sagin: as soon as you notice him anywhere, on the river or simply on the street, run from him as fast as you can, wherever your nose leads you! And be careful not to look back. It'll go better for you. No joke, Sagin, I'm warning you."

Volodka nodded in agreement and grew downcast. The captain coldly sized up his hunched figure.

"You had your hand in the cookie jar, now take what you have coming. Remember the popular wisdom: 'You're not guilty until you're caught.' Well all right, get going. You're free for now."

The words "for now" stuck in Volodka's heart like an icepick. He went out onto the street, perched on a bench, and became lost in thought.

Perhaps it was time. Yes, the time had come to call in a little debt. Was it for nothing that all these years he'd plied him with drink, fed him, and bedded girls under him?

Volodka had been saving an important person for just such an urgent, dire situation. Let him work off what he'd eaten up. What was it to him? One call, and the wheels would turn in the other direction. He would put an end to it at once. Who wants to come up against an important person? Arguing with him is the same as cutting yourself off at the root. He'll squash you without batting an eyelash.

Yes, perhaps it was time.

16

Sagin ran off to the white three-story building. It's okay, all's not yet lost: we, for you—you, for us. That's how it's been done in life since time immemorial.

What sort of wonder was this!? The office that had always been so hospitable now looked like an impregnable bastion. The double door was shut tight before the rushing Sagin. Was the report already in? Whew, now such a bloody mess has started that it's all or nothing. Save me, you snake!

The secretary snapped at Volodka like a fine German shepherd.

"No visits today! He's busy. I'm telling you in plain Russian."

Volodka stared at her in astonishment.

"What's with you, Alya, you off your rocker? Don't you recognize your old friends? It's me, Volodka!"

He tried to slap his old acquaintance on the shoulder. The secretary recoiled from his hand as from a white-hot iron.

"That's just it, you're Volodka," she blurted out without thinking. Alya immediately corrected him, however.

"Apparently it's you, citizen, who is off his rocker!" she yelled, darting an eye toward the door covered with Yugoslav leather. "The hours for personal matters are on Thursday, after six, and only with an advance appointment. Go to the doorman, there they'll tell you where to make the appointment."

And Alya began smartly banging away on the typewriter.

Volodka went into a frenzy. A month ago they were partying together without any advance appointments, and now...

He turned abruptly and yanked the leather door towards himself. Behind his back the secretary started to chirp piercingly, but Volodka, passing through the vestibule, was already inside the huge office.

He was met by the cold and ice of unblinking, glassy eyes swimming above a pile of papers. Sagin's fieriness abated somewhat.

"How did you get in here, citizen?" rumbled the calm, distancing voice. "I asked the secretary not to let anyone in. Today I'm not seeing visitors and I'm very busy. Come according to the schedule. Right now I'm requesting you to vacate the office."

Volodka was dumfounded.

"Aha," he finally got out, bumbling. "I guess you don't recognize me? It's me, Volodka from the lifesaving station. I have an urgent matter for you."

The master of the office was silent a while, then reluctantly pushed away the papers.

"I recognized you, I did," he muttered with displeasure. "Well, say what you need. I have a lot to do, so get it out and be on your way!"

Flabbergasted by the unprecedented reception, Volodka laid out his misfortune to the important person. The latter heard him out attentively and frowned.

"Well, what about it?" he asked, looking over Sagin's head. "So why are you telling me all this?"

"What do you mean, Why?" Sagin was surprised, still not believing the obvious. "After all, you just have to say the word and everything will change. Some chintzy little inspector! Call him in, hint that he shouldn't butt into other people's business... And I'll come to an understanding with the rest..."

The important person looked out the window, puffed a few times, and then his face began to take on a violet shade.

"What're you talking about?" he asked the startled Volodka in a hissing whisper. "Have you completely lost it? Why are you barging in here with your thieving business? You forget where you are? Forget what the weather's like outside now? I'm sitting here myself like on a bonfire, I don't know what'll become of me tomorrow! And you want to entangle me in some sort of machinations? Who was it who told you to come to me, who suggested it? Well, tell me!"

Volodka lost his voice from fright. This wasn't like spinning yarns on the divan. For the first time he understood the really huge difference in their positions. To wind up behind bars from this leather office was much easier than from the office he'd left not long ago. Mopping his cold sweat, Sagin babbled:

"What are you saying, what are you saying! No one suggested anything. Just by myself, on account of our old acquaintance, I decided to ask..."

"I'll give you old acquaintance!" thundered forth as if from a cloud. "Among my acquaintances there are no crooks or scoundrels! You crawled into the dirt yourself, now crawl out yourself! You barge in here like into your own barn! You show up here again, you'll have yourself to blame—within twenty-four hours you'll be out of town! Out of here!"

Volodka shot out of the office like a bullet. His fingers were trembling.

"What now?" he mumbled senselessly. "What now!?"

The secretary raised her understanding eyes from behind the typewriter.

"Kicked you out?" she asked sympathetically. "I told you not to go in."

"What's with him anyway?" Volodka brought out with difficulty.

Alya beckoned with a little manicured finger. He came closer.

"A commission has arrived," the secretary confided in a whisper. "From up there!" she pointed at the ceiling. "They're checking. Both the apartment business and in general. Immorality too. You know what they get burned on most. He's on shaky ground himself right now. So why should he care about you? He ordered all kind of... former acquaintances to be kept out," she said, hesitating a second.

Volodka grunted.

"So. Plain and simple. That means it's everyone for himself, and God for all?"

The secretary shrugged her shoulders.

"And what'd you think?"

Sagin understood that he'd have to get out of the tangle by himself. Help couldn't be expected from anywhere.

17

It was one lousy thing after another. But he had to live, to earn a kopeck. And Sagin decided to take a risk.

Night fell on the marshy bank of the Akdarya like a heavy quilted blanket. Shredded patches of clouds raced across the dark night. A stormy northwest wind came up in irregular gusts.

Sashka had gone down to the dock twice; he kept checking whether the net and fish sacks were well packed. Volodka waited patiently in his office for the time to go to work.

A soft, diffuse light spread from beneath the green shade of the desk lamp. A warm stream of night smells drifted into the open window, forcing Volodka's wide nostrils to quiver involuntarily. The aroma of ripe mint mixed with the hot smell of the air that had been heating up all day, faint gasoline fumes wafted from the distant asphalt, but the cool breath of the nearby river punctuated and suffused everything. From it came the barely distinguishable smells of rotting reeds and fresh fish.

Out of idleness, Volodka amused himself with the lamp. His finger pressed the off button and the light would go out. Several seconds passed and a sharp light plucked from the darkness a wide, feline face with reddish sideburns and the sharp slits of puffy eyes.

Finally Sashka, who was at the window, couldn't take it any more.

"So why are you flashing the light, why are you flashing it?" he muttered in vexation. "You'll catch it for your flashing. What a plaything you've come up with."

Volodka shuddered. His finger froze on the off button.

All day Sagin had been out of sorts. His temple throbbed unpleasantly. He felt ill. "Maybe I shouldn't go today," he thought vaguely. "Can trouble be far away? After all, I'm hanging in a spider's web. And what if they catch me again, then what?" Volodka grinned dryly. "Then it's biscuit baking and letter writing. On account of this greenhorn everything I've earned will go to pieces. For a good five years I won't be pawing Lyuska but some straw pillow instead. Go or not go? How can I stay?" Volodka took fright. "The truck'll be waiting. And the losses I've already taken. How can I make them up? And then how do I keep on living?! What do I do, hide every fish in my shirt and watch so young Ivan doesn't nab me by the scruff of the neck? Oh no, let's not fool around, it's better not to live at all than to live like that. I won't give in!" thought Volodka, his heart growing icy. "If he pops up on me at night, that's the young lieutenant's fate. It means his life has run its course." Sagin shook his head, driving off the dark vision before his eyes. "No, I won't give in! It's either him or me!"

Volodka glanced at his watch and got up decisively. It was time. Eleven-thirty. The right time had come.

It was so dark you couldn't see past your nose. Only once in a while the narrow crescent moon appeared between shreds of cloud. The night cool wafted into the wide-open windows, and even the mosquitoes had calmed down somewhat. Sashka was already busy by the dock.

It was a forty-minute ride in the speedboat to the Kiyarskaya hole. Each cast of the float net took about an hour. It was necessary to pack in two casts before four and make it back by five. The carp wholesaler was supposed to drive up to the OSVOD gates by five in the morning. It wasn't good to tire the client out with waiting.

The wholesale buyer got a ruble from Volodka for every kilogram of fish. Another time Volodka would not have even bothered with him, he would have taken the fish himself, but at the present difficult moment he had no great desire to take on a third job. The two he had were more than enough. So he was forced to bear unwarranted losses, grit his teeth, and put them down to young Ivan. His bill for the inspector grew not by the day, but by the hour.

Sagin curled up in depression, giving away the carp at half its bazaar price, but in his heart he knew that the trader's calculations were fully justified. Once he settled accounts with Volodka, the risk was all his—three hundred kilometers of open road with five or six GAI highway posts. Along the way, easily fifty kopecks came out of each ruble he received. The truck itself cost money, and there, at the distant market, in selling merrily by the piece, there weren't enough fingers on your hands to count everyone who greedily milked the profits. Each approach to the stand by an employee of the controlling trade organization cost a whole eighteen-pound fish and a nice ten rubles in the pocket. That's real fishermen for you. They never haul an empty net out of the muddy water. They always get something!

"So what're you doing?" Sashka said, interrupting his reflections. "Look what time it is! We've dawdled enough!"

Sagin heaved himself heavily over the aluminum side of the truck.

"Let's go."

18

Sashka's flat-bottomed boat was fastened to the patrol boat. On the pile of fish sacks lay a tightly rolled sack with the net.

"Well, God be with us," Sashka busied himself at the steering column.

Volodka untied the nose mooring line from the bronze ring and hurled it into the patrol boat.

"Start'er up," he ordered.

With one gasp, with half a crank, the mighty patrol boat started up from the first powerful pull. Volodka pushed his cap onto his forehead and got behind the wheel. He went from reverse to cruise. Overboard the sleepy water started to rumble grandly. Patches of moonlight began to play on the windshield.

They got to the place more quickly than they'd counted on. They stopped, looked about. Torn shreds of clouds cluttered the troubled sky. An even path of moonlight would appear on the fast-flowing water, then break up into fragmented, silvery drops. They waited for a moment, and another. All around it was quiet.

"Let's start," commanded Volodka.

Sashka pulled the small boat up to the side of the patrol boat and crawled over into his awkward trow. Volodka straddled the sack with the net and, pulling out the end cords of the tackle, passed them to Sashka. He tied the net slings to the stern of the rickety vessel and with light strokes of the oars began to guide the boat to the bank. Volodka, working the motor gently, held the patrol boat in place. The net went under the water with ease. After ten minutes a gray chain of floats, clearly visible on the black water, stretched from the patrol boat to the bank of the Akdarya. Employing the smallest turns of the engine, Volodka headed downstream. The line of floats swayed and began to form an arc.

Over by the bank, Sashka worked the oars like a fiend. It was important for him not to lag behind the patrol boat. The two linked boats started downstream. Now the 300-foot sparkling web of nylon, weights, and floats had completely come out of the sack. Volodka smartly snatched the end slings and wound them around an iron hook. The whole net went underwater.

Volodka whistled quietly. Sashka gave an answering signal. From the middle of the river, his heaving was clearly audible. The water by the bank was stirring a bit, and in order to keep pace with Sagin, who was going over the fast water, Sashka was forced to rotate the oars all out.

Volodka had almost killed the motor. He put an arm overboard and seized the taut, sinking cord in his fingers. The nylon vibrated tautly and sang a scarcely audible song in his hand. Now and then Volodka felt distant, dull blows coming over the line.

Thud... thud... thud...

Each of these blows echoed happily in Volodka's heart—those were sleepy Akdarya carp snugly setting their gills into the meshes of the nets. Then there was a stronger blow.

"Ho-ho, a hefty hog!" Sagin was happily surprised. "Maybe it'll reach eighteen pounds."

They covered another hundred yards. The line in Volodka's hand quivered and went into such a sharp spasm that it was just as if someone down there, beneath the water, had begun to jerk and pull the net in all directions at once.

Volodka increased the rotations of the engine, whistled sharply, and began to turn the patrol boat in towards the bank.

The cast produced a good haul, a whole carp family had gone into the net. Sashka's panting became stronger. Standing in the shallows, twisting like a worm, Sashka held onto the net. Volodka pulled the boat into the bank a yard away from him. He jumped out of the boat, handily seized his end of the net, and firmly set his soles in the slimy bottom: to pull a big, wet 300-foot sheet from the water with two dozen large carp trapped in the meshes was no joking matter. In just five minutes the laborers were steaming.

Hurrying to take up the net, Volodka threw the first fish into the bottom of the patrol boat. But they beat their sides so hard against the latticed wooden flooring, thrashed their wide tails on the thin aluminum sides causing such booms, that he was forced to distract himself from the main work.

At any minute the catch threatened to wake the whole surrounding area; the resounding metallic blows carried far over the quiet river.

Sagin lunged for the patrol boat and thrust open a sack with his teeth and one hand, while with the other he quickly started stuffing the sack with the writhing carp. His experienced fingers instantly found the angular hoods of the gill slits and the narrow anal openings on their slick and slimy scaled bodies. Hooking the fish with one finger at the head and the other at the tail, Volodka threw them into the sack with an imperceptible motion. Sashka joined in. The work went more speedily.

Very soon two fifty-kilogram sacks of fish took their place side by side along the center line of the OSVOD motorboat. The first cast took the fishermen an hour and a half.

However, they had to get in one more cast. The motor came to life once again. Volodka wiped his sweaty forehead with the back of his hand and listened closely. The chirping of the crickets and cicadas on Wolf Island melted into one indistinguishable, measured refrain. A fresh milk and fish scent wafted from the water. With his whole chest Sagin breathed in the sweet night air dense with danger and chance—this was real life!

The two boats, tied by a short halyard, quickly came out onto the main current. Far behind, Wolf Island shone darkly.

The second cast didn't go right from the very start. First Sashka got tangled in the wet net and for a good half-hour, cussing, he yanked the clinging nylon off the clawing wooden sides of his awkward trough. Then Volodka himself slipped on the slime-coated lattice and almost landed overboard. Finally they more or less straightened out the net and separated. They would have to hurry up. A damn heap of time had been lost for nothing. Sashka groaned heavily, rushing to draw the net across the river. At last this too was set right. Volodka began to settle down. No problem, we'll make it.

But he had no sooner thought these fatal, jinxing words, than the lower, weighted net sling gave a sharp tug and stretched out until it twanged. Volodka instantly cut off the motor.

"Fuckin' bitch," he swore crudely to himself. "As if it weren't enough! A snag."

On the other side, by the bank, Sashka began to splash with the oars, unsuccessfully trying to pull the net off the submerged branch. Volodka angrily hurled into the darkness:

"Stow your oars! Stop here."

"Looks like a snag," sounded faintly from the bank. "Probably ran up against a branch."

In a fit of anger, Volodka whacked his palm on the water:

"What a damn mess life is! When your luck's up, it's really up." The work was turning out badly. The second cast was certainly lost. Even without this, time was short, and now it was even unsure what was on the bottom, and whether the snag was bad. It would be good to yank the net off the underwater hook, if they could manage it, by pulling it upstream, but if not? Then what? You don't throw away your tackle on the river; until they freed the net there was no thinking about returning home.

Volodka glanced at his watch. Holy Mother, past three, and how long they would be forced to fiddle around was uncertain. And the main thing was, anytime now it would begin to get light, all he needed was to get messed up in another misfortune. Most likely young Ivan was just waiting for such a godsend.

Volodka raised his head, peering about. All around it was noticeably lighter. Sashka in his small boat became alarmed.

"Throw away the net!" growled Volodka. "What are you pulling on it for, like a fool? It'll only get stuck worse! Take the end to the bank, tie it in the reeds, and hustle over here, got it?!"

From out of the darkness Sashka muttered something incomprehensible. The time dragged unbearably before at last his vessel poked out of the gray haze.

"You ought to be killed!" Sagin cursed his relative. "What time is it now?! Don't you know to turn around faster?"

Sashka guiltily hung his head.

"Well, I just..."

"Okay!" Volodka interrupted him. "Finish it later! Crawl over to me."

They unhooked the net from the patrol boat, tied its end to Sashka's boat, and set off at a very low speed to where the snag was.

Volodka crawled into the water with a gaff, caught the net's float line that was submerged by the snag, and attempted to pull it toward himself. The line drew him down like a good steel spring, and Volodka realized that the net was stuck fast on the branch. Working the motor, he attempted to move upstream. And still the net did not give. The nylon sang out and stopped the patrol boat. Grunting, Sashka held onto the boat hook.

They had already been fiddling with the net without success for a good half-hour, and they were so preoccupied that they completely missed the quiet sputtering of another motor. The beam of a pocket flashlight hit them from a distance of ten feet.

"We've had it," was all Volodka could think when he heard a ringing, mocking voice in the inky darkness that caused a familiar pounding in his temple.

"Do you need some help? Otherwise, I see the two of you won't be able to handle it."

Sashka hiccuped and covered his face with his hand. Volodka straightened up and let go of the net. He was going crazy trying to make out whether there was anyone else besides young Ivan in the fish inspector's motorboat that had stolen up on them.

That they were goners he figured out right away; now a circumstance of huge importance would decide everything to follow: was the inspector alone in the boat or not? The previous times Ivan had operated in a mob, together with the old inspector and with volunteer helpers from the fishermen's society. But today? If the lieutenant was not alone now, then why fool around: night, the nets, sacks of fish, a state motorboat, the prosecutor couldn't have thought up anything better himself.

Anguish clouded Volodka's head. An investigation, trial, confiscation of property, the big house—clearly they would stick him with a hearty sentence, everything would go to the dogs, his work, position, the comforts of his home, and maybe the home itself, his family, stuff, car, and all his heavy and not so heavy labors—everything would go down the drain, into other people's grabby paws; snag a claw and then the whole bird is caught. But if the inspector, fortunately for Volodka, was alone? What then? Well, if he was alone, then... Sagin shielded his eyes with his hand.

"Put out the light, chief. You've seen everything anyway!"

The inspector laughed.

"That's true, citizen crooks. The law sees a long way in the dark!"

He gently brought his patrol boat up to Volodka's boat and wrapped the nose chain around his thwart. The flashlight went out. Volodka squinted, hurrying to accustom himself quickly to the darkness.

Young Ivan stood up, pushed his uniform cap onto his forehead, and unhurriedly came on board the robber vessel he had caught stealing at night.

"Ivan Sergeevich Nikitin," he introduced himself formally to the captured poachers, and politely put his hand to the visor of his black service cap.

The inspector was happy. Once again the treacherous thieves had fallen into his hands with a whole bouquet of irrefutable evidence of their robber trade.

Law and justice would be an empty collection of words if they weren't realized in action with such iron inevitability. The inspector ran his eyes over the wet, tightly packed sacks. Bastards—they were probably full of roe-laden female fish! What losses were inflicted on nature by these two jackals that had mistakenly received human form at birth. Thousands of unborn lives that hadn't yet shown themselves in this world by either a move of their mighty fins or a merry leap from their native realm, many thousands of lives were mercilessly interrupted, curtailed, and smothered in the stinking tightness of the robbers' sacks.

Streams of warm water peacefully flowed about the executioners' boat. Frogs thickly croaked on Wolf Island, the stars were barely visible, and Ivan Nikitin's heart hardened towards the destroyers of life who had fallen into his lawful power.

"You are under arrest," he said. "And the patrol boat too, and the fish, and the implements for illegal fishing. We'll go to the prosecutor right now. It's time to purge the Akdarya of robbers."

Volodka opened his eyes and they shone brilliantly in the dark. A light morning breeze chased away the remainder of the clouds. It began to get light.

"It's time to purge, time to purge..." Ivan's final words beat in his head. "It's time..."

The inspector was alone!

Sagin's heart thumped with fright and hurt in his chest; a foreboding of the inevitable drained the blood from his cheeks, but he clenched his frozen jaws tightly. Was Ivan's life worth more than the carp's?

"Start the motor," the lieutenant ordered the hushed poachers.

Volodka narrowed his eyes. The rainbow circles from the inspector's unbearable flashlight had completely vanished. Now he could see as well as during the day. A faint coldness grew imperceptibly inside Volodka's stomach.

From his position by the sacks of fish, Sashka started cajoling the inspector:

"All right, so what's the deal! Why light into us like this? Take as much as you're supposed to and lay off! Live and let live."

The inspector cut him off like a knife:

"I won't let you!"

Volodka just grinned. Oh, Sashka, you turkey, look who you're trying to sway. No, with young Ivan empty drivel is useless. You can't beg anything from him. You have to do a major job on him.

Sagin unhurriedly bent toward the aluminum side. There, below the curve in the metal body, an aluminum oar was fastened with two spring clamps. During the past year he'd had no reason to use it even once—thank God, the motor had been running like clockwork, but today, it looked as if its time had come.

With one movement Volodka pulled the oar out of the clamps and, straightening up, proceeded to take a swipe in front of him, aiming for the inspector's head. The patrol boat heaved under his feet from the sudden movement, and the oar blade grazed Ivan's cheek and ripped open his ear.

The next minute a mortal combat began in the dancing patrol boat. Volodka, seizing young Ivan by the collar with one hand, slashed at him with the edge of the oar, and tried to hit him on the head. He couldn't get a good hit because of the tank separating them and the lieutenant's upwardly outstretched hands warded off the oar.

Sashka, stunned by the unexpected turn of events, thrust himself in between. Trying to help Sagin, he seized the inspector by the arm, but tripped on a fish sack and was unexpectedly pinned between Ivan and Volodka.

Giving a wild whoop, Volodka slashed at the face flitting before him. Sashka gave a terrible howl. The blow had caught him. The inspector finally tore free of Volodka's grasp and, seizing Sashka by his striped sailor's shirt, he shielded himself from the deadly blade. The material ripped, and using all his might, Sashka tore himself from the inspector's hold, but Volodka, madly clenching his teeth and with a glassy look in his eyes, slashed away with the edge of the oar at the heaving human flesh before him. After each blow Sashka, maddened by the pain, wailed in an awful voice:

"Oh, don't! Oh, don't beat me! Oh, Volodechka, don't kill me! Oh, it hurts!"

At last Sashka emitted a truly deathly howl and tore himself away, so that his shirt gave way and ripped to the waist with a screech. Sashka hurtled to the bottom of the patrol boat, and the inspector went overboard. Volodka lunged towards the water and managed to get young Ivan with the oar again before he dove away.

Clutching his head in his hands and choking on his tears, Sashka wailed from the stern of the patrol boat :

"You've killed me. Oh, God, you've done me in!"

He passed his palms over his shredded visage and, raising his bloodied hands to his face, yelled for half the river to hear:

"Blood, it's blood! Look, brother, look, blood!"

Sashka shoved his wet, red palms under Volodka's nose.

"Why did you do this to me, brother?! Look, you've killed me!"

"Shut up, stupid!" Volodka furiously pushed him away. He stared intently at the water over the side.

"He'll get away, he'll get away," fearfully echoed in Sagin's brain.

Within thirty feet of the patrol boat a black shadow popped out of the water. With ponderous, sweeping strokes the lieutenant was slowly swimming downstream. It was obviously hard for him to stay above water.

"Oh, no, you won't get away!" a mad joy erupted within Volodka. He lunged for the wheel and turned on the engine. The roar of the motor rolled over the sleepy water like thunder. Startled by the sudden noise, the frogs quieted down. Volodka turned the patrol boat around almost on the spot. The patrol boat reared up and lunged ahead just like a wild stallion. The moaning Sashka almost fell overboard.

Volodka aimed the wide, flat nose of the patrol boat at the live ball bobbing on the waves. Picking up the growing roar of the motor, the inspector was about to turn aside when the heavy, long carcass of the patrol boat ran over him.

Ah-h-h-h!

The patrol boat's wheel jerked in Volodka's hands. For a second the boat halted. The motor's resounding bass became strained and tormented. You could hear the stress and effort with which the spinning propeller slashed the resisting, sticky mass beneath the water.

For several moments the deep, low wail of the engine continued. But then the water behind the patrol boat seethed and tatters of shredded rags and bloody flakes of foam flew to the surface, thrown up by the powerful force of the spinning knife blades. The water at the stern became a deep pink. Freed from its terrible engagement, the propeller instantly regained its full revolutions. The drive screamed and the patrol boat tore ahead.

Sashka, gazing spellbound at the shreds of human flesh that were coming up within a meter from the nose of the patrol boat, let out a cry and crawled along the side on all fours.

Volodka made a wide circle on the river and, cutting the revolutions, came up to the spot of the ill-fated snag of the net. He turned off the engine, caught the infernal net with a boat hook, and with several knife blows cut through it on both sides of the snag. Moving along the line, Sagin quickly took the bankside half of the net up out of the water, ripped out the end Sashka had tied to the reeds, and set off down the river after his brother-in-law's slowly drifting johnboat. The other half of the tackle he had cut free was tied to the boat.

Sagin shot a glance at Sashka. The latter was sitting by the fish sacks with his blank face turned away, keeping a sullen silence. Volodka was silent, too. He didn't bother to disturb Sashka. The first murder in life is hard for everyone. Everything inside Volodka himself was slightly aquiver right now. Let Sashka settle down and then it would be possible to have a talk.

While Sagin was taking up the bank half of the net, Sashka's johnboat had gone far downstream. It took about five minutes to catch up with it. Finally they reached it.

Volodka tied Sashka's trow to the patrol boat and began to take up the net. This one was hard to get out of the water. Volodka cussed:

"What's the matter, full of fish or something? Just the wrong time."

A terrible surmise flashed through the depths of his brain, his hands weakened for a fraction of a second, but Sagin got a hold of himself. That would have been completely... Having driven off the unwelcome thought, he applied himself to the net with redoubled energy. Sashka was sitting alongside in shock.

"Are you asleep or something?" Volodka hollered at him crudely. "You could at least help!"

Sashka turned a dumb, tormented face to him. Volodka glanced at him and turned away in disgust.

The net started to come more easily, then more and more easily.

Sagin involuntarily reeled from the side. He didn't want to know even mentally what was lodged, with broken, twisted arms, in his lucky nylon trap, and what was quietly swaying within ten feet of the side. Turning his head away and wincing painfully, Volodka cut through the net by touch. The last catch of the night slowly floated away from the patrol boat.

Writhing at Volodka's feet, Sashka let out a hoarse howl, unable to detach his crazed stare from the slowly sinking tattered flesh.

They made their way back in silence. The sun had already come up over the far horizon. The morning air fanned their weathered, swollen faces.

Once in a while Volodka shot a glance at his brother-in-law. The latter sat looking straight ahead, his arms wrapped around his torn and shredded sailor's shirt.

"Don't get cold feet, Sashka," Volodka said hoarsely. "It just turned out like that. We didn't want it, but it had to be that way. If we didn't get him, he would get us. And it was a deserted place. Nobody else happened to be there to see it. A day or two and those nice catfish will gobble him up."

Sashka shuddered in pain.

"And don't feel sorry for him, Sashka." Volodka softly admonished his brother-in-law. "Just remember, he didnt feel sorry for us. All he thought about was digging us a hole. Remember how he put it—I'll smoke you off the river with iron! So don't get too upset, don't think about it—it'll all be forgotten, you'll see. Time will pass and you'll say: 'Nothing really happened.'"

As if he were waking up, Sashka lifted his horror-filled eyes to his relative. His lips were trembling faintly. Volodka grew uneasy. "The fellow's not in his right mind," he thought fearfully. "I hope he doesn't pull something on the spur of the moment. I should watch him. Make sure he doesn't get out of my sight."

The nose of the patrol boat softly skidded against the dock boards. Volodka turned off the motor.

"That's it. We're here. Let's get out."

The sound of his voice seemed to release the tensed spring inside Volodka from its catch. The next moment Sashka, who had started to calm down, jumped out of the patrol boat and raced along the pier. Volodka, stunned, stared after him. All you could see were the shoulder blades working on his striped back. Several seconds passed before he grasped the full danger of Sashka's absurd flight.

"Stop!" he hollered.

By that time Sashka had managed to take off yet another two dozen yards.

"Stop!" Volodka roared huskily. "Stop, I say, you louse!"

Sashka increased his speed. Volodka raced after him. Sashka's broken wind from running and his alcohol-saturated lungs were good for less than a hundred yards; he hobbled the final length of road at a jog, and Volodka overtook his brother-in-law, who had fallen into a stumbling walk. He came down on Sashka like a ton of bricks.

"Gotcha!"

The first blow landed Sashka on the ground.

"Take that, you snake! Take that! You wanted to run! Took off for the cop station? You were going to turn me in! I'll show you how to run! Take that and that! I'll kill you, you snake! It's too late now!"

Sashka could only cry out weakly beneath the hail of weighty blows raining down on him. His lacerated hands tried to shield his mauled head. Suddenly he fell silent and stopped resisting. His hands fell.

Volodka's raised fist froze.

"What's with you?"

Sashka turned his tear-streaked, bloody face, consumed beyond recognition in one night.

"Vo-lo-dya! What have we done, brother? Ah-h-h? Why, we did in a ma-a-a-n!!!"

Sagin looked around fearfully and covered the driveling, crying mouth with his hand.

"Quiet! Quiet, I'm telling you!"

He relaxed his hand and, looking closely at Sashka's bobbing eyes, said with the great force of conviction :

"This didn't happen! Got it? Forget everything. You dreamed and imagined all of it when you were drunk. This didn't happen. Nothing happened."

Sashka, pitifully contorting his wailing mouth, tried to look into his relative's face.

"Dreamed it?" he whispered with mad hope. "Imagined it? It was nothing?"

"Nothing!" Volodka answered firmly without turning his sweaty face. "Nothing happened!"

20

By eight in the morning Sagin was already sitting in his private office, shiny with lacquered furniture.

The early sun bathed the world in tender light and warmth. Busy sparrows chirped beneath the eaves of the office roof. The new day was beginning amid quiet and calm.

And only in Volodka's head did the dark and bloody night still persist.

In the yard Sashka remained perched against the cottage's wall. He had already intruded into Volodka's office three times, supposedly on business, and the third time Sagin couldn't bear his brother-in-law's pitiful look.

"Get out of here! What're you sticking around me for? Sit outside and don't show your face in the street! Why hang around here! Slobbering all over..."

Such ghastly fear swam in Sashka's eyes, such guilt flowed from his entire hunched body, that Volodka's heart finally fell. He'll sell me, the dog... He'll sell me without a second thought. It's written all over his mug. He'll crack even before they start applying pressure.

He ought to get rid of Sashka quickly. His beaten look couldn't help but give rise to the most dire suspicions. But removing Sashka from his sight wasn't any less dangerous than keeping him around. No one could guarantee that his relative, who had been scared shitless that night, if left unwatched wouldn't run off to the authorities and squeal. Fear could push him to do anything at all. He was forced to keep Sashka nearby and once in a while impress on him that everything that had happened at night was illusion and dream.

Out of ingrained habit Sashka wanted to resort to his trusty remedy, but Volodka ripped the bottle out of his quaking hands.

"A fine time for that! Don't put a drop in your mouth."

As it was, the donkey didn't have much in his head, and now he was going to drench the sawdust he used for brains with vodka. As soon as he blabbed one dumb word while drunk—it would mean the clink! Yes, when the crunch came—a job for a tough man—his most trusted buddy turned out to be a wimp. And if he hadn't stopped him? Where would he have run off to? Just where had he headed? As it turned out, for the militia station. What could you do with him after that?

Only one possible hope remained, that the inspector wouldn't surface soon, and that by then Sashka would either have calmed down once and for all, or... Volodka frowned.

He fidgeted in the soft armchair. He just couldn't get comfortably settled. The two pieces of bad luck nagged at his soul, and no matter how Volodka tried not to think about them, nothing worked. With a heavy sigh he put his hand in his pocket and withdrew a small round mirror. The familiar sideburns were reflected in the cloudy glass. On the left side, below the curly growth, in the most visible place on his cheek, a great big scarlet welt stood out.

No good, thought Volodka for the umpteenth time. If it weren't for this chicken shit, how much easier it'd be. So what if Sashka's whole mug was mauled. Couldn't he have taken a ride alone at night? Couldn't he have had a face-to-face confrontation with somebody on the river? And precisely at that time Sagin, let's assume, was sleeping in the office, eh? Couldn't he have been? He couid've, you bet, if Volodka's snout were clean. It'd be hard for Sashka to talk to the cops if Sagin's visage was as unblemished as an Easter egg that morning. No good, Volodka sighed again, hiding the glass. A gnawing emptiness began in the pit of his stomach.

All morning Sagin washed the patrol boat. He ran a rag over the wide aluminum sides of the patrol boat, wiped the oar, and used river sand and some rags soaked in gasoline to swab the yellow propeller with its glistening sharp blades. Sagin winced as he recalled how the patrol boat's engine howled from the strain when the propeller's knife blades were slashing at the bloody pulp that a minute before had been a man.

After Volodka had thrown off his blood-smeared rags from the night before, he bound them up with a scrap of string and, shoving a rock inside, threw them as far as he could from the bank. He ordered Sashka to do the same and to wash with soap from head to foot.

And only now did he discover that other thing that had been nagging at him all morning. Volodka rushed to his brother-in-law, eyes white with rage.

"Why didn't you say so right away, you snake?"

Sashka sidled into the water, covering his head with his hands.

"I didn't see it right away myself," he protested in a weepy voice. "I just noticed it now."

Volodka grabbed his head and began to sway as if he were crazy.

"Come on, show it!"

There it was, half of the shoulder and breast on the left side of the sailor's shirt were missing. There had been only two striped uniforms on the entire Akdarya and in the whole town—one was Sashka's, the other, Volodka's. For years its dark blue and white striped edge had stuck out of the unbuttoned collar of his Navy jacket. The sailor's shirt had become as much a part of Sagin as his skin.

It would be nice if the unlucky rag with the sailor's stripes were lying somewhere on the Akdarya's clay bottom, snagged on a log, and the cold water below would cover it over with light silt. It would be nice if that were so. And if not? If...? Volodka became covered with cold sweat imagining the rigid, mortally clenched hand of the drowned man with the terrifying physical evidence squeezed in his blue fingers. Where would the detectives immediately rush to when they found the clue? It was obvious where. There was no need to think about it.

"And then Ivan went down right in the main stream," Sagin thought despairingly. A kilometer farther down there's a sandbank. In the middle the current is strong. It could very easily drop the body in the shallows in half an hour. And there are always plenty of fishermen there. It's the anglers' favorite spot.

"Oh, oh, oh," he groaned.

The sleuths could be expected in the OSVOD yard any minute now. Sailor's shirt in hand, the head slashed by the propeller, a shred of net—you didn't need a ton of brains to come to the unmistakable conclusion. They would sit on them for the time being and sort out the details later.

"Damn you, you parasite. You cut my throat without a knife."

Sashka raised his face, wet from fear.

"Maybe we should light out somewhere?" he mumbled pitifully.

Volodka made a dismissive gesture.

"Great idea. Couldn't you think of anything dumber?"

All they needed was to advertise their part in the deed. The only thing they had left was to trust in luck, in their usual good fortune.

"Sink all of the junk you have on," he ordered Sashka. "And don't take a step from me!"

And now Sashka was despondently hanging around the yard. The time dragged on slowly and agonizingly. In three hours Volodka burned up almost a pack of cigarettes. He had dog's breath.

At eleven-thirty (Sagin automatically looked at his watch) the phone rang. Volodka jumped. It was just like a shock to the heart. Don't pick it up! But he was scared not to. Only it seemed even more terrible to pick it up. As he wavered, the phone fell silent. Volodka weakly dropped the hand he had stretched toward the phone.

"Oof-f!" he sighed. "Maybe it'll pass?" After all, how many times had it looked like the end, curtains, life was over, but somehow he had gotten by, disaster had been swept aside.

Five minutes later another call came in. Volodka picked up the receiver with a limp hand.

"Yes," he whispered. "Sagin here."

There was silence on the other end.

"Hello, hello!" Volodka said hastily, breaking into a sweat. "Who's there?"

A busy signal came on right in the middle of his question. "O-hh," Volodka said quietly. The receiver fell from his hand. With instant, unerring perspicacity he understood the ominous import of the silent call.

"They're checking if I'm here," his dry lips pronounced all by themselves. "Now they'll come and get me."

Dazed, Volodka looked at the weakly beeping receiver. "Run, run, run as fast as you can!" the words beat feverishly in his burning brain. But his whole body was just like stone, he couldn't even move a finger. For ten decisive minutes Sagin remained motionless. The sound of a car pulling up to the OSVOD gates brought him out of his stupor. A police jeep stopped at the lattice gates of the office. Sashka, sitting against the cottage wall, two steps from the gates, froze. Two men in plainclothes got out of the car and confidently headed for the gates. One more man in a police uniform got out of the jeep. Sashka jumped up, shaking, and, squealing like a rabbit, hurtled toward the gate. The horror that gripped him at the sight of a police uniform turned out to be so great that Sashka didn't notice the two that were entering the OSVOD station.

It seemed that the detectives were taken aback no less than Sashka, but the next moment Sashka's hands were tied behind his back with a crunch, and his silly, hollow head was firmly pressed to the ground.

"I didn't kill him, I didn't kill him!" Sashka let out a heartrending yell, pouring out all of the horror he'd experienced in a furious howl. "I didn't kill him! He did it all, Volodka! He killed him with an oar, and the propeller! Not me! He forced me! He chopped me up with the oar! He hid the oar in the small shed. He sank his clothes. I'll show you everything! I know where!"

The terrible shouts hurled Sagin to the window. His hair stood on end. "That's it," flashed like lightning through his head. "Now there's no getting off. They'll shoot me."

He also could hear how Sashka's wild yelling became a moan; it was clear that the militia sitting on him had twisted Sashka's arm behind his back, and in the ghastly silence that ensued, just like nails in Volodka's coffin, came the simple and terrible words:

"Give me the cuffs, sergeant. Right! Here it is, the sailor's shirt. Like I said, we have to begin our checking with them."

The other one, in uniform, leaned toward the vehicle, got something shiny, and walked though the gate.

The mention of the sailor's shirt shot through Volodka like a bullet. It was as if a bloated hand with a shred of striped material pressed in its bent fingers had risen out of the water from the black, silty bottom of the river, and stretched towards Volodka's throat across the entire length of the Akdarya, and the wharf, and the gentle cool of the office. He caught at his neck, defending himself from the terrible vision. And from the yard once again came the calm order:

"Watch so the other one doesn't get away. Sergeant, you go to the window, and I'll go in the door. Lieutenant, stay by the prisoner. Everyone ready your weapons."

Volodka reeled away from the window. All that followed happened as if in a dream. What he did in the next seconds no longer depended on a rational effort; the unerring, highly resourceful instinct of self-preservation led him along the very edge of the abyss that yawned at his feet. Volodka rushed to the cabinet. He yanked a nice new *tozovka*—a small caliber, three-cartridge automatic rifle—out of its hiding place and dashed back to the safe. The boxes with cartridges were kept inside it. But on the way, within a couple of feet of the window, out of the corner of his eye he caught a glimpse of a police cap, and he understood that he wouldn't have time to get the cartridges. The next instant he dashed to the other window on the opposite side of the office, which opened onto a strip of corn planted by his thrifty brother-in-law.

Four mad heartbeats and Volodka, without having disturbed a single tall green stalk on the way, found himself at the edge of the patch. Five steps away a detective stood sideways to him with a lowered pistol in his hand; Sashka lay at his feet in irons. Behind the detective's back shone the opening in the gate.

Volodka cast a side glance in the direction of his abandoned office. The uniformed policeman, stretching his neck like a goose, was looking into the window of Sagin's private office. The second detective wasn't in sight.

"He's already gone into the office. You have another ten seconds," someone else said inside Volodka's brain. "The fence is ten feet high. If you climb it, they'll intercept you right away. There's only one way out." He seized the rifle in both hands by the forestock and below. He breathed deeply and froze for a second. "Go!" came the other's command.

Volodka covered the distance separating him from the detective so quickly that even this professional, accustomed to danger and trained in hand-to-hand combat, only had time to react to the sudden threat with his eyes. His eyeballs involuntarily jerked in Volodka's direction, but his brain didn't manage to pass a command to his hands.

"Wham!"

Volodka struck with the rifle barrel, like a bayonet. Blood spurted from the opened cheek. The detective was tossed sideways and the way was clear.

Just beyond the gate, over the narrow asphalt strip, began the famous unencompassable and impenetrable Akdarya *tugai*. The felled detective needed five seconds to leap from the ground and run up to the lattice gates—and those seconds saved Sagin's life. The belated cracks of the pistol shot only spurred his flight.

This time, too, the Akdarya saved its wild son.

21

Four hours later a flushed, cautious face poked out of the thick stubble of the shore *tugai* across from Wolf Island. Usually it was about two hours to this place on foot, but Volodka circled for a long time by way of a devious network of ditches, channels, and clumps of reeds. He was muddling his tracks, in the probable event that once the detectives recovered, they would set off after him with a dog. Anything could happen. They'd blown it once, but that didn't mean that they would keep it up. God helps those who help themselves. And Volodka made more than one rabbit loop and twist before daring to approach this hidden place. His eyes anxiously probed the surrounding river.

The noon heat was at its peak. It seemed as if the air itself had liquified. A light, transparent sheen quivered above the river, the low sandy tips of Wolf Island, grown over with wild *jida* and reeds, imperceptibly swayed in the blur of the overheated air.

The island stretched for a good kilometer of river. Its upper end, beginning with a sloping sand bar, rose sharply to the sky two hundred yards farther. Here, on the sandy mounds, besides *jida* there grew several elms and sickly acacias, planted God knows when and by whom. Then came solid, uninterrupted *tugai* formed from the thickly meshed growth of reeds, licorice, juniper, brambles, and again *jida*. The lower end of the island gradually fell to the clear Akdarya water. Just beyond began the Kiyarskaya hole, famous for its depth and its fish.

The place was extremely wild. Jackals lived on the island, and a long time ago a pack of wolves, which had given the island its forbidding name. Time passed, the wolves were taken away, but there were still jackals on the island.

Volodka listened attentively. A pair of mallards rose from the reach of river behind the island and passed with a whistle over his head. A drake cut the air and a duck followed behind, like an ideal partner, one wing drooping at an angle. On the far side the frogs were croaking in full voice.

Sagin stared at his intended hideout until his eyes hurt. His bramble-raked hand had a death grip on the forestock of the useless rifle. If you calculated it straight across the main channel of the Akdarya, then it was some hundred yards to the island. Volodka sniffed as he breathed the air. There was undisturbed calm all around him.

"Let's go!" he ordered himself.

Volodka made it across the channel in just a few minutes. When he got to the island he was without his weapon. He simply couldn't understand how the rifle had slipped from his hand. He reached the island *tugai* in one leap. The tips of the reeds waved and were still once again. He penetrated into the growth.

His water-filled shoes squished, the scorching sand ground beneath his feet, water ran off his wet clothing and was instantly consumed by the sun, thorny branches scratched his hands and got into his eyes; Volodka didn't pay attention to anything. Faster, faster! He hurried to a secret place he knew well.

A large black lizard dashed from underfoot. Sagin's heart stopped for an instant. He almost covered his pale lips with his palm, but the next second shook his head and stubbornly went on, forcing his way through the thick thorny growth.

The blue of an opening shone ahead. Volodka pushed aside a low branch that got in his face, stepped forward, and looked about.

Yes, this was the very place. He was standing on the edge of a small, sandy bald spot. The sickly stalk of a dried-up elm stuck up on the other side of the small bare island.

Volodka cast his eyes to the left of the tree. A huge batch of reeds loomed there, about the level of a man's height. Next to it was a batch slightly smaller in size. Volodka went up to it and wearily lowered himself onto the hot sand. Steam was coming off his clothing. It would be nice to rest up, if only for a while. He leaned his back against the batch of reeds and closed his feverish eyes.

Sagin was now not just sitting on the red sand in the middle of Wolf Island, he was sitting on his own life. Below, a few feet deep in the sand, directly beneath Volodka's moist place of repose, rested "something" securely concealed from others' hostile and envious eyes. This "something" had spurred Volodka to the attack that day. If it hadn't been for the constant thought in a remote, secret corner of his memory about the package buried in the sand on Wolf Island, he would have quite simply put up his hands and surrendered.

Volodka sniffed with satisfaction. He stood up. Before his drooping, tired eyes flashed a quiet Sunday evening at about this very time, a year ago, and Lyuska's attentive, caressing look. Sweet family coziness, the living room that his wife had cleaned until it shined, and two lilac packets with gummed strips of paper around them that Volodka had thrown casually onto the polished surface of a magazine stand.

"My life insurance," he had explained at the time in answer to Lyuska's silent question. "In case of the worst. If it comes to that, if they squeeze me so hard that I'm forced to run, I can always get back on my feet with it. This dough is sacred. I have to hide it and forget where it is."

Lyuska casually shrugged her shoulders:

"So it's sacred, fine. Where will we hide it?"

His wife's voice sounded businesslike and disinterested, but a certain unclear note in it forced Volodka to change his initial decision.

"I'll hide it in the right place myself," he answered. "Later I'll tell you. Now pack it up good. Put it in a plastic packet, and wrap a rag around it." Volodka nodded at the glass jar with a plastic lid that was on the stand, next to the money. "I'll put it in there and bury it."

Lyuska pursed her lips in offense and thought for a second. Then she got up and went to the kitchen.

Volodka wearily sank down in an armchair. Of course, he trusted his wife a hundred percent, but still it was better for Lyuska to pack up the money in front of him. Five grand—that's nothing to sneeze at. Better people than Lyuska had cracked because of such money. Volodka decided to wait a bit before showing his wife the place he would bury the jar. "I'll simply say 'on Wolf Island,'" he thought. "'Just where, I'll show you later.' So she doesn't get offended."

From the kitchen Lyuska brought a plastic packet with foreign faces printed all over it and a clean rag. She sat down on the sofa by the trumeau mirror and, digging in a pile of little boxes, got out a needle.

"I'll sew it up," she said to Volodka, "like a strong package. So it's more secure."

Volodka nodded and narrowed his eyes with satisfaction, sinking his back into the yielding foam of the armchair. "Oh, what a good housewife," he thought with great affection. "Not like others. Money runs right through their fingers like water. But mine doesn't lose hold of a wooden nickel. My wife is worth her weight in gold."

Lyuska took the packets of twenty-five ruble notes from the stand; her hands darted nimbly in the cool dimness of the room. The needle set to work. Right, left, across; across, right, left, and ever tighter!

The small package turned out amazingly neat. Lyuska ran her hand over the package for the last time, drawing the material tighter, and brushed tiny beads of sweat from her forehead.

"Why are you so flushed?" Sagin was surprised. "The fan's going full blast, it's almost chilly, and you're in a sweat. Are you sick, by any chance?"

His wife smiled weakly and shook her head "no." She took the glass jar from the stand and, raising it high overhead, tossed it inside the package.

"Look for yourself, doubtful Thomas," she said with a laugh, tapping the tight lid. "Don't let anyone gyp you out of a five."

Sagin grinned. His wife was obviously demonstrating her hurt.

"I'll stash away this dough on Wolf Island," he said conciliatorily. "There's one safe place there. Later, we'll ride over and I'll show you."

"As if I need that!" replied Lyuska, turning up her nose. "Don't I have enough to do without stomping around your islands! I have no interest in it."

Volodka took the jar and, hesitating on the threshold, went out. He was feeling somewhat guilty. After all, she was his lawful woman. It had turned out awkwardly. It looked as if he didn't trust her.

"I'll buy some earrings," he decided. "I don't begrudge Lyuska money. It's just that this money is vital. What if I get in up to my neck? It's all right. She'll let off some steam and forget it. It's over her head anyway." Sagin scratched his neck. "Now, you can count on it, she won't allow me to sleep with her for a week. She'll put on a show. Punish me. Fine," he decided, "for now I won't try her, but I'll buy some earrings and then..." he grinned. "Women are women. What can you expect from them?"

A shrike started to make a racket right by his ear and Sagin woke up. He looked around with wild eyes. Had he fallen asleep?! How long had he slept? Volodka glanced at his watch. His watch had stopped. His clothes were dried out. The sun was going down. "Damn nap," Volodka thought in a fright. "I threw away at least three hours. What a fool! Anyone could've taken me, barehanded. 'Look, the OSVOD director spread out for a rest. Just like at home on the couch.' Well," he sighed with distress, "I don't have a home any-more or a couch, and perhaps I won't for a long time."

While he was dozing like a total jerk, time was working against Volodka. Almost half a day had passed since the moment the two broad-shouldered young men in plain clothes had entered the office yard. By now the gigantic flywheel had been set in motion.

Volodka pictured how the teletypes were clattering, transmitting to all ends of the country the minutest details and information about Sagin. How the phones were ringing in the smoky police offices and auxiliary law-and-order places, how the patrol jeeps scurrying about the streets kept reporting to their invisible bosses that, "no, they hadn't run into the murderer and fugi-tive Sagin," how the huge fan of the federal investigation's fine dragnet was spreading out over the whole country. He pictured it and a cold sweat broke out on Volodka's head, scorched by the sun and these reflections. With horror Volodka sensed the terrifying hopelessness of his situation. His hands started to shake.

"It's all right, it's all right," he muttered, swallowing the nauseating knot that rose in his throat. "Even the cops are people. Even they have a few holes in their heads. If they caught everyone right away, then they would have been out of work a long time ago. It's all right. The main thing is I have money. I'll get out of it. It'd be another thing if I didn't have a cent. Then they'd nab me at my first step. Where could I go? The whole world is an enemy to a poor man. But as it is, I'll sit it out a year or two in a nice secluded place, and be-fore you know it everything will quiet down. After all, they try hard to catch you only the first week, and then they don't put out the same kind of nets. Then the meshes are bigger and it's possible to slip through. Afterwards I'll fix up new papers, and, well, we'll see..."

For the time being Volodka's dreams didn't go further than an initial shel-ter from the hunt—just so as not to jinx it!

He got up, thrust a hand into the middle of the batch of reeds, and pulled out a short sapper's shovel. The handle was worn white by the rains and sun, the blade was pretty rusty. Volodka smirked with satisfaction. See—every-thing was going as he had planned it a good year earlier. He calmed down a bit. Sagin might be half-literate, but nonetheless he clearly had a good head on his shoulders.

The sand easily yielded to the shovel. Quietly whispering something soothing to himself, Volodka shoveled it to the side. Then the metal loudly clinked against glass, and Sagin's heart leaped happily: it was there!

In another minute the cherished jar was in his hands. Volodka quickly peeled off the lid. It smelled of rot from the package inside. He pulled out the package, looked it over, and calmed down completely. He even recognized Lyuska's cross-stitching on the rag.

A warm feeling for his wife welled up in his heart. She did her best. As if she knew that the cursed time would come when her Volodka would be hunted all over like a mad dog. You could say she'd saved him. How was she back there now? No doubt, the cops are badgering her, pressing and pressuring her back and forth, telling her to turn in her husband, otherwise she, too, would be doomed. But no, they weren't up against that sort of woman. Volodka's woman wouldn't sell her husband for a cheap promise by a cop. "That's all right, the time will come, I'll free you from the enemy's clutches. We'll still have a life together, little woman, we'll comfort each other on a wide bed. Your Volodka doesn't sink in water or burn in fire. No matter what, I'll set my course in life. Don't be sad, Lyuska, will see each other again."

The rotten, decayed threads came apart beneath his fingers. Volodka quickly peeled the rag from the gaudy plastic packet, unwrapped the stash, put his hand inside and pulled a flat cardboard box of "Lilac" cologne out of the deep bowels of his treasure. Volodka looked dumbly at the box for several seconds, not understanding a thing.

"But where's the money?" he muttered to himself.

Finally his fingers moved, the top of the box flew off to the side, and Volodka stared, stricken, at the small, jolly yellow bottle sticking out of the tiny satin bedding.

"Ah-h-h!" the next second a wild, gasping howl soared over the island. "She swapped it! She robbed me! Sold me! Lyuska, you damn bitch, I'll kill you!!!"

22

After this blow Volodka's mind was impaired for a while. All of his mental powers waned pitifully. He hardly understood what he did all evening. It seems that he wandered along the shore-side edge of the island, looked into the water and, taking fright at the terrible, inhuman face which peered at him from the river depths, once more dashed into the thorny brush. Then he again tried to dig up the stash; he raised a whole mountain of sand, but didn't dig down to anything else, and gave up the senseless effort. It was simply a miracle that some fisherman didn't happen by and spot him then.

Volodka vaguely remembered that he tried to dig in the sand in two or three other places; then, for long hours his stiff fingers pointlessly stroked the rough cardboard surface of the sorry fake Lyuska had substituted for his treasure, and he cried copious tears and complained of his bitter hurt—to whom it was unclear—his dried lips sputtering a desperate woe.

Only towards dusk did he recover a bit. The despair that had shaken the ground beneath his feet was slightly dulled, and with difficulty and resistance Volodka began to be conscious of his unenviable position.

Suddenly all of his magnificently elaborated plans, calculated for years in advance, had crumbled. In case something happened, to light out for Kazakhstan, to a godforsaken country area far from people, somewhere towards the Alatau foothills; the very name—Alatau—sounded like an Eastern fairytale, like a denial of any official power. Well, of course they had some of their own local, petty tsars—Volodka could always find common ground with them, and after that he'd buy clean papers from the first drifter he met, and changing his appearance slightly if possible, he'd sit out a couple of years as a guard at a two-bit kolkhoz warehouse, or take off for other climes and there blend into the gray mass of seasonal workers in a far northern logging camp. There are lots of roads for a man on the run in such a huge country as our Motherland. Republics, regions, territories, districts, the devil himself couldn't figure out this administrative mishmash. And specific rules, laws, and customs flourished everywhere. It was a cinch for a little person to lose himself in such a melting pot...

Just like squirrels on a wheel, Volodka's thoughts kept returning to money. After all, it was the chief condition for salvation. Money solved everything. Having stolen the money, Volodka's wife had taken more than life from him: she had taken hope.

Volodka's ever-present instinct for life helped him withstand a blow of such destructive force and not break completely. There had been many dangerous reefs and treacherous whirlpools in his previous sailing, and he had navigated through them all successfully. And now he couldn't bring himself to believe that the time had come for a final reckoning.

"No," he muttered, clenching his teeth, "no, I won't give up!"

Volodka had staggered badly, staggered fatally, but he stayed on his feet.

23

Volodka awoke at dawn. It was as if someone standing on guard inside of him had poked him in the ribs: it's time!

As for his sleep, what sort of sleep was it?—nightmares and not sleep. Convulsive brain lapses, flare-ups of wild fear, endless and tortured flight from merciless pursuers, short pulsing sparks of words just like the shrieks of a last gasp:

"I won't give up..!"

With a weak hand Volodka wiped the cold perspiration that thickly beaded his forehead and took a cautious look around.

The gray shadows of the world's surrounding contours and objects stood out more sharply and clearly with each minute. As on an exposed photograph, out of the semi-darkness appeared the thick branches of the low juniper that enclosed Volodka's lair on all sides. Far beyond them a dark strip of water began to quiver, gradually acquiring a visible outline. A light mist rose from the water toward a gray sky that was growing light. In the opening among the tall reeds Volodka made out the long sandy spit onto which he had emerged from the river that night. The light coolness of night was subsiding. The sand beneath Volodka had cooled.

The terrible inner tension that had been with him for two days appeared to have let up somewhat. He limply waved off a mosquito that was pestering him. "I wish I could do that to the cops," he thought involuntarily.

Volodka raised his eyes to the sky. It'll be a scorcher today—sunup to sundown. In a couple of hours you won't be able to catch your breath.

A feeling of unbearable loneliness, of detachment from life, seized Sagin. He ran his palm over his chin. A two-day stubble rasped under his fingers. "Where can I show up with such a mug?" Volodka thought despondently. "It's plain I'm a fugitive now. Where can I go? Who's waiting for me? Only the detectives are on the lookout."

"Oh, Lyuska, Lyuska," he sobbed convulsively, "you fool, what've you done to me? Didn't I struggle all my life for you? And what'd you do?! Tear off my arms and legs."

Volodka began moaning.

"Oh, my sweet wife! Didn't I caress you and cherish you? Didn't I worship you from head to toe? Why did you do this to me? Did you think you had too little? Too little of everything? Wasn't a house enough, a car, a bank account, furniture and all the rest—you took all you could get. It was my life I hid and not five grand, my life, Lyuska, my life! And you made off with it before my eyes. What's left for me now, Lyuska? I'm dead. Well, tell me, go on, answer-r-r!"

Volodka fell face-down in the cold sand and pushed forward on his head as if he were trying to batter a hole in the mocking earth. His shoulders relaxed...

Time passed.

Suddenly Sagin tore his leaden head from the ground. Some incomprehensible change had occurred in the liquid, gray quiet. He didn't have time to realize what had alerted him, but the thick red hair on the nape of his neck stood on end, sensing a vague danger, his powerful short neck disappeared into his shoulders, and his small eyes darted quickly about, scouring the area.

From far away over the water came a quiet, indistinct sound. The next instant Volodka recognized it. A motorboat. And it sounded as if it wasn't alone.

In another minute he caught sight of several black spots moving on the water approximately one kilometer from the island.

Sagin rushed forward and parted the branches.

"One, two, three, four... My speedboat!"

He understood everything now. His hand shook, the branch was torn out of his limp fingers and swished back and forth in front of his face. So, she hadn't merely sold him, but bag and baggage, too! It was only Lyuska who could have pointed them to where he was hiding. Only she knew that his final desperado's trail would lead him precisely here, to Wolf Island, to the glass quart-size cucumber bottle with a stupid little plastic box inside!

And now the cops she had set on him were spreading the flanks of a cruel round-up at Sagin's hideaway. Death looked at him with its tin-colored eyes.

"I don't want to!" Sagin shook his head. "I won't give up!" He was about to start back but stopped in his tracks. "Wait, where am I going?"

Three hundred paces behind Sagin Wolf Island became a rounded, blunt, broad wedge of sand. Beyond the wedge, five yards from the spit, it was already five fathoms deep, the beginning of the Kiyarskaya Hole, with its thirty-foot covering of water extending a good two miles down the river.

On the left Wolf Island was separated from the mainland by a narrow channel of swift, roaring water. Endless cotton fields began just across the channel. It was possible to cross the channel in only a few minutes, but the place on the other side was as bare as a bald spot and the cotton rose but a hand from the ground, so it was suicide to take on the channel.

On the right the Akdarya's main stream, one hundred yards wide, washed the island with a lazy, almost invisible current. Sagin could have covered the main stream in two minutes. He would dive out of the bushes on the island, plunge into the water, tear off across the river with all his might, and there he would be, on the other, safe bank, in the dense *tugai* that extended for miles along the river: the same reeds as on the island, the same tangles of juniper, thorns, *saksaul,* and crooked elms—like finding a needle in a haystack.

But the cops knew their work, they sniffed out where he might take off to. Their motorboats were now going through the main stream. They moved briskly and aggressively, and in a minute or two would draw even with Volodka's hideout.

Volodka once again bustled about in one spot. Even if he dove in from the bank, he still couldn't cover a hundred yards underwater, and when he came up for air—there he'd be, like a watermelon on a plate, in plain sight of everybody from all directions. Go back? To the sandbank at the end of the spit? Where the channel and the main water merge and the Kiyarskaya Hole begins? The width there is more than half a mile. Where could he head? He wouldn't be able to cover even half the distance and the chase would be there. They could take him barehanded. So where, then?!

While he bustled about senselessly on his bare patch of sand, the decisive moments, when it still seemed that he might find a way out, passed by.

The first motorboat bumped its sharp nose into the upper end of Wolf Island. A second entered the channel, and yet another went downstream. Volodka's former patrol boat flew past on the Akdarya like a bird and, sharply cutting its drive, came in toward the island's lower end.

Craning his neck until it creaked, Volodka followed the round-up from a high sandy mound. Two policemen jumped from the speedboat onto the spit, and another remained seated at the wheel. Noises came from the upper end. Volodka turned in fear. Two more boats came in to the island. People were getting out of them, their guns flashing. In a minute several militiamen were standing on the spit where the first boat had got stuck. Next to one of them—Volodka unconsciously licked his suddenly dry lips—loomed a big German shepherd. Volodka got a bitter taste in his mouth.

"They're going to hound me down with that dog like a rabbit," flashed through his mind. "I'm in a bad way. You can't run from a dog."

Volodka started to give ground slowly. In a minute he was standing back in his secret clearing. His pursuers were visible from here too.

One of the militiamen standing on the spit put a bullhorn to his lips:

"Listen to us, Sagin," the cone blasted, echoing like thunder in Volodka's brain. "We know for a fact that you're here on Wolf Island. The whole island is surrounded and our boats are on the water. You have nowhere to go. Don't be a fool, come out on your own. We'll put it down as voluntary surrender. That's your only chance of saving your life. If you don't come out, we'll comb the island with the dog. There's nowhere to hide."

The bullhorn fell silent. Volodka was silent too. He clearly saw the excited dog furiously straining at the short leash. Its guide, one could see, was just waiting for the command to let the dog loose.

Volodka studied the posse, which seemed to be standing there indecisively, until his eyes hurt. What could they be waiting for? Why were they delaying? After all, they had machine guns in their hands. Why should they coax the unarmed Sagin to give up? Come and get him!

And once again there blasted out:

"If you're thinking of resisting or shooting somebody, keep in mind it'll be worse for you. We won't stand on ceremony, we have orders: in the event of armed resistance, shoot to kill! So better not fool around, come out on your own."

Volodka swallowed his thick saliva. "So that's it. They're afraid I'll chop somebody. They don't like that, I guess. They're used to chopping everybody down themselves. But how come this stuff about shooting? I don't even have anything to shoot with. Ah-h-h!" Sagin figured it out. "It's because they're afraid of the rifle I dropped. They don't know that the rifle's in the river and there weren't any cartridges for it anyway. They're scared I'll start shooting. Why, sure, who wants to get in the way of a stray bullet? Otherwise they'd rush me all at once. So that's it..!"

An indistinct hope of escape began to glimmer before him. And not of escape, but maybe simply some move as yet unknown to Volodka would be found, one which after all must exist somewhere in his ruthless fate. For he couldn't be broken completely when all that remained was—the end, collapse, death!

"Just make it somehow until night, until night," beseeched Volodka. "Then they can chase me with a thousand dogs, the night won't betray me, in a night I'll be far from here. Oh, I should have taken to my heels right away, to hell with it, the money, life is worth more than any money!"

The police stood a little while, talking among themselves, then, with obvious reluctance, they began to spread out in a chain. The bullhorn wailed again over the whole island:

"Sagin, come out, I'm saying it for the last time! Save your life! You won't have another!"

A faint trembling seized Volodka.

A sharp command was heard on the spit. Weapons flashed as the chain of policemen moved ahead. Their first step, as it were, ripped the catch off the spring of Volodka's silence. He didn't have time to figure out what he was doing when his hoarse voice cut the tense silence.

"Stop, you scum! I'll shoot you all!"

The following took place in the blink of an eye. The chain stopped suddenly, as if it had hit an invisible obstacle. The policemen pressed to the ground and thrust their machine gun barrels forward. The small, skinny man with the German shepherd quickly bent over the dog, unfastened the clasp on its collar and gave the sinister command: "Sic!" And the big gray beast shot into the depths of the growth with huge leaps.

Volodka involuntarily retreated. The frightened thought flashed: "Run!".

But with a tremendous effort of will power Sagin forced himself to stay put. Any fool could see how a race with a trained dog would end.

Volodka quickly shed his rumpled linen tunic with its OSVOD shoulder straps and wound it around his left arm. The sailor's shirt rose quickly and irregularly on his chest.

"I won't give up!" That one thought pulsed in his temple.

Volodka cast a glance over the area in front of him. The small, sandy clearing, the place of his shattered dream, had now become an arena for combat, the stakes of which were Volodka's life.

"Damn!" Sagin rushed to the edge of the clearing and grabbed the sapper's shovel he had left there.

When Volodka straightened up, the German shepherd was already five yards from him. At the sight of Sagin the gray, black-tipped fur on the dog all at once stood on end. Its eyes, red with rage, seemed to rip Volodka to shreds. With ominously hoarse breathing, the dog rushed at him.

Volodka, bending slightly and putting forward his wrapped arm, raced to meet the dog. Their leaps joined in a single, indistinguishable, lightning-quick movement. The sharp, yellow fangs closed on Volodka's upper arm. A desperate struggle continued in the air for several seconds, then the man and the dog fell on the cool sand. The shepherd's fangs pierced Volodka's arm through. With vicious growls the enraged dog jerked his head madly, trying to rip out a piece of Volodka's flesh. Sagin tried desperately to wrap his legs around the shepherd and pin it to the sand. For several seconds they rolled on the ground. The dog's nails raked Volodka's face until it was bloody and shredded the sailor's shirt on his chest.

For a minute the struggle continued with no winner, but finally the man overpowered the animal. Volodka got the dog underneath him. Groaning, he held its muscular, wheezing throat with the round shovel handle, and, giving a sharp grunt, threw himself upon it with all his weight.

The dog's neck bones crunched drily and broke under the rounded beech bar. The dog's fangs, which had had a death grip on Volodka's arm, suddenly weakened. Not believing in his victory, Sagin leaned heavily on the handle one more time. Beneath him the hot, powerful body beat convulsively.

Finally Volodka rose from the sand, freeing his arm with difficulty from the reluctantly parting steel jaws. He was breathing heavily. A vein in his temple throbbed sharply. Deep scratches and wounds covered his bloodied face, the sailor's shirt hung in tatters.

"So that's how it is. So they meant to hunt me down with a dog," Sagin repeated senselessly and pitifully. "Oooh, those cops, the swine! With a dog..."

Ahead, behind the bushes, there was a grinding of sand. Volodka rushed to an opening in the branches. The chain of pursuers was approaching his hideaway. Ten steps from Sagin a hefty police sergeant with a somber face broke through the thick, thorny brush. A snubnose commando submachine gun danced in his hand.

Volodka moaned painfully and ran back, seeing nothing in front of him. The sapper's shovel was clasped in his hand.

"I won't give up!" The spasmodic cry swelled inside Volodka.

He dashed out onto the lower end of Wolf Island while the master sergeant, sitting in his speedboat and bored by inactivity, was getting a cigarette. The cigarette just wouldn't come out of the full pack. Two policemen armed with pistols who were sitting side by side on the aluminum gunwhale were talking lazily. They didn't in the least expect that a seasoned, hounded beast would leap right out at them in broad daylight. The first second, all of them froze.

Volodka was a frightening sight—raked by the thorny bushes, mauled by the dog's claws, crazed from the chase, the rusty shovel still in his hand. He stopped for a moment, gazing mindlessly at his pursuers, his breath coming in hoarse bursts from his throat, and the shovel waving in his hand as if drunk. Then, with a pained and desperate yell, Sagin threw himself at the policemen, hoisting his one, sorry weapon over his head.

The pursuers, dumbstruck by surprise and fright, immediately fell into the patrol boat. The motor started up with half a crank. The boat, plowing the sand with its left flank, jerked and jumped into the water. The sergeant sitting at the controls clung to the wheel, with a desperate look the second policeman tore at the buckle of his empty holster, and the third was unable to calm his thumping heart and greedily gulped air through his panting mouth.

Volodka plunged into the water at a run. There wasn't a thought in his crazed mind now, only a constant muscular effort kept him on his feet.

The speedboat made a wide circle on the river and headed Volodka's way. He was able to get only a couple dozen yards downstream when his pursuers turned up beside him.

Volodka's frenzied eyes caught sight of the wide, flat hull of the patrol boat lifted above the water, with rivulets running down the aluminum, and the shattering roar of the overworked engine burst upon his ears. A terrible thought flashed through his mind: "They'll chop me to pieces with the propeller! Like I did to him, yesterday...!"

He turned sharply and dove. His eyes were wide open.

A huge sun wavered in the slightly turgid, yellow-green water, penetrating the heavy, lazy depths with bright strips of light. Right below Volodka's feet the bottom dropped abruptly into darkness. Here began the Kiyarskaya, the stupendously deep hole that Sagin knew through and through.

Slicing the water, the patrol boat's keel was speeding right toward Sagin, its propeller spinning madly. Behind the propeller stretched sparkling sprays of tiny silver bubbles.

Volodka tucked in his head and used all his strength to work his arms and legs, striving to escape down as far as possible. There, below, in the brownish, swaying semi-darkness, the black silty bottom of the hole was lost from sight.

A dozen or so big carp with dark green backs formed a single dense school that slipped by in front of Sagin on their way to the deep, and Volodka lunged after them.

"I won't gi-i-i-ve..." flashed in his brain, as the thought was extinguished.

...Down, down, towards the black silty bottom, where the quiet water barely disturbs the lion manes of submerged trees; down, down, where the cold bottom springs gush from the earth's hidden treasure chests to meet the warm surge of the powerful river flow....

Translated by Timothy Pogacar

Originally published in *Znamia,* January 1988.

Boris Ekimov

The Chelyadins' Son-in-Law

1

Everyone in the small village waited for the midday Saturday bus. Around the time it was due they poked their heads outside and tried to catch its rumble in the distance. They ran out of their gates, or even walked as far as the common, to the barns, meeting expected and unexpected guests on the way. On Saturdays the village, like an old mother, impatiently awaited the short weekend visit of her dear children and grandchildren.

Up rolled the bright yellow stubby bus, and its doors burst open like a ripe pod, spilling people out onto the road; it carried the others along the winding road to villages farther on: Vikhlyaevsky, Martynovsky, Deminsky, and also Bolshaya Golovka.

The noisy exchange of meetings, kisses, laughter and tears quickly simmered down at the bus stop's iron pole, and everyone scattered at once like water off a cabbage leaf.

On the roadside mound where red-sided seed drills, cultivators, and other broken-down machinery were rusting away just one passenger remained—a tall, young-looking man with close-cropped hair who carried a new suitcase. Nobody met him, and, more importantly, nobody recognized him. When everyone else had gone off, the man put his suitcase on the ground, slowly lit up a cigarette, and started looking around this place, where Providence had brought him.

Old log barns stood side by side on this wasteland, and a bit further away the village houses traced an intricate bow around the wasteland and barns. The houses stood above a small river whose course was charted by tall, spreading pussy willows. A small wood or, perhaps, a water-meadow shimmered in the distance. In every other direction there stretched field after field.

Just then, in that midday in June, they were lush shades of green and yellow, shot through with pink and dark violet, streaming away as far as the eye could see. And the fields were quiet and empty, and there was no sign of life anywhere. Grasshoppers chirped, the wheat field, which spread right up to the edge of the road, was rustling gently, and a large silent bird, also all alone, kept tracing indolent circles in the empty sky.

The newcomer grew uneasy. After the crowded, noisy places he'd had to spend time in, he found this solitude overbearing and eerie.

Out from behind the barns came Timofei Ivanovich, a well-known character in the village. He had been hurrying toward the bus in the hope of meeting someone, but had arrived too late. Guessing the newcomer was a stranger to these parts, and giving him a quick look over, he strode up and said, "You're not a s-spy, are you? C-come to f-find out our s-secrets?"

One glance at Timofei Ivanovich's face and the rest of him told the newcomer all he needed to know, and he asked, "What secrets have you got, then?"

"W-well, th-there's the st-store, for a start," Timofei Ivanovich hinted transparently. "I can show you."

"I'll make do without the store. Just tell me where the Chelyadins live here."

"Depends which ones..."

"Why, are there a lot of them, then?"

"Heaps. There's Mishka Chelyadin, Fetynia—the old woman, makes r-rotten homebrew, she does, Klavdia," he replied, bending one finger after another.

"Hold on," the newcomer stopped him, "or it'll be dark before you're through. It's Raisa Chelyadin I want. Know her?"

Timofei Ivanovich put two and two together in no time. First, he was speechless with excitement: his lips just smacked together and his eyes bulged. Then he got a grip on himself and stopped stammering.

"So, it's you, then, Raisa's penpal? From, well, you know..."

"That's it," the newcomer confirmed.

"So you're here at last!" Timofei joyfully threw up his hands and somehow his dark face even grew lighter.

"But how do you know? Are you family?

"Oh, around here we're all one big family. I'll take you there right now, we'll get everything laid on. We'll give you a proper welcome," prattled Timofei Ivanovich, looking forward to a good drinking session. "My mother-in-law's a cousin of yours, Martinovna. That makes us... I've been locked up twice for a day at the local station, too. Once Shuranya had me locked up..."

"That'll do, pops," the newcomer cut him short. "Know what I think of relatives like you? Show me and then beat it! Got it?"

His voice was imposing and icy—it was impossible not to obey him. Timofei Ivanovich pointed out Raisa Chelyadin's house and watched the newcomer set off; he was sore for a while but then realized it was no big loss. With the news that the Convict, as he had been nicknamed in the village, had arrived to see Raisa Chelyadin, he would be welcome in any yard and given a few drinks as well. And he went tripping off to Vasilisa Amochaeva's. They were fond of news there.

The newcomer sauntered off toward Raisa's house. Its white tin-plate roof sparkled invitingly in the distance.

At first glance the Chelyadins' property looked in very good shape, even though three widows took care of it: young Raisa, whose husband had died five years earlier; her mother, Martinovna, who was still quite strong and shrill-voiced, though getting on a bit; and the decrepit grandmother, Makunya, who had had trouble getting around the last few years and spent more and more time dozing and sleeping, preparing herself for eternal rest.

So the women did all the chores. The house, which had been built by Raisa's late husband, was painted orange and had blue shutters; some dark old hay was piled on the rafters alongside a fresh stack; the vegetable garden and potato patch were lush and green; near the yard there were quite a few white-feathered ducks swimming in a murky pond that was filled by a water-pump—everything looked just as it did in any good household.

But a close look would reveal at once that the fence was leaning over drunkenly on rotten posts and there were gaps between the beams of the tile-roofed cellar that obviously needed fixing, and summer after summer there were nettles growing all over the foundations of the outhouse, which the owner had started building as a summer kitchen but never finished. The tall television antenna was noticeably tilting, its winged crown swooping toward the chimney like some bird of prey. Yes, you can always tell a household run by women.

The Chelyadins ran the house and lived in it together, just the three of them—they'd sent off Raisa's children to live elsewhere. The boy was studying at a technical college attached to a factory in town; his younger sister had been recruited to work at a weaving factory a long way off near Moscow. So these days the Chelyadins didn't expect anyone on weekends, and the postwoman used to bring news of the children. She also brought other letters—from the Convict, as he was known. Alyoshka Borovskov, a good-for-nothing villager of theirs, who was serving quite a long sentence for robbing a store, had spoken highly of the widows in his village to his prison mates, and the good thing was that their addresses were simple, and they had no streets or apartment numbers. And then strange letters started arriving in the village. The first to reply was Faina Chertikhina, and then Skuridina. For some time there had been a serious shortage of decent men in the area, for a lot of them had taken to drink. But that didn't mean that life had to stop. The Chelyadins also started getting letters and they sent back food parcels to the prison. But there was little to hope for, and the future seemed pretty grim.

Mind you, Martinovna tried to justify what she was doing to herself and to others: "There're all sorts in there. Good men, too. If they don't get on with their wives or bosses, they get put away. It could happen to anyone." And others agreed with her. But the rather frightening word "convict" did not make her feel all that happy. So they just put their faith in God and waited. And now the time had come.

When the newcomer reached the Chelyadins' yard, only the two older ones, Martinovna and Granny Makunya, were there. Martinovna was in the shade, well out of the sun, knitting a fluffy scarf, while her mother, in a warm cardigan, had settled in the hottest spot and was making butter in a tall oak churn, firmly clasping the top of the ladle with her frail, withered hands.

The newcomer approached the yard, caught sight of the women sitting there, and began looking them over, trying to spot his penpal from a distance. One of them was very old, and the other not much good either, although in acquaintances of this sort anything was possible—sometimes they even sent photographs of other attractive women just as bait, and then hoped for the best.

Sensing that someone was staring at them from the street, Martinovna looked up from the scarf, noticed the stranger, and asked loudly, "Looking for someone?"

"Yes, I am," replied the man and strode toward their fence. "Does Raisa Chelyadin live here?"

"Yes, she does... What do you want her for?"

The stranger opened the gate, walked into the yard, and said, "My name's Konstantin. Kostya. Which of you is Raisa?"

The women stopped working, having guessed right away who the newcomer was. And it was not so much the name that helped them—Granny Makunya had absolutely no memory for recent events—they guessed by the different way he looked, by his short haircut and bold stare. He had a military look—tall, lean, and stern.

"Heavens," said Martinovna, getting up. "So it's you... It's... it's you, is it?.." she stammered, not knowing how to address him. "Raisa's at the lunchtime milking, with the cows. Come in, come in, no need to stand in the middle of the yard. Give me your things."

With more vitality than her large bulky body seemed capable of, Martinovna carried his suitcase to the porch, dragged over a chair, and put it down in the shade.

"Sit down, sit down... Take a rest. Raisa won't be long now. She's at the milking. You can hear them at it now."

The village was so quiet that you could clearly hear the gentle whir of the compressor at the summer camp by the dam.

"What'll you have to drink? Fruit juice or milk? Buttermilk or fresh milk? Maybe you'd like something to eat?"

"We'll eat when Raisa gets back. But I wouldn't mind some milk," replied the newcomer in a milder tone.

While Martinovna was running between the house and the cellar, the newcomer decided to get acquainted with the old woman, who, as soon as he arrived, seemed to freeze solid with fear; only her eyelids kept blinking. She had turned eighty and was, as they say, living out her days without any particular worries for her daughter and granddaughter. When drunk, Raisa's late husband had sometimes bullied his wife and mother-in-law, but he'd never laid a finger on old Makunya. She cried when he died. Widowed herself at a tender age and having gotten used to her daughter's early bereavement, she had not taken the business of her granddaughter's penpal seriously, putting it down to self-indulgence and too much good living. And whenever their neighbor happened to ask about Raisa, she would reply, pursing her lips, "Silly sheep, they're sending parcels. And he's a murderer or stole something from a store. Fiancé... Why, the likes of him'll never be let out."

One thing Makunya was sure about: good people didn't go to prison, but she didn't get too worked up over it, as she figured she'd be dead by the time the convict showed up.

But now, here he was, standing beside her and asking: "Still breathing are you, Gran?"

"Oh yes, son, yes," she just managed to gasp, afraid to raise her head and look into his terrible eyes.

"What are you working at?"

"I'm making butter."

The newcomer took the tall, dark-hooped tub out of the old woman's frail hands, lifted the lid and the grating, carefully looked at all the different parts, and, smacking his lips, took a gulp of the rather bitter soured cream from the churn.

"He downed half the churn in one gulp," she later told the old women next door. "Gurgling and smacking his lips."

"How old are you, Gran?"

"Very..." Makunya replied.

"And you're still working and helping out?"

"Try to."

"That's right, earn your grub."

Although she gave the right replies, Makunya had not the slightest idea what was going on. Only the last bit about working and grub struck home. It seemed to her that the newcomer was telling her off and ordering her to work. Gripping the top of the churn, she started pounding it very energetically. Her hands soon started to grow numb and she began to sweat, but her fear was so strong she couldn't stop.

Martinovna laid the table with everything she had at hand—milk, eggs, and bread.

"Have something to eat while you're waiting."

She sat down opposite her guest, watching how nimbly he handled the eggs, bread and milk. The man had large hands, strong fingers, and round nails like nutshells. No, his teeth were not his own, they all had metal caps, but he managed them fine and his angular Adam's apple kept bobbing energetically up and down. And, looking at his powerful hands, strong neck, and strapping body, Martinovna began feeling uneasy. "I ought to check his papers," she thought to herself. "Maybe he isn't the one who wrote but some other ox..."

She knew everything, she'd been to the Borovskys' herself, read the letters, and looked at the photograph, but from a long way off he hadn't seemed frightening to her. He had written that he was in prison for some trifle, that people had let him down. She had reassured herself beforehand that there were all sorts in prison. But now she could tell by his stare, his powerful build and manner, that he was no innocent victim and that he had been put behind bars for a good reason.

She wanted to check his discharge papers, but how? Perhaps she should call the farm brigade leader? She thought he was someone else—a stand-in—and that's why she was afraid that he'd come to their house.

Completely at ease, the newcomer ate everything offered him and lit a cigarette.

"Maybe you'd like to go down to the river?" Martinovna suggested. "It's very close—just down behind the vegetable plots."

"Wouldn't be bad to cool down," the newcomer replied, perking up.

Martinovna brought out a towel, showed him the path, and as soon as he had disappeared behind the trees, stopped pretending and rushed over to Granny Makunya:

"Mama, Mama... What do you think of him? You've seen a few in your time..."

Still energetically churning the butter, only now did Makunya come to her senses, and, tossing down the ladle, said in an undertone, "A typical convict. Mind he don't burn the house down. We got to hide the matches and warn folks."

Martinovna just flapped her hand dismissively, sat thinking things over for a few minutes, then went indoors. While he was out, she wrapped all their money, Raisa's ring and earrings, their savings book and the new passports they had just been issued in a small bundle, and carried it to a neighbor's, just in case. Only then did she set about getting lunch ready. There was a guest in her house, after all, and his arrival had already been announced all over the village by the loafer Timofei Ivanovich, and Raisa had heard the news, too.

At the summer camp by the pond above the dam the milking was nearly finished. The heavy black and white cows had passed through the milking stalls and were cropping the lush green alfalfa by the feeding troughs in the large corral. The last cows were being milked and the workers were carrying the last milk cans out to the delivery truck.

On a bicycle far too large for him, Amochaev's young boy came riding up on the road from the village. Wobbling along, precariously perched on the lower bar, he circled around the machinery and milking equipment without stopping and shouted out loudly, "Auntie Raisa! Gran's sent me to tell you your fiancé's arrived from prison!" Then he turned and set off back to the village the way he had come, the bicycle wobbling under him, for it was far too big for the boy.

Of course everyone heard the news: Raisa Chelyadin, the other women workers, the milk-truck driver, and the livestock expert, a stocky young man who drove to every milking in his own red Moskvich.

Raisa froze when she heard the news. After she had somehow managed to milk the last cow and let it out of the stall, she glanced around to check if all the others had heard, convinced herself that they had, and all of a sudden blushed crimson with shame, and tears actually welled up in her eyes.

Raisa Chelyadin had been born here in the village, and had grown up alongside her mother, Martinovna, a very bold, mannish woman. But other blood had got the upper hand. Raisa did not even look like her mother: slender, fine-boned, pale, she had the dainty step of a trim little white hen. And in character she was completely different... Whereas her mother could make more noise than anyone, Raisa from an early age had never spoken much. When she got married, she put herself under another person's control and power, and after she was widowed, she once again obeyed her mother in everything. That was just the way she was made.

Now she felt embarrassed and ashamed. The milk-truck driver called out, laughing, "Hey, bride, drag the milk over quick now! All you have to do is court, but I've got to work!"

The livestock expert smiled. The other women hurriedly had their say:

"Raisa, is it true, then? Why aren't you saying anything?"

"Why, I haven't seen anyone."

"He must have come on the bus. Those Amochaevs, why, they always know everything."

"You run along now. We'll finish things off."

"Run along where?"

"Why, to meet the man, of course."

"Mama and Gran'll do that."

"Gran..." they mimicked her. "Is it your Gran he's come to see, then? If you don't watch out, Nina Sitilina will swipe your fiancé out from under your nose."

Raisa only sighed in reply and carried the heavy can over to the truck. Then she started hurrying, and quick as could be, washed down the milking machinery and cans. The other women understood how she felt and moved away. But she was not in a hurry to get home. She just wanted to leave here as soon as possible and ride back home alone to get a grip on herself and to think it all through.

Once she had done everything, she got on her bicycle and pedaled off, but she had not gone far when she slowed down, took a detour, and rode the long way home, across the dam and meadow. Why hurry? What will be, will be. But there was no way of telling how things would go.

It was her mother who had started the business with the penpal. She would never have dared to herself. Her mother had found out the address, but it was Raisa, of course, who'd done the writing. She had sent a photograph and got another in return and sent some packages. And so it had dragged on...

From a distance, going by his letters, Raisa thought she liked the man. The photo showed a young, attractive man who, it's true, looked rather grim. But then, what was there to smile about there? Raisa felt sorry for her penpal and thought kindly of him. And she wanted another life for herself. It was no joy being a widow, and she hadn't even turned forty, so she had plenty of time to go.

She had been without a husband for five years. When he was alive, though he drank heavily, everything seemed to run smoothly: the firewood, hay, coal, and corn just seemed to stack themselves. Bit by bit the new house grew. But when he died, in women's hands, even hard-working ones, everything went to pieces. In five years they'd not been able even to finish the summer kitchen. And that was just one thing... It had taken old Arkhip all summer to knock together a porch to the house and he'd made a real hash of it—it looked more like some kind of birdhouse. But he took his money.

And it was so painful psychologically and emotionally to live without a mate... With her pretty face and a nature submissive as meadow grass Raisa attracted men. Married locals and men passing through tried courting her. She kept away from the locals, ashamed for their wives' sake, but sometimes went with men from elsewhere. One summer she lived with a visiting driver, another time with a vet on business. Both had promised that their intentions were honorable, and though she had not really believed them, she had given in. She had swallowed their lies like honey, responding to them with tender affection. They had promised much... But if truth be known, her casual men friends and even she herself had really been playing a game. They had families and children, and Raisa had two of her own, and her mother and grandmother on her back as well. What chance was there... It was as though they were trying to justify what they were doing—to themselves and others—by having serious plans for the future.

Local guys also tried to court Raisa, but they were all useless, heavy drinkers who'd been kicked out by their wives.

In short, during the five years she had been a widow there had been little happiness, and that's why she placed so much hope in the future.

The road Raisa took ran over the river, past the willow woods and the large wide meadow that stretched from Bullock Hill to the village of Yaryzhensky, Yaryzhensky Sands and, say, to the wood at the Buzuluk River. In the middle of this summer's day, after a good rainy spring, the meadow was lush and green, and its simple bright flowers—scarlet and white clover, daisies and buttercups—stood out against the green grass, stretching on and on.

The road did a loop but eventually came out by the village. It was time to head home—they were waiting for her there.

Raisa rode quickly through the village, her eyes lowered, for she felt every household had already heard and was discussing everything.

Meanwhile, their guest, or the new master of the house, whatever he might be, was making himself at home at the bottom of the garden by the stream.

The path Martinovna had shown him ran alongside the vegetable plot, where there were lashes of late cucumbers, knee-high rows of spring onions, and blossoming peas. The newcomer started looking for a cucumber, but, unable to find one, pulled up a white-tailed radish instead, wiped it and popped it in his mouth. In the green thicket of peas he pulled off a handful of pods and shelled them as he went along, sucking in the sweet young peas with his lips. Beyond the vegetable plot stretched the old garden with its impassable cherry orchard, prickly blackthorns, gnarled apple trees and tall old pear tree.

He left the path and started forcing his way through the garden undergrowth, sampling everything in his path, like a bird: sour apples, hard pears, cherries that were already red. On the edge of the garden by the riverbank he came across a tiny strawberry patch ablaze with sweet-smelling ripe red berries and white flowers. He lay down on the warm ground and lazily picked the berries, relaxing and growing pleasantly sleepy.

He didn't feel like dozing off and he certainly couldn't have just then. Through lowered eyelashes he could see everything: the deep blue sky, the long braids of willow branches trailing over the flowing water, the water lilies' flat leaves on the ripples, the crimson and blue dragonflies, their wings whirring as they flew about and landed very close by on the dry blades of grass, and the unfamiliar birds calling to each other and singing nearby.

After his long imprisonment and dull and cheerless life inside a barracks, he suddenly felt overwhelmed by it all: it was many years since he had seen so much greenery, such a vast sky, such silence interrupted only by the birds' singing and the voice of the wind in the light foliage—it reminded him of his childhood and summer camp. But his thoughts didn't linger on the past, for, after all, here right beside him was this day, this dazzlingly bright day.

He went right down to the river and sat on its bank, measuring it this way and that with his glance. Before he was locked up, he used to enjoy fishing and cooking fish soup outdoors. It had been a long time ago, but he still remembered it and this jogged his memory.

He had done six years at the labor camp. And Martinovna's doubts were groundless—it was he who had written and sent the photographs, and his name was Kostya—it was all true.

Kostya was thirty-five; he'd spent eight years in prison. The first time, he got a short sentence for some foolish thing he'd done in his youth; this time it had been for something more serious and the term was longer. He had grown up in town, had two children and a wife in the two-room apartment he had been allocated by the factory he worked in as a lathe operator. He had gotten sick of his job a long time ago and was in no hurry to get back to his wife and children, especially since the terms of his sentence prohibited him from returning to his hometown for several years.

Thinking things over in his spare time at the labor camp, he had decided to make a new life for himself. So here he was. It had started well enough: so far he had been given a good welcome, and now here was this bank, this strawberry patch, this clean river into which he dived now and swam about, unbothered by the cold springs, and then lay on the grass in the sunshine, cut off even from the quiet village by the dense old orchard that had run wild.

The only sounds came from the birds and the wind in the treetops, and every now and then from a fish splashing about, and something harmless rustling in the riverside bushes.

Things were off to a good start. And Martinovna was already calling to him in her deep booming voice, which rang out over the vegetable plot and garden: "Konstantin! Konstantin!"

She wasn't used to the name and found it hard to pronounce, and her voice sounded rather odd and unlike its usual self.

Chigarikha, a distant neighbor who was digging her vegetable plot, heard her and started wondering whom on earth she was calling. Unable to come up with an answer, she decided to go and ask.

They had lunch inside. Konstantin, after all, was from town, so they took the chicken noodle soup, curd dumplings, milk, homegrown greens, egg and lard from the kitchen into the front room.

Martinovna had invited along a nephew who was experienced in worldly matters. Prompted by his aunt, he checked Konstantin's discharge document straightaway and made sure everything was in order.

Then they sat down to lunch. The men split a bottle of white wine between them and hit it off at once, chatting about fishing and hunting. True, the nephew had never been behind bars, but he'd been through a hell of a lot when he had worked on construction sites in remote parts of the country. He was not so fond of work, but he did enjoy hunting with a shotgun and fishing.

After eating the soup, Granny Makunya grew sleepy and went off for a nap. The men went outside for a smoke and a chat. Left alone, mother and daughter kept exchanging glances as they talked.

"What do you think? Does he look good?" asked Martinovna.

"I don't know, Mama," Raisa replied with a shrug.

She really had no idea. She'd taken one look at him, recognized him from his photograph, and lowered her eyes. As she greeted him, she had felt his tremendous manly strength, and when she was sitting next to him, every time she had accidentally touched his warm shoulder, she had stiffened, not knowing whether to feel afraid or delighted.

"Just be firm from the start," Martinovna instructed her in a loud whisper. "'We'll see,' tell him, 'what you're like. Maybe you won't do. We need someone to work in the fields and run the house. We may throw you out on your ear.'"

She might say that but she didn't believe it. Sitting there next to the square-shouldered man, her daughter looked like a fluffy little quail. She didn't have it in her to be firm and throw him out.

Meanwhile the new master of the house felt completely at home: he drank and ate the chicken with gusto, talking loudly and confidently.

"We'll do fine... We've got hands and feet. Heads on our shoulders." And he already hugged his wife, or fiancée, whoever she was, reassuringly. "We'll do fine."

Raisa said nothing and only smiled shyly and sighed aloud.

Martinovna's nephew kept nodding, "You can get by here. If you're not stupid, you can do fine here. But in other parts..." And he poured out stories of other places that were hard to settle in. "If you've got a gun and something up here..." Then the conversation turned to hunting and fishing.

Konstantin—Kostya, as they now called him—was only too pleased to talk about this at the table and later outside when they went for a smoke. But Martinovna kept on at her daughter: "You're not afraid? And now?.."

She tried to imagine how things would turn out, but everything was all settled—this strong, tall man was sitting here at the table, chuckling and flashing his metallic teeth. He kept embracing Raisa and promising, "We'll do fine..." And he reassured Martinovna as well by saying, "We've got ten fingers and ten toes... We'll do fine..."

The meal went on a long time. Granny Makunya had her nap and got up again. Remembering his present, Kostya took some candies out of his suitcase as a treat for the women.

And then it was time for Raisa to go off to the evening milking, and Kostya followed, joked around and laughed, marveling how the cows lined themselves up in front of the milking stalls like circus-trained animals.

The other women took a liking to him and Raisa felt relieved. She bustled about the cows, washing their udders, massaging and clipping on the milking cups, while Kostya carried the milk cans to the truck. He did it as if they were weightless.

When the milking was finished, they set off home a roundabout way over the river, through the gardens, and by the time they reached home they were already a couple. They slept together in the double bed in the front room as man and wife.

Martinovna didn't sleep all night, afraid for her daughter's sake and her own, and for everything at once, even though she had taken the bundle to her neighbor's.

But the newlyweds awoke the next morning happy and relaxed. Raisa set off for work and Kostya dozed until she got back. The featherbed was high and made of soft goose down, the house was quiet, and only Makunya could be heard softly muttering her morning prayers. Among other things she prayed for their new man's health and well-being.

2

One morning shortly after he arrived, Kostya sauntered out into the yard, stripped to the waist, yawning loudly and screwing his eyes up against the sun, dazzlingly green grass, and trees. Bacon and fried eggs were sizzling on the stove and Raisa was putting fresh herbs and milk on the table. While she bustled about, Kostya had a look at the dilapidated fence and put it right in five minutes by driving two iron standpipes in as supports. He handled the sledge hammer with the greatest of ease and the pipes slid effortlessly into the ground. While he was fiddling about, he also tightened the supports on the television antenna so that it was now "as straight as a carabine."

Later the Chelyadins—Martinovna and Granny Makunya—boasted about it to their neighbors and friends.

"All in one go... You can tell the way he gripped it, he's a real handyman," droned Martinovna. "He did the fence and now it's as straight as a carabine."

"Yes, as straight as a carabine..." confirmed Granny Makunya.

What exactly a "carabine" was nobody in the village was really sure, but they understood because that is what their parents and grandparents used to say.

As far as the farm work went, Kostya was in no hurry to start.

"I'm going to rest up first," he told Raisa on the first day and promised to fix up things around the place.

"He's going to rest up..." Raisa obediently told her mother and grandmother. "And do some work around the place..."

"Let him rest up a bit," Martinovna repeated in her deep bass around the village. "We've got a lot of chores around the place that need doing. Mowing, finishing off the kitchen, the cellar roof."

The neighbors nodded sympathetically. Every household had no end of chores to get through.

How long he was going to rest was anybody's guess, but one of the first Saturdays and Sundays they went to the party the Alifashkins threw to welcome their son home from the army. As close relatives, Raisa and Konstantin were seated at the main table. And here the Chelyadins' new son-in-law really showed the whole village what he was made of, and made a good impression on a lot of people. He was a good singer and a great dancer; he enjoyed drinking but knew when to stop.

It was here, too, that Chapurin, the section manager or collective-farm brigade leader, as they used to be called, set eyes on him for the first time. They exchanged greetings and shook hands while getting acquainted. They had the same huge, tough hands and were both exceedingly tall—exactly the same height, in fact. True, the brigade leader was stouter and older.

They exchanged greetings and stood chatting about this and that.

"Planning to work, are you?" Chapurin asked.

"I'll have to," came Konstantin's brief reply.

"That's the right idea. You're a long way from retirement age. Got any particular skill?"

"You won't have work in my line."

"In that case you can work as a herdsman. We're getting a new young herd. It's going to be driven over here in about three days' time. There'll be Nikolai Skuridin and you. He's been off sick, but he's just getting back on his feet."

Nikolai was tracked down at one of the tables in the noisy crowded yard. Only just getting over his illness, he was still waxen-faced and terribly thin and drawn.

"Here's a partner for you," Chapurin told him.

"That's fine by me," Nikolai replied enthusiastically. "Can you sit on a horse?"

"Never tried to," Kostya replied.

"Well, never mind. We'll pick you a very gentle mare. A real rocking horse. And before you know it, you'll look as though you were born in a saddle."

That's how they settled things.

Nikolai came up to his new partner a couple of times later on at the party. He got drunk quickly because after being in the hospital he was still very weak.

"We're going to graze the herd together," he said. "I've spent my whole life with herds. We're going to graze them... We'll pick you a mare. Three hundred rubles a month guaranteed."

And his wife took him off completely smashed. But the Chelyadins' son-in-law spent the whole day at the party and then walked home on his own two feet.

At home Raisa and his mother-in-law said how delighted they were about his talk with the brigade leader.

"It's good work..." boomed Martinovna happily. "Herdsmen have an easy time of it these days. It's very well paid, too. You get three hundred rubles, even more sometimes..."

"You can have breakfast and a hot lunch," Raisa said solicitously. "And you can rest after lunch. And you can stay at home every other day. Other folks get by at it."

"And the pay's so good..." Martinovna kept on.

Kostya was not particularly bothered by money. What appealed to him most was that he could work every other day. In most jobs, say, as a truck or tractor driver, or lathe operator, he would be tied down all week. But here he could rest as well.

A few days later the young herd was driven over from the central farm. They found a gentle mare for the new herdman, fitted it, and off he rode.

For the first few days Kostya and Nikolai worked together, getting the herd used to the new grazing.

The village meadow was on the other side of the river and stretched all the way to Yaryzhensky and the sands. It used to get flooded in the spring but now was protected by dams. It was still a rich meadow, though. The spring rains and warm sun helped the grass grow wonderfully tall and strong. And in summer it was filled with simple wild flowers.

The two young herds—the milk herd and the villagers' cows—were now grazing in the meadow, and sometimes goats would wander in as well. But the goats really preferred spending their time in the salt fields and on the sands, munching the wild grass, wormwood, and young pussy willows. You could clearly make out the spots of two other herds in the distance, near Yaryzhensky. There were no restrictions on grazing.

Toward lunchtime, when the sun started pounding down and the heat became stifling, gadflies began droning over the still meadow. Hearing them, the cattle became restless and would shoot their tails up in the air and gallop off.

But in the early morning there was time to doze. The bullocks walked along, slowly cropping the grass. The meadow was huge and they didn't have to be turned around for a long while.

Nikolai Skuridin would doze on his horse. Over many years he had grown used to the saddle. Light and round-shouldered, he would hunch forward, let go of the reins, and doze with his head on his chest. Once in a while he would jolt up, look at the cattle and nod off again, like an old vulture in the heat.

But the Chelyadins' son-in-law, new to the saddle, sat bolt upright on his mare, fidgeting and rubbing his crotch. And he got down whenever he got the chance to, feeling more relaxed on the ground. He spread out his padded jacket and lay down, but could never drop off to sleep. The mare would disturb him when she jangled her bit, and he was bothered by the ants and other insects. Eventually he had to jump up and shake out his jacket.

"Shaking off the dust, are you?" Nikolai would ask.

"I kept getting bitten. All I need now is for some tarantulas to creep up."

"Some what?"

"Poisonous spiders."

"Here it's the women that're poisonous," Nikolai joked, "but they can't get at us here."

From here, far away, on the other side of the river, beyond the willows and overgrown orchards, the village seemed small. Behind the houses and cemetery the fields stretched on and on all the way to Vikhlyaevskaya Hill. There was a feeling of space and tranquility. The sun rose higher and started beating down.

"There aren't so many cattle now, so it's not such hard work," Nikolai would say. "You've just got to watch out the herds don't get mixed up. It's not such hard work. And the pay's not bad either."

During these few days Nikolai and Kostya got to know all about each other.

"We've got to put a couple of pounds on them all," Nikolai told him. "Yes, at least a couple of pounds, maybe more. But, then, on grass like this... And then we'll make a lot. Don't worry, you'll pay your alimony and have a bit left over."

The sun rose even higher and it became sultry. Sensing the gadflies, the cattle became restless. No more peaceful grazing.

"They may go crazy," said Nikolai. "And shoot their tails up in the air and streak off to the barns. And there's no way of stopping them, and if you do, they won't feed any more. They'll just run like mad with their heads in the air. But we won't let them go crazy, we'll fool them."

The wide open meadow was encircled by gently sloping hills scored with streams and gullies, and covered with grass—true, not as good as the knee-high grass in the meadow—but edible bluish-gray wormwood, yarrow, agrimony, ramsons, and wild basil, and here and there in the hollows and along the streams there was some very good grazing to be had.

"Here's Batyakin Gully, there's Thorny Hollow, Goat's Hollow, Luchki, Kargali, Krasnov Barrow, Merry Barrow," Nikolai pointed out the places around them, whose every nook and cranny he knew.

After turning the herd away from the meadow, they drove it up and out of the stifling midday heat toward the fresh steppe breeze.

"Always do this," Nikolai told him. "When the cattle get fidgety, drive them on to the hills over the gullies so they cool down in the breeze. One week, say, over Batyakina Gully, the next over Thorny Hollow, and then give it a rest. Don't crush the grass. Then try Lychka and Goat's Hollow."

They rode up and down, moving further and further away from the village. The luscious speckled green meadow remained down below. Further still, the riverside trees and shrubs loomed black and the river glinted here and there. The horizon grew wider, opening out with every step they took until they finally caught sight of the village of Vikhlyaevsky, surrounded by orchards, and the dark blue waters and white sands of Lake Ilmen. There, too, were the villages of Malye and Bolshie Gorodbishcha, Letnik, and, a long way off, Buzuluk, hidden behind riverside woods. The earth seemed to be opening up, taking more and more miles away from the sky.

Nikolai Skuridin had been ill for a long time. Twice he had undergone surgery at the regional center's hospital and nobody had believed he would pull through. But he did. And here he was, sitting on a horse. These first few days he was delighted to get back to normal everyday life. What had he day-dreamed about in his hospital bed, lying at death's door?.. About his children, his wife, his village, these places where he had spent his life. He yearned to be there. If he had to die, he longed to do so at home.

And now Nikolai was more talkative than usual with his new partner.

"I've got four kids," he said for the umpteenth time. "The doctors say I should stop working. But you can't keep a family on a pension. Once I start work, I'll get my health back."

He was thin, yellow-skinned and, to make things worse, hardly ever shaved. His gray stubble aged him a lot. So much for what he looked like, but inwardly he felt a new lease on life and was convinced he was going to get better.

The sun was shining, the horse's pulsating body seemed to be letting its hot blood into his veins. And Nikolai felt his strength growing. He spoke more animatedly, his face aglow with a smile.

"And we'll water them at Five Wells and Churkov Springs. I've made shafts there and put down pipes."

And it was as though Nikolai could actually see these sheltered, shady spots, the herd quietly waiting there for the midday heat to abate and himself spending the afternoon there.

"In summer this gets scorched..." he said, sweeping his arm in a circle. "It'll all get completely dried up. And we'll move away toward the wood. There're some good places there, I'll show you. We've got a young herd."

The steers were not bad-looking—broad-boned and stocky. At the central farm they had lost weight on the poor fodder, but they would quickly pick up again.

"They're good steers," said Nikolai approvingly. "They'll feed your children and mine."

He was the only breadwinner in his family, which included his four children, his mother-in-law and wife. They had spent all their money during his illnesses, and his wife kept nagging him.

"We'll earn enough for our kids and have enough left over for tobacco."

The young summer day grew hotter as it headed toward midday. A breeze was fluttering through the wormwood on the mounds, the herd was grazing as it moved slowly through the grass. Nikolai went on talking, Kostya kept glancing at his watch; the baking heat was exhausting and making him sleepy, but the time was dragging by.

They grazed the herd together for a week and then started taking it in turns to drive it alternate days, one day Nikolai, Kostya the next, the way it was always done.

Everyone in the Chelyadin household was pleased. Granny Makunya boasted to the neighbors, "He's working with Skuridin. We're going to get rich now..."

Martinovna was pleased, too, and Raisa even more so. And not so much with her new husband's work and the money on the way as with him himself. Kostya did not drink, he didn't raise his fists against her, and never even said anything nasty to her—what more could she dream of? Now only one thing bothered her—that Kostya would go back to his old family or fall for someone else in the village. Raisa was still pretty and well-groomed, but now she started protecting her face from the sun with a scarf pulled down so low you could only just see her eyes—the way village women looked in the old days. She took great care of her face, darkened her eyebrows, wore lipstick, and when nobody was looking, washed in milk.

So Kostya spent a real honeymoon in his village home. He liked the way nobody woke him up in the mornings and how Raisa used to come back from the morning milking and sleep with him.

He was amazed how silent it was. All you ever heard in the house was the occasional buzzing of a fly that had flown in and the old woman sighing in a far-off room. That was it. And it wasn't very different in the yard: the rooster would crow, the ducks would quack, a voice would ring out and then fall silent—a rare sound would instantly vanish and die away among the widely spread village houses, the green garden hedgerows, meadows, dense cherry orchards or simply among the nettles and burdocks towering over the wattle fences. The rare rumble of a vehicle somewhere near the forge or farm management office, or on the road to the grader dissolved in the green fields and blue skies without ever reaching anyone's ears.

Only the drone of an airplane sometimes reminded one that there was something else out there in the world. Konstantin remembered it well. The factory, the street, family life in a cramped apartment. Only once in a while was it possible to escape into the country for some fishing and live in quiet, green fields over a river for a couple of days.

His life now was like one long fishing trip. He kept thinking that any moment now it was going to end. But when he woke up in the morning, it was still there.

And Konstantin liked his new simple-hearted family—meek and mild Raisa, her rather mannish mother and, of course, her sweet old grandmother. Not for a moment could you even compare them with his old family. He had driven two stakes into the ground by the fence and straightened the television antenna, and they were thrilled to bits.

He was no good at mowing, though. He swung the scythe a couple of times, got the blade completely stuck up to the handle, and gave up.

"It's crazy," he said. "People are launching rockets, while everything here's like long ago."

And the women didn't nag him. He couldn't help it, after all, being from town, and they did the mowing themselves. Things didn't go too well with the new outhouse either. In the mornings Konstantin would slowly look over the rafters that his deceased predecessor had laid down, have a smoke and a think, scratch the back of his head as though he had some idea and was just working out the best way to tackle it, and then he forgot all about it until the next day. He had fishing on his mind.

The first few days he checked out the river, the village and neighboring ponds, and visited the warm Yaryzhensky springs, Panika Forest and the lake. He never came back empty-handed. They fried the crucian and made fish soup with the carp. Rumor had it, mind you, that he had checked out other people's nets and fish traps. Still, you're only a thief if you're caught red-handed, but as for digging up dirt on people—there were plenty of villagers who enjoyed doing that.

One day Martinovna plucked up courage and said to her son-in-law, "Our cellar is uncovered and the rains'll soon be here..."

Cellars in the village were covered with rushes. For some time now the Chelyadins' had needed attention. The old thatch had turned black and disintegrated, laying bare the rib-like rafters.

Kostya had a look at the cellar, grumbling to himself.

"We can get some rushes from the lake," Martinovna explained. "There's lots there. We'll have to fix up a horse with the manager. I'll go and have a chat with him and then between the two of us we'll..." she started, but Kostya stopped her.

"Got any homebrew?" he asked.

"For the horse? For the man who looks after it? Why, of course."

"Today's Monday," Kostya worked out aloud. "The builders will have arrived. Give me a couple of bottles and some lard."

For over a year now the regional construction office had been putting up two small houses in the village.

Martinovna didn't understand, but she did as she was told. With a bag in his hands Konstantin set off for the part where the houses were being built.

And half an hour later he came back dragging the slate along on a tin sheet as if it were a sledge. He put it on there and then. And then the cellar became a neat little white house in the barnyard—a treat for the eye.

Martinovna just threw up her hands in joy and kept repeating, "Now our little potatoes... How good they'll be..."

And she could already see the dry potatoes lying in a high heap in the dark cellar. She was simply overjoyed.

In the doorway Granny Makunya shook her head in amazement and said, "Now the cellar's good enough to spend the winter in."

Raisa was delighted too—for the cellar, for her grandmother and mother, and for her man. Kostya found it all highly amusing.

But when he started grazing the herd, he completely stopped doing the household chores. And the women realized he was working hard.

On the mornings when it was his turn Kostya would go and fetch his horse and then have breakfast while the gentle mare dozed by the gates, saddled up.

Instead of driving the cattle into the village at lunchtime, Skuridin watered them and kept them in a pen a long way off.

"Take some grub with you," he advised his work mate. "The herd's better off there. It's a sheltered and shady place. They have a good rest. But in the corral here it's baking hot and they get worn out. I've been doing this job all my life, pal..."

Skuridin urged him strongly, but from the very first day Kostya started driving the cattle his own way: lunch was lunch, and there were no two ways about it. He would drive the herd into the farm's corral and then go off for a hot meal and a nap.

Raisa was all for it.

"Skuridin doesn't drive them home for lunch because he won't get fed at home anyway," she said. "That's why he takes a packed lunch."

In the village nobody's affairs and goings-on were kept a secret for long.

Martinovna sided with her daughter as well.

"Of course, just think of it... Going without a hot meal all day. You might ruin your stomach."

And so Kostya used to go home for lunch and a rest. And he wasn't the only one. Other herdsmen also drove their herds into the farm's corral. Only Nikolai Skuridin did things his way. But that was Skuridin for you.

A week went by and then another. In the mornings Skuridin started noticing that the steers looked miserable, as though they were not getting enough food: tight-bellied, dull-eyed, they kept bellowing plaintively. And then his wife and mother-in-law started up. Although they'd never done a day's work on the farm and never stepped outside their yard, they still knew the answers to everything.

"It's the Chelyadins' convict... Folks say he has breakfast until lunch and lunch until supper, and you're doing all his work for him. You're just a fool, you are."

Nikolai didn't believe it: in the village they loved to grumble and find fault with people. Even so, he decided to go and see for himself.

In the morning when it was already late—he'd had time to mow while the dew was still on the ground and have breakfast—Nikolai set off for the Chelyadins'. All the cattle had been out grazing for a long time.

The Chelyadins' yard was on the other side of the common, but it could not be seen from the Skuridins'. He went down the street as though on his way to Aunt Lelka's on some business or other. From a distance he caught sight of the saddled mare hanging her head and dozing by the Chelyadins' gates.

"You son-of-a..." he swore aloud. "You could have at least hidden your mare, but it's there for the whole village to see."

Martinovna came out of the yard to meet Nikolai.

"Where's the herdsman, then?" Nikolai asked.

"Oh, I think he's having his breakfast..." she replied with a sigh.

"It's already time for lunch and he's still having breakfast. You might have told him..."

"Tell him once, and you might not want to again," replied Martinovna and walked on by.

She really had spoken to him. As soon as her son-in-law had started working on his own, she'd noticed that he was in no hurry and had said, "You must get them out now. This is the best time for grazing."

"There's no hurry, they'll still eat their fill," her son-in-law had retorted.

She said the same thing another time and then a third, and then she was sorry she'd mentioned it.

Kostya stood blocking her way, eyes hardened, his voice sounding downright military.

"You're talking a lot, Mother," he said. "It's me who's looking after the herd, isn't it? Yes, it's me. So don't you go poking your nose into everything. I don't like it. I don't like it one bit." He looked straight into her eyes and she wanted to look away but couldn't—she was too frightened to move. "Understand? Not one more word. I don't like repeating myself."

Then off her charming son-in-law went, and for a long time she couldn't stop shivering or get warm, and she complained to her mother, "Oh, that son-in-law of ours..."

Makunya heard her out and then muttered reproachfully, "It was you who lured the man here... What do you expect? He's served time. And you're not thrown in there for nothing. Maybe he killed someone. Don't you touch him. Maybe, God willing, he'll go away."

Martinovna then spent a long time agonizing over whether or not to tell her daughter. She decided to keep quiet. She felt sorry for her only child. Regardless of everything, he was at least a man and seemed to treat Raisa all right. Maybe he would settle down in the end. As for the grazing, well, there were no end of herdsmen like him these days. Cunning, that is.

So that was why, when she met Skuridin now, she answered the way she did. Having had her say, she walked off—let them sort it out themselves, man to man.

Kostya was fixing a bicycle in the yard.

"What are you doing?" Nikolai asked.

"Well, I'm busy with this," replied Kostya. "I've glued the inner tube, I'm off to the lake tomorrow."

"But look at the sun! When's the herd going to graze? And then, the gadflies. Boy, you really ought to..."

Skuridin felt awkward telling off a man not much younger than himself and failed to come up with the right words.

"I'll drive them out now," replied Kostya. "They'll get their fill, the grass is good."

He didn't want a row either, especially here in the yard, and so he got up from the bicycle and started off. Untethering the mare, he clumsily mounted and rode off—not at a gallop but at a brisk trot, jogging up and down in the saddle. Once he had left Skuridin some way behind, he slowed down.

Nikolai's reproaches, and those of his mother-in-law, weighed heavily on him. He had shut her up and now it was time to tell his partner where to get off. So that he'd understand once and for all. He knew one should never put off such things.

And so in a couple of days, when Skuridin came up to the Chelyadins' yard at the same time, the saddled mare was standing by the gateway just as before, being devoured by the flies. She kept flicking her tail and jingling her nickel bit.

But the master of the house was nowhere to be seen in the yard. Martinovna was weeding the potatoes.

"Where's Kostya?" asked Nikolai. "Is he sick or something?"

"He went down there with his rods," Martinovna waved her arm. "Down to the river."

"With his rods?" repeated Nikolai incredulously.

"That's right," Martinovna affirmed, looking down.

Skuridin stood stock-still, blinking. He was on his way to Aunt Lelka's to sharpen the scythe and hadn't intended checking up on his partner, figuring Kostya would be ashamed of having been ticked off and for at least the next week would be driving the cattle out on time. And now he simply couldn't believe his eyes: Kostya's mare was standing by the Chelyadins' gates.

He thought at first Kostya must have fallen sick. After hearing about the rods, it took Nikolai a while to come to his senses, and then he didn't know whether to run after his partner and hunt for him in the riverside bushes or go straight to the manager's office.

After a few moments' thought he set off for the riverbank. Martinovna gazed after him, puckering her lips bitterly.

He was in no hurry: he was not looking forward to it at all, and, more importantly, he was completely baffled. Here was the hungry herd standing in the corral. Standing there, just as it had the past few days. And here was this man, his work partner, happily fishing, repairing his bicycle and sleeping. Nikolai had been around for forty-odd years. His children were grown up. So you could call him a grandfather, really. He had knocked about for many a year and had seen all sorts of people in his time. And all sorts of cattle, too— hungry, unmilked, outside in mid-autumn and winter, belly-deep in mud and snow. But for a sober and sane man to be out fishing while the cattle were bellowing their heads off with hunger, that he couldn't understand. No, it just made no sense to him. It was something he simply couldn't figure out.

Kostya was sitting on the bank on a black willow stump. The willow had been sawed down sometime or other and the stump had been left. It was comfortable to sit on. Hearing Skuridin some way off, he asked without turning around, "Come to chase me down?"

Just then the float jerked, sending ripples across the smooth water. Kostya froze, waiting for the float to bob down, and then, feeling the weight of a fish, hooked it with a slight tug.

The heavy crucian shone like burnished gold with red streaks. Kostya unhooked it and tossed it into the bucket along with the rest of his catch. Next he washed the slime off his hands, wiped them slowly and only then turned around.

Skuridin stood there, emaciated, stooping, his hooked nose sticking out from under his peaked cap, a wistful look in his eyes.

"What do you want?" asked Kostya, standing up. "Why are you here? It's your turn to rest."

"The cattle are up there. Do you really not feel sorry for them?"

"The cattle. The cattle are up there," affirmed Kostya. "But it's people I feel sorrier for. I mean, like you, you fool."

He strode toward Skuridin, who could tell by Kostya's eyes and bared teeth that he was going to strike him. He wanted to protect his sick stomach, recently stitched up and still not healed, but he had no time to.

Kostya struck out quickly, but didn't hit him. However, Nikolai was already doubled up with pain and fell, writhing; he only came to his senses a few moments later. The pain had gone, but he still found it hard to breathe and his head still felt strange. He kept seeing green and red dots before his eyes.

Kostya lifted him up by the scruff of the neck, supporting his full weight, it seemed, in his large fist. And he only let go when he was sure he could stand up on his own.

"I haven't laid a finger on you, and you're already toppling over," he said. "But if I do lay a finger on you? What then? Eh? Watch out—and don't make me repeat it. I don't want to hear another word from you. I don't teach you how to run your life, so don't you teach me. I'm not going to tell you again."

That was that. Getting his breath back, Nikolai couldn't tell whether Kostya had touched him or not. It seemed as if he hadn't. He was about to go off when Kostya called to him.

"Hang on..."

Nikolai stopped and a moment later simply could not believe his eyes or ears. Kostya was embracing him, helping him along and saying in a friendly tone, "You should get some treatment at a health resort. You're wearing yourself out, you know. Take it easy and live the way you like. But don't bother other people; they may have their own way of looking at things and don't want anyone else's."

They walked along the path through the old orchard and vegetable garden and in the yard Martinovna gawked at them in surprise—here was her son-in-law all cheerful and happy as could be.

"I've had a great time fishing, Mother. Thank goodness Nikolai's come to see me. Time's flying. And the fish is for Nikolai. His kids'll eat it. We've got plenty."

He dropped his catch into a plastic bag and handed it to Skuridin, then they left the yard together.

"I don't like being nagged. You understand me, I hope, Kolya. I'm not going to repeat myself," Kostya said outside the gates and, climbing into the saddle, rode off toward the corral.

And Nikolai found some old homegrown tobacco in his Aunt Lelka's yard, rubbed together a couple of leaves, and lit up. To start with, he felt dizzy and was racked by a cough that hurt him somewhere deep down in his stomach where he had been operated on. He hadn't smoked for some time. At first, he was all but dying and when he came around, he wasn't up to it. Besides, the doctors had warned him he would die if he went on smoking. But then he stopped coughing and felt better. Now he could think better and see everything in a clear light. But what was there to see? Clear as day, it was. And now, nearly an hour later, his side was still aching, and so was his chest, and his head was buzzing. But then, he actually hadn't touched him probably. Just scared him. But what if he were to? Strong as an ox he was, and he had learned a thing or two inside. If he touched him, Nikolai was done for. And his kids would be left orphans.

He finished his smoke and went straight to the manager. He decided not to complain, but how could he keep quiet about the cattle? Sooner or later they were bound to find out. And what had the steers done to deserve it? He might not complain, but he certainly had to say something. Ask for another partner or move to another herd himself.

Chapurin was standing by the office building. The car had broken down, and the groom was saddling a horse. Except for the two or three times a summer when it was his turn to graze the villagers' cows, Chapurin hardly ever rode. He didn't sit very well in the saddle: his long legs got in the way and at over two hundred pounds he was on the heavy side. He'd already clambered into the saddle and didn't want to get down again, so he listened to Nikolai from where he sat, hemming every now and then.

"Right," he said. "You did right. You've got to do it right now or else he'll get out of hand. I'm not going to switch you, you can keep on, but I'll go and tell him off right away."

Chapurin had already heard how the Chelyadins' son-in-law was grazing the herd—his wife had told him.

"I'll have a talk with him today," he promised, touching his horse.

The horse galloped off, its sides heaving.

The manager disliked putting off such things for long, so that very evening he set off for the Chelyadins'. Instead of going straight into the yard, he called out from the street:

"Martinovna! Is your son-in-law at home?"

"Yes. He's resting after work."

"Call him, will you?"

By the fence there was an elm log whose bark had peeled over the years and had worn to a shine. Chapurin sat down on it. Out came Konstantin, stretching and yawning. Since he had arrived in the village he had put on quite a bit of weight, his face was tan, and his metal-capped teeth glinted even more brightly when he smiled.

"Good day, Sir Cossack," Chapurin greeted him and stretched out his hand.

And just like the first time at the party, they tested each other's strength as they shook hands. Kostya was the younger and stronger of the two.

"You're good at patting butter," muttered the manager, "but you're a lousy herdsman. You drive them out late, take a long time over lunch, and drive them home early." He glanced at the setting sun. "The people's private herd is just coming back now, but when did yours get back to the corral?"

"You're right, I'll do better..." said Kostya with a smile.

"That's more like it," replied the manager, softening. "You're a tough fellow and you've got a good partner. You can do it. And look at the steers you've got—real Herefords. As long as you graze them, they'll grow real fast. And the pay'll be all right. Do you need any money?"

"Yes," replied Kostya. "You've got plenty, and just look at the house you've built yourself."

Large, attractive, painted, with a slate roof, the manager's house stood out among all the rest. Chapurin had taken a long time building it and had done a proper job. He would be living in the village for the rest of his days and then his heirs would get it. In short, it was for good.

"It's a fine house," smiled Chapurin. "I'll say so without boasting. Why don't you build something? Just earn a bit, and then build onto this."

"It's not worth it," Kostya replied. "It's so hot just now. You can go on building and building, having a hell of a time, and use up all your money. And then some fool drops a match," he lowered his voice. "Just one match and no house."

Chapurin looked up and was about to open his mouth, but froze. There was an evil glint in the eyes of the Chelyadins' son-in-law. "He's going to burn it down," Chapurin was instantly convinced. And he looked over toward the house. The sun was setting in crimson flames. Its reflected light was flickering in the windows of his house. For an instant he caught his breath and then exhaled it. But the chilling sensation in his chest remained and his heart stabbed sharply.

"It's me you're getting at just now," Kostya continued calmly. "But what about the others, how do they graze their cattle? One's taken to drink and not shown up at work. Another's got a hangover. But I won't go on a binge. I guarantee that. So let's live and let live."

That was the end of their conversation. Chapurin went home.

He didn't want to think the worst, but he couldn't help it. So much money had gone into this house, so much hard work, so many nerves. He would never manage to build another, never. But it wouldn't take much for this fool just to drop a match, and that would be that. Then he would say how sorry he was, showing all his metal-capped teeth. Then prove he'd done it! And even if they did and he was locked up, what good would it do? He couldn't get the house back.

His heart stabbed again. He stopped and listened to it. And without meaning to, he started thinking about how the Chelyadins' son-in-law wasn't so bad, after all. He didn't drink too much, and he'd started working right away. There were worse devils, there really were. And who could match Nikolai Skuridin? Let him look for a partner himself. Why should they run to the manager for every little thing! They had started coming to him like little kids, but he was only human, wasn't he? He wasn't only a brigade leader, after all! He needed some peace and quiet too, and he had his health to think about. He wanted to make it to retirement and then live in peace for a while, look after his garden, and go fishing. Try doing that here!

Nikolai Skuridin was sitting on the bench by the gate near the back of his house. He was just the person Chapurin didn't want to see just then.

"Resting?" he asked with a sigh.

"I was waiting for you, really. I figured you might have had a word with him."

"I have. I did ages ago," Chapurin replied irritably. "As if all I spend my time doing is talking to different people. I talked to him at lunchtime," he lied. "Then I phoned the board and asked their advice. And they told me straight—you've got to educate him yourself. Put him under someone and teach him. But nobody'll let you sack him. So try to get along somehow. He's not that bad, and he doesn't drink. He's just gotten out of hand. He'll mend his ways. Has the chairman called me?" he yelled across the fence to his wife. "How about the chief agronomist? He has? I'm looking for him too," he explained to Skuridin. "The harvest's being brought in, but he's..."

Nikolai understood everything. He stood up and set off home.

It was noisy in the common. A herd of horned goats was clattering across the dam and galloping toward the farm. Lost kids and she-goats were bleating loudly and young children and old women were separating their livestock into groups, searching for the stragglers, chasing the restless ones with switches, and pulling others by their horns. Reddish dust was billowing over the common and anyone would have thought it was a Mongolian horde roaring into the village, not a herd of goats.

Catching sight of their father, Nikolai's youngest daughters called out:

"You get the cow, Dad. There's a kid and one without horns missing. We're going to look for them."

"All right," Nikolai replied and stayed on in the common.

The cows came later at dusk. The Skuridins' cow, Marta, a good milker that was keen on her food, usually headed for home by way of the barns, where grass grew in between the abandoned rusting farm machinery. So Nikolai went there, sat down on an old mower, and started waiting.

Once the goats had gone by, the village fell silent again The sun disappeared behind Vikhlyaevskaya Hill. Pink and crimson light illuminated the high feathery clouds. "Red feathery clouds mean rain's on its way," Nikolai recalled his late grandmother, Fyosha, and automatically glanced towards the cemetery. They'd buried her there a long time ago.

The sky blazed yellow, promising a long sunset. As dusk stole toward the village from the strip of pasture along the river, the cows came wandering along the road, bringing with them a warm cloud of soft dust and the acrid smell of livestock.

Nikolai spotted his Marta. She took one look at her master and put her head down to graze.

Nikolai remained sitting: there was plenty of time, the evening was long. He kept thinking about the cattle, the convict, about Chelyadin—in a word, about what was happening now and what lay in store. The day was drawing to a close and the next would soon be here. He would get up early and graze the herd till late. But then...

Kostya, the Chelyadins' son-in-law, was sitting on the warm elm log in his yard, waiting for Raisa. After the brigade leader left, Kostya had laughed. "How easy it is to frighten them... Kids, kids..." He had a laugh and that was all. Then he started thinking about the next day. His bicycle was fixed. He would go somewhere in the direction of the Panika Forest river and spend the day there. There were some big black hunchbacked perch to be caught there. He would cook up some fish soup and grill the perch in its skin over hot coals. The sun set like a seething yellow fire, and the crimson and orange sunset spread across half the sky. The village and all the surrounding countryside were already slumbering in the quiet of evening. The only thing disturbing the silence and the high golden sky was an airplane you could just make out high overhead as it streaked away somewhere.

So the day ended. The next went as planned: Kostya spent his time fishing in Panika Forest, while Nikolai grazed the steers until dusk. During the day the steers fed well, their sides filled out, and they were a joy to look at.

But later that night Nikolai slept badly. He couldn't stop thinking. After hardly any sleep, he woke up when it was still dark and started getting ready. It was Kostya's turn, not his, but he got ready without saying anything to his family, took some bread and lard, and drove the herd out into the pasture at the proper time. Kostya, of course, was not there—he was still eating his breakfast.

Nikolai knew there would be a row and maybe something even worse. But he just decided to drive them out, and that was that. That day and others, too. Because it wasn't the herd's fault, and he had to feed his family. There was also a faint hope, there really was, that maybe his conscience would prick him. After all, a person has to have a conscience. He may have steel teeth, but his soul, just like everyone else's, is human and alive.

Translated by Jan Butler

Originally published in *Novyi mir,* March 1986

Natalia Sukhanova

Delos

On the trolleybus this morning a child was singing. Not Robertino Loretti.[*] And not "Santa Lucia." It was something like "La-la-la," sung pensively and methodically. It was still quite early. Everyone was sleepy. So no one paid any attention to him or bothered him with stupid adult conversation. His mother was sleepily silent and didn't hear him—he himself might have barely heard or been conscious of what he was doing. He'd sing, then after a moment's silence would trace little paths and pits in the window's velvet frost with his finger and his breath. He'd sing while pale blue and yellow colors swam in his squinting eyes—the pale blue light of dawn and the yellow glow of streetlamps. Bright sparks flared up in the frost. People dozed off, swaying, while above us all wafted this pure "la-la-la."

This morning's impression stirred a feeling of bitterness in me. Bitterness, irritation, spite? At what or at whom? At myself? "You've been weighed in the balance and found wanting." The feeling was there, yet not realized. It slipped through my fingers. It appeared, and then slipped away, unbegotten.

The pain was momentary and then it receded. Only sadness remained. Anything in the world can turn into plain old sadness, after the sharpness of the pain has gone away.

... An incident that my colleagues and I had analyzed a long time ago. There was no evidence of a crime, as they say. On the contrary. Well, the assistant was a bit late. It happens even to astronauts. It would have been better, however, if I'd replaced him with our Maria Ivanovna, even with her average medical education and painful swollen legs. But I'm not the Lord God who foresees everything. Besides, how could I express a lack of trust in a colleague

who's the same age and has the same experience as I have? And was he the
only one at fault? What is each person's share in a case of collective guilt?
Possibly we were one or two days late with the operation. Or, on the contrary,
we rushed it. No, there wasn't any "rushing it"—we just about made it. A sur-
geon goes to a complicated operation the way an ancient commander used to
go to battle, invoking all the gods and heeding their voices within. At the
time I wasn't good at discerning those vague voices. Moreover, it just so happened that I was the brand new head of an old maternity hospital. I was per-
suaded to take the job and agreed. Of course I had consultations and did
operations and was called whenever there were complicated births. But that
wasn't the main thing. The main thing was the walls, the ceilings, the roof,
the operating rooms, and the toilets. The walls got wet and the chimneys
sometimes filled up with soot, and sometimes they worked. Babies got sick
and various antiseptics would prove ineffective, and it was easier to change
the chief administrator than the roof, the walls, or the chimneys. Every day
something stopped working: water pipes, plumbing, electrical wiring. I'd go
to the public health department, the executive council, the local Party
branch—no one would listen: "You must be kidding? You just had repair
work done! A major overhaul! Go ahead and fire anyone you want! Hire anyone you need. But no repairs!"

I didn't fire anyone. I called in the head nurse and ordered her to start
keeping a record of breakdowns. A detailed one, twenty-four hours a day.

March 22—the toilet on the first floor got stopped up and won't work.
March 23—the sewer pipe in the operating room has started leaking.
March 24—the toilet on the second floor doesn't work.
March 25—short circuit on the first floor.

In a few months I put two ordinary cloth-covered notebooks full of such
entries on the desk of the secretary of the local Party committee. I got a real
major overhaul and put it to good use. I finally managed to get the latest
equipment too.

But that came later. At that time, battles of a local and strategic nature were
in full swing. No one relieved me of my usual cares. Every day at eight on the
dot I held a five-minute meeting. Until then—la-la: "my son and I divided the
apartment," "he said to me," "I said to him," "kicked my husband out," tights,
children, drinking, marketing, meat. There was a small radio on my table that
was hardly audible. But as soon as it started to chime eight o'clock, I'd turn it
up full blast. Then whoever wasn't already in place would start running, fastening up their coats on the way, so as to get a foot in the door on time. Then
there was the overnight report, which, of course, couldn't be crammed into

just five minutes, even if you left out superfluous words. The doctor on duty reports how many entered the hospital, how many gave birth, and how many were in labor. The head nurse of the children's unit reports how many babies we have, which ones have turned blue and which haven't, how another one has taken the breast, how often it's soiled its diapers, what kind of bottom and belly button it's got.

And we'd be off, full speed ahead.

"Anton Apollinarievich, please come look at this mother—she's bleeding more than she should."

"Anton Apollinarievich, Dyagileva's fetal position is transverse, the contractions are weak."

That means we have to make a decision about Dyagileva. This is her first pregnancy, a full-term baby, only it's lying the wrong way.

"Nina Andreevna," I say to Dyagileva when she enters my office, grimacing with pain, "Nina Andreevna, listen to me carefully. Your baby's not lying with its head down as it's supposed to. It's not lying bottom down either, but sideways. It's doubtful you'll have a successful delivery without some help." Twenty-year-old Nina Andreevna looks at me tensely.

"There are two possibilities," I continue slowly and clearly. "The first is to operate, do a Caesarian section, which means saving both the child and you. The second is unassisted labor, in which case we'll quite likely lose the child."

"The operation... the Caesarian section...is it dangerous?" asks Dyagileva.

"It's an operation like any other. It's not that unusual. But for a period of about three years afterwards, you shouldn't get pregnant again."

"I can't have the baby without help?"

"Probably not. There's a possibility that the baby will get into the right position, but it's a slight one."

Dyagileva's apprehensive eyes shift from one person to another, but no one can help her now.

"Does that mean you'll cut the baby out?"

"Yes, if you can't give birth. But you're still very young. You'll have other babies."

"Can I talk it over with my husband?"

"You can and you should, Nina Andreevna."

We call in the husband. In the labor room someone is screaming loudly. The scream turns into a strained howl—labor isn't far off.

First I talk with Dyagileva's husband alone. The guy is frightened, but he's very robust, very solid. I catch myself thinking how I'm beginning to look at men through the eyes of women giving birth. I explain the situation to him.

"She won't be able to deliver the baby without help?"

"Here's a door," I tell him, "and here's a wardrobe. If the wardrobe's turned toward the door this way, then it'll pass through. But if it's on its side... And this is a room, you can turn a wardrobe around in it. But your wife's got a tight muscle-bound sack."

"You can't turn it around?"

"We can try, but it's unlikely."

"Can't the child turn around by itself?"

"That can sometimes happen with active labor. But your wife's contractions are weak, few and far between. So there's very little hope."

"Is the operation dangerous?"

And so on and so on. He crumples his cap in confusion. "Your wife's coming now," I tell him, "Think about it, talk it over."

"Is she permitted to walk?"

"Yes."

They don't sit down, even though I invite them to make themselves more comfortable. She stands on her feeble legs, shoulders slumped, in bedroom slippers and a bathrobe that covers a long yellow disinfected nightgown.

"So what should I do?" she asks.

"I do-on't know. Whatever you want, Nina. Whatever's best. The doctor says the operation's not so risky."

Shaking her head, she explains to him as you would to a silly little boy:

"Then for three years we'll have to be careful. I can't get pregnant or have an abortion."

"I don't know," he mutters again. And says to me: "Doctor, what if we don't have the operation?"

"Of course," I finish his thought for him. "She's still young, you'll very likely have other children."

There's a call from the executive committee inviting me to a meeting. I explain that I can't come.

"Well, have you decided?" I ask, putting down the receiver.

He looks at her in silence.

"There's no need for the operation," she says.

"Have you thought it all over? Because you're not in great pain now, dear, but later it'll become really painful and you'll say: 'I want the operation,' but it'll be too late."

They're both silent: he looks at her and she looks at the floor.

"There's no need for an operation," she says just as flatly as she did the first time.

"Well, okay," I say as though I'm somewhat relieved. "Nurse, tell Alla Borisovna that she can go home. There won't be any operation. And you," I say to Dyagileva's husband, "you get going too. Don't worry, we'll do everything we need to."

Looking at Dyagileva as she walked away—she was stepping gingerly, holding onto her stomach with both hands—I thought of another twenty-year-old who exactly twenty-four hours ago in this very same place was sobbing, begging us to save her baby. Save it from an abortion. She was an unmarried college student. Her mother and father had talked the girl into an abortion, but when she was already in the operating room she came running to me. A complicated situation: of course I'll help, I'll explain to her parents, but, you know, she's still a child herself, hasn't lived on her own, it's her first love, and that's the kind of person who suffers most, you know. I kept trying to calm her down: no one has the right to force her, but has she thought it all through? Essentially, there's no baby yet, only an unconscious embryo, and God willing, she'll give birth yet to a bunch of kids. The girl kept shaking her head convulsively: "I can't! I don't want to! Tell my parents some lie, tell them it's impossible. Only leave the baby alone." I was all for it. As soon as she began speaking, I was for it. I'm almost always ready to come to the rescue of the unborn. And if she herself wanted it...

I called in the parents and made them understand that forcing someone to have an abortion is punishable to the full extent of the law. And I hid her in my office under some pretext. Her and the baby she was going to have.

Down the hall a baby carriage was whisking the live bundles off to their feeding—to the sweet sounds of sucking and whimpering. You know, most likely the one who's right isn't me or the student, but the sensible Dyagileva. My student will have a rough time with her fatherless child. Her parents will end up taking it and will love it even more than their own daughter, but they won't be able to replace a young mother and father. Now Dyagileva, by soberly choosing those pregnancies that are most convenient for her, will keep her husband and give birth to a pair of strong, healthy children, will give them everything they need, and will forget about this baby, which she's carried to term and which is alive. What can you do, it wasn't conceived right, it's not in the cards.

Yes, it was precisely on the day that Dyagileva refused to have a Caesarian section. Because she was the one I was thinking about, and it was about her that I struck up a conversation with Alla Borisovna, who had dropped in to say good-bye after her rounds.

"What, Dyagileva refused?" There was a touch of curiosity, a touch of surprise in Alla Borisovna's voice; she had the same thought that I had: after all, it was already full-term. Curiosity and surprise—yes. But not censure. At times, however, I feel like such a dilettante next to these women who, so many times in life, soberly and without undue reasoning and speculation, decide the question of all questions: whether a person is to be or not to be. Whereas I'm like a child who demands a particular toy right there and then, this very minute. And the despair when the answer is "No! not now! later!" is as acute as if it were for the first time. I know of nothing more beautiful than a pregnant woman! I never, either on public transportation or on the street, confuse a women who's simply fat with a pregnant one: her face has such a special charm, even if it's marred by spots and tiredness, her stomach has such an ideal—cosmic!—roundness, heavy with new life! There's no miracle that's smoother or more rounded! The Son of God also lay clasping himself with his arms and legs, his head down, in the weightlessness of his mother's fluid. A world within a world, and a woman surrounds this universe that's expanding inside her—her spine's pushed back so as to bear her along, her legs are tired and swollen, and her face shows that she's spiritually turned inward. I know nothing more degrading than the obligation to help a woman get rid of a baby! Surely I'm not the only one? How many times have I scolded our staff for their hostility toward women seeking abortions. After all, every one of our female employees has made the same decision at least once. And yet they still have that attitude...

Alla Borisovna yawned broadly.

"I'm going to have a good night's sleep." Then she added on her way out: "Anton Apollinarievich, have you had a look at that woman who came in yesterday? Grigorieva. There's something funny going on with her."

Then she left.

A woman in the labor room was screaming so loudly that even the experienced Maria Ivanovna got upset. When she was checked, everything was normal. Then some other problem arose, then still another.

I must confess that on top of all this urgent stuff I was also thinking about Dyagileva. And not without irritation. Didn't she have any feelings for the baby? How could she be so certain that there'd be another one? What if she doesn't have another baby? This one already exists. Oh, how we squander the miracle of life! Even so, I'm afraid she's right. When a female kangaroo is being pursued, she tosses her young out of the pouch, for if they stay together, neither the mother nor the young can survive; she alone will be saved and will give birth to other kangaroos—the species will go on and kangaroos won't become extinct. A simple statistical calculation. A wild sow, before crossing an open space with her litter, pushes one of the young out in front to reconnoiter, so to speak, because it's better that one of them perish rather than all the others together with the mother. Neither the kangaroo nor the wild sow thinks—generations of survivors are "thinking" inside them. Those who acted differently have long since disappeared. A woman who worships her newborn child doesn't even recall her unborn. "You can't give birth to them all," women say. And they even condemn those with lots of kids "who'd do anything to give birth, but then let them grow up on their own, like weeds. You can't bear them all—what's important is that the ones who are born have brains." You can stay sentimental only by closing your eyes to fully half of what goes on in life. As at my maternity hospital, when the dissolute Dudarikha crushed her "love" child with her legs—right in the middle of labor, when you'd think that she'd only care about giving birth. The books don't mention such cases. The books are very correct: if it's motherhood, it must be sacred; if there's cruelty, it's the devil incarnate. And in general it's considered improper to write about such things as labor and pregnancy—that could put a damper on male passion. We prefer to know a woman in the throes of passion and not while she's carrying a baby and going through labor. Occasionally we even contrive to separate passion from "pure," "elevated" love. Our masculine reasoning tells us that labor is not an appropriate subject for literature. But it's the women who pay for this reasoning in the delivery rooms. Oh, yes, you pre-human, you want to stand upright on your two legs and have a good look around? You want to think? Well, your mothers, wives, and daughters will pay for that. There's a reason why the Biblical legend has a woman choose the fruit of knowledge—whoever pays is the one who gets to choose. Whoever gets to choose is the one who pays. It's precisely the woman giving birth who pays the price for walking upright and having a large brain. The pangs of labor are the price paid for equality with the gods.

Now here's a young woman on the delivery table. Crazed eyes. Her thin leg quivers in the stirrup. Her pathetic legs look different in the act of love. Her large mouth is quivering. Her whole face is quivering. Her hand is quivering. A group of student stands at her side. The women are unmoved; the men are actively compassionate: their eyes, peering out over their masks, express sympathy.

"Come on now, Lenochka," one of them whispers. "Give it all you've got, Lenochka."

That's just the way Yurka Borisov and I were (how many years ago?) when we joined the maternity hospital as interns. At the time I was attending two institutes. First, because this gave me twice as many ration cards for grains and fats, and second, because I enjoyed studying at both places. I was having a hard time making up my mind what I wanted to be. But I was going to have to decide: mechanical drawing was taking up so much time that I had to choose. I wanted to drop medical school and stay in engineering. Yurka's girlfriend tried to talk me out of it: "What's with you, Tosha? You'll be a doctor somewhere in Sochi, wear a white coat and hat. Each morning as you leave

for work the sun and the sea will be shining. You'll ask people, 'How are you
doing?' and they'll answer, 'We're taking it easy.' 'Well, keep it up,' you'll say
to them. But life as an engineer? Clanging, grinding, dust, grime! Think about
it, Tosha!" And I did. But while I was trying to make up my mind, our turn
came to go to the maternity hospital. Before that we'd only seen pictures. The
pictures had left us devastated. But this was something else! So much for
clanging, grinding, dust, and grime! The male and even female students just
barely managed to get out, holding onto the wall, and then they would sit
down right on the floor in the corridor, while someone shoved ammonia
under their nose. Or they'd throw up in the toilet. Yurka turned out to be just
like that. Later he always stood in the back or gladly ran off on errands. But I
was hooked. My internship ended, but I stayed on. At first they started by letting me do the initial examinations, then the uncomplicated deliveries, and
then they let me put in stitches. I also did night duty. I'd curl up on a cot
somewhere for a nap: "If anyone goes into labor, wake me..."

"Lenochka!" the students cheer her on, "Push some more, Lenochka, come
on!"

"There's something I don't like about her heartbeat, Anton
Apollinarievich," says a concerned Maria Ivanovna. "Listen."

In fact it sounds rather muffled—has the umbilical cord gotten twisted
somewhere or has the placenta started to peel away?

"God, it hurts like crazy, and you keep squeezing me," Lenochka groans.

"Lena, listen carefully. When the contraction comes, push, try as hard as
you can and work to the count of four, okay? That's it. Take a breath, but
don't gulp it down, then take another right away. That's it, that's it, that's it. It's
coming, it's coming, it's coming. Is that it? Has the contraction stopped?
When it stops, don't push any more, take the mask and breathe, give the
baby some air. Yes! Yes! Here it comes, here it comes!"

A student who's holding onto her bony knee says:

"Come on, come on, Lenochka! It won't be long. Come on, come on!"

A bluish gray ridge is visible now—the child's coming out. But that's all,
the contractions have stopped and the little head retracts. We can't wait any
longer or we'll lose the baby. Another contraction. Lena doesn't notice the incision. The stethoscope on her stomach caused her pain, but she doesn't feel
the incision. The little blue head is now outside, in a loop made by the umbilical cord, but the tiny body is still inside.

"Come on! Come on!" the students moan, "Lenochka, again, again!"

A tiny pale hand and tiny body. Maria Ivanovna is already suctioning off
the mucus with a tube. She splashes cold water on the tiny chest. Squeezing
the tiny face in her hand, she massages and pinches it. Suddenly the child lets

out a faint wail—it's come to life! The female students remain unmoved, while the male students laugh loudly with joy:

"The little guy's alive! A great little guy! See, he understands!"

"Listen, Lena, labor isn't over yet..."

While Maria Ivanovna takes care of the little guy in the bassinette, I keep an eye on Lena, just in case. Nowadays women have so many abortions, even the very young ones who've never had babies. Abortions rarely are done without aftereffects. Bleeding during labor has become more common. And once bleeding begins, we start counting the seconds.

Everything worked out fine.

As we were leaving, I complained to Maria Ivanovna:

"There was no need to draw off the mucus. Babies can catch all sorts of things, even if nothing happened in this case."

Maria Ivanovna knows what I'm talking about. Only she's got no time to think about it. When you're trying to save a child's life, you don't think about yourself.

Once I'd left the delivery room, I remembered what had been on my mind the whole time. Of course, Grigorieva, Ekaterina Semyonovna. Thirty-three years old. Married since she was twenty-two. She's a "cleaning super" of two five-story buildings in a new development, that is, the one who cleans the stairs, landings, and entryways. Two full-term pregnancies with normal labor. Three abortions. All average statistics. But there was something peculiar about this pregnancy. In the eighteenth week, she was seized by terrible pains at work. She was taken to the hospital but released because they couldn't find anything wrong. About two and a half months later, the pains came back and she was hospitalized again. They couldn't find anything wrong, but kept her for a while, then sent her home to carry the baby to term. Now, finally, when she was already in her last month, the pains came back again. Tersely diagnosed as being "in danger of premature labor," she was assigned to us.

I noticed the newcomer as soon as I entered the ward, but didn't go to see her immediately because I was checking up on the others. As always during rounds, a respectful silence reigned in the ward. The newcomer smiled gently as she looked at me, as though she recognized me and was glad to see me. She was a pleasant, mature woman with light hair and no makeup. Small, bright eyes, a rather large mouth, and a face that was pretty, serene, and friendly. And in fact she looked somewhat familiar to me.

Finally I went over to her bed.

"Any complaints," I asked, adding with deliberate slowness, "Ekaterina Semyonovna?" As though the very process of pronouncing her name would clear something up for me. I even added once again (these little medical tricks!): "E-ka-te-rina Se-myonovna..."

She smiled with satisfaction, as though this was just what she needed to hear, someone thinking about her and her name. But she didn't interrupt my thoughts and didn't even answer right away:

"Complaints? Right now I've nothing to complain about... I'm just lying here."

"What happened, Ekaterina Semyonovna?"

"These pains came. I thought I was in labor."

"How's that?" I muttered warmly, but distractedly. "How could you suddenly go into labor? It's not time yet. You've given birth twice and were just fine, and now suddenly there's this whole mess."

She smiled even more broadly, even more happily, and was about to say something, but once again refrained.

I examined Katya.* I could feel the entire fetus, I felt the tiny head, I heard the heartbeat, and found everything just as it should be. Then I left, with no idea of what was wrong, just like the others before me. Something subconsciously bothered me, giving me no peace, but I didn't know what it was.

The rest of the day I was distracted as much as my work allowed. Irritable too. I yelled at a med student whose coat wasn't spotless and then went to apologize to him.

And then, when there were no examinations, or women in labor, or equipment breakdowns to note in the log, no dinner menus to approve or telephone calls to make, I remembered Grigorieva as I was having a cup of coffee. That's why her face seemed so familiar to me: she'd given birth about six years ago, not here in this maternity hospital, but in my former one...

An angry midwife had come running in:

"Anton Apollinarievich, there's a woman here who hasn't had any checkups, hasn't been to see any doctors, and has no medical record. Where should I put her?"

I went to see her while the midwife was filling out her case history and a lab technician was taking a blood sample. Grigorieva answered all the midwife's questions with that absent, vacant expression typical of women who are having contractions. Hardly had the lab technician let her go when she started pacing up and down between the beds with big, heavy steps, pressing one fist, then the other into the small of her back. The midwife had to repeat each of her questions twice. Sometimes Grigorieva would break off her answer to squeeze the bed's iron frame and lean over it. Then she'd start running up and down again. According to her answers, she should have been only in her seventh month of pregnancy. I looked doubtfully at her huge

---

*Informal shortened version of Ekaterina.

stomach. There was no point in setting up a delivery now without prior permission, but the indignant midwife couldn't restrain herself:

"We do live in the twentieth century! How can anyone be so careless?"

Grigorieva didn't answer.

I had just reached the doorway when I heard a hoarse moan and a thump behind me. With a loud sigh, the woman had fallen to her knees, squeezing the bars on the bed. Her water had broken.

The Greeks, incidentally, wrote the following about childbirth:

> And as soon as Eileithyia, the helpmate of women in labor,
> set foot on Delos,
> Birthpangs seized Leto, and the goddess readied to give birth;
> She cast her arms about a palm tree and kneeled
> On the soft meadow while the earth smiled beneath her.
> Then the boy leapt forth into the light...[*]

Maternity hospitals don't have names, but I would have given the name "Delos" to some maternity hospital. In memory of the Greeks who wrote about childbirth. In memory of the floating island of Delos, which, despite Hera's prohibition, gave shelter to the pregnant Leto. In memory of the beautiful twins born there: Apollo and Artemis. Joyful Phoebus-Apollo became the protector of the arts, but also a healer and soothsayer. The virgin Artemis was Goddess of the hunt, and also, surely, in memory of her mother, the protectress of child-bearing women. I love these twins and their mother Leto.

I also remembered Grigorieva after she had given birth, in the post partum room. Her relaxed, serene, fresh face. Her plump neck, full breast, and wide, dark nipple.

"How much does your little boy weigh?" I inquired. "Wow! How's that possible: a premature baby weighing that much?"

"Why premature?" she asked gently in surprise.

"That's what you said, my dear."

"Did I really say that? Well, I must've gotten mixed up from the pain. It makes you forget not just time, but even your own name."

"Forget such a splendid name? Ekaterina Semyonovna!" I remember saying that then, smiling happily for no reason at all. Of course that's why she smiled knowingly today in response to my deliberate "Ekaterina Semyonovna." But only now did I actually remember. I read about Leto then to the women in the room:

---

[*]From the Homeric hymns.

Shall I sing how Leto bore you to be the joy of men,
As she rested against Mount Cynthus on that poor rocky isle,
In sea-girt Delos? While on either side a dark wave
Rolled on landwards, driven by shrill winds....

There were seven women in the room. They perked up and began to bar-
rage me with questions: what was the poem, who was the goddess, what was
the island. They asked why the rocky island was poor one moment and
boundless the next. Whom did the goddess give birth to? They even asked
about my middle name, Apollinarievich. Their questions showed how curious they were and also that they wanted to play up to me a little. Katya was
the only one who didn't ask anything, but she blushed with embarrassment
and pleasure. After all, she had "kneeled," if not on a "soft meadow," then at
least on linoleum repeatedly washed with Lysol.

I was on duty that evening. My favorite time is the forty minutes before the
morning meeting and those one or two leisurely hours in the evening. There
are no distractions, so you can reminisce and think things over. When I'd finished going over a couple of pressing chores, I called Ekaterina Semyonovna
into the examination room. Someone was screaming once again, but for us it
was just common background noise. In the corridor right outside the door
leading to the room an impatient woman was trying to cajole Maria Ivanovna:
"Honey, you haven't forgotten about me, have you?"
"How could I forget!"
"Oh, it's so painful!"
"Well, what can you do if it's not due yet. Once you've delivered, it won't
hurt any more."
"Oh, God, maybe you can do something?"
"It's not me, dear, but nature who's in charge of when your time comes."
"I'm gonna go crazy."
"Now, now, no one's gone crazy yet."
"Maybe it's time? Maybe I should go to the delivery table?"
"It's still early."
"Oh, it's starting, it's starting!"
Katya was also listening to this; she was pensive, apparently remembering
her own labor.
"Well, madame," I said, "Ekaterina Semyonovna, can we talk?"
I asked her a number of questions, not so much to check her medical his-
tory as to lessen her suspicion and concern at being called into my office. I
asked her how her boys were, what illnesses they'd had, how many abortions

she'd had, whether they'd all been done in a hospital. I also recalled the first time we'd met, when she came to have her baby without any previous medical care. She told me how that had happened, she told me "ab ovo," as the saying goes, from the start, the whole thing, because, as I've often observed, a woman has a hard time telling things any other way, since everything in a woman's life is connected—husbands and children, work and abortions, pregnancies and everyday life.

"I had the first one, Dima, with my husband gone," she recalled. "He'd gone off to the army, and I'd gotten pregnant right away. Everyone kept saying the same thing: 'don't have it. Look, Andrei's younger than you, he mightn't come back to you after the army, and you're takin' on this extra burden—you'll be sorry the rest of your life.' After a while I started running away from everyone. Couldn't take it when they'd talk to me like that. I grew up without no mother around, I went through a lot. Now here I was about to be a mother, alive and healthy—how could I even think of...? So, I had it. Sure was hard, all by myself with him—standin' in lines, goin' to the market. Andrei came back from the army—and I just wasn't real careful. When he'd gone off, you know, I wasn't really a woman yet. Even though I'd just gotten pregnant, I didn't sense anything. What a dummy. They don't come any dumber, you know. I was gonna have Dima, but I had no idea about havin' a kid. Didn't feel scared, didn't know nothin'. So I carried it and carried it, then all of a sudden I'm supposed to have it, but I didn't know how. Still felt no pain. The water'd just broke, and I still don't get what's goin' on. My landlady says: 'It's starting, go to a maternity hospital.' I didn't wanna believe it. I'm thinkin', they'll send me right back, and holler at me to boot: why'd you come, you're not due for a week? Then it was like they forgot I was there. I found that real surprising. If I'd come when I was supposed to, why weren't they doin' something to me? I walked 'round and, jeez, everyone's in pain but me. It was real embarrassing. And, I'll tell you, pretty funny too. Then they gave me a shot and the pain really got to me. I wanted to run. I thought, why'd they make such pain for me with that shot? I wasn't all that young, you know—I was twenty-two—but what a silly goose. And not just about havin' babies. Even more so about family life. Who could've explained anything to me? I had no mama growin' up. I was ashamed to talk about such things, really hated such talk. I hadn't fooled around before my Andrei. I didn't look my age somehow: people would ask me, what grade are you in in school, missy? It's only now I've filled out a little. Well, my Andrei, he returned, but I wasn't no longer a girl. Like a winter apple, I'd ripened separate from the tree, in my lonely bed with a baby in my arms. We didn't have time to be careful and I got pregnant again. I wasn't sure I should have it. It wasn't just that we didn't have a penny to our name—no winter coats or a decent dress, no wardrobe for our stuff—besides that, after the army Andrei started drinkin' a lot at work. He's a carpenter, does a lot of moonlighting. He didn't have time to make us a wardrobe, but to drink he sure did. They'd carry him home, or else drive him home, or I'd have to go down to the police station to get him myself. I started thinkin' we'd never get on—I'm not standin' for it no more, I'm leavin' him. It's a lot easier to manage with just one child on your hands than two! While I was thinkin' and havin' doubts, it got too late for a legal abortion. So I went and explained and begged and pleaded and finally got permission. I was already at the hospital when the baby goes and stirs and then I just couldn't. I ran out of the hospital. It was already alive, you see, its little heart was beatin'. Come what may, then. Well, then Andrei comes to his senses and his brother got him work here. Helped with a place to live. I was carrying Artyomka, but didn't go to see no doctors. I was scared the whole time that they'd come lookin' for me from there, from our old place, since I'd gotten permission to have an abortion and then up and left all on my own— first I beg and plead, then I run away. I was scared of the police. Like I say, I was a dummy! The pains had started up and I says to Andrei: 'Wait a bit longer till I can't stand it any more.' Waited as long as I could. Then I showed up at the very last minute."

I didn't just listen to all this, but applied it to the current situation too: "So to the very last minute she put up with it and didn't give in. Why would she suddenly start carrying on this time? No, sirree, she felt real pains for the first time at eighteen weeks, and then a second time, and now, too. She had pains...so ? How come? Why?"

"So that's how it was!" I said meanwhile. "Then you scared yourself into thinking that they'd put a warrant out for your arrest. But you haven't tried to get rid of the child, to terminate the pregnancy, have you? You know it's rare nowadays to have three. Your husband, he's not drinking, is he?"

"No. But to tell you the truth, Andrei didn't want it at first. Not because it's hard—though, of course, it's not easy. But, you know, it's not as hard as it was before. He's just embarrassed! 'We're not rabbits,' he says, 'to keep on havin' one kid after another.'"

"What he's saying is wrong."

"I don't know, doctor. Maybe he's right. I just have a hard time with abortions." And her light brows knit together and her round face, mottled from pregnancy, grew heavy with the thought.

"Why, do they scare you?" I asked almost absentmindedly.

"Yes, of course they do."

"Can abortions really be more painful than childbirth?"

"No, of course not. There's nothin' more painful than childbirth. Unless maybe torture. But it is torture. It's torture to have a baby. But childbirth is somehow meant to be. What nature intends."

I'd often heard women say something similar: deciding on an abortion was more terrifying than giving birth—you're scared of giving birth, but somehow it's different.

"It's not that an abortion is all that scary," Katya continued pensively. "You only have to put up with it a few minutes or so. But the main thing is that I'm so stupid."

"Ekaterina Semyonovna, why are you always going on about being stupid?"

"Well, it sure seems to be the case, doctor. Andrei says so too: 'You sure act strange.' For example, other women don't consider aborted children to be real children. But I reckon them among my children."

"What are you going on about?" I lost my own train of thought, though I'd meant to cut her off and get on with the examination.

"It's stupid, really stupid! I know that. Well, okay, I'll tell you: I haven't told another soul, but I'll tell you. I dream about them, doctor. Not all the time, of course. But before an abortion, I'll dream about the baby for sure. And after, too."

"That's just your nerves!"

"I don't think so. But those dreams. I dreamed of the first one as if I was looking in a mirror, and from behind my back, there's a face in the mirror—it's not clear, but like in a shadow. I saw my own face real clear, only I wasn't lookin' at myself. But from behind my back—there's his, my son's, face. Not a child's face any longer. And it's like I know, this is how he woulda turned out if I... And—I'll tell you this too: he was the best of all my children. I know. And then the mirror, it got all clouded up. Or it moved away, the face did."

"My dear, that is mysticism."

"And my two other unborn children, I led them by the hand to a green meadow. To the same place and time. Right before an abortion I dream of them. They show up for the last time when it's all over. All grown up, like they woulda been... And then they disappear."

"That's your nerves, Katenka. Putting ideas in your head. Believe me, Katyusha, children aren't born with an exact plan for how they'll turn out. What they'll grow up like depends on a lot of things. Even their looks can turn out any number of ways. It depends on an awful lot of things."

"Maybe that's how come I see them so dimly."

"Drop it, Ekaterina Semyonovna, forget it."

"Well, I don't remember them often. Only when one is due."

"And now?" For some reason I asked this dumb question.

"Bad dreams, doctor."

"Heavens, dreams again. Why don't we examine you and listen to your baby instead."

As soon as I picked up the stethoscope, I forgot about both Katya and my own uncertainty. Once again I heard the fetus' heartbeat, and heard it very well. I could also feel the tiny head and the other parts of the fetus. Then suddenly it became a lot clearer—wasn't it too close? The fetus was right under my hand. Then and there I broke out in a sweat: Lord, isn't this a *full-term ectopic pregnancy*?!

But that's nonsense, it's got to be, absolutely! *A full-term ectopic pregnancy!* Can a tree of paradise grow in the desert? On stone, in magma, on an asteroid, in a thermonuclear fire? Of course not. Since the time of Hippocrates, how many people have been born? Say, ten billion, twenty, even! And throughout the history of billions of people, of countless births, each instance of a full-term ectopic pregnancy is an unbelievable event, an extraordinarily rare thing.

When we were still raw student recruits, we asked our professor, the venerable Aram Khachaturovich, how often a full-term ectopic pregnancy occurs, and he said:

"Well, my dear students, in prin-ciple—I say, in principle!—such a thing can happen. It can hap-pen! Because there's nothing that is impossible. If you and I were possible, my dears, and life and humanity, then, yes, it's possible. But it happens—allow me to put it this way—rarely. It's a great rarity. An extreme rarity. I hate to disappoint you, but it happens so rarely that it's practically—I say, practically—out of the question. Consider it something that doesn't happen. Like the line in that joke: 'It exists, it exists... we just never have it.'"

I remembered Aram Khachaturovich very clearly: his words, his gloomy eyes and soft, cheerful voice, his face, with its strong, sharp features, and the weariness and sadness that permeated his eastern graciousness and playful humor.

Recently I took a look in a mirror and got unnerved—it wasn't me staring back at myself, but old Aram Khachaturovich, who long departed this world. I never thought that with my Polish and Russian blood I would look like this Armenian some day. Or is it a question of one's profession and age rather than one's individual features? We thought of him as an old man, but he probably was no older than I am now.

All this came back to me in an instant, on the surface layer of my instictive consciousness. But, deeper down, my mind feverishly groped around in the depths and brought to the surface the signs of an ectopic pregnancy. As it was, I hadn't needed this stuff before, and I shouldn't have ever needed it. But our consciousness apparently is prepared even for the most incredible things!

I recalled that one of the most reliable tests for full-term ectopic pregnancy was being able to feel a bulge—the uterine fundus—next to the fetus. And, what do you know, there it was, a bulge next to the baby!

Everything fit, all the indications were there. It was enough to make a donkey laugh: imagine, in my very own practice, a full-term ectopic pregnancy, of which there are so few recorded instances in human memory!

Now I pressed her with more questions: what were her abortions like, what happened after the abortions? Aha, the last abortion was accompanied by a break in her menstrual cycle and anemia. Apparently they had scraped her clean and, just as when humus from the fields is washed out or thrown to the wind, there was nowhere for the roots to go. "And the earth was a formless void, there was darkness over the deep." And after this third abortion she didn't get pregnant for a long time. Till now. She was even pleased, so long as it was a girl.

"Did you feel dizzy during those attacks, Ekaterina Semyonovna?"

"I really don't know. I felt bad, like I was about to faint. Yeah, dizzy."

I take another look, think again, then ask her more questions.

But I already know. There's little doubt about it now.

That night I got a call from Yurka Borisov. We call each other from time to time. A holiday was coming up and our wives had already got in touch.

"Hold on, now!" said Yurka assertively. "Wait a minute, nothing will happen with your pregnant mothers if you spare a couple of minutes for an old friend. Well, what's going on there, arches giving way or something?"

An amateur buffoon, he always thought it professionally smart to make some kind of crude joke with anatomical details. Overall, he was a gentle person, so he liked cruel jokes all the more.

Some character darts out on top of a trench wall and shouts at the top of his lungs: "What are you doing? Where are you shooting? There are people here!" Yurka's jokes are full of characters who have no idea what life's all about. They're herding children into a gas chamber. A little boy is carrying a kitten, hugging it to his chest. One policeman says to another: "Look! What a sadist! So young, but already a sadist: taking a kitten to the gas chamber!" Yurka's favorite jokes have to do with medicine... All at once he swore at me: "A fetus on your tongue!" And I stopped listening to him.

All sorts of stuff was buzzing in my head, darting in and out.

Horton the Elephant hatching a bird's egg in the sun and snow, in rain and hail, to the sound of laughter and hoots.* Only he couldn't stand the mockery, so he climbed down from the tree and wandered off.

> But at that very instant, the egg burst apart!
> And out of the pieces of red and white shell,
> From the egg that he'd sat on so long and so well,
> Horton the Elephant saw something whizz!
> It had ears
> And a tail
> And a trunk just like his!

And—how does it go?
"My egg!" shouted Horton. "My egg! Why, it's hatching!"

It's true, it's only at such moments that snouts with tusks and big ears can ever ever become faces!

Horton the Elephant with his radiant face flashed through my mind, like an alpha particle that once in every few billion years breaks through an impenetrable wall of atomic energy. Only once in every few billion years, just as only once in every few billions of billions of years, does life assert itself despite the supreme mechanical inertia that levels everything to the nothingness of death. Life asserts itself, and with a child's negativism says "yes" every time these laws say "no," and "no" whenever the laws say "yes." And it continues to say so until its "no" and "yes" themselves become laws. That's all there is to it. What keeps nature alive is the fact that her laws can turn somersaults that transform them into their opposites. It's not a question of impending doom, but simply, as Jerzy Lec† would say, "Knowing how to turn your little cubby hole into a spaceship's cabin."

The delightful thought flashed through my mind that there's a phenomenal difference between "rarely" and "never!" I had obviously read this before somewhere, but what did I care then! Life also builds its freedom from what's at hand. "God himself wouldn't have created anything had he not had something to start with." You can make practically anything with what's already there! All you need is for there to be something!

———

*From Dr. Seuss's *Horton Hatches the Egg.*
†A popular Polish writer known for his aphoristic sayings, which have appeared in Soviet newspapers.

I'm a poor reader when it comes to the "anthropic principle." Whatever I read, I end up comparing it with my own profession, translating everything into pregnancies and childbirth. It was in one of my son's popular science books that I read about the alpha particle, which once in a few billion years contrives to bend in such a way that it can penetrate something impenetrable. Indeed Lucretius was right: the path to freedom in the world is crooked, not straight. I imagined the alpha particle as a baby's head that has to pass through something narrower than itself; the bones of the skull press together then, and the flattened head emerges, like a bluish-gray crest, through a passage that should have been impassable.

I read about the "fine tuning" of the independent structural units that comprise the universe in some other book from my son's room: about the possibility that our Solar System may be the only universe in which life and reason are feasible; that they may exist only on Earth. And I thought in alarm: it's fine, of course, if some God or a happy coincidence or the very makeup of things brought the two together. But something had spoiled the healthy earth, a healthy woman: was it chemicals, abortions, influenza, an over-ventilated room or drafty staircase landings? Did her husband give her an infection, or did she allow some quack woman doctor to scald her with iodine? The violated earth and a rather unprotected woman became infertile. Life was resurrected, nevertheless, and fragile, uncertain life flickered into being. You led three of them off to that flowering meadow, Katya, but you decided to bring this one to term. Your little one has taken root in the wrong place, however. I'm afraid it's going to die and take you with it...

Yes, it was a miracle, and why me, why was I the one entrusted with saving the ill-positioned baby? But who should answer that if not the one who knew enough to ask the question? It was as though it had all been planned in advance: whoever asks the question should have to answer it. Really, who should have to answer, if not the one who guessed where and what was conceived and was in danger of dying? And Horton the Elephant suddenly acquired the face of Aram Khachaturovich, with his dark eyes, which looked tragic or tired, or simply blurred with age, and his face wasn't spoiled by his hook-nosed trunk. And Horton the Elephant's voice was courteous and low and husky. In general Horton the Elephant was dark-skinned and tragic, like a black saxophonist, and his trunk was curved like a saxophone...

Racked by anxiety, I glanced into Katya's ward: she was quietly sleeping on her side, and next to her and inside her slept her baby, who was definitely not fated to live. Her baby and her possible doom: the mother and baby were sleeping, fused by love, a decision, and chance.

As soon as it was possible I arranged a consultation to confirm or refute my diagnosis. I presented the case to the other doctors. They called in Katya and examined her. I wrote down: "A full-term ectopic pregnancy." According to such and such data. Then I asked:

"Well, doctors, my esteemed colleagues, do we agree?"

"It certainly looks like it," said my colleagues.

"Then sign."

They hem and haw. They're not inclined to believe it. They're afraid of bringing shame on the whole city. Not just the city, but the whole country! If they're wrong, they'll be a laughing stock for years to come: "How did you, out there in Timbuktu, come to diagnose a full-term ectopic pregnancy!" And no matter how much they'd defend themselves later, saying, "You know we had this quack, Anton Apollinarievich, who dreamed this up, and convinced us, fools that we were," it would still be a real embarrassment. But the prognosis is such that if it is in fact ectopic, then any delay carries very grave consequences, for it means certain death. They hem and haw.

"So, are there any arguments against? What else can you suggest? What do you think? Let's hear your diagnosis."

They're silent. With a brief sigh, they nevertheless sign, one after another, and leave hurriedly—what could they say now? Until she was opened up, nothing more could be known.

I certainly didn't feel much like talking either. Now I'd be happy if it turned out to be a mistake. After all, if we were right, if it really was a full-term ectopic pregnancy, then no matter which way we turned and no matter what we decided, there were potential disasters everywhere. We had to try and foresee everthing, not be too late and yet not rush ahead. That's the way it always is with miracles—they require incredible foresight and effort.

I obtained permission to operate in the second gynecological hospital—they've got better equipment: an artificial respirator, a device for administering anesthesia, all the latest technology for emergency assisted delivery. And I also got permission to do the operation myself.

They gave me a whole surgical team. The hospital's chief physician assisted. I was assigned a first-class anesthesiologist.

We started. Katya fell asleep, cut off from the world outside. It was as though all that remained of her were monitors—the jagged lines of her pulse and her breathing. And her body carrying her child.

I see that my assistant is doing everything he should, but without confidence. I don't care whether he's confident or not, so long as he does what's necessary. We go inch by inch. We still don't know what's ahead of us. We can only guess. The last cut, a careful one, and here it is, the uterus, and alongside it—alongside it, not in it!—is the live baby. The membrane covering it is like cigarette paper. And her water is right in the abdominal cavity. My God, it would've been easier for life to appear on Mars, Venus, or on a rocky asteroid, than for this baby to develop in the abdominal cavity. Yet here she was, a baby girl, alive and growing. Now in retrospect we see it as something startling and amazing. But at the time it hit me only for a second that I'd guessed right. And then we quickly removed the fetus, cut the umbilical cord, and handed the baby over to the second assistant. The nurse wiped the sweat off me. Because we were in mortal fear of Katya's death: the placenta was lying on the intestines, intertwined with them. If we ripped it out, then immediately dozens of vessels that were feeding it would start gushing at the same time, and it would be impossible to tie them all in a matter of seconds. That would mean the end of Ekaterina Semyonovna. Should we leave parts of the placenta, and hope that they would gradually decompose? That was also risky.

"What shall we do, colleagues?"

We left it, and treated her.

Weeks passed before I stopped worrying for Katya's life.

All this time I hardly thought of the little girl whom a slow assistant let slip away. I had no real right to blame him—in the confusion of the moment, he wasn't able to clear the respiratory track instantly, while the baby, just feebly hanging on, wasn't yet breathing, and the umbilical cord which had fed it had already been cut. An instant's delay, and it was all over.

And yet—should I say it?—whenever I caught sight of him in the city, I would turn away to avoid him, for I couldn't bear to see him. I'd avoid him and forget. For the time being, at least.

But as soon as I stopped worrying about Katya, I was overwhelmed by the thought: we could have saved the child, we could have, but didn't! I didn't! I was overcome with profound anguish and pain. I didn't know what to do with myself and couldn't concentrate in my restlessness. I even went to see a psychiatrist.

"You're overworked and exhausted, Anton Apollinarievich," he said to me in a professional tone of benevolent gentleness. "You have no reason to reproach yourself, my friend. This is simply nervous exhaustion and depression. Let's try some mild anti-depressants."

I tossed out the anti-depressants. That proved to be a mistake, because it was precisely then that I had an ugly scene with Yurka Borisov. I ruined the evening for everyone who was relaxing over shish-kabob and dry wine outside, in the bosom of Mother Nature. After all, he had only the best of intentions, concern for a friend's honor: how come I still hadn't written an article about our case of a full-term ectopic pregnancy, of a diagnosed full-term pregnancy, a daring, splendidly confirmed diagnosis, a rare case, and the woman's life was saved!

"The baby died," I explained.

No one paid any attention.

"The little girl died," I explained.

By now everyone was a little tipsy and full of goodwill, so several voices piped up:

"It wasn't your fault!"

"You weren't responsible for the baby!"

Like a conductor reducing the orchestra's volume, Yurka made a gesture that silenced the objections. He wanted to establish the basic fact that the baby's death rate in full-term ectopic pregnancies is eighty-five percent.

"And, by the way, the death rate for the mother, as you well know, Anton, is also rather high, especially when, as in this case, the placenta is lying on the intestines!"

What could I tell him? That I wasn't dealing with percentages, but with Ekaterina Semyonovna and her baby? That it wasn't percentages that did in the baby, but a slow assistant?

"And finally," Borisov said with the triumphant tone of an erudite, "consider the fact, my dear old man, that fifty percent of ectopic children are born de-fect-ive. So that eugenics—which is neither stupidity nor pseudo-science, my dear man, you can trust my sober judgment in that—would consider the preservation of a fetus conceived and grown under such inauspicious circumstances ir-ra-tio-nal!"

Even at this point I restrained myself. Who's to judge whether a baby should or shouldn't live? Should the thinkers decide, then? Should some people act while others think and decide? That means that some bring life into the world in mucus, blood, and torment, while others decide whether that life should exist? And what about humanity—what should we decide about humanity? How much cruelty and stupidity, not to mention torture and humiliation of those like ourselves, are man and mankind answerable for! So does that mean we should annihilate them? Let's rid the Earth of them, deprive them of food and air, scrape the Earth down to its stone layer, and then, perhaps, after billions of years, a new humus will form, and, who knows, perhaps the next version of mankind will prove more successful? We've got lots of space, and planets, and stars, and universes, eugenics is no fool and good sense is nothing to be sniffed at.

But that's all I could say. I had no watertight arguments, I didn't then and don't have now...

Borisov continued holding forth with verbose complacency. And it was then that I started cursing; I cursed foully, hopelessly, then left them all. I heard them looking for me, but I didn't want to see anyone. The one thing I knew for sure was that Horton the Elephant had crushed the fragile bird's egg. Crushed it. And he was completely disgraced and wrong.

Dyagileva, by the way, had the baby; she gave birth without any help to a strong, healthy baby. Her contractions grew strong, and the child moved into the right position. So, not she, but I deserved to be reproached for my secret annoyance and haste. In such cases women say: it was fate. Or: it wasn't fate. Very convenient—there's no need to get tense and torment yourself and feel guilty. The baby is born and that's it. Intuition? Chance? It was lying horizontally and shifted into the right position.

And the student whom I had released from my overly tender care when my concern for Katya overshadowed everything else nevertheless let her loving parents take her to another hospital for an abortion, which apparently was also the right thing to do.

I buried myself completely in administrative matters. Although I still had consultations with patients, as before, for some reason I listened more attentively to the opinions of others.

I didn't send an article to the journal. My assistants did, however, including the one who let the little girl slip away. He let her slip away, but, it turned out, possessed a gift for words and a vast knowledge of obstetrical theory. The scholarly journal, it's true, eliminated all his beautiful words, leaving the bare facts, but it sounded even more impressive.

One evening during my shift a female colleague from another hospital who'd had an abortion that day at ours, dropped in on me. We talked about this and that as we chatted. She complained about a woman in the ward who was no longer young, a mother of grown children, and the forbearing wife of a long indifferent husband. Her late pregnancy had made her whole family uncomfortable and annoyed. So she obediently went to have an abortion. After all, who has a baby at her age, at fifty? During the brief period on the morning of the abortion, women don't usually bother to get to know one another—they're not in the mood. No one particularly noticed her: getting on in years, quiet, on the silent side. But after the abortion, she began crying, at first quietly, trying to hide it, then almost at the top of her lungs, with lamentations.

"Just imagine, she carried on all day long!" my colleague marveled. "It was unbearable! They gave her some valerian, and for about two hours she was quiet. Then she started again. The damned old woman really got to us," said my colleague, who herself was only slightly younger than the "damned old woman." "'My poor little tyke,' 'my unborn one,' and 'surprise,' and 'gift from heaven,' and 'forgive me, your foolish mother!' What a gift for colorful expressions, I thought, nobody speaks like that nowadays. She went on, 'He would've been my consolation and joy. No one needs me—I'm there just to clean, feed and provide, I'm alone for days on end, just the TV and me, two old fools they can turn off when they don't need them.' And 'I'll put an end to myself,' and 'I'll hang myself,' and 'what use am I to anyone!' A menopausal mental case, I swear!"

A little later I went to the ward to see this poor woman—she also had Aram Khachaturovich's eyes, like me in my premature old age. I chatted with her as best I could: what's the sense of having children at our age, when the kid could be born without fingers or something even worse. To everything there is a time, to everything there is a place, and she should be thinking about grandchildren now. It turned out they don't trust her with her granddaughter, she's poorly educated, so they don't want the kid to start talking like her, using the wrong words. I remembered her "colorful expressions."

But what could I do? Whatever I might say or think, in general old age is not a happy time—however many things you have overcome, you must experience defeat sometime, because that's the law: death, and mechanics, and friction, which extinguish one's passions. I, too, am not the man I was. In Kazakhstan I got called out on an emergency once—a woman was having problems with her delivery and our driver had gone for a walk. I couldn't wait, jumped into the car, turned it on, took off, overtook the driver, and got him in. I'm racing along when a big car comes toward us. We've got an ambulance, but it didn't even occur to me to stop or step on the brakes. I swerved to the side under the beam of a telephone pole. The driver pleaded: "Anton Polinaryich, for God's sake, let me drive." We drove up, I washed up in two seconds and, dashing to the mother's side, pulled the baby out by its leg. Energetic, fearless. Everything worked out. Then I likely could have saved them both: Katya and the baby girl.

So we talked. This woman got to the very marrow of my bones because of what we had in common: we were both doomed to old age and extinction. But after that, for some reason I felt better—I began to be aware once again of the smells that the wind carried and what kind of clouds were in the sky.

About half a year passed. And one day toward evening the entire Grigoryev family showed up at the hospital with flowers: the lean, tanned, well-built husband, the large, light-haired Katya, with her simple, homely, sweet face, and two tow-headed boys. The one thing the boys had in common was the flaxen fairness of their straight hair—the same shining hair Katya must have had as a child. The older boy was sturdy, full of calm dignity. The other, the one who had shifted in her womb just in time, had two different eyes: one eye was light blue, the other reddish-brown. The older one's face was a little more handsome, but the younger one had so much vitality and suppleness, that I couldn't help staring at him in admiration.

"You saved me twice," said Katya, though that wasn't true.

"Thanks for saving mama," said the older one.

And suddenly, between the boys' markedly different figures, I clearly imagined the little girl, lithe as a wildcat, one of those who grab onto their skirts and, locking their knees in place, hang upside down on a horizontal bar, their straight platinum hair hanging down to the ground, and their bright eyes looking strangely from their upside-down faces. That's how I saw the little girl, hiding behind her brothers' backs in embarrassment and at the same time hanging upside down on the horizontal bar in some children's playground.

I rubbed my eyes, chased away this vision, and drove away the desire to ask Katya whether in her dream her unborn daughter had looked as I imagined her.

Translated by Charlotte Rosenthal

Originally published in Novyi mir, *March 1988*

Nikolai Shmelyov

The Fur Coat Incident

The last light went out across the street in the nine-story high-rise apartment building—tomorrow was another working day. The clock in the main room struck twelve.

Viktor Ivanovich had come to the conclusion long ago that the best moments of his life were these half-hours every evening by the window in the kitchen, when he would smoke one or two cigarettes in solitude before going to bed. His family usually went to bed before him, and quiet descended on the apartment as soon as their footsteps fell silent along the corridor from the bathroom. He would not turn on the light in the kitchen. He preferred to sit in the dark so he could more easily see the empty street and the trees on the square across the street... That's the way it was when Natasha, their daughter, was little, and when she was growing up, going to school and then the institute, and when she got married and moved in with her husband and he and his wife remained, just the two of them. That's the way it was yesterday, and that's the way it would probably be tomorrow, and the day after tomorrow, as long as he lived.

In the summer, greenery rustled in the open window, the sound of someone's hurried footsteps on the asphalt drifted in, and he could hear the rumbling of the street-cleaning machines or the distant whistle of a trolleybus as it picked up speed on the boulevard. In autumn he watched through wet glass as the wind tossed and battered the branches of craggy apple trees that had grown old before his eyes. In the winter, as now, the street and square were covered with clean, crisp snow that sparkled in the slanting light of the street lamps.

But today he wasn't there simply out of habit. He hadn't been able to settle down all evening. He could barely sit through the nightly episode of a long television series and even made a couple of clumsy attempts to send his wife off to bed early. He was impatient to be alone, so he could finally think over calmly, without interference, what he had been told at work that morning, what he hadn't been able to get out of his mind all day.

Viktor Ivanovich Grebenshchikov worked in a large specialized equipment assembly bureau. He was considered a good engineer and was on friendly terms with both the management and his co-workers—he really didn't have any subordinates. He'd enrolled in an institute before the war, was drafted into the army in his fourth year, fought in the artillery corps, earned the rank of captain, was seriously wounded in a bombing raid (six months in the hospital), was demobilized, and in '46 he graduated from the same institute he had started in. Immediately after graduation he came to his bureau, which had just been opened, and ever since—nearly thirty years—he had worked there at the same desk, and essentially at the same job. He was often praised, awarded bonuses, and his picture was put up on the Honor Roll bulletin board many times, but he was never given any significant promotions nor sent on any long business trips. The latter was important because in their system a person could get ahead, as a rule, only one way—if he were trusted to direct the assembly of a major construction project in the provinces or abroad.

Recently Viktor Ivanovich had begun to feel his age quite keenly. He often dreamed about his childhood, and sometimes he complained to his wife about his health: something ached a bit inside, usually after he'd had rich food. It was nothing very definite, but it seemed to be well-entrenched, deep inside, next to the old wound in his abdomen. In the evenings now as he sat by the window he often thought about his pension, how he would live, what he would do, where he and his wife would go on vacation. These thoughts didn't frighten him at all; on the contrary, they calmed his spirit and banished those exhausting, annoying, petty grievances that added up by the end of every living day.

The important question was the size of the pension he could expect. With his current salary there was no way he could even get the standard maximum pension, and naturally that was what he wanted. In fact, he didn't want just that—he wanted a special pension that would be slightly higher than the regular one and, moreover, a distinction. Life had never spoiled him with a surfeit of distinctions. Of course, his sense of pride had faded long ago, but not to the point that he was completely indifferent to everything that distinguished people from one another.

Grebenshchikov knew that he ought already to be taking steps to arrange an independent posting somewhere far from Moscow for at least three years or so. No matter how much he thought about it, he didn't see any realistic way to arrange a good pension. Now, at this point in his life, he could allow himself to leave Moscow for a while without any ill effect: Natasha had married well and seemed to get along with her husband; his wife, who had once been a very active woman, seemed fed up with her work; and he himself would even welcome a change of scenery and a chance to live in a new place awhile. After all, other than the usual trips on vacations and business, he had not really traveled since the war. "It's time. I need to move around a bit. Water doesn't flow under a stone," he told himself more and more often as he contemplated his options.

It just happened that a very appealing position had recently opened in a major project. Grebenshchikov heard about it indirectly and decided that it was exactly what he needed. Of course, he wasn't without contacts—several of his classmates had worked with him and now held rather high positions. He had never taken advantage of those friendships, without even knowing why. Perhaps it was for the best—in any case, now he could turn to any of them with a clean conscience, and he knew he wouldn't be refused.

He was closest to Grisha Shokin—his very oldest buddy. The two of them had whiled away many long hours in beer halls and other places, happily spending their paltry student stipends. Once in a while now they would reminisce about the old days when they'd get their pay or bonuses and stop in a quiet and rather out-of-the-way establishment that was further away than their co-workers would usually bother to walk. As he had expected, Shokin not only agreed to help, he truly sympathized and promised to do everything within his powers.

But this morning Shokin had stopped him in the hall. Without looking Grebenshchikov in the eye, he asked, "Listen, can you tell me what the incident with the fur coat was all about?"

"With what fur coat?" Grebenshchikov asked blankly.

"I don't know what coat. That's why I'm asking. Come on—think back. But for God's sake don't try to hide anything—we're beyond that. I should say that our chances aren't bad, but everything depends on that coat."

"But what coat? Can't you at least tell me what you're talking about?"

"I told you—I don't know. All I know is that in your personal file 'the fur coat incident?!' is written in red pencil across the cover. It's underlined and there are two punctuation marks at the end: a question mark and an exclamation point. And that's it—no clarification on the cover or in the folder. There's only a date—December 1947. I tried to find something out, but no one knows anything more. I even went to—well, never mind who it was. We've got our own Pimen the Chronicler here, the keeper of the legends. He remembers everything... But he doesn't know about this. All he remembers is that back then, during those years, you were never promoted, and the reason was the same every time: 'What was that incident with the fur coat?' Management asks—no one tells them anything, everyone's silent. Maybe no one really knew anything, or maybe they didn't want to get mixed up in it...

Anyway, you know the rest: 'What? No one has anything to report? All right, let's put it aside 'til the next time. We're in no hurry.' And then they stopped asking... Who wrote it, why he wrote it—no one knows. Maybe the person who wrote it died a long time ago. But the written words remain, and they have power! Nothing will come through until you and I erase that pencil mark!"

"Good God, could it really be that?" Grebenshchikov wondered when he was finally alone. Out of habit he moved his stool toward the window as he sat down, but he remembered that the kitchen door was open and got up to close it so the tobacco smoke wouldn't seep through the apartment. Some mornings his wife griped at him, insisting that even the curtains in the main room smelled of his tobacco.

The building was old and quiet, with thick walls: as midnight neared and life died down, if he strained, he could just barely hear the faint sounds of a radio coming from somewhere above him or on the same floor. The house was so quiet that about ten years ago a cricket moved into the crawlspace in the kitchen. Viktor Ivanovich soon got used to it, and loved it, especially since the cricket, smart little devil, rarely showed himself to others, but preferred the hour when he and the his host were left alone together. Then one summer when they didn't spend too much time in the city the cricket disappeared and never came back.

"Could it really be that? Could it be the incident that happened twenty-five—no, twenty-seven years ago?" Grebenshchikov thought. "It can't be. It's like a bad dream. But what else could it be? There hasn't been anything else..."

Ever since that day his wife couldn't bear to hear about any fur coat, and every time her coat wore out she had a tailor she knew on Petrovka make her another one with a fur collar. Back then, on an overcast November day, he was shopping with Lina (her full name was Alina), carrying an amount of money that was rather large in those days. Lina's father had wanted to give his daughter something substantial that she really needed for her household as a wedding present, but in the rush he couldn't find anything, got upset, and finally thrust an envelope with money into her hand: "Go spend this on whatever you think you need—you know better—after all, you're the ones it's for, not me..." There was talk of a currency reform that autumn. The public was rabid, grabbing up everything that appeared on the shelves. As they entered a fur shop on Sretenka, at first he and Lina could not believe their eyes: a rack of faux sealskin coats was hanging behind the counter, and there was no crowd. It must have been right after the lunch break: Sretenka Street probably hadn't had a chance to sniff anything out. Lina tried on a coat, it fit her, Grebenshchikov paid the cashier and took the wrapped coat. Then something inexplicable happened: how and why he put the bundle down on the counter, what distracted him, why he turned away, at what moment it happened—he could not remember anything in detail either then or later, and Lina didn't notice anything either. The bundle had disappeared.

When he told the people at work what had happened, everyone, of course, sympathized with him, especially the women. But for most of them a fur coat was something so unattainable that the whole story sounded more like something out of the life of Mary Pickford or Greta Garbo. He sensed that it wasn't that some people didn't believe him, but they simply felt uncomfortable and uneasy for him and even began to regard him as odd—not a liar, exactly—but as someone who had suddenly developed a penchant for daydreams and visions. In time he began to have doubts himself: don't be silly, did it ever actually happen or did he dream that damned fur coat? No, clearly he didn't dream it, if its trail turned up in his dossier... "Should I tell Lina or not?" he wondered. "If I tell her, she'll be upset and withdraw. She's gotten strange. She's miserable, she cries over nothing at all, she gets home from work, lies down and just lies there, and nothing will budge her. What's she crying about? She herself probably doesn't even know. She's getting old, no one needs her any more... Except me... Natashka is also a peach—she might take an extra minute to call and ask: how are you, still alive, old folks? She wasn't raised in a barn, as they say. But I really should tell her. Alina Georgievna, this might explain a lot that happened in our life together. A long life and not an easy one..."

They started out so happily, but later... Well, what about later... Later it all went as it probably does for everyone. But no, that's only what we say—"like everyone." Actually, everyone has his own life, his own pain, and it's no consolation that other people don't have it easy either, that things didn't work out for them, that it didn't work out at all for some people.

After they married Alina walked around like a queen, and her girlfriends openly envied her. The war had just ended, there were few fellows around— or rather there were men, but they were all seventeen-year-old kids or invalids: demobilization hadn't yet gotten fully underway. Grebenshchikov wasn't bad looking, and against that background—a black-haired, slender young man in an officer's uniform with ribbons on his chest, calm, even-tempered, speaking to the dean and professors as equals—he naturally attracted attention all around. Even very pretty girls who knew they were pretty and had never deferred to anyone before were often disconcerted and turned away when they caught his eye somewhere in an auditorium or on a staircase. Not to mention those gray mice; there were more of them, the ones who huddled in corners, not knowing what to do with their chapped hands, workworn beyond their years. Later his marriage to Alina was the subject of endless gossip in the institute. Many thought it was a misalliance on his part; in their opinion, he could have found someone more special.

When and how she conceived of this casual disdain for him, when it turned first into covert and then overt contempt, when the contempt was replaced by indifference and submission to her fate—even now, after so many years, he simply couldn't say. Looking back, he saw only the long sequence of years, blurred, faded, and so alike that they were indistinguishable.

Perhaps it all began after their daughter was born? Lina had fallen into a state of dull, unremitting bitterness: the close quarters, the crying in the night, bottles, warming lamps, endless basins of washing, clotheslines with diapers all over the apartment, every conceivable and inconceivable illness of that tiny, constantly wailing creature—it seemed that it would never end. In those days the only thing he aroused in Alina was constant irritation at his clumsiness and incompetence. If he had been swallowed up by the earth, she probably would only have sighed with relief: at least she wouldn't have to think of what to feed this outsider, this extraneous person who was taking up so much space everywhere—in the kitchen, in the room, even in the stairwell, where she shooed him out to smoke and where each time he crashed into the carriage they kept at the entryway. When he came home from work, he was greeted at the door by a mindless, unseeing gaze, her washed-out housecoat was invariably buttoned wrong, and any attempt he made to tell her something, to share something with her, always ended the same way: without listening to the end of his story, she would jump up and run either to the bathroom or to their room, where once again something wasn't right and once again a cry resounded. That lasted a year or two, until they placed Natasha in a child-care center.

And yet that wasn't when it started. No, not then... Viktor Ivanovich recalled that quiet summer when he and Alina were finally by themselves. The old folks had moved to the dacha and taken Natasha, who had already begun to walk.

Something came over them both, some sort of despairing, unquenchable thirst suddenly gripped them. If they so much as touched each other, they both felt throbs from head to toe, clothes flew in every direction, and, wild-eyed and panting, they immediately fell into some kind of oblivion. And if all the cannons in the world had thundered in their ears, if the house had burned down, if anyone at all had come in and stood over them—nothing could have torn them away from each other in those seconds, or stopped that agony for the sake of which a person forgets everything... Then they went away together on vacation to a village east of the Volga. And it was the same there as it had been in Moscow: "the grim, dull flame of desire" overtook them everywhere—on the beach, in the woods, on the porch steps of the tumbledown shack they were staying in together. How long had that lasted? For a long time, probably. In any case, he could still recall their impatience as they waited, even that autumn, for Natasha and then the old folks to fall asleep on the other side of the wall.

But then it left the way it came—by itself, at no particular time, for no particular reason...

After that upheaval, months went by, even whole years, that were essentially unmemorable. He worked, he took Natasha to the day-care center and then to school, he bathed her, told her fairy tales at night, drank with friends, watched television, took groceries out to the dacha (his father-in-law always rented a dacha in Kratov for the summer), and sometimes in the fall he went to the forest to gather mushrooms. What else was there then? Stalin died, and after three years they released everyone who had been unlucky enough to be arrested, then there was some absurd escapade with corn... Of course, he was upset then, too, and argued with his father-in-law and friends, tried to visualize the future, tried to imagine where and what it was all leading to, how it would end, what was temporary and what was lasting and would endure until the end of his life and even longer. But to tell the truth, he was not noted for his imagination, and he was incapable of seeing the scale of the events, their enormous, awesome significance. Each time these thoughts typically ended by gradually turning elsewhere, to whatever concerned him that day or to the near future. It probably worked out that way because that was not the most important thing for him at the time. But what was most interesting for him, what was most important of all—now, two decades later, he couldn't say. But was it just him? In those days people were born, married, died, rushed about their business, attended soccer games, lounged on the grass, looked at the sky...

It was hard for them during those years—they lived from payday to payday. His parents had died, and they could only thank her folks for using their last kopecks to build another apartment and leaving them this one. He could not let himself—a front-line officer, a man a with higher education, and over thirty years old—be supported by someone else! It's true, once in a while Alina would tide them over with a hundred or two from her mother, but he got angry with her whenever it happened, and he has to give her credit—it happened rarely.

The hell with it, though... He didn't want to recall their youthful poverty... Constantly short of money, clothes sewn together out of rags, humiliating pangs of conscience over every extra pack of cigarettes, over every bottle drunk on the sly so his wife wouldn't find out... He remembered how they spent nearly an entire summer discussing whether to replace the broken desk lamp with the pay he'd just gotten or to wait until fall when they couldn't manage without it in the early evening darkness...

While it was hard for everyone else around them, Alina basically accepted it as unavoidable, and he couldn't accuse her of a single fight or even quarrel over money. But life changed, and gradually her eyes showed bewilderment, a question directed not into space, but directly at him: "Well, what's with you? How are we going to manage now? Can't you do anything? You, who were so powerful and prominent when we got married?"

One day they were invited to his classmate's, a fellow he hadn't seen for several years. Alina came home ill that night. She was devastated by the fantastic, inconceivable finery of the apartment they had just visited. The carpets, the chandeliers, the matte-brown furniture, the crystal on the table, the silver champagne bucket... She lay on the couch for a long time and cried, burying her head in the pillow. In those days she was still ashamed of her tears. She didn't respond at all when he tried to console her, but only turned to the wall. There was one phrase that he could make out in her disconnected sniffling and muttering: "He was the worst in the class. The least likely to succeed. Trash..."

It's not that Grebenshchikov immediately accepted his modest lot in life. After a while when he understood that there was no light at the end of the tunnel for him at work (as they said then), he made several attempts to find something else. He filled out applications and once even conducted very serious discussions with very serious people. But... He would have had to change everything, to leave a place he felt at home in, and naturally no one could guarantee that the new position would be better. So he would have to take a risk, to cast off the comfortable and habitual for some vague, indefinite hopes. Every time he thought this over he backed down, and then, when he approached forty, he completely stopped looking for and discussing a new job. This was apparently his fate. Besides, he really liked to walk through the same doors every day, greet the regular security guard, climb the stairs to his floor with a group of co-workers, and then, when he heard the bell, lay out his papers on the desk without bustle or bother, and slowly, using the silence at the start of the day, submerge himself in a world where everything was precise and clear, where there were formulas and technology, and where any misfortune or mistake could not only be caught and understood but also fixed.

There was a period in his life when he earnestly resolved to straighten out his affairs by finishing his dissertation: he chose a topic, hauled home a stack of journals from the library, bought a variety of necessary and unnecessary books. Then, after several years, Alina mercilessly tossed them all out in the dump: he didn't even protest—he just grinned. Why did it work out that way? Damned if he knew. The war had claimed all his strength, or maybe he never had any.

Like everyone else, at work Grebenshchikov had to sit from the first bell to the last, and had only evenings and Sundays left for all his personal hobbies. For a month or two he tried to manage a double load, but he quickly soured on it. People who had been through this already advised him: "When you get home, have a bite to eat, sleep for an hour, and then sit at your desk no matter what, no matter what happens at home. There's nothing so terrible about that. They'll wait, this is important, it's for their sake—they should understand." It's easy to say "they should understand." But Natasha would greet him at the door with such a look in her eyes, she was so genuinely glad to see him. When did that expression in her eyes disappear? Before she started school? No, there was still something in them her first years in school. It was about then that he discovered he had a talent: he had a knack for carving funny little figures out of wood. Natasha was ecstatic over them. She took them to bed with her at night and refused any other store-bought doll from then on. And every night he also had to make up a new fairy tale for her; he usually told her the most unbelievable nonsense, which he was even ashamed to recall now, but she waited for those fairy tales and would not go to sleep without them. After he said good-night to her, he would finally sit down at his desk. But, as if on purpose, the telephone would start to ring, then his wife would call him to tea, and before he even had a chance to look around, it would already be twelve and time for bed—he couldn't go to work the next day with a foggy head. "What does it say in the Gospels? A person's family is his enemy? Yes, that's a deep thought... But is it really true? What's more important before God, if He exists? A dissertation no one needs or contemplation about saving souls, or playing with Natasha on the floor by the couch in the bedroom?"

There—that's where it all started. No, that can't be it. Why then? This didn't start simply, it didn't come out of nowhere...

One day Alina came home late from work, gloomier than usual. He still couldn't say what had snapped in her that evening. Natasha and he were sitting at the table in the main room making a Turk out of wood. He recalled that he was trying to fit the freshly carved turbaned head onto a dowel sticking out of the pot-bellied torso. Other toys he'd made stood on the table, where Natasha had dragged them in from the bedroom: an old man with a sack and cane, a bagel-seller, and an organ-grinder with his parrot. Alina stood beside them for a long time, looked at them, and then suddenly, without a word, swept them all off the table with a single abrupt, wild gesture, and bolted out of the room. The Turk's head rolled under the couch, the bagels scattered, and the old man broke right in half. Natasha and he were dumbfounded. Then Alina cried for a long time, begged them both for forgiveness, saying something about being tired and having frayed nerves.

Soon after that she took a lover. Viktor Ivanovich quickly suspected that something was wrong: nothing had really changed and there was no proof, but suddenly an inexplicable, gnawing melancholy gripped him and he felt uneasy. He wanted to grab his hat and dash out into the street and go somewhere. Where? Nowhere in particular. Wherever he felt like going. Maybe her gaze had changed and turned inward: sated, calm, filled to the brim; or maybe she held her head differently, like someone else; or maybe there was some restraint, some heaviness in her arms when she would still occasionally embrace him, as if it were an effort to lift them and an effort to put them around his neck, requiring the ignition of some transmissions and levers.

Then it went from bad to worse. At first there was still some kind of inept lie, and then no lie at all. Alina became more brazen every day. She came home near midnight, sometimes drunk, all mussed up, disheveled, with either her stockings slipping down or her bra unhooked. Once she came home without it altogether, and she always smelled of someone else's sweat and something else that made him blind with fury... What was the problem—didn't the fellow have a bathroom? Sometimes when she got home, without saying a word, she would immediately get in bed with him (he had taken to sleeping in the main room), and he—he didn't refuse her.

Maybe the contempt started then? Whatever you say, women are a harsh lot. So she fell out of love with him and took up with someone else—why not smooth things over and make it easier, have mercy on him? After all, this man is here with you, he's the father of your daughter. But no, she had to crush him completely, destroy him, stomp him into the dirt: "I'm home, you're lying there waiting for me; I'll get in bed with you, and you won't refuse me because you're nothing and my power over you is absolute." Once he couldn't stand it. One night he lost his mind and his humanity and beat her savagely. He closed the door to the room tightly and beat her without a word, he beat her unsparingly against the corners and walls of the room. The next morning she was a terrible sight. For two weeks she lay on the couch and didn't show herself anywhere; they told everyone it was a car accident. After that it got worse. Alina completely let herself go. Now she would telelphone to give instructions on what to feed Natasha in the morning and she didn't spend the night at home at all.

It wasn't difficult to find out who she was with: it's a small world. It turned out to be a young buck where she worked, younger than he, and even younger than she. He supposed that he didn't intend to marry her or else she would have run away with him. What can you say: she was already over thirty then, and he was rumored to be a slick operator, a slippery one. He was sorry for her, and ashamed for her, but there was nothing he could do: only wait for it all to end, wait for the fellow to throw her out for good. After all, wrinkles had already started to spread under the woman's eyes and her body had started to sag. So he waited. How many cigarettes he smoked at night by the window in the kitchen, how he went over it and over it! He considered everything: walking out and starting all over again, running after the fellow and beating the life out of him. He even wanted to kill her: damn it to hell, sometimes things just didn't work out. The old folks would raise Natasha without them, they'd provide for her. But in his rare lucid moments he realized that he wouldn't go anywhere, he wouldn't do anything to her, and in the end he would forgive her everything. What could he say? He loved her. What can that word explain—he "loved" her? It was time to change all those words—that's what. They don't mean anything. He felt sorriest of all for his home—it was his home in spite of it all, and she had always been and was still home for him.

One time he and Shokin had been drinking in a restaurant, and got so thoroughly drunk they left a briefcase and folder there and had to go back for them. Grebenshchikov told him everything. He didn't have the strength to bear it any more, he wanted to hear just one kind word, and there was no one to be embarrassed before, it was just the two of them.

"Well, leave her," Shokin said after hearing him out.

"I can't."

"Well then, forgive her."

"I can't."

"You know you'll forgive her."

"Yes, I'm lying, I'll forgive her. And I know I will."

"I wouldn't be able to."

"No—but I can."

Shokin was silent for a long time. Then, somehow suddenly sad and sober, he looked at him and said, "Vitya, do you know what you are? You're a great man. You are a truly great man. The only one I know. No, there was one other great man. But that was in literature."

"Who?"

"Alexei Alexandrovich Karenin."

"Why's that?"

"Because he was magnanimous, that's why. He was surrounded by all sorts of slime and small fry. Like me. I, Vitya, am not a great man. I'm shit. But I love you."

It went on for about two or maybe even three years and then, imperceptibly, everything began to fall in place again. Everything more or less calmed down, blew over. She almost never disappeared in the evenings, and she very rarely smelled of wine when she came home. She once again began to drag him to visit relatives and to various social functions at work and got angry when he shrugged them off. She made him change his shirt and tie and was furious when she couldn't find something she needed in their constant disorder. She shouted that she wasn't his and Natasha's maid who had to pick up after them, that they couldn't even be left alone for a day. She was soon elected to a committee at work, and now she spent the evenings on the telephone, discussing office intrigues and squabbles. But Natasha and he quickly got used to it and didn't pay particular attention, except for an occasional understanding smile between them. Usually he only turned up the sound on the television, because Alina's voice was not very pleasant—it was rather sharp, and when she got carried away it was so piercing that you wanted to cover your ears or cut her off altogether.

You couldn't say that she began to treat him more kindly. No, it was more like: "This person is living with me, I don't mind that he is, God bless him, what can I do with him? I can't throw him out on the street." Sometimes when she came out of the bathroom in her robe, she would silently take him by the hand and lead him into the bedroom. Instead of the old sagging couch there were now two shiny wooden beds. "Just like regular people," he couldn't resist sneering when they were delivered. They never spoke about what had happened: that was their tacit agreement, and they observed it, although, of course, they both thought about it often and at night, too, especially at first. For a long while afterwards he noticed tears in her eyes, although he saw no reason for them, at least from his side.

Later he thought she had something else going—with another man or other men, if, of course, his senses weren't deceiving him. But these new passions seemed quite unthreatening, not very serious compared to what had been. They didn't change anything in their life, except for making Alina a bit more lively, and he wouldn't have been surprised had he discovered that there was nothing to them but sighs and long goodbyes at the gate—it was just a little something, a bit of nonsense, done quickly, on the spur of the moment, while a friend's apartment keys jangled and the time was constantly checked.

But she aged almost overnight, in one year, when she was already over forty and he suddenly saw—God knows why, but he saw very clearly, like a light suddenly flashing on in the dark—that he was living with an old woman who had grown fat, who had a heavy behind and thick legs and waddled, who had badly dyed hair that was always covered with some ridiculous hat that made him uncomfortable, even ashamed to look at. He always suffered over those hats when they were invited out, but he decided not to say anything to her: in the end he felt sorry for the old girl. Besides, you can't change anyone at that age.

She apparently looked at herself soberly at last and finally decided to give up. That was probably the start of her indifference to everything, an indifference that sometimes made him melancholy but for the most part, to be honest, suited him. It was more peaceful this way, and that was crucial—after all, he was tired too, and all he wanted now was quiet: the war alone had cost him so much, and after the war he certainly hadn't had a life of balls and galas. Life hadn't been easy, that's for sure.

And he hadn't been a saint, either. Of course, he'd had brief affairs... Who hadn't? Life is life, anything can happen, and he was just like everyone else, no better and no worse. But he was blameless in one sense: none of those affairs had ever touched his family—not with a harsh word, not with money, not with anything else, so that neither Alina nor Natasha had any grievances about him and his conscience was clear. True, there had been a moment when he could barely keep from chucking it all to hell. But he took hold of himself and backed down. Did he have to back down? That's a good question, but an idle one. What happened, happened, and there was no point now in tormenting his soul—the past could not be recaptured.

He had met his dear Vera in the dentist's chair, while some of his teeth were being fixed and some extracted to make his first dentures. He couldn't have been a very pleasant sight: a forty-year-old guy, beginning to go bald, eyes bugging out from fear and a mouth full of holes and the remnants of small teeth, black from smoking, sticking up on the sides. For about two months while his dentures were being fitted, he was unaccountably so ashamed of himself he could barely stand it, as if he were to blame for his bald head, for not having many teeth left, for the bags under his eyes that never went away, even if he hadn't been drinking the night before.

Vera was a nurse in the office. Soon she began to smile at him like a friend, and once, when the doctor was called out of the room for a long while, they chatted very warmly about nothing in particular, and by the end he had already decided to invite her out for the evening. He recalled how she gladly accepted the invitation without any hint of affectation. That evening she was right on time, not a second late, and—damned if it didn't really happen—when she saw him, she pulled a bouquet of hyacinths from behind her back and handed it to him. This was in March. Later, in the restaurant, the bouquet lay on the table all evening, and, when they were leaving, he wrapped it in paper so it wouldn't freeze and took it with him.

She was about twenty-six or twenty-seven, slender and good-looking. In her own way she was even pretty, with a beauty that wasn't striking, but was quiet, gentle, unthreatening. It didn't put people off, but, to be honest, neither did it especially attract anyone. Why did he invite her out that night? Probably because he wanted to prove that he was still good for something, still needed, that his life wasn't over and that there was still something to look forward to, that it was too early to be put out to pasture. After all, man is

stupid by nature: to think about being put out to pasture at forty and to get
sad and upset about it—what would you say now? If someone then, when he
was forty, had shown him himself today: here he was, on the verge of retirement, no doubt about it, and he didn't have to prove himself to anyone, it
was enough to look in the mirror.

She was a sweet, affectionate person, and her room was always quiet and
pleasant. To be sure, it was a communal apartment, actually a half-basement,
but somehow she managed to arrange it so it was cozy and light. Nothing was
jarring or disturbing to the eye—her entire room was as attractive as she herself was. There were white muslin curtains on the windows, prints on the
walls, bookshelves, a big, easy chair in the corner where—if they cuddled together tightly—they could both sit. Vera lived alone. She had been raised an
orphan, without parents, under the supervision of a rather odd aunt, an old
maid, one of those you can still sometimes see in the health food store on the
Arbat. At that time the aunt was already half-blind, and Vera would visit her.
Viktor Ivanovich usually walked her right up to her aunt's building, and beforehand they always stopped in the Prague Restaurant store to buy something to eat and, without fail, a box of pastries—eclairs, if memory serves,
which her aunt loved.

How he waited for those rendezvous! How impatiently he stared at the
clock, waiting for the damn bell, so that he could practically fly down the
stairs and be at her apartment in ten minutes—no, seven! His salary had finally just been raised, and considerably, but he told Alina free-lance work had
turned up that was reliable and permanent—it would be a sin to lose it, so he
would have to stay an hour or so after work. Maybe she believed him, maybe
she didn't—who knows. In any case she didn't object and he didn't elabo-
rate—that wasn't their way. Vera never demanded anything of him, and that
extra money was enough for everything: for some little treats for her and a
dinner in a restaurant every once in awhile, and at home they soon felt that
money had eased up. What a happy time that was! Perhaps the only happy
time in his life.

All Vera needed was any good fortune, even the slightest, to put her in a
good mood for the entire evening and often even for days. At first he didn't
believe that people could be like that, and, to his shame, he sometimes
thought that for some reason she was pretending.

"You know," she would say, smiling, to him at the door, "you know who I
saw today? You won't believe it."

"Who?"

"Lemeshev! Right there on the street. He was in a fur coat, and there was a
lady with him, really elegant."

"So then what?"

"What do you mean, 'what'? It was the first time I've ever seen him in person. He's gotten old, of course. Wasn't that great? Why don't you say anything?"

"Why Lemeshev? What Lemeshev? What's he to me?" Viktor Ivanovich wondered, expecting further explanation. But she didn't try to explain anything, apparently not understanding how such things could be explained, especially to him. Of course, he could have shrugged his shoulders then as now and said, "Nonsense, that's nothing, really. So what it if was Lemeshev?" It really was nothing. But what is life made up of if not trifles? Oh, we all know how to feel pain—and *how*—but to feel joy—are many people capable of that? Do many people have the gift to feel joy, especially over something trivial? No, except in hindsight, looking back, when everything is already over. But what kind of joy is that, when it's already gone? That's not joy, that's suffering. It would be interesting to know if she had kept this sacred gift, or if life had crushed her, too, as it did other people.

They were so content on their own that they rarely left her half-basement. Who cared what was happening up there? Hadn't they seen it all? So there was snow, so there was slush, so people were bustling here and there. But it was warm here, and they didn't need anyone else, and how lovely and nice to realize that no one in the whole world knew they were there. They could hide completely from everyone by closing the curtains and turning off the lamp, leaving on only the small night-light in the corner.

Here's where his years were needed: he could hold her close and protect her—it wasn't important from whom or from what, it was just clear that she needed protection from someone or something. Well, he could protect her. Once she admitted to him that after they started meeting she didn't have anything to say to her peers. "Vitya, if you only knew what fools they are. Good God, such fools..." she repeated, and it looked as if she might cry.

But time was moving on, and he had to decide, to decide in earnest. Grebenshchikov knew that he was wasting her youth, that she wasn't seventeen anymore, and he was tortured by that thought, he condemned himself, cursed himself, but he couldn't make up his mind. Why are good people unlucky? Take another look—the other one was ugly as sin and as greedy and mean-tempered as a ferret. It was a miracle that she had snatched up this prize. What did he, fool, see in that witch? Nothing could be done about it—that's life. That was true, of course. But, to tell the truth, realizing it doesn't make it easier for anyone...

So Vera, an innocent soul, didn't expect to get what she wanted from him. The day he feared inevitably came. That evening, he recalled, he had put on his coat when she said:

"Vitya, someone proposed to me today."

Everything swirled before his eyes, his heart skipped a beat and instantly fell, and he held his breath for a long time before it occurred to him to get a Validol tablet out of his side pocket. "Who?"

"One of our doctors. He's been interested in me for a long time."

"And what about you?"

"I don't know, Vitya. I don't love him, but I'm thirty, after all..."

That night, for the first and only time in all his married life, he didn't come home. The next morning they sat at the table, smoked, drank coffee. "That's it. It's all over." That was the only thought in his head. Later another thought inexplicably flashed by: "What if Natasha died? Is this what it would feel like?" But he drove the thought away. He did not expect life to be merciful to him in the future. Ahead there lay only one path, one straight, short path... Where? He knew where—straight ahead, without swerving off the road, without deceiving himself or anyone else.

Now he had two favorite pastimes: hunting for mushrooms and ice-fishing. Actually, that was all he had lived for in the last years: he worked five days, and disappeared in the woods for two, or, if it was winter, he went to a lake about 100 kilometers from Moscow. It was especially fine in autumn, in September. At that time he usually sent Alina off to the sea while he took his vacation in the forest beyond Kostroma. And an old couple that lived on the edge of an abandoned, run-down village—a garrulous, half-drunk old man and his gloomy, God-fearing old lady—somehow, at the end of his life, became the closest people to him on earth.

Why are people afraid of being alone? It's hard to understand. It's best to be alone in the forest. It's not that thoughts are somehow special in the forest—not at all. They are generally about the same: there's a bird over there chirping, the dew is dripping from that bush, glistening in the sunlight, a mushroom is hiding there—let me get it... But in the forest you don't need to think. A person feels at home in the woods: he, and the tree, and the bird are all the same, and it's easy to feel one with them, not alone. A person isn't demeaned, nor does he have to look for his place in the world. Yes, all the mystery of life that unrelentingly torments a person in the daze of city life seems suddenly uninteresting and contrived in the forest: there's no mystery. There you are, and where you came from and where you're going—isn't it all the same? Wait and see. It cannot be that this harmony, this whole that is as graceful as everything surrounding you, doesn't have something ordained for you for eternity, a kindness that can only be sensed, felt in the lingering fog, in this white, smoky twilight...

He was careful to pick good mushrooms. He wasn't greedy and never picked more than one basket. Then he would slowly return home along the copses, skirting the forest. Sometimes he would lean up against a haystack along the road, lie down, chew on a straw, watch the black rooks in the field, squint at the blue sky and the autumn sun, and sometimes even doze off. At home he would empty out the basket on the oilcloth table cover, and with the old man—who usually managed to have a few drinks before noon—chattering disjointedly in the background, he and the old woman would slowly, without hurry, pick over the mushrooms he'd brought home: this one to dry, that one to salt, this one to fry.

One day the old lady reached over with her blackened fingers and plucked a good-sized mushroom that looked exactly like a white boletus. She showed it to him.

"Don't pick any more like this one. They're poison. Look here, it's kind of pink here on the bottom."

"What sharp eyes she has! She saw it right away, and at her age! I'm an idiot... That was a close call," he thought, "and it looked so harmless. How many people have died because of that mushroom? But who thinks about them now or how many of them there were? They're gone, gone for good, God rest their souls. I won't pick that kind of mushroom anymore, that's all there is to it. But there are tasks, many of them even more trivial than this mushroom, and yet even they require someone's death, maybe even many deaths, so that those left behind can live more easily. What was the point of my life, I wonder? What did I do that was worth doing?"

However you looked at it, he had fought in the war thirty years ago, and something had filled all the years that followed—he'd done something, lived for something...

In the war he had gotten used to death, gotten used to counting numbers instead of people. But there really was no way to keep a good count: in order to count, you'd need to know every person, and who knew that? So they had estimated: a battalion of the enemy was destroyed, or, the other way around, our troops sustained considerable losses. But how many casualties there were, who was the casualty—try and figure it out. No one could. There's no other way it could have been: war is war. Once when he was hauling an artillery tractor along a muddy road, he looked out of the cabin and saw a body lying in the ditch, another one next to it, and more bodies in the field—some were ours, some were the enemy's. It was fortunate if they were picked up later, but sometimes they rotted there in the rain—people couldn't always get to them. If one of your own men was lost, a man from your division, you'd be overcome by grief: how could this have happened? A man lived and now he's gone; we had just been sitting next to each other, we had just been together. But then you would forget the next day; some came, some went.

It's strange how a person changes with the years: he was no longer used to counting numbers—he couldn't count the same way anymore. Instead of a

number, some Ivan Ivanovich who was just buried yesterday floated before
his eyes. Was it yesterday? That's right, yesterday. He was lying in the coffin so
peacefully, so calmly, yet he'd once been feisty, raised quite a ruckus, had always been striving for something, making all kinds of plans...

"Okay. What's the point of philosophizing? Life turned out this way and
not another, and what's done can't be undone," he thought. "Be thankful that
you're still alive: how many were massacred and how many in vain? Who
counted them, and when, and who'll count them now? You can't count them
all, so there's no point in trying. What difference does it make if there's one
more or less? They're buried and forgotten. You were lucky. The doctor did a
good job of sewing you up. You've lasted thirty years, and, God willing, you'll
last a few more... Only it's a shame. The war didn't use me up completely—
some powers remained. But what's there to say now! Whether it's your fault
or somebody else's—there's no telling now. And even if you could figure it
out, what would be the point in the end? Maybe Alina is right: if I'd banged
my head against the wall I might have gotten somewhere. But I didn't! And I
won't! Go ahead, just think of me as one more who's gone to pot... But what
good does it do anyone? Who's better for it? That's the question..."

The night ended. The clock in the main room struck six. On the table in
front of him was an ashtray full of cigarette butts. His head ached, and he had
a sour, sick taste in this mouth. The water pipes whined somewhere above
him and a snowshovel scraped outside the window: the street sweeper was
up and scraping at the ice in the dark, probably cursing the weather and her
life. Shuffling footsteps sounded in the corridor—Alina had gone into the
bathroom.

"So, should I tell her or not?" he thought. "No, I won't tell her. What for?
No, I'd only add to her misery. There's nothing she can do. And there's nothing I can do, either..."

The switch clicked on; the abrupt, unceremonious light blinded him for a
second. Alina walked into the kitchen.

"What made you get up at such an ungodly hour? Good Lord, you've already managed to smoke up the place—I can hardly breathe. Shall I put the
kettle on?" she asked as she wrapped her robe around her and yawned, leaning against the door.

Translated by Michele A. Berdy

Originally published in *Oktiabr'*, May 1988

Vladimir Tendryakov

Donna Anna

Summer, 1942.

In the sky the dark, swarthy sunset was fading. A light breeze wafted the fresh night air and an insistent bitter smell of wormwood across the entire twilight steppe. Somewhere on the edge of the earth, right beneath the sunset, gunshots rang out gaily, crackling like burning brushwood.

In one spot, beneath the sunset, the exchange of fire was thicker. From time to time thudding shouts came from that direction, as if someone were beating the dry steppe with a blunt pick. Shells were bursting. Lieutenant Mokhnatov's fifth company was entrenched there, across from the lonely poultry farm.

The sunset faded, twilight began to spread over the steppe, and the war fell into a semi-sleep. There was movement in all corners of the steppe amidst the fragile calm, as things big and small got under way, things that the daylight interfered with. Tractors roared and some batteries moved into new positions. Trucks with dimmed headlights crept along the roadless steppe, feeling their way along as they transported ammunition. The field kitchens, loaded with the same old millet gruel, could drive right up to the trenches, whereas in daytime they could only crawl toward them.

This business evidently wasn't suitable for daylight either, even though it was called instructive. They had summoned us here from all the sub-units—privates, sergeants, even some junior officers.

We sat on the bristly hillside of a gently sloping ravine, which was still warm from the day's sun. A cool, slightly bitter breeze was blowing on us.

Down below a covered truck stopped. Several sturdy soldiers jumped out one after the other, moving swiftly. They wore peaked service caps. They all looked alike but were completely unlike us, the listless, dirty men in the trenches. In a businesslike manner they helped a small, gray, disheveled soldier get out of the truck. His field shirt was unbuttoned and his boots were without puttees.

This little soldier, looking as limp as a quail that had been mauled by a dog, was to be the focus of the "instructive" lesson. In the bottom of a gully ten feet away from the truck, in defiance of regulations, a trench with a dusty clay parapet was waiting for him—a grave.

The commander, tightly strapped up in shoulder and waist belts, just as sturdy and brisk as his subordinates, issued orders in a low but energetic voice that the soldiers in the caps obeyed. The man-quail appeared at the edge of the grave in an unbuttoned undershirt, in skivvies that were almost falling down. Without orders, the soldiers lined themselves in a small file opposite him, squared their shoulders, and leaned their rifles against their legs.

At that moment a fat, somewhat sluggish man appeared who wore a commander's uniform but carried himself like a civilian. He took a piece of paper out of his map case, found the right angle so that he faced us, the viewers, and the defendant, and so that the receding light fell on the paper.

We already knew everything, even more than what was written on the paper. The fellow standing in his underwear with his back to the grave was a certain Ivan Kislov, an animal-transport driver from the transport company. While working on kitchen detail, chopping meat, he'd chopped off the index finger of his right hand.

This happened back in early spring, during training. It was the middle of summer now, our regiment had taken up its defensive position a week ago in the middle of the steppe. In the first two days we lost half of our fresh troops, but we stopped the Germans who were rushing toward the Don. We thought we had stopped them.

And here this Kislov was being dragged from behind the lines all the way to the front for an instructive lesson.

"In the name of the USSR, the Military Tribunal!.."

Kislov, convicted of intentional self-mutilation, stood below in oversize government issue underwear. In the twilight you couldn't see the expression on his face.

Just yesterday I had two friends, Slavka Koltunov and Safa Shakirov, a loud, lively Bashkir, as small as a teenager. Yesterday the three of us were eating chaff from the same pot. Slavka was killed on the spot while on the line, and I sent Safa by truck to the field hospital just two hours ago, with a bullet in the stomach. Who knows whether he'll make it or not.

"...An investigation has established that on the fourteenth of March, 1942, Private Ivan Vasilievich Kislov, assigned to kitchen detail..."

The sunset was fading. The young guys in the caps were standing in a pose they'd learned in training, while opposite them an absurd figure swayed, as limp as a sheet in the wind. The grave behind him was waiting.

But Slavka Koltunov was probably still lying somewhere in the middle of the steppe. There was nobody to dig his grave.

The fact that in just a minute five armed guys would kill a sixth who was unarmed and defenseless didn't bother me in the least. It was just one more death. And how many of them I'd seen in just one week! I never ate from the same pot with Ivan Kislov from the transport regiment. Did they get Safa Shakirov to the field hospital alive? Would the doctors save him?

"Why show us this bum?" The question came in an angry whisper. The commander of the chemical platoon, Junior Lieutenant Galchevsky, was sitting next to me.

We had become acquainted in the troop train on the way to the front. I was on telephone duty in the headquarters car. It was night, and the top regimental command had received orders not to move out until morning, so they went off to sleep. A guard by the safe was breathing noisily and shifting from one foot to the other. A guard from the commander's headquarters was sitting at the rickety table by the light of a wick lamp. He was a young fellow with a white neck like a young girl's, his hair cut like a cadet's, with the small cube-shaped, ruby insignia of a junior lieutenant in the tarnished braid of his field uniform. He was deep in thought and excited, writing something, probably letters home. He kept breaking off, staring wide-eyed, with a devouring look, at the lamp, then desperately attacking the paper again, his pen rustling in the quiet like a swarm of enraged cockroaches.

I was sprawled out on the floor near the phone, on top of my tent-raincoat, from time to time sending out long distance the dendrological recitative: "'Acacia!' 'Acacia!' This is 'Oak!' 'Maple!' 'Maple!' 'Rowan-tree!' 'Firtree!' 'Firtree!' Have you fallen asleep, blockhead? This is 'Oak.' Testing."

The door of the car was half-open, and night peeped in through the crack. The moist, damp darkness was so dense you could reach out your hand and feel it. Houses with curtains on the windows were hiding somewhere in its midst. Out there people were getting ready for work in the morning, worrying about their problems—how to get hay for the cows, where to buy firewood... If you jumped out of the car into the darkness right now, why, in about ten minutes you could run to that paradise with the curtains on the windows. Ten minutes! How close that was! And how unattainable! Right then, the unknown front, lying hundreds of kilometers from here, somehow seemed closer. It was night, and my heart ached for something I couldn't explain: either for something simple like walking barefoot across a newly-

washed floor, or for something improbable, miraculous, beautiful...
Something in the face of which the war would seem insignificant.

It was time again for me to call out my incantation "Acacia!" "Acacia!" But
instead of this I defiantly recited:

> At dawn it is cold and strange,
> At dawn the night is dim.
> Maiden of Light! Where are you, Donna Anna?
> Anna! Anna!—Silence.[*]

The chair I'd pushed away fell with a crash, the light from the lamp flickered, and for a second the car was thrown into darkness. The guard at the
safe straightened up, and froze at attention while the junior lieutenant
jumped up from the table and looked at me with his dark, cavernous eyes.

"Hey, you there! Yes, you! Do you like Blok?"... He was panting.

I liked what I knew, and I knew something from Blok, something from
Esenin, and from Mayakovsky. I liked Gregory Melekhov and old Shchukar,
D'Artagnan and his friends, and the incomparable Sherlock Holmes. The junior lieutenant had a contemptuous hatred for some of them, like Esenin, for
example: "He's bourgeois! A lumpen-proletariat! The soul of a drunk! Imagine
being a whiner during the Revolution!"

But he also liked Blok, Dumas, and Sir Arthur Conan Doyle. He particularly liked the cinema, not comedies, but movies about the Revolution and
the war. He raved about the scene in the movie *We're from Kronstadt!* where
the sailors are executed. He'd lean his whole body toward me as he said with
a shudder, "That's how one should die, looking the enemy right in the eyes,
laughing at him!" His face was narrow, with fine features and a capricious
twist to his thin lips.

I was unenthusiastic about the cinema, especially about war movies. There
was already more than enough war without the movies adding to it. And I
didn't want to die, no matter how beautiful the death, no matter how I looked
the enemy in the eye, but I was ashamed to admit this even to myself.

"Maiden of Light! Where are you, Donna Anna?" The soldiers were talking
about broads, about broads and grub, the eternal inexhaustible topics. They
talked about grub more often, perhaps because our military rations were
scanty, and moreover the sergeant majors and cooks stole from them without
a twinge of conscience. We were always hungry, and, in this case, not for
women.

---

[*]The lines are from the penultimate stanza of the poem "The Commendatore's Footsteps" by the
Russian poet Alexander Blok (1880-1921). The lyric recounts a famous moment from the Don
Juan legend.

Maiden of Light! Where are you, Donna Anna?
Anna! Anna!—Silence.

We'd stumbled upon one another, and he started turning up almost every day right outside our car and asking me to come out to exchange a few words. He sought me out when I was on phone duty at night, he would sit there for hours, and if everyone around us was asleep he'd tell me about his mother:

"Believe me, there's no one saintlier on this earth!"

His eyes widened, his lips curved with pain, and, suffering together with him, I loved his wonderful mother... And then for a long time I'd be exhausted with memories about my house, about my own mother, about Father, who'd left for the front before I did. Soon it would be a year since his last letter arrived: "A horse was killed from under me. I was sorry for it. I'd gotten used to it. I saw my first air battle..." My father had gone through two major wars, World War One and the Civil War, but that was the first time in his life he had seen an air battle.

I didn't know whether I should thank Galchevsky for all those memories or curse him.

"For God's sake, call me Yarik, like they do at home."

I was a junior sergeant, and he a junior lieutenant. In the army building set up according to rank, his office was a whole floor higher than mine. I always felt guilty before him because I didn't know how to respond in kind. I was always tense, watching myself, careful not to overstep the bounds so I wouldn't accidentally do anything that would cause him to not like me. For some reason I was frightened by the capricious twist of his lips.

I didn't see him the whole week we were at the front. That week I lived through more things than I'd ever done before in my whole life.

He saw me there and sat down beside me, thin, lanky, his neck touchingly childlike.

"Why are they showing us that bum? To frighten us!? Us? With death? That's a laugh!" Again that twist of his thin lips that one sees on the faces of martyrs. It seems he, too, had seen his fill of horrors that week.

Did they bring Safa Shakirov to the field hospital alive? Would they save him?..

———

A brisk order rang out:

"Present arms!"

The young guys who'd arrived in their fresh new caps raised their rifles.

A lonely man stood undressed before us in the still, dark steppe. He was no longer a soldier, and had only a few seconds left as a man.

You could hear the roar of the tractors in the depth of the dark steppe, on the outskirts of which shots kept crackling merrily. A stubborn wind was blowing.

No, this death was still different from the ones I'd seen recently.

"For a traitor to the Motherland!.." sang out the commander of the gallant crew.

The tractors were roaring and I heard my heart beating in my chest.

"Fire!"

I was waiting for the boom of the proverbial thunderbolt, but there was only the unimpressive sound of a ragged, discordant shot. The twilight shadows quivered from the fire that shot out from the five rifle butts. The ghostly white figure stood for a while as if bewildered, but long enough to feel a whole series of reactions: first the thought, "But they missed!" then a senseless relief, and finally, hope: "What if they were just scaring me with blank shots? They'll pardon me now...," and his faith in the latter started to surge swiftly, but didn't have time to develop. The man in the underwear, shrouded in twilight, swayed and fell headfirst toward the soldiers who hadn't yet lowered their rifles.

They summoned you to watch a performance. Five men at ten paces away, firing virtually point-blank—it would have been hard to miss.

Ducking from habit, our medic with his bag ran over to the man who'd been shot. He had to verify that everything had been done properly.

The spectators got up. Someone zealously worked his homemade lighter, striking the flint to get his cigarette lit. In the silence someone said loudly and expressively to no one in particular:

"Our cause is just! The enemy will be crushed! Victory will be ours!" Galchevsky twitched at these words, but immediately relaxed and gritted through clenched teeth:

"That's the joke of an idiot."

"Let's go," I said.

For all I knew Yarik could jump on the joker and start teaching him a lesson.

Down below in the gully the twilight was thickening. You could hear a car rumbling and the relcutant clinking of two shovels.

Again I remembered that right then Slavka Koltunov was lying somewhere in the middle of the steppe with no one to bury him.

The cabin door of the truck slammed, the gears scraped, the motor roared into action and the car headed back.

The shovels continued to clink. Our men were doing the digging; the new arrivals only did clean work.

Where earlier the dawn had been dark, the sky now glimmered with a despondently monotonous ash-gray light. The light from an illuminating rocket slid along the ash-gray ravine, like a bright drop of rain down a grimy window. It was shining over Lt. Mokhnatov's company.

Yarik Galchevsky walked beside me and fumed:

"Some bastard fucked it up. What a time to say 'Our cause is just.' Those petty juridical manipulators are a fine bunch too. Their attitude is 'We've got you all together here so you can see what would happen to you, too, if you.... Fear us more than the enemy!' Ugh! The front-line soldier has a real horror of these rearline wonders who call the tune."

Galchevsky fumed, while I listened to him with half an ear as I kept turning that phrase, which was sacred to me, over and over in my head... If our cause is just, then the enemy will be crushed. The enemy isn't right—we are. If we're right, then we're strong. Truth always triumphs in the end...

"You know, I want to quit the chemical platoon for good. Right now I'm neither fish nor fowl, and there's no way out. The regiment already has a chief officer of chemical units, why do you also need a commander of the chemical platoon?"

Another rocket flew over the area where Mokhnatov's company was stationed, but this time it resembled a green, iridescent crystal.

I didn't like Yarik Galchevsky when, like now, he got all fired up over nothing, and I didn't like those guys in their parade caps and the efficient way they had dealt with the transport driver Ivan Kislov, and, of course, there's no way I could like Ivan Kislov, with his attitude of "Who cares, as long as I save my butt!"... But I think I liked myself least of all. I was deluded about something really simple: "Our cause is just! The enemy will be crushed! Victory will be ours!" It's as plain as day! Truth always conquers, but say what you will, the enemy—the wrong ones—had reached as far as the Don.

"I'll take the rifle platoon! Your average rifleman is the vertebrae, the small bone in the army's spine on which everything depends!"

Tumbleweed silently rushed past us like a beast without a body, a ball of thorns whirling away into the darkness, into the desolate infinitude of the steppe's plain.

But the infinitude of the steppe is deceptive. About ten feet farther on, the steppe dropped sharply from under our feet into the thickets of prickly bushes that grew along the dried-up creek's stony bed. Several foxholes—the headquarters of our regiment—were hidden here in the undergrowth of the wild hawthorns. I had no foxhole, only a trench, a long slit in the earth, where two packs, mine and Slavka Koltunov's, were lying unattended. There had been a third—Safa Shakirov's—but I'd sent it along with its owner to the medical battalion. This trench was my home. I'd make my way to it and squeeze myself into the rock-hard clay walls, wrap myself up in my tent-coat and collapse.

The only happiness left in my life now was to sleep.

"'Clover' 'Clover'!"

"Clover" didn't answer. Somewhere in the parched steppe the thin thread of the cable was broken. When I slept, this was gone.

A greasy, mustily sweetish smell. Inky-black corpses were strewn about in the crushed wormwood of the steppe, with clouds of satiated flies buzzing triumphantly overhead... When I slept, this was gone.

No Slavka Koltunov, returned from the line... No sweaty face of Safa or his slanting, shiny black eyes with their expression of a helpless, suffering bird. No! No! I slept.

While I slept, there was no war.

It was a pity that lately I could sleep only two or three hours a day.

It was also a pity that now I slept as if in a faint, without any dreams. If I could just see the threadbare curtain drawn across the window of our house and, outside, the pink dawn with the rooster crowing in the garden... Or the float submerged amidst the platelike leaves of the water-lilies, or the struggling golden perch pulled out of the water in a rainbow of spray... Or my mother's face as she bent over me, her soft voice saying: "Volodya, get up. You'll be late for school."

"Don't, Mom, don't wake me up!" As soon as the dream finishes, the war will begin again.

Night over the steppe. The distant exchange of fire. I haven't made it to my trench yet, I'm not sleeping yet, but already I feel happy. Blessed be nature for giving us, the living, the gift of forgetting about life for a while.

But this time I didn't, couldn't fall asleep.

There were a lot of soldiers crowded in the ravine, with rolled-up greatcoats hanging around their necks, with packs, rifles, and helmets—in full battle dress. Their boots crunched as they tramped on the red-hot pebbles of the dry riverbed. The commander of the communications company swooped down on me as he passed.

"Junior Sergeant Tenkov! You're now under the commander of the Second Battalion! On the double!" An order from the commander of communications!

Everything was clear. Our regiments had losses every day. Every night non-combatants were transferred to the rifle company: transport soldiers, cooks' helpers, and rearline quartermaster dimwits. Even the infantry reconnaissance platoon, who, as experts in attacks by night, were the aristocrats of the regiment, now took up a defensive position, just like common riflemen.

There are never enough communications men in a regiment. The heavier the fire, the more often the connection is cut off. So there I was, a radio operator without a radio set, a telephonist who was grabbed on the spot.

I climbed down into my trench to get my pack and greatcoat roll. To the trench where I returned every night and which I considered my home. Maybe I'd be able to grab an hour's sleep before dawn in some other trench. Sometimes I could and sometimes I couldn't.

"Tenkov! Volodya!"

Yarik Galchevsky was looking for me. Hey! He too was in his helmet and coat, carrying his pack.

"They're sending us together. To Mokhnatov's company," he told me excitedly.

Well, I was ready.

The steppe, baked to a rusty-brown, crawled lazily upward toward the wrenchingly blue sky. Standing on a crest beneath the sky, you could make out even with the naked eye the rugged line of their trenches. Behind the crest was a poultry farm. It was probably a small farm, several adobe houses, whitewashed with lime, and a dirty little pond surrounded by muddy, trampled banks. Probably like that... None of us had ever seen the poultry farm, but everyone had heard of it.

The poultry farm was the highest point in the flat steppe.

All the Germans had to do was haul their tanks and motorized infantry through the farm and head straight for us.

The poultry farm was a trampoline from which it was very convenient for the Germans to pounce on us.

Mokhnatov's company occupied the defense across from the farm. Everyone talked about Lt. Mokhnatov, from the regiment commander down to the last animal transport driver in the train.

I imagined him as a hefty fellow, his face unshaven after his long stint in the trenches, with long arms dangling down to his knees, almost like a gorilla! Mokh-na-tov—the very name evoked a furry beast!

A few feet ahead of the common trench, in which you could walk without stooping, a narrow deadend ditch had been dug in the direction of the enemy. Inside, the earth had been pressed together to form a step that was used as a perch. This was the company commander's observation point. A young man in a faded white tunic was perched there, his dusty boot resting against the wall. His dirty oval face had a swarthy mat skin. A dry wisp of hair stuck out from his forage cap, and his hoarse, croaking voice sounded at times like a rooster's.

"Telephone operator!" he yelled with uncertain aggressiveness. "Get that fat bastard on the line!"

The "fat bastard" was the company sergeant-major, who hadn't brought in enough water during the night for the unit. Mokhnatov was threatening to bring him before the firing squad.

The transparent air above the company commander's dusty forage cap was suffused with fiery heat: heavy shells hissed and lisped as they flew over us, bullets whined and groaned, and the ominous whisper of stray shell fragments spread along the line. But down below, where the company commander was standing, on the level of his long-unpolished boots, in the narrow confines of the cool trench, the efficient, lively activity of the line of defense continued. Mokhnatov's orderly, Vasya Zablik, whom I knew, was running around, stooping as he jogged along. A down-in-the-mouth soldier stood respectfully at Mokhnatov's boots, with the buckle of his canvas belt slung to one side, his tunic spotted with machine-oil, his pants drooping, his puttees sagging, and his face streaked, unwashed, and unshaven for a week now, ever since our life at the front began. This was Gavrilov, the best machine gunner in the company, and maybe in the whole regiment, who was an expert at demolishing the enemy's firing points with his Maxim machine-gun. He was the one who'd just now got Mokhnatov angry at the master sergeant when he told him that soon there wouldn't be anything to pour into the casing of the machine-gun. Next to him stood Dyozhkin, the commander of the left-flank platoon, an elderly senior sergeant with the face of a sad bookkeeper. He had been standing there for almost half an hour, patiently trying to get Gavrilov's machine-gun team from Mokhnatov. "There are too many against us. We need to give 'em a scare." Mokhnatov, however, wouldn't say yes or no, but diplomatically cursed the sergeant-major with excessive fervor:

"He got that fat belly gorging himself in the transport train! His mug's fatter than a soldier's ass. You can't find that beauty even in broad daylight!"

"Medic! Medic! Where's the medic?"

They were leading a wounded man along the trench. He was naked to the waist, with dazzling white bandages clumsily wrapped around his right shoulder and black rivulets of dried blood on his protruding ribs and bluish skin. A soldier right behind the wounded man supported him by holding his good elbow. A second one, strapping and loud-voiced, walked ahead, swinging his arms emphatically, as if readying for a fight, and calling the medic.

Mokhnatov turned sharply to him from his perch:

"Why two of you? Why not take the whole company?! Dyozhkin! Are these your heroes?"

But Dyozhkin didn't have time to answer. Mokhnatov tumbled onto the head of the machine gunner Gavrilov, who was standing respectfully under him. The trench shook from the explosion, sand fell from the walls, and a momentary shadow fell across the cloudless sky.

We weren't considered under fire if the helmet placed on the parapet didn't fall with a clatter back into the trench. But even in quiet moments like these, you didn't lean out if you didn't need to—"you'd get dust in your eye."

Usually the helmet fell all day long. But sometimes the lead and steel simply caused the parapet to shower earth into the trench, which shuddered feverishly from the explosions, and the helmet would start falling before you could count to ten.

"'Clover'! 'Clover'! Can you hear, 'Clover'?"

I still had the same telephone contact, I'd been yelling, "'Clover'! 'Clover'!" to him yesterday from above—from the regimental headquarters. Now I was yelling from below, from the company. And no matter how much they shot, no matter how the ground shook from the explosions, no matter what shell fragments showered over the parapet, as long as "Clover" heard us, everything was fine. We were alive and we were safe, the shooting even made it cozier. In the ground it was just like being in the bosom of Christ, just try to get us!

And now this:

"'Clover' 'Clover'!"

Not a sound on the line.

I nudged my buddy, who wasn't awake yet, and shoved the receiver into his hand.

"Hold this, I'm going 'for a walk'."

In the daytime we would "take a walk" in strict order. My buddy "took a walk" the last time the connection was broken. During a calmer period. Now the helmet was falling... You dive across the trenchline as if it were an ice-hole.

The thin thread of the cable stretched across the steppe. Above your back, above your unprotected, exposed back, above the back of your head stalked death with its many voices.

The language of death at play is simple. You begin to understand it during your first hours at the front.

If the bullets sing tenderly and yearningly as they dissolve into the dense air, you don't pay attention to them—it's no big deal. But if a bullet screams quickly and fiercely, making a shower of earth sting the skin of your face as it splatters on you, that means they're shooting on target; that means the second or third bullet could be for you, and you should get away from that damned spot and run. Not on your feet, though, but on your back and on your stomach, moving fast across the steppe, seeing nothing but sky and wormwood, sky and wormwood—until the bullets start to whine soothingly again, high above you.

There was the dry hissing whisper of a shell fragment moving somewhere right by us; if you felt around, you could find it. It wasn't scary either. During its long transit across the blue sky, it had lost its power to kill. It could hit and even wound you, but not fatally.

A soul-crushing howl, a howl that drills through your brain. There's nothing more terrifying in war than when this howl breaks off. A short second of deafening quiet. After this quiet, a lot of men never hear anything again. But the man who didn't repeatedly grow numb at that silence wasn't a front-line soldier yet.

The cable stretched across the steppe. There was no one around, the men were far away, and if you got wounded, help would be far away. At those moments that were most dangerous for him, the telephone operator fought all alone.

The cable stretched across the steppe... Stop! It didn't! Here was a break!.. The ends of the cable had been split by an explosion.

"'Clover' 'Clover'!"

There was no 'Clover,' but there would be soon. To find the end that had been thrown aside and join it together just takes a minute! Sometimes, it's true, the fragments tear the cable into bits, but even then it's not a big job to pull them together and join them. It's getting there and back that's the big deal.

When you get back to the trench, your buddy greets you with a look of respect and gratitude. Even if he makes those trips himself several times a day, right then he's still in awe of me as a man who has wandered close to the next world.

The two of us operated this beat-up little wooden box with the receiver. The only thing I knew about my buddy was that he was a Siberian and had the strange last name of Nebaba.

But how many times I'd waited for him under heavy fire, miserable with tension! How many times had I felt joy at his return, and seen the very same joy in his eyes. He was like a real brother to me, as I was to him. I didn't doubt that. But what kind of man was he? What were his likes and dislikes?

Was he married or a bachelor, an easygoing sort or a whiner? I didn't even know if he was young or not. Under the layers of trench dirt we all looked like old men.

We lived in crowded quarters and took turns. When one of us was on duty, the other always slept. When one of us jumped out and made for the line under fire, the other stayed by the receiver. We only saw each other in the middle of the night, when the field kitchens arrived, as together we ate the hot gruel made of millet chaff from our mess bowls. During those brief moments we didn't talk about ourselves, but about other people and the business at hand.

"Two more got wounded in the first platoon. Something's wrong with our set. The batteries must have worn down."

"Check the grounding. Maybe it's corroded."

Close yet distant, as closely attached as brothers, and at the same time complete strangers.

I've described this in great detail, as if we'd been sitting in our trench week after week. But only two days had passed, days that were as painfully endless as waiting, as exhaustingly nightmarish as the war itself, and as monotonous as humdrum existence.

At the end of the second day I heard some sounds of life on the line.

The distinctive bass of 0-1—in our code, the commander of the regiment—made contact with me, "Cornflower," from the distant "Rye" station. After that they started issuing "Clover" commands every minute: "Call Ulibochkin to the phone immediately!" "Send the orderly to Ulibochkin!" "Give me someone from Ulibochkin's household." I knew the whole regimental and battalion roster of leaders, both by their last names and by their numbers. Ulibochkin was not among them. Finally a new sister joined our plant family—"Thistle." And this "Thistle" began to worry right away about "coals for the samovar." I understood this meant they had attached a mortar battery to our battalion.

At night Captain Pukhnachyov, the battalion commander himself, appeared. He crawled into the trench to see Mokhnatov, and in a second out jumped Vasya Zyablik. In the quiet night, a chorus of voices rang out over the foxhole-riddled steppe and the trenches:

"Dyozhkin, go to the Lieutenant! Master Sergeant Dyozhkin! Junior Lieutenant Galchevsky, to the company commander!"

Mokhnatov summoned his platoon commanders.

Nearby, about ten feet away, our machine-gun operator—it must have been Gavrilov—let loose with a deafening burst of machine-gun fire, as if to say, "I'm not sleeping! I'm keeping watch!" The enemy answered the shots from the other side. I was sitting in the bottom of the trench, but I could clearly imagine how the tracer bullets were flying over the dark steppe.

"Is that you, Volodya?" Galchevsky bent over me. His face was swallowed up by a big helmet, his pointed chin looked gray in the twilight, and a heavy submachine-gun was hanging awkwardly on his thin neck. He had just come from a briefing session. "Our orders are to take the poultry farm tomorrow," he said, sinking down beside me. "Captain Pukhnachyov just brought word to Mokhnatov."

I nodded. Heck, I'd guessed that a long time ago. For me, the telephone operator, that wasn't news.

"Mokhnatov doubts we've got the guts for it."

"Mokhnatov knows," I answered evasively.

"All the same, he's of little faith."

Again there was a deafening burst of machine-gun fire, which again was answered from the other side. It was the usual listless nocturnal exchange of fire. As long as the firing remained like that, it was quiet at the front. You could crawl out of your trench, stand upright, go to the field kitchen, get your portion of gruel, and believe and quietly enjoy the belief that you'd live, at least until morning.

During quiet moments like these it seemed as if some kind of disturbing electricity was emanating from Galchevsky. He twisted his helmet, twitched his shoulders, and finally began to speak breathlessly at full gallop:

"We're getting used to submissiveness! Every blessed day we learn only one thing—weakness! A shell whistles and comes at you—do you stop it! No! You're powerless! Fall down, cringe! And what about our life on the front line? Don't dare move, even to go take a leak! Just sit there, like a submissive prisoner, in the hole you dug with your own hands... Buried alive, submissive, as meek as can be! How I'd like to show them! I'd really like to show them!" Galchevsky gestured with his helmet in the direction of the Germans. "Hell, I'd show them how I can rea-ea-lly hate!" And suddenly he recited:

> Through thickets and forests,
> We'll scatter to let pass
> Beautiful Europe! We'll turn
> Our Asiatic mugs to you!*

This bookish pathos had a false ring to it at the bottom of a trench, and evidently Yarik Galchevsky realized that himself, for he said:

"Ah, that's all nonsense! It's just putting on airs from boredom! All his life he ate off silver plates. There's only one thing that's not nonsense! To walk

---

*The quatrain is from Alexander Blok's poem "The Scythians" (1918).

straight and tall instead of crawling on your belly. Why did they come to us? Why did they pull me out of my home, didn't let me continue my studies? Why did they have to make my mother worry? She's got bad heart problems... I h-a-t-e them!"

"You need a rest, Yarik."

He got up, puzzled, and stood silently for a second, then said haltingly, his voice quivering tonelessly:

"You said exactly what my mother says. You even used the same intonation."

"'Cornflower' 'Cornflower'!" came through the receiver.

"'Cornflower' speaking!"

"How do you feel, 'Cornflower'?"

"Normal so far. Ask me the day after tomorrow."

The switchboard operator on duty at the regimental headquarters laughed sympathetically. God only knows if I'll live through tomorrow.

"I'm off." Yarik crawled out of the trench. He stopped when he got to the top. "They asked us to pass it along to every soldier: there'll be a general attack when they send up a red flare. Mokhnatov will give the signal to begin."

Again I barely nodded in response.

"If I fall in this attack, I'll fall head first because I h-a-t-e them!"

"Better not to fall."

"I'm not sorry for myself. I'm sorry for my mother." He left, walking with light, uneven little steps.

There sounded the threatening, indifferent thunder of a machine-gun blast. The German gunner obediently answered from the other side. Everything was okay; it was quiet in our section.

Yet today even Yarik's step had an unusual swaying gait, like that of a drunk.

From the steppe came the sounds of scraping and clinking. Soft, elated voices, verging on exultant, flew from one end of the trench to the other: "It's the kitchen! The kitchen's arrived!"

"'Cornflower' 'Cornflower'!"

"'Cornflower' here!"

"Call 29 to the phone!"

"He's not here! He's up ahead."

Number 29 was Lieutenant Mokhnatov, sitting, as always, astride his commander's perch five feet away from me, a dirty-faced little boy with wispy bangs sticking from under his cap. He was glued to his binoculars, the clumsy handle of an antiquated gun sticking out of the pocket of his breeches. It was a loaded flare pistol.

Without hesitation I lied onto the phone that number 29 was not on the command post. Mokhnatov heard me but remained glued to his binoculars.

In the morning, an invisible swarm of shells buzzed and lisped over our heads. Behind the crest where the poultry farm was located you could hear the rumble of shots, reverberating as if they came deep from underground. Right near, in back of us, began to croak the mortars from Ulibochkin's new equipment unit, called the 'Thistles' in telephone code. The Germans answered us with artillery from mortars and machine-guns that flew over our heads, to the rear, and right at us. The helmet fell with greater zeal than usual.

That's when Lt. Mokhnatov's single combat with rear headquarters started.

"'Cornflower!' 'Cornflower'! Give us 29 immediately!"

I'd obediently hand him the receiver.

"They want you right now, Comrade Lieutenant."

He would climb down unwillingly from his observation perch and begin speaking in bored tones with 16, battalion commander Pukhnachyov: "It's absolutely impossible, 16. It would be murder! There's no offensive. We'll fall by our own trenches. Under arrest? Go ahead, Comrade 16. Come on and arrest me. You're welcome to! Don't delay!" He'd carelessly shove the receiver at me and snort, "I'm not here. I went to the platoon."

Finally the commanding bass of 0-1 roared into the receiver:

"Get out of there! On the double!"

The commander of the regiment himself! This time Mokhnatov didn't dismiss it with a gesture of his binoculars. He crawled lazily off his perch and waddled up to the receiver, but answered in a brisk voice according to military protocol:

"Yes, sir, Comrade 0-1. Yes, sir! Sir! We'll try, Sir. We'll do our best."

Before handing the receiver back to me, he leaned over and looked me steadily in the eye. It was the first time I really saw his eyes, transparent and bulging, with needle-thin pupils and irises as gray as the trenches, the skin under the eyes sagging like an old man's. How many times had they seen death close up—both his own men's and the enemy's too? How many times had they gazed out coldly like that, those clear, dangerously empty eyes?

"Listen, sweetheart," Mokhnatov drawled softly, looking me straight in the eye. "I don't like slow-witted people."

I tried to be quick-witted after that.

"'Cornflower!' You're not carrying out orders! You wanna be shot, you motherfucker? Where's 29?"

"They've already sent three men after him! They can't break through—there's heavy fire out there."

Meanwhile Lt. Mokhnatov sat on his perch, his dusty boot resting against the clay wall of the trench, and closely surveyed the field. The antiquated handle of the gun loaded with the flare pistol was sticking out of his pocket, but none of the soldiers scurrying past spared it the slightest glance. Not every loaded pistol gets fired, even at the front.

"'Cornflower'! Pull the line forward immediately! 'Cornflower'! You're ordered to stay at Mokhnatov's side! Not fall behind by a single step! 'Cornflower'! Repeat the order!"

"Pull the line forward, Sir! Stay near 29, Sir!" I repeated deliberately and loudly and looked questioningly at the back of the lieutenant's head.

He advised carelessly over his shoulder:

"Pull out the friggin' connection and send it to hell!"

Mokhnatov was getting me into a dangerous game. To break with my very own hands the connection that had been repaired, and in the heat of battle... If the high command should find out about it, there wouldn't even be a tribunal first, I'd be shot right on the spot for sheer sabotage! But the high command was far away and Mokhnatov was right here.

"'Clover'! 'Clover'!" I informed them, "I'm signing off."

"Just do it quickly, 'Cornflower'. Quickly!"

I yanked out the rifle bayonet that had been stuck in the ground and used as grounding, and hung up the receiver that was now deaf and dumb. The line was repaired and the equipment was repaired, but there was no connection. My buddy Nebaba, who was standing to one side, looked at me with sympathy. He was usually lucky, but I had bad luck even when on duty.

Nebaba's eyes left my face and widened in alarm. I turned around. Behind me stood Junior Lieutenant Galchevsky, holding himself straight as a ramrod, the steel visor of his helmet low over his eyes, his pointed chin jutting out over his visor strap, his eyes beneath the helmet fixed on Mokhnatov's back. He held his heavy submachine-gun in his hand next to the white, tarpaulin top of his boot, the barrel pointed downward.

Yarik Galchevsky stepped over my outstretched legs and shouted:

"Lieutenant Mokhnatov!"

With his chin jutting out, his narrow shoulders squared, and his heels together, he seemed to be standing at attention and you expected him to finish with the words always used at drill, "At your command, Sir." Only this time he had his submachine-gun in his hand, the barrel pointed downward.

"You are foiling the attack, Lt. Mokhnatov."

Mokhnatov stared silently at Galchevsky. Yarik could see his eyes up close. Clear eyes, dangerously empty!

"You're not obeying the orders of the command, Lt. Mokhnatov!"

"Go back to your platoon, you fool!" Mokhnatov said in a tired voice, without anger, too much like an adult speaking to a child.

"To save your own skin you're...

"Junior Lieutenant! Atten-tion!!"

Galchevsky's back, which was already tensed anyway, jerked convulsively. "About face!"

In response Galchevsky cried in a voice like a bird's throaty shriek, "You're a coward, Lt. Mokhnatov! I despise you!"

Mokhnatov's elbow moved back very slowly, his hand reaching toward the strap of his holster.

"You lousy coward! You're only out to save your own neck! You're a traitor to the Motherland, Mokhnatov!"

The steel barrel of the pistol Mokhnatov held in his hand flashed sky blue.

Galchevsky flinched and jerked his gun. His narrow, skinny back shook as if he had a fever to the short rat-tat-tat of machine-gun fire, followed by the belated sound of a discharged cartridge case.

Mokhnatov slid off his perch and, with an unnaturally serious and stern expression in his clear, wide-open eyes, stepped forward, and, as if he had broken apart, fell on his knees and butted his head against the clay gravel under Galchevsky's tarpaulin boots.

Then I saw Vasya Zyablik, the signal man, who'd left the bottom of the trench and run up to us, his shoulders stooped as he jogged along. His thick-lipped peasant face looked unusually rigid just then, and his eyes had acquired the same transparent emptiness as Mokhnatov's. Vasya Zyablik was lowering his gun from his shoulder.

Galchevsky lurched jerkily toward Mokhnatov, then, just as abruptly, straightened himself up after throwing his wide-barreled flare pistol up above his helmet.

Vasya Zyablik raised his submachine gun, aiming at him...

Galchevsky fired. A thick, dense cloud of smoke shot forth and a semi-transparent drop of manganese hung suspended in the blue sky.

"Com-pa-ny!" Galchevsky shouted with a sob in his voice and, gathering momentum for the jump, leaped up out of the trench.

Vasya Zyablik kept his rifle aimed.

The machine guns that had been shooting on the flanks choked and the trenches fell silent.

"Com-pa-ny!"

Galchevsky stood on the parapet, incredibly lanky, his huge tarpaulin boots so close I could touch them if I stretched out my hand, while his small head hidden in his helmet reached up to the skies. Just a little higher, in the engulfing blue of the sky, hung an iridescent crimson drip.

Vasya Zyablik watched him spellbound from the trench, his gun ready, and a strange, inspired expression on his face.

"Listen to my command! For the Mo-ther-land! For Sta-l-i-i..."

The incredibly elongated, lanky, clumsy figure swayed and disappeared.

"Hur-rah!"

It wasn't my ears, but my whole body, my skin and bones, that picked up the commotion in the trenches, feeling through the ground the movement and panting of the soldiers crawling out from under the ground into the open air.

"R-rah!"

Vasya Zyablik suddenly began to bustle about, his thick-lipped face suddenly losing its dangerous rigidity and becoming simply worried. He hurriedly jumped up on the parapet and for a split second his round-shouldered body blocked off the sky, looking unusually powerful as he dashed forward... And then the earth seemed to swallow him up.

"Hur-rah!"

The dull-gray, rusty steppe sloped just like the top of a school desk. There was something poignant about its leisurely, persistent movement toward the sky: the arid and unkempt aspiring to the immaculately pure and unattainably elevated—poverty dreaming of grandeur.

Probably because the steppe itself is too great and vast, people seem too inert in its infinitude; they don't hurry, but wander tiredly toward the blue sky. They wander and try to encourage themselves with the forced, uncertain shout of:

"R-rah!"

In the midst of the pilgrims wandering toward the blue sky a dirty-yellow wadded ball appeared.

"Ah-h!..." Then silence.

A sharp blast hit me softly in the face. The wadded ball fell apart, then sailed off over the red, dreary ground, its tufts of dirty smoke brushing against the men who'd scattered. The distant sky above the unkempt steppe cracked in several places and poured forth a "Rat-ta-ta-ta-tat!" In the steppe something started spinning again, as somnolently sluggish and confused as before. Another explosion, and another! Tufts of dirty-gray.

The trench heaved and the land reared, hiding the steppe, the people, and the tufts of smoke from me. Tremors started shaking the trench. There was gray, greasy smoke with a life of its own, coiling and swelling, and through it the earth streaming upward in a long torrent. The sun began to play hide and seek, hiding in the smoke one minute, then gaily peering out the next. Shell fragments rang out all around. A hailstorm of dry clumps of clay rained down on the parapet, on the dusty bushes of the pitiful wormwood, and on my shoulders.

Somebody behind me tugged at my leg.

"Junior Lieutenant!.. Junior."

The eyes on Nebaba's sallow face were wide-open, whitened by the sky. Only in the bottom of the trench did I realize what had happened: the German artillery had blocked the path of the men who had tried to run back. You couldn't break through the wall of smoke filled with shell fragments and upturned earth.

And the sun played hide and seek, shining one minute, hiding the next.

The clumps of earth still continued to fall in a sparse, tired shower from the burning, cloudless sky. A sound that was a cross between an annoying tinkle and an ingratiating whine could be heard. I didn't realize right away that it was the ringing in my ears. From the silence.

I remembered the phone—the grounding had been pulled out! I stuck the rusty bayonet to which the wire was tied into the ground.

"'Clover' 'Clover'!"

Silence. The invisible fourth dimension where "Clover," "Rye," "Buttercup," and "Lily of the Valley" were located had disappeared. There was only a blank wall.

Nebaba in businesslike fashion set his helmet on his head. He always put his helmet on before leaving the trenches to go on the line. It was his turn to "take a walk."

The puttees of his boots flashed above me against the sky. There was a thin silvery tinkling sound in my ears, the melancholy sound of bullets flying overhead, the echo of an explosion somewhere; by the dry, crackling sound you could tell it wasn't a shell, but a mortar. Then silence! My God, what silence!

Only then did I suddenly realize that I was alone. Completely alone in all the trenches. About ten minutes ago there had been a hundred and some men, maybe even two hundred. They lay in the steppe now, far away from me. I was alone in all the trenches, alone in the face of the Germans. Small and weak, I'd never fired at anyone, nor killed anyone, and only knew how to wind and unwind the cable reel and shout into the phone. And how strange it was that someone as peaceful and weak as me was alone before the terrible enemy that had cowed all of Europe, a Europe unknown to me. I didn't even feel horror at that, only a numbing, chilling anguish. Alone.

He was still at my side. I had managed to forget about him. He lay in the bottom of his commander's ditch, huddled up, his knees pulled up to his stomach, his tangled hair buried in the ground, his right arm broken in an odd place, the unbuttoned holster gaping at its side, and the burnished steel pistol lying behind him, next to his unpolished boots. He had fallen there during an exchange of machine-gun fire such a long time ago that I had already managed to forget about his death.

Silence! The tinkle of little silver bells. I felt through my skin the empty, senseless, lifeless pits surrounding me on all sides.

"'Clover' 'Clover'!"

"Clover" was silent; I had no hope of being saved from my solitude. I felt wildly jealous of Nebaba. Again he was lucky! He was alone too, but not in the empty trenches; he was in an ordinary situation. A telephonist who jumps out of the trench to repair a broken line always confronts war face to face. That's normal.

I heard the sound of steps and the rustle of clothing. I spun around as if stung: there, with his cap in shreds, his strap buckle twisted to one side, his tired and hopelessly despondent face streaked with dirt, stood Gavrilov, the machine gunner.

Lord! How dear he was to me at that moment!

I couldn't calm down, while he just stood there, frowning and scratching his unshaven cheek, as he asked matter-of-factly:

"Maybe we should all group together in one spot?"

"You... You didn't go into attack?"

Gavrilov looked at me with dull amazement, his baked lips twisting.

"What about you?"

"I've got to stick with the phone."

"Like me with the machine gun. You can't run with the Maxim. The others were hand machine gunners—they all..." Gavrilov blew his nose sadly. "Dyozhkin also has a machine-gun station on the left flank. There are two men there—just like us."

How little you need to be happy! I wasn't alone, and I rejoiced—inwardly, of course.

"Only five left from the whole company..."

"Six," I cheerfully corrected him. "My Nebaba went off to fix the break."

"Give it a try. Perhaps he's already..."

"'Clover' 'Clover'!" Not there. He's been gone a long time. The break must have been far away.

Gavrilov sat down next to me, but hurriedly got up again and moved to the other side. He saw Lt. Mokhnatov in the ditch, his bare head butting the ground.

"Petka Gubin, my number two, is also slowly losing his mind. He says his prayers aloud: 'Lord, save us, your people.' But maybe everyone else on earth has gone crazy and Petka's the only of us who's normal?" Gavrilov fell silent and kicked a hole with his heel. "'Lord, save us, your people.' Yet he keeps the machine gun going. They're not exactly chocks either, they're dying too!" He fell silent again for a moment, then with dreary, vicious conviction, concluded: "There's no life for a peace-loving person in this world!"

A shower of earth fell into the trench on one side, followed by a tearful sob, and a black, disheveled body limply tumbled in, twitched, shifted restlessly, then grew still. The only thing you could hear was a heavy, sobbing breathing.

Gavrilov rose very slowly and sighed:

"He's come from there."

I rose too.

His breathing was strained and punctuated by sobs. You could see the movement of his shoulder blades under the brown tunic and the wrinkles on his brown neck, which meant he wasn't young.

"Hey, buddy, are you wounded?" asked Gavrilov.

The guest "from there" moved with an effort and sat up, his face black, the whites of his eyes clear and almost burning, his lips a bloodless blue. He pried open his lips and said with a tearful wheeze:

"Don't know."

"Who else is alive there?"

"Don't know."

"Maybe there's someone wounded we can drag out?"

"Don't know."

However, he made an agonizing effort to think back, a vein pulsing tensely on his blotched forehead, and he started to speak:

"I saw our company leader... Dyozhkin... He was crawling, but he didn't have any legs. Crawling, and not a drop of blood in his face. Give me some water, guys."

And then I saw another one, who emerged from around the bend in the bottom of the trench and limped toward us. I recognized him by his round-shouldered carriage—it was Vasya Zyablik. He behaved very strangely: he'd run five paces, limping, then floundering blindly, climb up out of the trench, peer somewhere into the distance, then jump back in, and five paces later he'd climb out again... He was all askew and looked a mess, his pant legs torn, with no helmet, no gun, his ears sticking out in bewilderment from his dusty, smooth head.

"Why, it's him, the bastard! It's really him!" he said in stunned staccato tones. "He's alive, the son of a bitch!"

And he climbed up again and stuck out his neck, his mouth opened wide as he pricked up his protruding ears.

"It really is! It's him! Walking around... Take a look! Look! It's him!"

Gavrilov and I also climbed up.

The steppe. It was just the same: dreary, rusty, desolate, stretching toward the sky. It hadn't changed in the least. You couldn't see the shell holes from here, nor could you see the corpses either.

A solitary figure was walking—upright—along the steppe located beyond the beyond. They were firing at him, and you could see the dust raised by machine-gun fire on all sides. He didn't duck, but walked with an irregular, unsteady gait, as if dizzy. His awkwardly lanky form was very familiar to me.

"He's alive! Can you beat that! Alive! Because of him they're all dead, while he—he's alive!" Vasya Zyablik was dumfounded, the words tumbling out in a rush through chattering teeth.

"What is he, bewitched or something?" asked Gavrilov.

"Shit doesn't sink... But never mind! Never mind! If the Germans don't get him, then I will... With pleasure... Don't you worry..."

"Forget it, buddy! Don't get excited! He got excited and look what happened—the company wiped out without a trace."

"He plugged the lieutenant! For the lieutenant's sake I'll get him. Don't you worry."

"If he stays alive, that'll be even worse for him!"

Bullets started kicking up dirt in front of our parapet, whining hotly as they cut down the bushes of wormwood. As one man we quickly slid down to the bottom of the trench. Junior Lieutenant Galchevsky was coming closer, bringing the fire with him.

He suddenly loomed up above us, his small head in the huge helmet outlined high against the sky. Bullets whined, crackled, and ripped the air into shreds, but he loomed there, in the earth, with a look of aloof melancholy. His bony little gray face in the depth of the unfathomable universe looked important, like the face of God. Then he bent over and sat down carefully on the edge of the trench, with his canvas boots dangling beside us.

We stood on either side of his dangling boots and goggled idiotically at him.

"Here I am," he said and suddenly shouted tearfully, in the same voice as when he'd call the company into attack: "Kill me! Kill him! Whoever made *If There Is War Tomorrow*, kill him!!"

We continued to stare up at him as if in a trance and didn't understand a thing, while he just sat there, his boots dangling over the edge, howling in a sobbing voice:

"K-i-l-l!!"

Vasya Zyablik grabbed him by his boot and jerked him into the trench:

"Cut it out!"

"'Clover' 'Clover'!" I bent over the telephone.

Silence. I put the receiver down and climbed out.

Nebaba was lying just ten steps away from the trench, his face buried in the dusty wormwood, his left arm flung over the wire that was stretched across the steppe. Just a little bit farther along the sun-baked ground was a crater that had scattered earth in all directions. It had the uneven, spiked star shape of a mine-crater, not a shell-hold.

He was lucky. He was as close to me as a brother and at the same time was a total stranger. We didn't have time to get acquainted.

That was the beginning of our retreat. To the Volga, to Stalingrad....

I saw the Don crossing: the trucks burning near the riverbank, the raised gunbutts, the unshaven faces with bared teeth, the foul language, the shots, the corpses falling into the murky water, and the wounded lying on stretchers, forgotten by everyone, yet neither calling anyone nor even moaning as they maintained a doomed silence. The wounded men were silent, but the wounded horses screamed dreadfully, the hysterical sound resembling women's shrieks.

On the other side of the Don I saw generals without regiments, wearing dirty tunics and torn boots with leg wrappings, majors and captains wearing only skivvies. There was a young fellow near us walking around for a while with nothing on but his birthday suit. Somebody gave him an old coat out of pity. He kept grabbing at our chief's sleeve, assuring him with tears in his eyes that he was the personal adjutant to General Kosmatenko. He begged to be put in touch with Army Headquarters. None of us had the slightest idea who General Kosmatenko was or where the Army Headquarters were at that moment. Everyone laughed with cruel contempt at this adjutant who turned up out of the Don's murky waters, a contempt that only someone who's dressed can feel for someone who's naked. From under the naked adjutant's raincoat stuck out the light, muscular legs of a sportsman.

"Our cause is just!..." The monstrously unjust enemy had advanced almost as far as the quiet Don. And how pathetic we looked, we, the just ones... The naked just, arrayed in skivvies.

And is the one whose cause is just always strong? Maybe it's the other way round? The just are always weaker; they're constrained by something: you don't shoot in the back, you don't hit below the belt, and you don't kick a man while he's down. The unjust aren't handicapped by such constraints. But that means that unenlightened scoundrels will take over the world. Those who inflict pain, who ravish, who deceive. Cruelty will become valor, goodness—a flaw. Is it worth living in such a hideous world? It turns out that the world is not wise, and justice is not all-powerful, life is not precious, and our sacred slogan, "Our cause is just, the enemy will be crushed," is a useless phrase.

But even the general conflagration did not burn Yarik Galchevsky out of my memory. At times I would still see him sitting there on the parapet, and I'd shudder inwardly at his shout: "Kill him!"

Whom? Why, whoever made *If There Is War Tomorrow*. Strange.

Maiden of Light! Where are you, Donna Anna?

Yarik loved poetry, but he loved movies even more. He knew all the famous and lesser-known actors by name. *If There Is War Tomorrow...* There was such a movie before the war. "If Tomorrow..." The war was right now, the war was going on, and the enemy was on the other bank of the Don. "Maiden of Light! Where are you, Donna Anna?" "Kill him!"

It turned out that I wasn't the only one who remembered Galchevksy then. Someone else did too....

A clear moon with the pockmarked face of a Ukrainian cart driver crept out above the steppe. The soldiers slept even on the run, jostling against one another in their sleep; they didn't even have strength to curse each other.

For the fifth day our regiment, which had dwindled considerably, wandered around the steppe, sleeping only two hours a day and trying to find some mysterious Rallying Point. Every time we got close to this Point, it was moved to another place, deeper into the rear, a little farther from the enemy that was driving us back. God helps those who help themselves, of course, but in a soldier's case it's all up to him.

Once the moon was out, it meant that we'd soon be allowed to halt. This was the longest stop during the night. And indeed, the advance detachment had already turned off the dusty track. A closed truck, bouncing along the uneven road, rolled past as it overtook us.

The steppe, which looked turbid in the moonlight, was at rest. Somewhere in the far distance was a rumbling. It was far away, so you could barely hear the war. But you could still hear it, even though we were moving away from it as we stumbled along, hurrying and wearing ourselves out, with only two hours of sleep a day.

They led us up to a truck that had stopped in the middle of the steppe, and lined us up in ranks as best they could, but for some reason they wouldn't let us sit down.

Major Sanochkin, acting commander of the regiment, was annoyed and kept shouting at the men near the truck:

"Okay, but hurry up! Get a move on, for God's sake! These men are tired!"

And then they brought him out... In the dim moonlight, in front of the regiment that was in a stupor from exhaustion.

"Only, for God's sake, don't drag it out!"

These weren't efficient young fellows in the stiff peaked caps worn at the rear. From the midst of the confused ranks they hauled out six soldiers from the commander's platoon, stumbling from exhaustion, just like all of us.

Six soldiers, so tired they stumbled blindly over each other, lined up across from him. He held his head high; it looked small and smooth on his thin neck. He was wearing an unbuttoned tunic and the navy blue riding breeches of a staff commander, but he was barefoot. Behind him lay the boundless steppe, undulating turbidly in the moonlight.

"Come on! Get a move on!"

The six young guys from the commander's platoon knew Junior Lieutenant Galchevsky, the commander of the chemical platoon, by sight, if not personally. Now he was no longer a junior lieutenant, and he had only a few minutes left as a man.

These weren't efficient young fellows who knew their job well. They hadn't stripped him to his underwear, and hadn't even dug him a grave.

Two men immediately stepped forward. One of them held a flashlight over a piece of paper, while the other one solemnly began to read:

"In the name of the Union of Soviet Socialist Republics, the Military Tribunal..."

For some reason these solemn words brought peace to one's soul. It turned out that even in the hectic confusion of retreat, somewhere order was preserved, someone didn't forget his duty; some kind of discipline was alive, the army was alive.

"...has examined the case of the accused, Galchevsky, Yaroslav Sergeyevich, serviceman, Junior Lieutenant, born in 1922..."

Behind him the steppe looked dim in the dispersed light of the moon. The air infused with the smell of wormwood was permeated by the heavenly odor of boiled pork spiced with smoke.

This afternoon our troops detained some quartermaster's trucks on route, that's why even now we could smell the long-forgotten aroma of pork. An amazing smell, it dispelled our tiredness and revived us. The cook from the commander's platoon was the famous Mitka Kalachev, who left his field kitchen on the other side of the Don during the retreat. But he was a crafty old devil! He got the bright idea of using a washtub that he'd acquired to boil the pork in while we were on the move, so that we wouldn't have to wait so long for it to cook when we made camp.

"...And has found Galchevsky, Yaroslav Sergeyevich guilty!" He fell silent and his comrade turned off the flashlight.

The moon was hanging over the boundless steppe as it rested listlessly, and in the far distance you could barely hear the rumble of war. He stood beneath the moon, his thin neck protruding as he picked at the loose overall of his tunic.

The organizers hesitated, scuffling around and whispering to each other.

"Have done with it! What's the matter with you?" Major Sanochkin pitched into them again.

"Give your men the command!"

"No way! Spare us! It's your affair. Just get a move on, move it—our soldiers are dropping from exhaustion!"

Then the one who had read the sentence stepped forward heavily and shouted in a tinkling voice, totally unlike that of a combatant or someone in command:

"As an enemy of the Motherland!.."

Without hearing the usual command to stand ready, the soldiers clumsily raised their rifles to their shoulders in confusion and without any coordination.

At that moment Galchevsky straightened up, tensed, and his ringing voice washed over the moonlit steppe:

"I'm not an enemy! They lied to me! And I believed them! I'm not an enemy. Long live..."

"Fire!!"

The barrel of one of the men in the shooting squad was loaded with a tracer bullet. It shot out in a fiery streak, passed through Galchevsky's thin, fleshless chest, and came blazing out through his back.

He fell on the hard wormwood, on the grass that looked blue in the moonlight.

His mother had a bad heart...

The air smelled of boiled pork. A smell that promised life.

The next day we arrived at Sadovaya Station on the outskirts of Stalingrad, a city that hadn't been destroyed or burned yet and was still bustling. We defended it. In this city the enemy was crushed. Our cause is just and victory proved ours...

December 1969-March 1971

Translated by Lila H. Wangler and Helena Goscilo

Originally published in *Novyi mir,* March 1988

Lyudmila Ulitskaya

Lucky

Every Sunday Berta and Matthias would go to visit their son. Berta would make sandwiches, pour tea in a thermos, and neatly tie a paper string around a broom. She'd take a jar, just in case, and pack all of this in a bag that Matthias had repaired. Matthias would help her on with her coat or her raincoat or jacket, and they'd go to the market to buy flowers. Then they'd wait a long time at the tram stop for the infrequent tram.

With time Matthias was getting more and more squat, and increasingly resembled a mahogany cabinet; you could tell he was a redhead by his dark-pink skin and the brown freckles on his hands. Berta apparently had once been the same height as he, but now she was half a head taller. Unlike her husband, she somehow became less unattractive with the years. Although the wispy mustache that had spoiled her looks when she was young had grown a lot, it had become less noticeable on her old face.

They were bounced about by the tram a long time; inside it was either hot or cold, depending on the time of year, but it was always stuffy. They'd sit impassively; people always let them have their seats. Even when they'd just gotten married, people were already letting them have their seats.

Their route, which left no room for any doubts, took them to a brick fence, led them under an arch, and left them on a neat melancholy path, along which, amidst the greenery or snow or soft damp fog, they would meet old acquaintances on both sides:[*] Isaac Bentsionovich Galperin, with his bright blue little eyes, crimson cheeks, and pale blue baldness; and his wife Faina Lvovna, a thrifty woman with a tightly pursed mouth and shaky hands. Also Ivan Mitrofanovich Smerko, a colonel in the engineer troops, with the broad shoulders of the epic hero Ilya Muromets, who sang and played wonderfully on the guitar and was so young, poor thing; then Borenka Mednikov,

[*] In Russian cemeteries a photograph of the deceased is frequently put on the grave.

two years and two months old, with his faded grandparents, his face vague and distracted; the unlikable Kraft family, burly, clumsy, white-bodied, who announced themselves in elaborately graceful Gothic lettering; the unusually affable old Rabinowitch couple, with their rhymed names—Chaia Raphailovna and Chaim Gabriilovich—in a perpetual embrace, with light-gray hair that had thinned out with age in identical fashion; dry, light, almost festive, they had ascended here in a day, leaving all witnesses to the miracle baffled...

Past the turn, the path narrowed and led them directly to their son. Vovochka Levi, seven years and four months old, had already met them many years earlier with a smile, chosen for the occasion, that parted his lips and exposed a little line of square baby teeth, between which there was a dark gap left by a tooth that had fallen out.

All the other expressions of his pleasant, wide face, in revenge for the fact that they weren't chosen for representation, imperceptibly stole away, leaving once and for all just this one smile from the countless multitude of facial movements.

Berta would take out the package with the broom, undo the bundle, and would fold over four times the newspaper in which it had been wrapped, while Matthias used the broom to sweep the dust or snow off a simple little green bench. Berta would spread the folded newspaper and sit down. They'd rest a little, then tidy up the house—skillfully, without hurrying, but quickly, like good housekeepers.

Berta would spread a paper napkin on the small rectangular table, then pour tea into the slick plastic tops, and make a little stack of identical freshly made sandwiches. This was the weekly family meal which over many years had become the core of the whole ritual, starting with the wrapping up of the broom and ending with screwing on the top of the empty thermos.

The profound silence filled with shared reminiscences wasn't broken by any casual word—other hours and years were set aside for words. After they finished their service they would depart, leaving behind the smell of freshly washed floors and aired rooms.

At home during dinner Matthias drank his usual Sunday half-bottle of vodka. He poured it three times into a large silver glass with a crude design, a Passover glass belonging to Berta's father; three times Berta, who didn't know how else to respond to him, would heave a profound, cow-like sigh. Then she'd take the dishes to the kitchen, wash them a special way, with soap and liquid ammonia, wipe them with a clean old towel, and they would stretch out on the tall bed they shared.

"Oh, you old man, you," Berta said in a whisper, her large lids closing over her little eyes.

"Never mind, never mind," he muttered, and with a strong, heavy movement of his left hand, he would turn his wife, who had turned aside, toward him.

They had the same dreams they usually had on Sunday after dinner—of the incredibly happy eight years they'd shared as a threesome, starting from the unforgettable day, full of sudden changes, when, exhausted by terrible thoughts, she had gone to a gynecologist with her swollen chest and other unusual symptoms without telling her husband. The old doctor, a sister of a friend, poked around for a long time, squeezed her nipples, and after several shameless medical questions, told her:

"Berta, you're pregnant, and you're far along."

Without putting on her bra, Berta sat down on a chair and, wrinkling her old face, burst into tears. The large tears flowed rapidly down the wrinkles on her cheeks, caught on her mustache, and dripped coldly onto her large white chest with its dark nipples thrusting up.

When she told Matthias, he looked at her in surprise—he'd known a long time ago, for his first wife had borne him daughters four times, though the smoke from their bodies had long since dissipated over the pale fields of Poland. He had interpreted her silence his own way, to mean "what's there to talk about?" He had no idea that she didn't know what had happened.

"I'm forty-seven, and you'll soon be sixty."

He shrugged his shoulders and said tenderly: "That means we old fools are going to be parents in our old age." For a long time they couldn't choose a name for their boy, and until he was two months old they called him "ingele"—Yiddish for "boy."

"We should name him Isaac," said Matthias.

"No, children aren't called that nowadays. Better let him be Jacob, in honor of my late father."

"We could name him Judas, since he's red-haired."

"Don't talk nonsense. The baby's really beautiful too, but we're not about to name him Solomon."

They named him Vladimir. He became Vovochka*—reticent, like Matthias, and meek, like Berta.

When he turned five, his father started teaching him what he'd been taught himself at that age. In three days the boy learned the twisted letters that resembled each other, like ants, and in another week he started reading the book which his father had read, from right to left, all his life. In a week he was also reading Russian books with no difficulty. Berta would go into the kitchen and wash the dishes in distress.

"Oh, what a boy! What a boy!"

*Vovochka is an affectionate diminutive for Vladimir.

She was enchanted with him and was terrified of what exuded from him—like the thin, cold trickle of air emitted in the winter from a sealed window frame which touches your bare, hot hand like a needle.

She washed her dishes, whipped cream, which her neighbors could never do, baked pastries and made patés. She developed something of a passion for recipes and completely forgot about insipid wheat kasha swimming on the bottom of aluminum bowls, or watery green cabbage soup, which she used to cook with the young stinging nettles picked behind the collapsing two-story houses, in which at the beginning of the war lived forty-eight, and by the end, eighty eternally hungry, sick, and dirty children. She forgot about the pale blue, endearingly rough heads of the boys, their exposed ears protruding defenselessly, and the thin collarbones and the blue veins in the girls' necks. Her keen love for all these children in general was now focused sharply on Vovochka.

Each day of her life she enjoyed having the chubby redhaired boy near her; she'd often touch him with her hands to convince herself that he was really hers. She'd be bathing him and he'd be screaming, and she'd gaze with delight at his disproportionately large feet and his secret little cone.

When he got older she took the same delight in watching his child's games, which resembled real and boring work: for hours he'd weave little rugs from strips of cloth in various colors, cleverly fastening them together. A Warsaw tailor trained in Paris, Matthias worked in a special atelier that serviced the Party and brought his son scraps of cloth. He helped Vovochka cut them into ribbons...

In her heart of hearts Berta was afraid of her inordinately intensified love, and considered it even a little sinful. Not being prone to self-analysis, she didn't bring her feelings to that threshold where they would need verbal definition, and she lived, inwardly avoiding doing so.

Matthias would come home from work, have dinner, and sit on the couch. Vovochka would ensconce himself beside his father, like a little pie baked from leftover dough next to a big red pie. They read and talked while Berta, full of superstition, left to wash her sparkling dishes.

In her dreams she'd enter the past as easily as the next room, and she'd move about in it easily, happily breathing the same air as her son. The silent presence of her husband, Matthias, with his Stalin-style mustache, was the main component of the scenery. These dreams resembled a show whose charm was like a drug, which she had seen many times and which had been on for a long, long time and always ended fifteen minutes before Berta carried Vovochka in from the street in her outstretched arms—a pale Vovochka, with a fresh scratch on his cheek registering his morning efforts over an airplane model that had replaced the cleverly, smartly woven little rugs. The collar of his striped shirt was undone and in his neck, which was fully exposed and elongated becaue his head was thrown back, not a single vein was pulsing.

It had all happened instantly and recalled a bad scenario—the large red and blue ball had rolled abruptly into the middle of the street, and the boy flew after it as if shot from a catapult; there was a screech of brakes belonging to practically the only vehicle that had passed that whole Sunday, and the ball continued its lazy movement after cutting across the path of the truck and losing all interest in movement, while the boy, with arms outflung, lay on his back in final immobility, still absolutely healthy, his fresh blood, of which not a single drop had spilled, still continuing to circulate in his fingertips, but he was already irreversibly dead.

Matthias was standing by a small mirror on the wall, his cheeks lathered and chin raised as he tried to get at a difficult spot on his neck with the heavy blade in his right hand...

The old folks woke up some time after six o'clock. Berta thrust her thin gray feet into her fur slippers and went to put the kettle on. They sat at the round table covered with a tablecloth as hard as plywood. A festive bowl with homemade honey cakes taken from the sideboard presided in the middle of the table. In the corner behind Matthias stood a highchair, on which, for the fifteenth year now, was hanging a boy's brown sports jacket that Matthias had made with his own hands out of his own jacket. The left shoulder, the one that faced the window, was badly faded, but now, in the light of the lamp, that wasn't noticeable.

"Well, come on then, deal," Berta said and reached for her glasses. Matthias was shuffling the cards.

Translated by Helena Goscilo

From the author's manuscript

Vyacheslav Kondratiev

At Freedom Station

*To those of my generation who found it more diffi-
cult than the rest to fight, but who fought no worse, and
perhaps even better, than the others.*

"Heading west, fellows?" Andrei asked.

"Most likely... Why are you looking like that? Are you jealous?"

"Sure. I've still got a year left here."

"There's nothing to be jealous about. Things are getting hot in the west."

"Well, if it gets started there, it's gonna be a fine kettle of fish here too."

"That's for sure..."

The troop train started to move. Andrei watched as at first slowly, and then faster and faster, the boxcars sailed by with wide open doors, and within Red Army men were standing behind a wooden railing—a whole military unit was heading west.

He stood a little longer, gazing after the train... He could hardly believe that in little more than a year he too would be setting off back home to Moscow, now so distant. When the train disappeared from sight, he went into the station building.

"Where've you been wandering, my boy? Our train is coming soon," said Pogost, who was sitting on a small bench in a careless pose with his legs crossed, and displaying his enormous, ugly army shoes to general view without any embarrassment.

"I was on the platform. Two troop trains heading west passed through." Andrei sat down beside him, but he drew back his legs in their wraps, hiding them under the bench.

He felt awkward in them, especially here off post, in a crowded station, where every now and then women would pass by and they seemed very beautiful, no doubt because he hadn't seen any for so long. In nine months of duty he'd got a pass to go off post only once. And now it seemed almost like a holiday to him to be traveling with Pogost on assignment to the town of Freedom with the opportunity to ride on a passenger train along with civilians.

He and Pogost were just pretty lucky. They had graduated early from regiment school, been given the rank of sergeant, and posted to a railroad checkpoint not far from a small town. And their assignment was hardly tough: to stand guard on a railroad bridge and regulate passage of the troops during maneuvers. The regiment school cadets envied them because the school would have summer camps, where, as the senior staff said, they would make it hot for them—endless marches over volcanic hills and tactical exercises.

Andrei pulled out some cigarettes with long tips and offered them to Pogost. Andrei's mother had sent him the cigarettes. She filled them herself with good Choice brand tobacco; this made it much cheaper than packs.

"Are you nervous, Andryusha?" asked Pogost.

"No, I think I know everything fine. What about you?"

Pogost started to laugh, and Andrei understood the stupidity of his question. Why should Pogost—a construction engineer—be nervous before some sort of exam for the post of bridge supervisor that they would be taking that day at the Amur Railway Directorate, the reason for their trip to Freedom? For him it was peanuts, but for Andrei the exam was important: at least it involved some specialty, and it was especially important because he didn't know if he'd get to study in an institute after the army.

As he smoked Andrei kept glancing at the shoe that Pogost was displaying for effect, and he felt as if everyone walking by was looking at that ugly shoe. He couldn't stand it:

"What are you putting that beauty on display for?"

Pogost burst out laughing again.

"Do you really care about such trifles, son? Forget about it! Look on all of this as an amusing adventure. We'll mark time for one more year and return to our own business. I still find it funny that I, the head of a proper construction bureau, am suddenly summoned to the military commissariat, ordered to show up with my things in a few days, then planted in a cattle car, hauled clear across the country to this Godforsaken hole, forced to wear this overcoat, issued these famous shoes with leg wraps, and forced to do stupid drills and to subordinate myself to our matchless platoon commander with a fourth-grade education. Isn't it funny? And for what? It's good that that's all behind us now and at least we have a job to do. It's true that for now our duty on the bridge is a real cushy job... Well, Andryusha, I think we earned it by laboring without sparing our strength and by the sweat of our brow, amusing ourselves with the game of soldiers within the walls of our illustrious regimental school."

"A lot of trains are heading west, Pogost."

"Well, let them, and good riddance."

"I don't understand you; you're a lot older than everyone, but..."

"But what? Finish what you started to say. I'm not easily offended, you know that. Did I take offense at your idiotic guffaws when I was hanging like a sack on the horizontal bars? Or when our company commander poked me in the stomach, which I couldn't pull up and stick somewhere, no matter how much I wanted to?"

"You weren't mad, that's true. I was even surprised."

"I just admired you young red-cheeked idiots who are incapable of understanding that the main thing in a man isn't swollen biceps but something else, even if it's the number of convolutions right in this spot"—he made circles around his head with a finger. "So finish what you were saying."

"I wanted to say that you somehow don't take anything seriously. Like the article in *Red Star* on 'The Myth of the Invincibility of the German Army' that took up a whole page, and these trains going west..."

"I understand, Andrei, but I don't want to think about war. I was pulled off work on a big project to do marching drills, wind on leg wraps during alerts, and do all kinds of nonsense that's completely unnecessary to me. And you want me to take all this seriously. It's incredibly stupid. I'd have been much more useful in my construction office... And as far as *Red Star* goes, you'll recall that not very long ago it carried articles like 'The Infantry Platoon in an Offensive,' signed by Captain von Paul such-and-such. Remember?"

"Yes."

"So what do you make of that?"

"I don't know," Andrei shrugged.

"Me neither. And we won't rack our brains. Our train will be here soon." Pogost looked at his watch. "On the way back from passing the exam I'll treat you to a beer in the dining car. Any objections?"

"Of course not."

An attractive girl with a braid sat opposite them in the coach, and as soon as Andrei sat down he immediately hid his feet under the seat. Pogost, who noticed this, also refrained from displaying his shoes, as Andrei feared, but he didn't pass up the chance to smile ironically and wink at Andrei, as if to say "I hope you appreciate it—I'm doing it for your sake."

A general conversation didn't get started for a long time. Pogost gazed rather indifferently out the window, and the girl leafed through some magazine, while Andrei opened the newspaper in which he had wrapped his text-books, put them at first on the little table so the titles would be visible (they were institute textbooks!); and then, picking up *The Strength of Materials,* opened it to a marked page and, while pretending to read, cast occasional glances at the girl. The institute textbooks had not made any impression on her; she didn't even give them a passing glance, and Pogost smiled ironically again.

"Quit cramming, Andryusha," he put his hand on the book. "You can't get your fill of breathing right before death. Better tell me how your Moscow sweetheart's getting along, and what she writes. I recall that you got a big love letter recently."

"The letter wasn't from her," Andrei answered dryly, sensing that Pogost would now start to spout nonsense, but not having decided yet how to react to it.

"Not from her?" Pogost feigned astonishment. "Aw, too bad that it's not from her. How can that be? We're tempering ourselves unsparingly here in the rigors of army daily life, we're learning by the sweat of our brow to defend our Homeland, while there in Moscow, under the neon lights, they are start-ing to forget us little by little and writing less and less often." He shook his head as if stricken.

"Cut it out, Pogost," implored Andrei.

But this conversation interested the girl a great deal more than the institute textbooks that had been put out for show, and she glanced at the embarrassed Andrei. Pogost didn't let up.

"You see, miss, here we are in the rigors of daily army life, while they, there in Moscow..."

"Under the neon lights," she continued with a smile.

"Exactly," Pogost burst out laughing.

Andrei smiled too, even though he found the conversation unpleasant.

"Tell us, miss, are you all really so forgetful? Don't you have a friend serv-ing in the army?" Pogost asked.

"No. But if I did, I'd write him often."

"You hear, Andryusha? She'd write often. But yours..."

Andrei stood up abruptly and headed for the platform. As he passed, he heard the girl say reproachfully to Pogost: "Why did you do that? Maybe for him it's something really serious?" Pogost burst out laughing and retorted de-risively: "What can be serious at nineteen?"

The last letter from Zhenya had been a month before New Year's; Andrei remembered it by heart: "I met (imagine—on the street!) a very engaging man. He's a lot older than we are—over thirty—but he's very intelligent. You can have a very good conversation with him about literature, and just in general. Apparently I made an impression on him. But for me he's interesting only as a person. You understand? As a person! For New Year's (even though it's still some way off) he's invited me to a restaurant. To the National! I haven't been there even once! I'm asking your permission to go—may I? You understand, I'm so depressed. There are only girls in the institute, and the available boys are all rejects who weren't drafted into the army. You can't even get a group together to celebrate New Year's. So tell me, may I go? My father's given his permission!"

Of course, her father would allow anything if only she would break off with him, Andrei thought, as he stood on the car platform. He remembered very well the conversation they had before the army. Her father had summoned Andrei into his study (they had a three-room apartment) and, after seating him in a leather armchair, studied him long and silently; then he began without ceremony:

"You understand of course that I don't have anything against you personally, but I can't approve of your relationship with Zhenya due to circumstances you're aware of. So while you're in the army, while fate itself, so to speak, keeps you apart for a long time, I'm asking you to restrain your feelings and try to forget Zhenya. It will be better... for her, and probably for you, too."

"And what does Zhenya think?" Andrei smiled wryly.

"Don't worry about her. We'll try to see that this passes more or less painlessly for her. Only you don't have to write to her from the army. Have we come to an understanding?"

Andrei shrugged and left the study without answering.

It was Zhenya, though, who wrote first to him in the army, cautioning him to reply in care of general delivery. They had been corresponding, although infrequently, but since that letter before the new year there hadn't been anything from her. And all this was serious to him, even though he was only nineteen, but he would never say anything about it to Pogost, who generally didn't take anything seriously except the work he'd left unfinished at the construction office.

When Andrei returned to his seat after having a smoke on the platform, Pogost greeted him with exaggerated joy.

"Our star pupil of combat and political training has finally returned! We were afraid you might jump off the train out of pique. By the way, Andryusha, our enchanting traveling companion's name is Nadyusha. I recommend her to you. Kindly introduce yourself."

"Shchergin... Andrei," he said inertly, still not having put aside his painful recollections...

Upon leaving Zhenya's father's study with a face as red as if it had been slapped, he immediately encountered her mother, who approached him apparently knowing what sort of conversation had taken place in her husband's study.

"Don't pay any attention to it, Andrei. I'm your ally. Zhenya will wait for you. As for my husband... you know his situation. But let's not go on about that," she said with a wave of her hand; and then, coming right up close to Andrei, she quietly added: "In my opinion, he's afraid... of the same thing. You understand?"

"Yes," he nodded. "But I won't come by any more, or call. Let Zhenya herself..."

"Of course, of course," she said hurriedly. "I'll tell her."

Very late that same evening Zhenya came rushing over to his place.

"You gave me up? And did you ask me?" she set upon him right from the doorway. "It turns out I don't mean anything to you?"

"I didn't give you up. I just can't come to see you."

"Rubbish! You will come! I'm grown up! And nobody, nobody can keep us from being together. You understand?—nobody! You want me to stay with you tonight?" she suddenly asked, throwing her arms around his neck. "Do you want me to? I'm not afraid of anything! You want me to?" she ardently whispered. "Just don't be a coward. I'm not afraid!"

"But my mother... Right now my mama's supposed to come," he mumbled, disengaging himself from Zhenya, who had pressed close to him.

No one knows what might have happened had his mother not returned from visiting friends. But even now he couldn't forget Zhenya's dilated, wildly-flashing eyes, her half-open mouth, her crazy words, and his heart would start at the thought that she could be like that with someone else.

"In the summer I'll be in Moscow," said Nadya meanwhile. "My papa and I travel every summer. He's a native Muscovite, but for ten years now we've been in the Far East. He doesn't want to live in Moscow; he says that in two months of vacation he gets more from the city than he got in the years he lived there. And it's true, we go to all the theaters, all the museums. If you want, Andrei, I'll stop by your girlfriend's and say that it's not good not to write letters to a person who..."

"Who in the rigors of army daily life, unsparingly and by the sweat of his brow...," chimed in Pogost, and they all burst out laughing.

"There's no need to see Zhenya, but if you would kindly stop by my mother's..."

"Gladly," Nadya quickly agreed.

"Mama's very lonely; we have few acquaintances and..."

"What's there to explain? Of course I'll stop by," Nadya interrupted.

"And maybe, Nadyusha," Pogost began with a smile, "you'll permit my young friend to write to you? And then to hell with all those Moscow maidens there, under the neon lights..."

"If Andrei wants to, let him... write," she replied, somewhat embarrassed.

"As if he wouldn't want to!" Pogost guffawed and slapped Andrei on the shoulder. "Can't you see he's dying of happiness?"

Here Andrei too became embarrassed, and he mumbled:

"Well, if you allow it, if I may... I'll write."

"Then we're agreed!" Pogost exclaimed. "Thank old Pogost, because you're a bit timid for a lad from the capital."

Nadya became curious about Pogost's surname. A *pogost* is a cemetery, so how did the name originate? Pogost explained, and she remarked that in spite of his name there was nothing morbid about him; on the contrary, he was a very cheerful fellow.

Andrei didn't participate in the conversation; he was looking at Nadya and suddenly caught himself wanting to kiss this girl. She noticed his look, apparently sensing something, and fell silent, embarrassed. Andrei became uncomfortable, for it seemed to him that the girl had guessed his wish. "I'm going to have a smoke," he said and got up.

He smoked unhurriedly on the car platform, biding his time, having concluded for some reason that Nadya would come there, and then they would talk without any witnesses, but she didn't come. And why had he thought that she would come? It was just a simple farce started by Pogost and of course it was as a joke that she talked about a correspondence and about how she would visit his mother, and he took it all seriously, now wasn't that stupid? His conjecture was confirmed upon his return when he heard animated voices and Nadya's laughter: no doubt Pogost was again making jokes about him, Andrei. He frowned and sat down on his seat.

"I was telling Nadya about our famous Captain Ivanov," Pogost said. "So don't think that we were picking you apart," he added, smiling.

Andrei smiled too—Captain Ivanov was worth telling about...

When he and Pogost had gotten off the train at a platform marked "77th km," they were struck by a sense of wilderness and desolation: a river, hills, silence, and absence of human life. There were just two lieutenants who got off here and headed in the direction of the bridge, while on the platform near the ticket window stood some elderly captain, whom they decided to ask for directions to the railroad checkpoint.

"Will you permit an inquiry, comrade captain?" Andrei came to attention.

The captain turned around. He was bulky, and his poorly tightened wide belt hung on his bulging stomach; his face was flaccid. He glanced at them with dissatisfaction.

"Wadd'ya want?"

"How do we get to the railroad checkpoint, comrade captain?"

"Ah, I understand. So, you're reporting to me. Bridge specialists?"

"Yessir!" barked Andrei, and the captain frowned.

"Your papers, please…" the captain kept repeating as he examined their documents. "Well, let's get going."

They set off from the platform toward the little checkpoint buildings visible not far away. After going a short distance, the captain suddenly asked:

"What's your attitude toward the female sex? Are you real skirt-chasers or not?"

The unexpectedness of the question confused not only Andrei, but Pogost, too, who shrugged in perplexity and muttered:

"In regard to me, comrade captain, I'm… I'm probably not much of a 'skirt-chaser' as you expressed it, insofar as I've been a bachelor 'til now. And this boy"—he nodded toward Andrei—"in my opinion still has no conception of such things."

"Uh-huh," said the captain, smiling oddly. "I brought it up because I have a young wife here. Very young." It was unclear if the captain was speaking seriously or joking. "And you yourselves can see the crushing boredom here— it's an isolated spot, there's no human contact, a passenger train comes through just twice a day… You can do yourself in."

They listened to the captain without understanding why he was baring his soul to them. Was it heartfelt candor or was he mocking them?

"You, comrade…" he poked Pogost in the chest with his finger.

"Pogost, comrade captain."

"You, comrade Pogost—that's a strange kind of name… I'll dispatch you to the 73rd kilometer, beyond the river. It's the same distance to the bridge as it is from here."

"Yessir, comrade captain. I'm flattered, of course, since I never thought I could pose a threat…" Pogost began, but the captain wearily interrupted him:

"There's no room for two at the post. Get it?"

"Yessir," replied Pogost.

"Did you have breakfast at regiment headquarters?"

"No, we didn't manage to. We were afraid of missing the train."

"We'll find out from the cook if there's anything left."

They continued walking in silence while Andrei studied the captain with interest. He was somehow very civilian, with his belly, loose belt, unhurried, ambling gait, and his strange candor regarding his wife. And very unlike the commanders from the regiment school, who spit out orders crisply, with metal in their voices, and who, of course, didn't engage in heart-to-heart talks with their subordinates.

The 77th kilometer checkpoint consisted of an ordinary railroad shack of prerevolutionary construction, like the ones which stand along all our railroad tracks, and two contemporary army-style buildings—a canteen and a Red Army barracks. They approached the former along with the captain.

"Vasek!" the captain shouted, opening the door. "Anything left over from breakfast? We've got to feed two commanders."

Andrei was surprised at the address to the cook by name, the familiar tone in which it was expressed, and the cook's cheerful, informal response:

"We'll find something, comrade captain. We'll feed 'em."

"After you've eaten, come see me," the captain said casually, in response to which Andrei and Pogost came to attention and barked in unison: "Yessir! to report, sir, comrade captain!" They barked so loudly that the captain covered his ears with his palms and winced.

"A little quieter, fellows. This isn't your regiment school."

Apparently out here at the checkpoint they didn't stick all that closely to regulations and military formality.

"Well, how does the captain strike you?" asked Pogost, wolfing down kasha with meat gravy. "An interesting guy. And in spite of his simple manner, I think he's well educated, possibly from the ranks of prerevolutionary officers."

In fact they soon found out from Sashka Novikov, the platoon vice-commander, that their captain had been a staff officer in the Imperialist War,* and had commanded a regiment in the Civil War, that he had the Order of the Red Banner, but had been demobilized, and only in the 1930s had been called up from the reserves; but he had been given a minor rank then, and assigned insignificant duties. Actually it was rather insulting to be commander of a company, and a railroad security one at that, after having commanded a regiment, but the captain had been working a long time on getting a transfer to the infantry and a higher command.

Andrei saw the captain's wife the second day. She didn't seem all that young to him, for she was rather thin and pale, with frightened eyes; she certainly was no beauty. But the captain always accompanied her to the platform and the ticket window where she sold tickets before the arrival of the passenger trains; while she was there he would pace about the platform, keeping a sharp eye on the window, and as soon as some lieutenant or other would dawdle at the ticket window, he would direct his heavy steps toward it...

When Nadya learned where they were stationed from Pogost's story about Captain Ivanov, she said it was quite close to their town, and letters would take only two or three days, not like to and from Moscow, which required almost two weeks.

*World War I.

"So you were serious about corresponding?" asked Andrei.

"Of course."

"I thought you were joking," Andrei uttered with relief, and the thought came to him that Nadya evidently was a very fine and unpretentious girl, un-affected, and it would be splendid to correspond with her.

He glanced at her sweet, already tanned face, her honey-blond braid, falling forward across her shoulder, and a feeling of tenderness toward this girl enveloped him, so that once again he felt a desire to kiss her.

"I expect that our renowned Captain Ivanov will let us come into town, and then, my boy...," Pogost broke off meaningfully.

"By the way, we don't live far from the station," Nadya remarked.

"You hear that, Andryusha? Not far from the station! That means you have tremendous prospects awaiting you, so let them there in Moscow, under the neon lights...," Pogost gestured and again started to laugh.

"Haven't we had an awful lot of the 'neon lights,' Pogost?" said Andrei with a slight laugh.

"You're right—I've overdone it," agreed Pogost good-naturedly, and he turned the conversation to another subject.

They sat and talked about this and that, about Moscow and about their "cushy job" at the 77th kilometer checkpoint... Andrei boasted of climbing to the topmost beam of the bridge superstructure and from there in good weather enjoying the view of the town where Nadya lived. She in turn said that their town was very beautiful and fairly ancient, that the Amur River on which the town stood was very broad and mighty, but through binoculars one could easily view the Manchurian settlement on the far bank, and in the recent past Manchurians and Koreans would come across in their little boats on market days and trade in the town...

When Andrei got ready to go out again for a smoke, Nadya also got up.

"It's very hot... I'll go with you onto the platform."

Andrei opened the door on the platform. The blast of air lifted Nadya's braid, ruffled her blouse, and billowed her skirt, revealing her knees. At first they didn't say anything, but after Andrei had closed the door Nadya asked:

"Have you been in the army long?"

"Less than a year... But Moscow and my former life have receded some-where so far away, it's as if they never existed."

"Come on, that can't be."

"It can. In regiment school we were like machines; we had only twenty minutes of personal time per day, otherwise we went from reveille to taps without a breather. There wasn't even time to think about anything. But I had the good luck to wind up in the technical section."

"So that's why you have institute textbooks!"

"You did notice, then. I'd planned to master the first-year institute course work on my own during my army service, but apparently it's not going to work out. Now maybe during the second year..."

"And which institute are you in?"

"The Moscow Railway Engineering Institute. I knew I'd be called up into the army but I took the exams anyway, although..." he thought a moment, "although I don't know if I'll get the chance to study."

"And why not?"

"Just because of... various circumstances." He took a last drag on the cigarette, then discarded it. "Yes, we've grown completely wild in the course of the winter. We got a pass only once. And right now it seems strange that I'm out of formation, riding in a passenger train, talking with you... It's just that this is embarrassing." Andrei touched a hand to his close-cropped head and then pointed to his leg wraps: "I'll never get used to them."

"What nonsense," Nadya smiled. "Can that really be bothering you?"

"It's killing me," he sighed. "I asked my mother to send me boots. Maybe I'll get a package soon..."

"Don't agonize over it," she continued to smile. "Intelligent people don't pay attention to such trifles."

"Nor do you?"

"Nor do I."

Andrei felt relieved, although he still couldn't imagine that anyone might like him in those ugly leg wraps. He decided to boast again and said that he had already been swimming.

"Wasn't the water terribly cold?"

"It was fine... But there was a very strong current; you couldn't swim against it. A little way downstream from our checkpoint there's a small island, and when I was swimming toward it I was almost swept past. The island is completely primitive, and it was very interesting to wander around. It even seemed that some sort of prehistoric monsters would suddenly appear..."

The sudden wish to kiss Nadya that Andrei had felt in the coach had gone now that they happened to be alone on the platform. He just found it exceptionally pleasant to be standing with her and talking... He began to tell her about a certain evening that he couldn't forget. Captain Ivanov had invited him and platoon vice-commander Sashka Novikov (also a Muscovite) to his quarters, treated them to the pipe tobacco that he himself smoked, and after several officers' jokes from the days of the First World War recounted by the captain and conversations of no particular significance, he suddenly frowned and asked them quite seriously, without his usual ambiguity, whether it seemed to them that this year they would have to do some fighting. That wasn't the impression they had. Then the captain sighed: "No, boys, my heart tells me we'll have to. That's why I'm not pushing you. Relax for now, gather your energies. There's going to be a hard war. The Germans will start it, of course, but then the Japs might start to stir as well."

"Is it really going to happen after all?" Nadya asked.

"I don't know. Right now in the daytime when the sun's shining you somehow can't believe it, but then at night sometimes you think about it."

"Are you afraid of war?" Nadya began, then started to laugh. "What a thing to ask! Would a man admit it? But I'm afraid, I don't want war, and I'm not ashamed to admit it, since I'm a woman."

"I'm probably not afraid of it," Andrei replied seriously, so seriously that she stopped smiling immediately. "And I'm not showing off. You understand, I can't tell you everything about myself right now; I'll just say that after a war something has to change. That's what I think."

"What has to change?"

"Oh, I don't know specifically, but something has to."

"And possible death in war? You're not afraid of it either?"

"Death? Of course I'm afraid," he smiled, "but at present I can't imagine it in reality."

They were silent a while, then Nadya asked if he liked the Far East.

"I do. Except it literally is so far. You feel a kind of wrenching separation from home that I've never experienced before... It's very beautiful at our checkpoint: there's the river, the hills, the great breadth..."

"Yes, there's so much space...Really, I couldn't live in a big city... under the neon lights..."

"Well, I'm a city man. Big cities are beautiful, especially in the evenings. I've visited Leningrad; it's more beautiful than Moscow and somehow more historical, even though Moscow is a lot older than Peter.* You wander along Nevsky and you find yourself thinking: this is where Pushkin walked, and Gogol, Dostoevsky, Blok, Esenin... Cities are full of the past, full of history. I roamed around Leningrad even at night, and I imagined that suddenly on one of the white nights I would meet... well, Raskolnikov, for instance."

"How interesting!" she exclaimed. "You probably have a great imagination."

"No, I'm more likely too rational, but Peter, the white nights... you involuntarily start to fantasize. You just can't help fantasizing. Do you understand?"

"I do. Even though my father is a railway engineer, he's terribly imaginative and inventive."

"Where did he finish his institute studies? Not in Moscow?"

"In Moscow."

*Peter (*Piter* in Russian) is an old colloquial term of affection for St. Petersburg (later Leningrad, and in 1991 renamed St. Petersburg).

"Do you know in what year?"

"In 1920, I believe."

"And mine in 1918! It's possible our fathers were acquainted! That's great!"

"You tell me his name, and I'll ask my father. Anyway, when you get leave, come straight to see us. All right?"

"Thanks, Nadya. Of course I'll come by, if only I get leave. You know, it's so good that we got acquainted. I won't feel as lonely now in this remote Far East," Andrei said warmly and sincerely. "You can't even imagine what it means to be in a family's home after barracks life, to sit a while in a home environment. We've all developed such a longing for our homes."

"I can understand..."

Overcome with feeling, Andrei involuntarily touched Nadya's hand, and she did not pull it away. Then he lightly squeezed her fingers. They kept standing like that, holding hands on the breezy car platform, until Pogost intruded upon their isolation.

"Are you all right, kids?"

"We're all right," Nadya smiled.

"That's very good that you're all right. I'm making myself scarce," said Pogost, and he vanished.

Andrei squeezed her fingers again, and blurted out: "I really like being with you!"

"Me too," she said simply, and squeezed his hand also.

The cars clattered, and the nondescript scenery of a monotonous plain floated by; only to the left of the train were there volcanic hills very far off, which appeared blue... And the kilometer posts were flashing past, inexorably bringing the end of the journey closer, and with it also the end of their encounter. Andrei didn't want to think about it; he wished that the trip would never end, that the little town of Freedom would be somewhere at the end of the world.

"Nadya, if for some reason they won't give me a leave, can you come to see us at the checkpoint?"

"Of course I can. But how would I manage to get back? The next train isn't until the morning of the following day."

"We can go to the closest bypass and I'll put you on a freight."

"That's an idea!"

"But we'll have to arrange by letter that you don't come on a day when I'm on duty. They won't let you onto the bridge; it's under guard." He was briefly silent. "If only nothing happens that's... unforeseen."

"And what can happen?"

"A lot of things. What if suddenly there's war?"

"I don't believe in any war. You must have read the TASS communique."

"I did, but our captain just shrugged in response to it."

"Never mind him, that captain of yours!" Nadya tossed her head. "We won't go on about it."

And indeed, why think about bad things on this day, so exceptional for him? He would be corresponding with this sweet girl, and maybe also meeting her. He began telling her that he would certainly take her by boat to the uninhabited island he had spoken about, that they would wander there like the first people on earth; he spoke of other things also. The train meanwhile was nearing the station; the drawn-out whistle of the locomotive had already sounded at the approach semaphore, the clicking of wheels had slowed, and the hissing of brakes was heard.

"We've arrived, my young friends," said Pogost, as he entered the platform and handed Andrei the textbooks wrapped in newspaper. "Are you traveling on, Nadya?"

"I am," she answered in a dejected voice, and squeezed Andrei's hand.

"Your address, Nadya," Andrei remembered to ask about the most important thing and he pulled out a pencil.

The train came to a halt. They stood silently looking at each other for several more minutes until Pogost nudged Andrei. "It's time to go, my boy."

They hopped down off the car step... Andrei was tormented by the thought that he had not said something to the girl, and it was only when the car shuddered, the buffers clashed, and the train started to move that he shouted: "If we don't manage to meet, I'll still remember you!"

"I will too." And she started to wave her hand.

They stood a while longer on the station platform, watching the train leave.

"Is that incredibly serious also?" laughed Pogost.

"Very," Andrei replied.

"What can I say, except that I envy your nineteen years... By the way, has standing on the car platform with an enchanting girl driven all the rules for technical utilization and instructions on signalization out of your head?"

"I guess not," Andrei smiled.

"Well, let's tramp off, then, to that famous administration. We still have to ask around where it's located."

Freedom turned out to be an uninteresting little town, gray and plain, dusty and dirty. There were wretched wooden dwellings even in the center where the railroad administration was located. As they walked around the place Andrei, filled with impressions of the unexpected acquaintance in the car, was not thinking at all about the examination facing him. He was picturing to himself future meetings and correspondence with Nadya; Pogost was not distracting him by conversation, thus giving him the opportunity to daydream. Only when they were right at the administration building did Andrei come back to reality, and the familiar chill always sensed before examinations passed through his breast.

But the exam turned out to be ridiculously easy. Andrei knew much more than was required of him, and the examiners smiled approvingly. On the whole this examination, conducted by civilians, took him back temporarily to his previous life before the army, and a feeling of calm settled over him: the year of army service would soon fly by, and then Moscow, the institute, and the beginning of a real, normal life.

Pogost remained in the building after the examination for some instructions, while Andrei went out into Freedom's little streets in an elated mood, gratified by his brilliant exam performance. He and Pogost had agreed to meet at the station.

He walked along the unappealing, village-like streets, inhaling deeply, pleasurably sensing the springiness of his steps, the strength of his well-conditioned young body, and he even felt like taking a run. He wasn't embarrassed now by his leg wraps or by the clumsy shoes on his feet, for even with them Nadya apparently had liked him a little; she wouldn't have hung about with him on the car platform if she hadn't found him interesting.

He turned off from the main street leading to the station and, whistling, walked along some dusty, unpaved alleys, past small one-story houses. The station was somewhere nearby—one could hear the engine whistles and the signals of the trainmen. Andrei had to turn left, and he looked for some passageway or cattle track leading to the rail line. Such a lane soon appeared; he turned into it, went a short way, and then...

At first he couldn't make sense of anything. In front of him something gray spread... Spread was the right word, because people—and these were people!—were kneeling with their backs toward him and their faces toward a long line of boxcars. And glancing in both directions, he was barely able to discern the ends of this enormous stationary rectangle that sprawled out in front of the cars... Then he caught the sharp odor of unclean human bodies, a distinctive odor of damp padded cotton jackets that never get dried out, of dirty leg wraps, and also the smell always given off by a large number of people jammed together, dirty and hungry.

Andrei reeled... He retreated toward the fence so that the guards wouldn't notice him. The scene began to swim before his eyes, and he couldn't tell if this gray mass was actually moving or if everything in his vision was shifting. From somewhere seemingly distant a command was heard, and the enormous gray rectangle that had been sprawled on the ground started to stir and to move toward the boxcars... Dust boiled up, raised by shuffling knees, and it hung as a gray, hot haze over the people, making everything around spectral, indistinct, nightmarish. This movement on the knees was unnatural, and therefore terrifying...

A shouted order rang out again, and the rectangle froze... The front rows had already moved right up against the boxcars, the black holes of their open doors gaping. Then—another order, and at each door one person got up from his knees. At the next order they got into the car. The rest crawled again on their knees, moving toward the line of cars.

Andrei's vision went black. He pressed a hand against his mouth so that a moan or cry wouldn't escape and stood, lacking the strength to avert his gaze from that mass of dust-covered human beings... But no, not human beings, rather some kind of unknown creature... some astounding monster... "A monster most ponderous, fearsome, enormous..."—the lines of Radishchev's epigraph floated up for some reason. "My God... Father... Can it be that he's like that too—on his knees?" His father—and on his knees! Andrei pressed his hand even harder against his mouth, barely suppressing a moan.

"Go on, get outa here, there's nothin' here to look at," someone's voice reached him.

He raised his head. One of the convoy guards was approaching him, a young fellow with a pockmarked face.

"Go on," he repeated.

"But why... why are they on their knees?" Andrei asked with dry lips.

"Don't you understand, or what? So that the scum don't scatter off. All right, beat it," said the guard in an almost friendly manner, and tramped off.

Andrei cast a final glance at the dirty jackets, the shorn heads, the gray winter caps, and he left, barely able to move his legs, which felt like cotton and refused to obey him. He staggered, and after a few dozen steps halted, leaning on the garden fence in front of some house. He felt sick and he bent over, trying to get rid of his nausea.

Occasional passersby looked with surprise or disapproval at Andrei doubled over, white, his hand still on his mouth. Some probably thought he was drunk. With trembling fingers he pulled out a cigarette, but couldn't light it, for the matches kept breaking. He threw it away and pressed himself even more heavily against the fence.

"Are you feeling bad, sonny?" An elderly woman in a kerchief had halted near him.

"N-no, it's o-okay," he barely managed to utter with trembling lips.

"Let's go to my place; I'll give you some water. Well, come on, let's go," she urged and took him by the sleeve of his uniform, but Andrei shook his head in refusal. "You feel bad, son, I can see that. Your face is blank, you've turned white as a sheet."

They entered the house, and Andrei sank down heavily on a chair. The woman filled a mug for him, and Andrei greedily drank some water, then pulled out his cigarettes.

"Go ahead, go ahead and smoke," she replied hastily to his questioning glance.

Andrei inhaled deeply, then again and again, but the deep draughts did nothing to help him recover. Suddenly the woman asked:

"Who do you have... over there, dear?" and she pointed in the direction of the station.

He started at the unexpectedness of the question and didn't reply, whereupon she continued:

"I saw how you were standing there beside the tracks, and so I guessed. Looking at such a thing for the first time is horrible... But we've seen our fill. They often drive them along our street. So who is it? Your father, probably?"

Andrei nodded.

"So that's how it is," she sighed and shook her head in grief. After a little while she quietly asked:

"How will you fight, son, if a war starts?"

He raised his head. What was she getting at? He didn't understand the connection between what he had seen and the woman's words. He frowned, trying to figure it out, but wasn't in the right frame of mind, for what he had seen loomed before his eyes.

"What am I saying... maybe God will grant that there won't be a war." She crossed herself and offered him more water.

"Thanks, I'll be going." Andrei stood up.

He made it to the station staggering, but didn't enter the building where he had agreed to meet Pogost. He didn't care about him, or anyone else, for that matter. Pogost would wait for the train on which they were supposed to return and could get back alone. Andrei walked out onto the station tracks, sought out a freight train heading east, climbed onto the brake platform of one of the cars, sat down on the bench, and only then did the long-suppressed cry of anguish burst forth.

Soon the train set off. The cars started to clank at their couplings, and occasionally the drawn-out, melancholy whistle of the engine would jar his ears. Andrei sat hunched over, holding his head in his hands—he had never experienced such despair and hopelessness. Not even when his father was arrested. "My father... on his knees, my father... on his knees..." kept pounding in his head, and the car wheels seemed to hammer out the same thing.

He thought about his father constantly. Just as constant was the pain, but until the sight he had witnessed today he had not imagined, nor could he have imagined, the full horror and nightmare of what had happened to his father... Andrei, like everyone else, knew about the camps only from the movie *The Convicts*, where the barracks looked almost like a picture postcard, where the reeducated engineer-saboteurs were well-dressed, with neckties and silver cigarette cases, where the irresistible jailbird Kostya the Captain guzzled vodka and the romantic thief Sonka, accompanied on guitar, sang the heart-tugging ditty, "My wings are all smashed and broken, my whole spirit has been gripped by quiet pain, all my roads have been buried by the silvery dust of cocaine...," where the camp administrators were wise and charming... There was nothing, nothing frightful in that movie. And Andrei had thought that his father, too, of course, was working in his specialty, supervising some sort of camp construction or else designing it, like those engineers in the movie. Especially since in his infrequent letters he would write that everything was fine and that he didn't need anything.

And here was that "fine"... Again there floated before his eyes the enormous gray rectangle of a thousand people on their knees stirring in the dust...

And he, Andrei, young, strong, was completely powerless to change anything, to help. He didn't even know who was to blame for all of this and what it was all for. He was certain that his father wasn't guilty of anything, but, then, what was going on?

Towers appeared on the right side of the track, and soon the train sped by gray barracks encircled with barbed wire... And here Andrei remembered the woman's words: "How will you fight, son?" "Yes, how will I fight?" he repeated to himself. "How will I fight?"...

Nine days later the war began...

1981

Translated by Louis Wagner

Originally published in *Iunost'*, June 1987

Daniil Granin

The Forbidden Chapter

It was 1978, and Ales Adamovich and I were working on the second part of *The Blockade Book*. I forget who directed us to B-ov. The siege survivors we interviewed passed us along from one to the other. We'd heard a lot about B-ov from a number of people and had been trying to reach him for some time, but it was a while before we succeeded. He lived in Moscow, and as the first vice-minister of an all-Union ministry, he was a busy man. During the siege B-ov had been an assistant to Alexei Nikolaevich Kosygin, who was sent to Leningrad as a representative of the State Defense Committee. It was important to us to talk with B-ov in order to survey the blockade from the somewhat different angle of the government efforts to supply the besieged city and to evacuate the population and anything of value. So far we had dealt with individual fates and stories of everyday life, but we felt that the reader should be given a chance to view the entire picture from the perspective of the higher-ups and see things that the siege survivors who froze in their icy burrows did not know.

B-ov put us off as long as he could, but finally he gave in and generously spent a few evenings with us. He was touchingly conscientious about every fact or figure he provided, and when Kosygin was mentioned he meticulously checked some sources for dates, itineraries, names of enterprises. You could clearly sense B-ov's training and the respect he held for Kosygin. This same training, however, precluded any show of real feeling. What it demanded was a precise report, an account, an explanatory note. What did personal feelings have to do with it? Emotions were in the way. Nor was there any place for independent reflections, impressions, conjectures.

We never did get B-ov to tell us about the seven desperate months he spent in the besieged city amid bombardments, fires, and corpses. He appeared only in his official role, Kosygin's assistant and nothing more. He did not consider it possible to act independently, on his own. He was Kosygin's assistant, they were all Kosygin's assistants. Well, what about Kosygin himself? How did he react—was he alarmed, afraid, did he suffer? How did the blockade affect him? After all, his garrison life in wartime Leningrad took place before your very eyes.

He gave us a puzzled look. Such questions had never occurred to him, and anyway... He was somewhat embarrassed and could not imagine how having such feelings might affect his boss's reputation. After all, we were talking about the present chairman of the Council of Ministers, and even during the siege Kosygin had been deputy chairman of the Council of People's Commissars. With persons of that rank one doesn't... And anyway you can't speak for someone else. And then it struck us—why not ask Kosygin himself? Write down his story! Just as we had written down the stories of others in the siege. In this particular case he was just like all the rest. B-ov was obviously flabbergasted by the thought that you could interview and record the chairman of the Council of Ministers as if he were an ordinary survivor. At first he made fun of us, since that was easier than objecting. We insisted, and verily— to him that knocketh it shall be opened; soon he hesitated, groaned, and squeezed forth a fuzzy and cautious "I'll see what I can find out."

In our provincial simplicity we assumed that all B-ov had to do was to pick up the phone, crank out a call to his former boss on the Kremlin hotline, and tell him what he wanted. They were practically front-line buddies, after all, and B-ov wasn't exactly small fry himself. B-ov winced at the impossible nonsense we were suggesting.

I have no idea how our project wandered from that point on through the labyrinths of power. From time to time B-ov would tell us that it was "being cleared up," "considered," "something had to be checked," "things were moving"... Then they stopped moving. And then they moved backwards. We were never told the why and wherefore, and Kosygin's name was never mentioned in our telephone conversations. We spoke in allegories. We figured that we were entering a special sphere of governmental communication. Who the heck knew—maybe their constant secretive and jittery "Not something I can discuss on the phone" was in the normal order of things.

Now we were sorry we'd gotten B-ov involved. If only he would give us a clear yes or no and stop beating around the bush. But it turned out that something had clicked somewhere, and there was no going back.

One day B-ov called me in Leningrad and asked me to come to Moscow the next day. Getting a ticket on such short notice was not easy, but I realized that not even B-ov—much less the person he represented—could take such trifles into consideration.

I went to Moscow. Toward evening B-ov picked me up, and we set off for the Kremlin. On the way he told me that they had agreed to see only me, and there was nothing to do about that.

Noiseless corridors, guards, staircases, passages—everything clean and glistening. We arrived at the waiting-room right on time; we were expected and were immediately ushered into the office.

I had been aware of Kosygin for many years. He was there among the portraits that we carried in demonstrations and in the ranks of portraits that lined the streets: they were always dressed in the same black suits and the same ties; only the medals were different—some Heroes of the Soviet Union had one gold star, others two. They stayed around for years and decades without aging. Invariably benevolent and severe, on television these men would file in to the Presidium, start clapping at the same time and finish at the same time. What did we know about them, their personalities, opinions, passions? Nothing at all. Nothing about their wives, or their friends, or their children. No one had ever heard about them going out on their own for no particular reason to buy something in a store, take the trolley-bus, chat with passersby, go to the movies or a concert. Their individual identities were carefully concealed. However, Kosygin was different in some respect. Perhaps it was his gloominess that made him different. He did not attempt to conceal it, and that had a certain appeal. His gloominess seemed to run counter to all the eulogizing and chatter and promises of impending triumphs. By piecing together the most trivial little facts and vague intuitions, we ignorant little cog-wheels developed a certain sympathy for this harried workhorse straining for all he was worth to drag his load up onto the road...

The face beneath the short bristly hair was knotty, weary, unsmiling. No preliminaries, just the matter-of-factness of a man used to deciding things quickly and not merely chatting. But that was exactly what I had to do—chat, get him to reminisce, disturb his matter-of-factness. So instead of asking questions I began examining his office. Not attempting to conceal my curiosity, I purposely gaped with the interest of a writer at the oaken wall panels, the enormous desk in the middle of the room, the strips of carpet, and the heavy armchairs. Somehow this spacious office and tall windows and view seemed familiar. As if I had seen all of this, but when?... Kosygin noticed my confusion. "This used to be Stalin's office," he said.

So that was it! But of course. How many photographs and films we had seen of Stalin puffing his pipe and pacing this carpet beside this table. He worked here for many years.

Immediately I was on my guard, taut and bristling.

"M-m, yes," I drawled with feeling—not with awe, but something I didn't understand myself. Kosygin threw a glance at me, and his faded little eyes grew cold.

The three of us—Kosygin, B-ov and I—sat down around a little table near the entrance, some distance from that desk. There was a white telephone on the table. Not once in the course of the evening were we distracted by a call, and no one came into the office.

I got out my tape-recorder, the little tried and tested tape-recorder that had served us faithfully during a hundred interviews already. But Kosygin shook his head disapprovingly. "No recording!" Why?—I stared at him in bewilderment. "No recording," he repeated. How about taking written notes? That was allowed. And he announced that before the edited notes were included in the book he definitely wanted to read them. Further, mention of his personal contributions was to be minimized, his role was not to be inflated. All measures were taken in collaboration with the Military Council and the city organizations.

All of this was set forth drily, unemotionally, with no explanations whatever. From the very outset I was given to understand that this was not such a simple matter, would it please me to note. He waited inquisitively to see whether I would refuse.

Well, then, what did I want to talk about? I enumerated my questions. It was a known fact that by the winter of 1941 two thousand railroad cars loaded with valuable equipment and non-ferrous metals for the munitions factories had piled up in the Leningrad switching yard. Why? Couldn't they have been sent off before the blockade closed the city? Why did the State Defense Committee have to send its representative, that is, Kosygin, to Leningrad? How was the Road of Life organized to evacuate both all sorts of machinery, tools and scarce supplies and at the same time starving children, women, skilled workers, scientists? How were choices made?

B-ov sat straight, silently aloof. A witness, perhaps? It seemed as if we were engaged in some sort of legal proceedings, a kind of ritual intended for person or persons unknown.

Kosygin began answering in a roundabout way. Soon I realized, however, that he was not answering at all, but merely telling what he wanted to tell regardless of my questions. The siege survivors we had interviewed similarly would talk not about what I had asked them, but about what they thought was interesting. That was fine with me, especially since it really was interesting. And he told it well—succinctly and to the point.

A commission was sent from Moscow to Leningrad in late August: V. M. Molotov (Chairman), G. M. Malenkov, L. P. Beria, A. I. Kosygin, N. G.

Kuznetsov (Navy Commissar), P. F. Zhigarev (Commander in Chief of the Air Force), N. N. Voronov (Commander of Artillery).

"We went by plane to Cherepovets. We couldn't get any farther that way because of the air battles. In Cherepovets we took a locomotive and a railroad car. Not far from Mga we came under bombardment. We got out of the car and took cover in a ditch. Up ahead we saw the glow from the burning station and warehouses and settlement. The rails had been demolished. There we sat. 'Let's take a look at what's going on up ahead,' I said to Kuznetsov. Off we went. There were repair crews here and there, but they were barely stirring. There was a troop train and guards. We went up to them and asked about it. A sentry shooed us away with an oath. Just think—a People's Commissar and me, vice-chairman of the Council of People's Commissars!" he exclaimed with benevolent surprise. "We demanded to see the commander of the train. He appeared and asked us to excuse them. It seems they were a Siberian division bound for the front. Through them we managed to get in touch with Voroshilov in Leningrad. He sent an armored train to get us—two cars and anti-aircraft guns."

I wrote all this down verbatim. It was quite an impressive picture: huddling there at night in a wet trench were practically all the highest officials of the government and army—there amid wailing bombers, thundering anti-aircraft guns, and blazing fires. It was the first time in their lives they had been in such a scrape. They hunched up and hugged the ground. I know myself the terror of the first bombardment at the front. It makes you wonder how they behaved—the all-mighty Beria, and Malenkov, and Molotov—how they acted when they got even this little taste of the war.

Toward morning they reached Leningrad. They went to the Smolny and assembled the command. Voroshilov, commander-in-chief of the Northwest Axis of Operations, reported on the situation at the front. The German attack had not been halted, and armies were advancing on the city from several directions. The situation was confused, and control of the fronts was breaking down. In the evening the commission summed things up. Having several military councils—for the northwest front, the city, the Krasnogvardeisk fortified region—created a muddle. It was decided to set up a single military council, establish an independent Karelian front, and allot it such and such units.

Even at that time it became clear that the leaders of the city failed to understand the danger threatening Leningrad and had not bothered to provide for the evacuation of the population and industry.

Kosygin's assessment was cautious. One could have made a more severe judgment. The attitudes and propaganda Adamovich and I had encountered from that time, for example, encouraged bravado and portrayed leaving the city as cowardice and lack of faith: "We, true Leningraders, will not desert our city!" And this had made organized evacuation difficult.

The commission had to decide whether Voroshilov should be left in command and how to coordinate the army and the Baltic front. And behind all this was the fateful question—can we hold the city? The worst scenarios had to be foreseen. If they could not, then what was to be done with the navy, with the population, with the city? The next day they broke up into groups. Molotov took charge of the Smolny, Beria of the NKVD, Kosygin of industry. Molotov told Kosygin: "You stay here: Stalin's orders. We'll get in touch later." Kosygin remained to organize the eastward evacuation of enterprises. The specialists had to be sent along with the factories.

Soon Headquarters recalled Voroshilov, and Zhukov took command in Leningrad. "We gave Voroshilov a warm send-off with a friendly dinner in his honor, so that everything was quite decent and not the way some novels have described it," Kosygin emphasized. He tried to arouse sympathy and respect for Voroshilov: "His very name was an inspiration, and his visits to the front raised the morale of the troops."

I recalled our retreat in August, the September battles near Leningrad, the retreat from Pushkin. There was no communication with the staffs, we weren't supplied with shells, no one knew what was going on, the officers gave orders every which way. Tales of Voroshilov's legendary exploits met with sneers and even abuse. Somewhere, we'd hear, he had roused the troops and led them on a charge. What the hell did we care about the great warrior and his charge! Two months of combat had taught us a lot. We understood that if the commander of a front leads a charge it's out of desperation rather than valor. By the middle of September the front crumbled completely. We abandoned Pushkin; we simply ran. The enemy could push right to Leningrad through our sector with no obstacles whatever. That was what we soldiers had gathered from what we had seen along our segment between Shushary and Pulkovo.

I could have told Kosygin another thing or two about what Voroshilov got us into and about changes we felt even in the trenches when Zhukov arrived. I didn't interrupt, however, because I realized that Kosygin was no military man and knew nothing about the Leningrad front. As to the siege, he knew things unknown to anyone else...

He gradually warmed to his subject, describing with obvious relish the scale of the aid reaching the besieged city (it was already January 1942), how he managed to mobilize the Party committees of various provinces to gather provisions and arrange for the reception of evacuees. He remembered names, quantities of foodstuffs and machinery, names of enterprises. He had a remarkable memory. Judging by the freshness of the pleasure he was experiencing, I think that he was telling about all this for the first time. His impassive voice mellowed and he got carried away into digressions that did not seem to be immediately relevant to our topic. But he found them interesting. One concerned October of 1941 in Moscow—the most critical days of the war. Moscow was hurriedly being evacuated; the diplomatic corps had left for Kuibyshev; performers, the Academy of Sciences, People's Commissars had already been sent off... Among the leaders staying behind were Stalin, Malenkov, Beria and he, Kosygin. Incidentally, when he organized the evacuation Kosygin put Nikolai Alexeevich Voznesensky in command of the train carrying the government officials. Voznesensky was irritated by the task. He had a hot temper and people were afraid of him, particularly since he was one of Stalin's favorites. Stalin received him every evening. Voznesensky threatened to complain about the idiotic mission Kosygin had given him. It should be noted that Voznesensky was already a candidate member of the Politburo, and that meant a great deal.

"I didn't back down, and soon Voznesensky gave in: 'To hell with you then, I'll take charge,' he said. But I wasn't afraid—we'd been friends since our Leningrad days..."

Suddenly Kosygin fell silent, interlocking his fingers as he checked himself. Hardly anyone had heard of Voznesensky. Everything had been done to make sure he would be completely forgotten. The same went for the "Leningrad affair." It never happened. It left not a trace, especially since it was not preceded by any debate or opposition, and no one was unmasked. And in fact there was nothing to unmask. There was no public trial. They were liquidated in silence. There were hasty denunciations and condemnations, but no one really understood why or for what.

So they were friends... Nikolai Alexeevich Voznesensky—one of the best educated and talented in that Politburo. "One of"—I said that out of habit. He was in fact the best educated, most talented and competent economist around. At the same time they liquidated his brother (the RFSFR Minister of Education and a former rector of Leningrad University) and his sister, Party secretary of a Leningrad district committee, their entire remarkable family. They were all simply lumped together with the Leningrad leaders—P. Popkov, Ya. Kapustin, and A. Kuznetsov, who at that time was already a secretary of the Central Committee. This happened four years after the war, in 1949-50. Those who happened to survive and returned from out there in the sixties told me how Kuznetsov and the others were tortured. They were forced to admit involvement in a conspiracy to set up a separate Russian Central Committee, make Leningrad the capital of Russia, divide and split the Party... In other words, a sloppy cock-and-bull story even for those days. It was Malenkov who came bearing it to the Leningrad Party organization, and he did not worry much about its plausibility—what the hell, they'll swallow it anyway.

Who was struggling for power with whom—Malenkov with Beria, or perhaps both of them against Voznesensky—is anybody's guess. Getting rid of Voznesensky suited the others as well, since Stalin seemed to be thinking of him as a successor. The machinery of slander was very refined.

Kosygin, of course, knew the details of the terrible repressions that emptied Leningrad and spilled over into Moscow and other cities. They took former Leningraders, and not only them. By some miracle, Kosygin survived—almost the only "big" Leningrader who did. During that winter of 1949-50 they could have come and taken him away at any moment. Outwardly he remained on the pinnacle of power. He was respected, feared, but he himself lived day and night in constant fear of arrest. To him, death was something quite different from death to us soldiers at the front, where it came in desperation or by accident with the whistle of a bullet or the burst of a shell; nor was it death in the siege—quiet exhaustion, a dying away... He knew very well what they did to his friends, he knew about death amid torture and mockery...

Did he realize the infamy of what was going on? Or did he forgive everything because it passed him by? No, it would seem he had not forgiven... But did he excuse Stalin? How could he excuse him? Did he let himself think about it? Or perhaps he drove such forbidden thoughts away to keep them from interfering with his work? Did he become accustomed through the years to driving them away, to not giving anything like that a thought? Where do they go, these suppressed doubts driven into the underground of the mind; what do the old fears become? It was impossible to read anything on his hard, tidily arranged face.

"Why was he..." I started to say about Voznesensky, "If he was in Stalin's good graces, then why..."

But Kosygin would not let me finish. As if there had been no pause and I was interrupting him, he held up his hand to stop me and went on with his story. Later I realized the meaning of this deterrent gesture.

One after another he presented fascinating details of the evacuation of the central government Sovnarkom Building on October 16—the doors of the offices wide open, piles of papers rustling underfoot, telephones ringing everywhere. Kosygin dashed from office to office, shouting hello into the phones. No one answered—silence at the other end. He realized that they were checking to see if anyone was still in the Kremlin. And so he ran from phone to phone. To let them know that at least someone was there...

Here I interjected a story about our company lieutenant, who ran from machine gun to machine gun as we retreated, firing off bursts to make the enemy think we were still in the trenches.

One of the callers had identified himself. He was a well-known figure. "Well, are we going to surrender Moscow?" he asked matter-of-factly. Kosygin lashed back at him: "I suppose you're prepared to do so?" And cursed. He never cursed, but now he did.

He went to Leningrad again in January 1942. This was decided shortly before New Year's. On December 31 he was visited by Chairman of the Leningrad Party Committee P. Popkov, who was in Moscow on official business. He and Kosygin were friends—they were from the same part of the country, and Kosygin had once held the same post in Leningrad. It grew late as they talked, and Kosygin suggested that they eat dinner together. At that point Voznesensky phoned and asked where he was planning to greet the New Year. "I don't know." "Come over to my place." "All right, but I'm bringing Popkov with me." "Good enough." They agreed, went to Voznesensky's, ate dinner there, and their host suggested going to see a comedy. After all, it was New Year's, so they went to a special viewing on Gnezdnikovsky Street. They were sitting there watching and laughing, when suddenly the man on duty came in and told Kosygin he had a phone call. "Comrade Stalin wants to speak to you." And in fact it was Stalin looking for him. He asked what Kosygin was doing. "Watching a movie." "Who with?" He listened, paused, then asked: "How did you happen to get together?" Kosygin explained in detail what had happened. Stalin said: "Leave them and come on over to see us." Kosygin went. It was three in the morning. Sitting around the table were Malenkov, Beria, Khrushchev, someone else. They drank, everyone was in a good mood. Beria was joking about how they had huddled in the ditch. And at this point Stalin said: "Kosygin, it would be a good idea if you went to Leningrad. You know everything about the place, and we have to get the evacuation organized."

"And that was how I got my mission."

"Well, well," I said. "Stalin was quite a guy, suspecting his loyal comrades-in-arms every step of the way."

I blurted this out involuntarily, for I felt sincere sympathy for Kosygin.

He glowered and suddenly banged his palm on the table so hard that the telephone bounced.

"Enough! What do you know!"

His shout was crude, angry, rash—a slap in the face quite out of keeping with the entire interview.

I flushed red. His bloodless gray face broke out in crimson blotches. B-ov lowered his head. The silence rasped like a phonograph needle on a record. I put my pencil in my pocket and banged my notebook shut. To hell with the interview and my notes and the information. We'll get by without it. I don't have to take this high and mighty crap from anyone.

But Kosygin was ahead of me. He didn't exactly smile, but his face changed. He shook his head as if to admit that he had flown off the handle and said in a conciliatory tone of voice: "It's best we don't talk about Stalin. That's another story."

And immediately and with no transition, he began telling about his preparations to go to besieged Leningrad in January 1942—how he organized convoys for the Road of Life, got drivers, repairmen, buses. In that cold, after all, women and children could not be transported across the lake in open trucks.

I took notes mechanically, still unable to regain my composure. Why the devil did he tell that story about Stalin? You'd think he would realize that anyone would have reacted just as I did. If you've got a pain somewhere, why the hell keep picking at it? Is he a Stalinist or what is he? Why, in fact, had he left everything in this office just the way it was? Out of respect? Out of fear?

Out of the corner of my eye I again examined the bulky furniture—gloomy and solid, devoid of any embellishments or distinctive marks, a triumph of bureaucratic style... The massive door behind the desk through which the Leader of the Peoples would noiselessly step in his soft boots.

A quarter of a century later his spirit was alive and well and could be clearly sensed among these ordinary surroundings. I don't know whether such spirits of the past exist or inhabit the places in which they once lived, but I could feel some such devilry hovering there, and the present occupant must have been all the more aware of it. He, after all, could vividly picture how Voznesensky, and Popkov, and Kuznetsov, and the thousands of others liquidated in connection with the "Leningrad affair" had their fates sealed here in this room. He knew that here it was decided to deport the Kalmyks, the Chechens and the Balkars from their homelands, that here was where the different campaigns were launched against adulation of the West and cosmopolitanism, against the various Shostakoviches, Zoshchenkos, and Akhmatovas.

Good Lord, what prayers and curses sped to the walls of this respectable office from all the jails, camps and prisoner convoys. These bloody specters of the past wandered about here, restless to this very day. Where else could they go? Telephones rang, papers rustled, ministers, vice-ministers, briefing staff held their meetings, and secretaries darted about obligingly among the fleshless apparitions. The past operated invisibly, like radiation.

A Stalinist, not a Stalinist—such simplistic labels were inadequate. It wasn't necessarily because of Stalin that he flared up; here too you have to try to probe a little deeper: you have some facts presented to you, you're given a striking incident—go ahead and interpret it as you wish. But not out loud! And don't ask for conclusions! Facts are sacred, interpretations are free... This is not exactly caution but a condition of survival. Mention not and thou shalt remain unmentioned. That's been learned, become a habit, gotten into the blood. Any doubts about the Leader's righteousness are dangerous. The higher you rise the more cautious you have to be, the more thoughtfully you have to behave. Weigh every gesture, every glance. A false step meant a fall, even death. No wonder most of the members of the Politburo perished.

It was an expensive education. As you rose your personality was planed away and disappeared. Fyodor Raskolnikov once rather aptly described how Stalin trampled the souls of his confederates, how he forced his brothers-in-arms to wade in torment and disgust through the pools of blood of their former comrades and friends.

There was plenty of fear to go around. For everyone. Out of nowhere suspicions would raise their monstrous heads: Ah, a foreign agent, perhaps? Fear paralyzed the most honest and decent.

"That was the whole trick—give them a scare. Everyone was afraid," young people chime in scornfully.

Just try to explain to them that besides fear there was faith, deification, hope, the joy of accomplishment—all sorts of things tied together in a tight knot. Even my generation cannot understand it, and later ones do not even attempt to try. "Respect?" young people ask. "For what? Show us!" Their simplifications are presumptuous, insulting, unjust, but that is probably how the past is always treated. It's either glorious or worthless.

When he got to Leningrad he concentrated all his efforts on the Road of Life—the only artery through which blood was still feebly pulsing to the dying city. Day in, day out he set things into rhythm, straightened out the bottlenecks and chaos on both sides of Lake Ladoga. He had to get rid of the superfluous orders and empty chatter, and resolve conflicts between civil and military authorities, sailors and infantry, sick and healthy. These whirlpools had to be channeled into a smoothly flowing stream to get two, five, fifteen times more people out, and flour, canned goods, grain and meat into Leningrad. A pipeline was laid across the lake to supply the city and the front with fuel. They sent coal to the power stations. Communists on the eastern shore of Ladoga were mobilized to get supply depots in order, because the storage of foodstuffs was in an awful mess. Back and forth he travelled along this road. When the ice broke up he took a launch. Once he came under heavy machine-gun fire from the enemy shore and barely got away with his life. He told about all this rather in the casual manner of the combat veteran. It was a bothersome job done on the run, with no office or paperwork, and it was a front-line mission that yielded precise results—so and so many people saved, including those evacuated to the rear and those who were supplied with food. The greatest months of his life were spent among stacks of light, hunger-dried corpses, bombardments that came like clockwork, the wail of sirens, artillery shelling, sleep in the stuffy, musty bomb shelter at the Smolny. Strange to say, most of the blockade survivors I interviewed thought that this tragic, most terrifying period was at the same time brightened by a sense of elation. Never had they breathed such freedom; people everywhere opened up and were their real selves. This seemingly impossible combination of grief and happiness is present both in Olga Berggolts's poetry about the siege and in Dmitry Sergeevich Likhachyov's notes, where he says: "Only people dying of starvation truly live; only they are capable of the greatest vileness and the greatest self-sacrifice."

In Leningrad Kosygin was his own boss. He was spared the daily oppression and to some extent, at least, was a free man. So he remembered this time differently—with gratitude. He scurried about the factories selecting machines, presses, equipment, and specialists to be evacuated. As quickly as possible he got children, parents, anyone who could still walk, ready to be sent off—by trains from the Finland Station, then on to buses and over to the other shore, and there they had to be received, fed, given medical attention, and then these hundreds of thousands of starving, exhausted, helpless people on their last legs with their scanty baggage, their clothes, photographs, remnants of their former lives, had to be sent off deep into the rear. A coordinated system had to be organized between the army, the militia, the doctors, the railroad...

Suddenly he remembered something and stopped short: No, no, everything, of course, was a collaborative effort, with the Military Council or the city Party committee... He enunciated this distinctly, as if it was meant not only for me... The collaboration was all the more intense since he was surrounded by old friends and comrades such as A. A. Kuznetsov (he was even some sort of relative), and Yakov Kapustin, and V.S. Solovyov, and V.S. Yefremov, and B.S. Straupe... half-forgotten names from the Petersburg Old Guard that were still around when I returned from the war. The stratum that remained after the Kirov affair. When Kirov was murdered there were also mass reprisals in Leningrad, and almost all of these Leningrad leaders, specialists, and economists perished.

During the "Leningrad affair" purges again began to mow people down left and right. There was no stopping them. Everyone notable, original, everyone who had survived the horrible war years with honor intact, who had advanced in the system, was ripped out by the roots. I was working for the Leningrad Power System at the time. You'd come to headquarters and find that this person or that person wasn't there. Where is he? Silence. Power station managers and chief engineers disappeared. Next door, in the District Party Committee at the Smolny, it was the same thing. The city fell silent. Yet another calamity—who knows how many that made. One fire wasn't out before another flared up. What had this great city not gone through—before the war, during the war, after the war. Punishment upon punishment—not a single bitter cup passed it by. They tried to force it to bow down, turn it into a provincial backwater, make it look like all the rest.

Kosygin was a native of Petersburg. I don't remember apropos of what, perhaps of nothing in particular, he mentioned he had studied at Petrovsky Real, now the Nakhimov School, the one with a black bust of Peter the Great high up in a niche of the building. He happened to have been in Leningrad the previous year and had dropped in just to take a look at his childhood classrooms.

"Just think," he said with irritated perplexity, "they have bunk beds in the dormitory. As if there wasn't enough space. The aluminum spoons in the dining hall are all bent. What's the matter—can't we take better care of our future officers?"

What irritated him the most was that the place was shabbier than during his school years.

It is risky to go back to the places of your childhood, for they usually hold only disappointments. And yet if you do not look in on your childhood now and then it will become choked with weeds and die. I was pleased that he should like his childhood and want to return to it. Boris Borisovich Piotrovsky, director of the Hermitage, relates that Kosygin came to the museum once and asked to be guided through the old exhibition, through the rooms visited by tours before the Revolution. They found someone on the staff who knew the layout of the old Hermitage. Kosygin confided that he would very much like to look at things his grandfather had once shown him. And for a long time he browsed from room to room—stopping, recognizing, amazed at how many of his own childhood memories he had retained. During the entire time he had been director, Piotrovsky could not remember a single high-ranking leader who had visited the Hermitage—not with a delegation, but on his own, simply to admire its treasures. Kosygin was the first. Not even the secretary of the Leningrad District Committee had found time in all his years there to take a stroll through the Hermitage.

What was the most complicated part of his work in the besieged city? That was what I wanted to find out. You are always on the lookout for clashes, conflicts of personalities and opinions, difficult problems. Sure they were friends, but he still had to get hold of Kuznetsov and Popkov and get them moving to keep the Road of Life in operation. And things were not so simple with Andrei Zhdanov, either, especially since Zhdanov never visited the city or the frontline detachments and knew little about local conditions. There were many complaints about this from others we had interviewed. What were the disagreements between the two men? That there were some was common knowledge. It is no coincidence that in his account Kosygin did not once mention Zhdanov in any context.

"Disagreements?" Kosygin looked over my head out into the distance, and his wrinkles slowly joined in a humorless smile. "There was no room for any disagreements... No room at all," he repeated with insistence. "General Khrulyov, for example, helped us in all sorts of ways."

He switched the subject to Khrulyov, then went on to the Leningrad militiamen, who continued working even though they were dying of hunger. Beria had to be pressed to send fresh detachments, which were of enormous assistance.

"Beria didn't want to... Things between Stalin and Zhdanov weren't going so well by then," he interjected as if in passing. "That was Beria's doing..."

We touched on the foodstuffs that went through Mikoyan. Here as well, I gathered, there was friction between Mikoyan and Zhdanov, and Zhdanov had reason to complain to Stalin about him. All of this made supplying the city even more difficult. Kosygin was forced to maneuver and take into account the complex relationships between the leaders. From Leningrad it wasn't so easy to get a good look down the corridors of power. His sparse remarks illuminated a little bit of it—just enough light to let you take a single step without stumbling. I found it difficult to picture those corridors of power. What came to my mind was another image more familiar to me—a transformer substation, high-voltage switchgear, hanging wires, insulators, copper bus bars. The air is saturated with electricity, there is crackling and humming all around... In violation of all the safety rules, I worked once under the high-tension wires, right at the bus. Slowly, keeping your eye on the dull copper, just inches away from its baritone drone, you raise your hand. You measure each movement, your muscles contract, all around you you feel the electrical field ready to pierce you with a lethal bolt at any moment. We felt something of the same protracted, impossibly tense fear once as we crawled through a minefield...

Kosygin went on with his story, skillfully skirting the forbidden places, cleverly maneuvering, not letting me examine, penetrate, inquire... There was a row of locked, sealed doors on either side. But why? Who was being locked out? He? We? He should take advantage of the opportunity. There is not much time left. Who knows when he will have a chance to travel this road again. He's in his seventies—a critical age, when nothing should be put off. His memory has retained an enormous body of materials on the blockade, the war, the post-war years. Tell it—why wait? There won't be a second chance. The people trusted you in those critical years to take charge of industry, the government, events. So please, let's have your report. Write or tell the story.

Especially since you made this history of ours in secret, behind closed doors, without revealing your doubts or mistakes to anyone. Once society had a historical consciousness. Public figures great and small alike understood their responsibility to their children and grandchildren, and realized that they were part of history. Where has this feeling disappeared? People have begun dying so mutely, as if they felt guilty of something. But why? After all, they did a lot of good. If something is not as it should be, that is all the more reason to share it with others... You are the last of all your comrades-in-arms. None of the Leningrad district secretaries of those years has survived; none of the members of the Military Council is still alive...

The longer I listened to him the less I understood what he was trying so hard to avoid. What did he have to fear? Our eyes met.

"You can't do this, you can't do that—what can you do?" I blurted out.

He understood what I was getting at, and he realized that I understood what our eyes had said. He did not answer, but merely grunted either at my stupidity or at the fact that I was unable to see.

The silent telephone stood between us on the empty table. Its presence was bothersome. It stood there like a spy, an eavesdropper.

Good Lord, if he'd at least changed something in this office. I felt sorry for this old but still strong and intelligent man who seemingly could do so much and wielded such enormous power yet was so inhibited. Still, one thing had to be cleared up at any cost. I would not retreat until I found out how choices had been made during the evacuation. The choice between people and equipment. Between the starving and the machines and apparatus needed for the war industry. Airplanes, barges, automobiles were used, but vehicles were in short supply, and it had to be decided whether people or metal should be sent out first. Whom to save, whom to help—the front-line soldiers with tanks and airplanes, or the citizens of Leningrad? Well, then, what were the scales in which need and urgency were weighed?

"Both people and equipment were evacuated—simultaneously," replied Kosygin.

"Of course simultaneously, but that's all by and large and on the whole. In practice it had to be decided in each case how much of what."

"And it was decided—both," Kosygin insisted angrily. "What other choice was there?"

"But a choice had to be made!"

I persisted and he persisted. I realized that here was the whole problem—he could not choose. It was this dilemma that tormented everyone: they could not choose and they could not help but choose. That was the admission I was after—that the situation was agonizing, heartrending. He was being ordered to get the factories shipped out as quickly as possible, and for the sake of that goal they were ready to do anything. Yet at the same time he had to evacuate the people, for thousands were dying every day. And out on the front lines we soldiers gazed into the skies and waited for our fighters to appear. This was the battle that had to be waged. If he just could have said a word or two about all this. Just a word about the bitter feel of it, about even the faintest twinge in his heart. There must have been something—someone he helped or pitied, some rule he broke. Or, on the contrary, someone he failed to help...

But no, I couldn't get anything out of him. The thought of the choices that had to be made flashed a scene before my eyes, and if our conversation had taken a different turn I know I would have told him about it. It was then, incidentally, that I first saw Zhdanov. It was in the winter of 1942. We were summoned straight from the trenches to army headquarters and put through a nitpicking inspection. The day before we had gotten new field shirts, scrubbed our boots, sewed on fresh undercollars. Headquarters was on Blagodatny Prospect, which meant we had to cross the entire city to get to Smolny. We rode standing up in the one-and-a-half-ton truck so we wouldn't get dirty. A group of about sixty of us had been gathered together from various parts of the front to receive medals. I was so excited that I didn't see or notice much. They took us into a little hall. Sitting at a table were civilian and military commanders I didn't know. The only one I recognized was Zhdanov. During the entire presentation he sat quiet and motionless; I remember how flabby and sleepy he looked. At the end of the ceremony he rose heavily, congratulated us, and gave a speech about the inevitable defeat of the German invaders. He spoke with feeling, but his round, pale, smooth and shiny face remained indifferent. At certain points he raised his voice, and we dutifully applauded. When I returned to the battalion I had a hard time retelling what he had said. It all came out nonsense, with nothing new or interesting about either the second front or our airplanes. Zhdanov did not ask us about anything, although we had been coached by the political division and were ready for him. This was the first time any of us had seen him. He had never been to any of our units, and in fact I never heard anything about him ever visiting the front line. Word would have gotten around if he had.

I did tell the guys about our dinner—how they took us down to the dining room and gave us a fancy meal. We knew that they would give us something to eat, because that was the way it was done. But we had a tablecloth, and china dishes, and silverware. We had pea soup with meat in it, then chops and pearl-barley groats for the main course, and pink kissel pudding for dessert. The portions were tiny—barely the shadow of a real dinner—but we had forks and teaspoons. Most touching of all were the three pieces of bread and the piece of candy in a green wrapper on each plate. The candy was an extra touch—a little surprise. We put it in our pockets or field bags to take back to our buddies. Of all the dinners I've ever had, this is the one I remember best. Afterwards a group from Moscow gave a concert. A large woman in a long décolleté silk dress sang, someone read Nekrasov, and I remember an accordionist and a woman dancer. I was struck by how fresh and rosy they looked. The room was warm, and some of us got drowsy and began snoring. After the concert a guy in a khaki field coat called us over and gave us a talking to. "We," he says, "came all the way from Moscow to entertain you, and people are out there snoring. It's offensive. Our plane was shot at, our performers risked their lives in the hope that... This concert came at a high price..." And so on and so forth. Someone said something apologetic about our not being used to such things. One of Zhdanov's aides (as we later learned) approached and stood there listening. Then Vitya Levashov, a platoon leader in artillery intelligence, put his hands in his belt, cocked his head to one side, and asked: "How much do you weigh, comrade?" The speaker was struck dumb. Levashov looked him over: "Not under 155, I'd say. With the other performers and your accordion to boot, a good half a ton. So here's a question for you: if they'd brought us half a ton of flour and canned goods instead of you, we could have fed almost a whole regiment. As for civilians, those supplies would have saved a thousand. We appreciate the performers and we're not blaming them. But you're right—anyone who can sleep through a concert that cost half a ton of supplies ought to be punished!" Everyone chuckled; even the head of the troupe smiled; only the aide glowered. If it hadn't been for Viktor's medal, he would have been in hot water. They rode him for a long time afterwards. It may have only been a joke, but it made the rounds among the troops and got to people. After this we started weighing things up in our minds.

I knew several warm and friendly anecdotes about Kosygin. One of them I had heard from Mikhail Mikhailovich Kovalchuk, a doctor on Lake Ladoga. I tried to bring it up, but Kosygin shrugged his shoulders indifferently. It appeared he had forgotten. He had also forgotten the dying little boy at the gate of the Kirov plant—as if it were just a trifle, a momentary weakness. Yet in fact he had tried to help him. His memory evidently jettisoned everything that was not related to his work.

Probably in order to evade my questions, he told about a letter from his father asking him to look in on their Leningrad apartment, which had stood empty after his parents were evacuated. While you're there, his father wrote, feel around the shelf above the door. Fortunately, the building and the apartment were still standing. Some of the windows, of course, were knocked out, and the walls were covered in frost. Kosygin stood on a stool at the door,

thrust his hand deep into the shelf and extracted one quarter-liter bottle of
vodka after another. It seems that his father had been in the habit of hiding "a
little one" at New Year's in memory of the year before. Some of the bottles he
pulled out were from the tsar's days, with an eagle on the label. He collected a
whole bag of them and treated everyone at Smolny.

That was the extent of the personal details he remembered. All of his feelings were concentrated on the Job. About the Job he could tell you all you
wanted to hear.

It was after eight in the evening. I envied his stamina. The office itself was
an exhausting strain, and I was drained by the twists and turns of our conversation. The time had come to get up and say thank you, I couldn't really take
up any more of his time, especially after working hours, and so on and so
forth. Kosygin stood up and wished me luck in publishing the book. To
which I replied that we were going to have problems with the second part.
Our Leningrad Party supervisor had declared of the first part that no one
needed such a book, that the siege of Leningrad was all about bravery and
heroism, but that for some reason we were describing suffering, deprivation,
and death—examples that teach us nothing. His remarks, of course, were
hastily conveyed to our Moscow publisher; alert to the opinion of his superiors, he had backed off.

"All he wants is heroism. Another expert," said Kosygin with the irony we
front-line soldiers would feel as we listened to civilians explain the war.

"And no one will intercede," I was encouraged to prod him on. "Well, we'll
see what we can do," he was supposed to answer. He had read the first part—
it was only then that he had agreed to meet me. That meant that he had no
objections. Surely he could call our bosses or anyone else to account—make
them ashamed of themselves, give his approval. All he had to do was tell an
assistant to phone the editors. Nothing more. The matter would be settled...

But his knotty face revealed not a trace of sympathy. On the contrary, it
lacked any expression whatever and showed only stony indifference, as if this
meeting and our shared experience of the siege had never been, as if the person standing before him were an outsider pestering him with requests. He
shook his head disapprovingly—he was not about to get involved. Publishing
was none of his business, and that was that. His hand was warm, soft, bone-
less.

B-ov and I silently passed the carpet-lined corridors, the staircases, the
passages, the guards. Searchlights blazed in Red Square. The evening crowd
of tourists milled over the paving-stones. It was spacious, free, noisy. I inhaled the air and its gasoline fumes with relief. I stretched the muscles of my

numbed body and face, and felt myself grow limp inside as nerves and feelings that had been tensed to the limit relaxed. B-ov also straightened his shoulders, took out his handkerchief, wiped his neck, and reproachfully observed the faces I was making as he loudly blew his nose.

"You're a fine one. I vouched for you, set things up, and you..."

"What did I do?"

"You let me down. Those questions of yours! You got me into it with every one. You put me in an embarrassing position every time. You mean you didn't feel it? I was so ashamed I was in a sweat."

"Because of the questions, right? What about the answers?"

"Now, was it tactful to ask about his disagreements with Zhdanov? Try to understand—Zhdanov was in the Politburo at the time."

"And Kosygin?"

"He wasn't."

"So what? Now he..."

B-ov waved his hand and grimaced at my intolerable ignorance. There are rules, there is a hierarchy, finally, there is etiquette—ceremony, if you will. And people of that rank simply are not asked about their personal views. Where have you heard or read anything about their moods or illnesses? Sorry. It's not done. So there must be reasons.

What's he talking about? If I made a mistake it was that I was too reticent about it! Too ashamed, and so I came away from the table hungry, so to speak. Surely it wasn't my questions. Questions or no questions, Kosygin was being tight-lipped. He doesn't trust himself. According to him, no one was guilty of anything; there weren't any conflicts, no mistakes, a million Leningraders died, and everything was irreproachable. Except for the Fascists, no one was guilty of anything. What's the use of digging up the past, they told Adamovich and me—the important thing is that the city held out; never mind the price—victors aren't asked to explain; look for the guilty and you'll lose sight of the righteous, and so on and so forth. We had set such hopes on Kosygin, and he set about covering up for others. Why? Why should he time and again give the credit for his services to the Military Council and tell us not to mention his name too often? Doesn't he realize that literature is about people, not organizations? Why the hell all this modesty, this evasion and beating about the bush, this pussyfooting? Anything just to keep from stirring up or frightening all the vampires and demons still cluttering our imagination...

At this point B-ov couldn't stand it any longer and leapt to the attack. If I had been in his office at the Ministry he would have pounded the desk, screamed at me to shut up, and thrown me out. But here on the square there was no desk to pound, and he couldn't throw me out. "You and your writers," he cursed. "You scribble up a storm, but you haven't got what it takes to try to understand real people."

What is there to understand? It's quite obvious that he doesn't dare do anything for our book! And it's not "ours"—it belongs to the voices of the dead, the memory of everyone in the siege. He betrayed his own reputation with his bureaucratic "none of my business." But he did make sure to follow all the awe-inspiring rules.

"...All you hear is words, Mr. Philosopher, not the heart. Goddamn you anyway!" B-ov interrupted me and stopped short as he realized we had started shouting. He glanced over his shoulder at the windows of the Kremlin, took me firmly by the arm and quickly dragged me off the square. As we came to Gorky Street and the anger in his voice changed to humble patience, he asked whether I really didn't understand what was going on here. Suppose Kosygin had met me halfway and had interceded on behalf of our book, that is, the book that would contain the reminiscences I had heard. Just suppose. As everyone knows, however, another book with other reminiscences came out not long ago—about the "Little Land."* It paints a picture of heroic defense, deprivation, exemplary political work and leadership. The book is being studied, read over the radio and television, translated into foreign languages; your writer friends are out of breath praising it. Today it is the *big* book. When the second part, *Resurrection,* appeared, it was the same thing. And so here, out of the blue, comes another memoirist. Well, well, now, here I am, how about me? I also have an epic , and what an epic tale it is! It has sweep, and merit, and authenticity—better told and more heart in it too. Just how nice do you think that will be? Right away they'll say that he pushed *The Blockade Book* out of personal interest. He tried to get it published out of spite, to belittle others. Rivalry, a dirty trick, a challenge—they'll twist it into something mean. No problem finding someone—there are plenty of bootlickers around.

"In fact, do you want to know how it looked? As if you were trying to set them against one another, demanding that they oppose each other!" he concluded almost in horror.

Suddenly I saw our interview in a new light—through the eyes of both of them. I imagine that my expression must have become puzzled, maybe even idiotic. Who would have thought that was behind it all? So here was the key to the riddle. Pretty simple and convincing. No, things hadn't turned out well. I looked down at our feet striding in step over the worn asphalt.

---

*The allusion is to the title ("Malaia zemlia") of Chapter 3 in Leonid Brezhnev's *Memoirs* (1979/83), which incorporated his shorter earlier reminiscences (*Little Land,* 1978). It recounts Brezhnev's wartime experiences on the southern front, especially the Soviet seizure in February 1943 of the 30-km. beachhead called "Malaia zemlia," which they defended from the Germans until September 1943.

"So it's not clear who should be accusing whom," B-ov pressed on. Did I realize now that the whole meeting was a bad idea? That's why they kept dragging it out. And yet they weren't scared and decided to go ahead. Real courage means you have to think too, you know. Someone else would have concluded that, sure, he's hard as flint, but there's a heart you don't see in the man, just as there's fire you don't see in flint.

I am reporting only the gist of his triumphant lecture, because his nimble mumbling, punctuated by sighs, interjections, and winks, let him dispense with names. He did not mention Brezhnev or others, and instead of Kosygin he used the third person plural—"they."

"All right, don't lose heart," said B-ov more calmly. "There's an art to be learned here."

"And what an art it is," I said. "You have quite an eye."

They really are good at calculating in advance. Their telescopes and sensors anticipate each move; all the possible answers and variants have been thought through. They've got the knack, these seers... I felt the anger inexorably welling up in me, because for over two years now I had been living amid the desperation and starvation of the siege recalled in stories broken by sobs, where there was no room for calculation, where, scheme as you might, you couldn't wangle an extra crust of bread or bowl of gruel. Where did such people get the courage to live by their conscience?

"You know what they were afraid of? They were afraid of losing their humanity!" I said. "You were there yourself. Death was nothing to you..."

"Everything's relative," said B-ov.

"No, not everything... If Leningrad owes anything to anyone, it's to Zhukov and Kosygin. He could have behaved..."

B-ov stopped and gave me such a look that I shut up.

"My, aren't you the warrior... Actually... It would be better for the time being to keep quiet about the visit," he said with a warm and solicitous smile.

We kept quiet.

But, all the same, the chapter with Kosygin's story did not get into *The Blockade Book*. B-ov did what he could to no avail. We were never really told why. Deletions made no difference—it was not going to go through, and that was that. Kosygin was ill during these months and could not intervene. Or so Adamovich and I assured ourselves and others as we waited and played for time...

Kosygin died soon after. We had to rework the chapter, omit direct speech, transform the story into a collection of anonymous information. Quite a few passages that meant a lot to us were deleted from *The Blockade Book,* though we were able to salvage some things. But some losses were particularly painful, and this chapter was one of them. If we could not accuse the guilty, we at least wanted to give credit to the man who in such difficult conditions organized the evacuation and saved thousands and thousands of Leningraders. They would not let us. Perhaps it is good that Kosygin never saw his story in such a mutilated, faceless form.

Years passed. The omitted, forbidden chapter that we had fought so hard to save could be resurrected. But something happened to it. Now you could clearly see the blank spots, the evasions—that is, the silences and indistinct patter, everything I had tried to dodge, everything that had gone on during the interview. At times the false tone grated unbearably, especially next to the artless stories of the others we had interviewed. It was not only Kosygin's fault. What I myself had written had gone stale. It became obvious that I was not trying to get clear answers, that I was inhibiting myself, that I did not dare. And that made it dry. Most important, there was no understanding my own attitude toward Kosygin—on one page I condemned him, on the next I revered him.

Today, the chapter we thought was so superb and honest has now unmasked us. Both me and my interviewee. I saw before me his interlaced fingers, our gloomy parting, him standing there with his hands at his sides, all tight and tense, as if he were tied. Something shifted in my perception—the way a beam of light is refracted as it enters another medium. Perhaps the whole problem was that we had entered another time. Suddenly, almost physically, I felt within me this refraction and transition, both happy and painful...

Sometimes it seems to me that if Kosygin had known that evening how soon he was to die, or how close the end of that time was, he would have felt freer, wouldn't have talked the way he did, wouldn't have been looking over his shoulder like that. It is sad, of course, if it is only such knowledge that can liberate us.

Translated by Charles Rougle

Originally published in *Znamia,* February 1988

Vyacheslav Pyetsukh

The Ticket

The drifter called Pasha the Saint can be seen any day of the week around the village store, at the bus stop, by the Contract Mine office and on Drifters' Island, which stretches like a sausage along that point where the Luiza Creek flows into the Burkhalinka River, and he's not at all your usual drifter. He's properly dressed in a gray suit, a slightly worn sweater and brown army shoes, and a cracked ballpoint pen—"Made in China"—sticks out from the breast pocket of his suit. The expression on his face is an ordinary human one without that vacant, weary look you usually see on drifters' faces, especially when they're sober. In short, if it weren't for his deep tan, something like the color of a ripe plum—the same as you find on drowning victims—you would never say Pasha was a drifter.

Within the brotherhood of drifters at Contract Mines Pasha the Saint occupies something like the position of chairman, and this is an honest-to-God puzzle because around here drifters don't recognize any superiors. Nevertheless, along the whole route from Marchikan to Ust-Nera, that's to say, within those geographic confines where the drifters respect no authority, Pasha the Saint carries about the same kind of weight as the neighborhood cop and the dedicated hard worker do in the ordinary world. This is especially odd considering that Pasha is a relative neophyte and hasn't been a drifter very long, it's maybe a year and a half since he finished his sentence— start to finish—for embezzlement.

Pasha the Saint has occupied something like the position of chairman for the following reasons: first, he's a rather well-educated man, albeit self-educated; that's to say he's read through the entire camp library several times; second, he's a decent man, and when he owes somebody twenty kopecks—even if he has to turn himself inside out—he'll give it back; third, he's a decisive man, in fact, so decisive that in only a year and a half he's been able to establish more or less real order among his fellow drifters. The most surprising thing is that he did this without taking any special measures. Whenever the drifters started some nasty trick, he simply told them with tears in his voice (he almost always speaks with tears in his voice; apparently it's a nervous habit of his) that they were doing something nasty, that good deeds are good, that bad ones are bad, and that in all circumstances a human being must remain a human being: in short, he cranked up an old, old tune that was, nevertheless, a novelty to many. Either the drifters took his words to heart or the very fact that a real man personified a real morality stunned them. Whatever it was, underwear hung out to dry on unattended lines soon stopped disappearing in the village, feudal wars ceased, and the borders of those staked-out claims where the so-called crystal was mined were seldom violated. Nevertheless, drifter Nikolay, nicknamed the Serene, drifter Kuzkin, the son of a Vlasov follower, and drifter Frenchy, baptized the Frenchman because he knew the first verse of the *Marseillaise* in French, went on making trouble for a while, but in the end the other drifters got together and blocked them, and they moved first to Sladkoe, then eventually to Kartkhala. True, Frenchy came back later and started up his same old stunts again.

About a week after Frenchy returned, a series of events occurred in Spring Mine village, which, in an unexpected and unforeseen way, crisscrossed and then snarled into a knot, and within a short time developed into a certain ugly, but instructive story. Some of the drifters played a part in this ugly story, as did the chief engineer of the mine, Novosiltsev, his son Novosiltsev Junior, a certain sergeant of the militia, the cashier of the village store, and the assayer Kazakova.

And so, shortly after Frenchy returned, a series of events occurred in Spring Mine village that unfolded in the following sequence... One day in early August a routine survey carried out at the claim on the Mirt Creek headwaters showed not a single gram of gold. At the village store a lottery ticket was foisted off on Novosiltsev Senior: he usually threw them away, but this time, out of forgetfulness, he put it in the breast pocket of his blue suitcoat. Frenchy, meaning to sew himself some britches, had stolen a sheet somewhere, for which Pasha the Saint gave him a good chewing out. Frenchy quietly nursed a deep grievance over it. The telephone at the Novosiltsevs' apartment was being fixed. Finally, thanks to the neglected state of the sewer pipe, the abandoned repair shops that the drifters had occupied for a long time were flooded. True, this event was notable only for the fact that Pasha's respectable gray suit got soaked through and through and he went off together with his fellow sufferers to Drifters' Island to dry out. There, by joint effort, they got a bonfire going and stood around the fire languishing and waiting for the store to open. Only Masha Shalyapina, a baby-faced thirty-year-old with the hands of a hardened laborer, who wore a jacket cut off from a nylon raincoat, a chiffon scarf, a cotton batting skirt, with a lisle stocking on one leg and a wool one on the other, and worn-down rubber boots on her feet—she alone wandered around the island and talked to herself. Meanwhile, despite the morning chill, Pasha the Saint threw off his suit and hung it out to dry on some branches near the fire. The suit was already beginning to steam, and even to smell, when Frenchy found his chance to take revenge: on the sly he tossed Pasha's suit onto the fire with a twig. Pasha let out a sorrowful wail of distress and rushed to rescue his clothes, but it was too late—the flames that had crept over his pants and coat turned to ashes and it was clear to everyone that Pasha wasn't going to wear that suit anymore.

Frenchy didn't go unpunished for his sabotage, however, since Masha Shalyapina had accidentally noticed his manipulations with the twig and betrayed, so to say, the guilty party. Frenchy caught all the rancor that had been boiling up at the time and was almost beaten up, but in the end it was decided to run him out of the group for good. It must be noted that, to Frenchy's credit, he was quite shaken by his fellow drifters' unanimity; he told himself that if the drifters drove him away, then that would be the end of everything, so he got down on his knees and fervently offered to pay, with interest, for his guilt.

The drifters grumbled, but agreed.

That same evening Novosiltsev Senior returned home from the mining office, puttered around a bit in the cold frame where he grew tomatoes and cucumbers and sat down to supper with his son in the big room, which, southern style, they called "the dinner hall." Just as he grabbed the kind of crusty heel he liked the most from the breadbox, the telephone gave a deafening ring and the crust of bread slipped out of his fingers into his borsch. Novosiltsev Senior snorted, got up from the table, went to the phone, and raised the receiver. The call was from the office; the controller said that assayer Kazakova had slipped up and that the last survey at the most productive stake hadn't yielded one gram of gold. In terms of the mining company this was a small tragedy: it meant that the quarterly plan, as our administrators put it, had crashed, and Novosiltsev Senior returned to the table dejected and gloomy, as if a great misfortune had befallen him. He was about to reach for another heel when he suddenly froze, his eyes bulged, and he collapsed from his chair onto the floor. Novosiltsev Junior rushed over to his father and turned him on his side: this movement caused a puff of air to escape with a rattle from his body. Novosiltsev Junior, a hydraulic monitor operator at the mine and a strong fellow, went over to the mirror and looked into it for a while as he wiped his eyes with his fist, then hit his own reflection with all his might, smashing the mirror into silver smithereens.

Novosiltsev Senior was buried two days later. The weather on that day proved nasty as if by special order. It was cold, windy, drizzly, and two remotely acquainted down-and-outers nicknamed the Yellow Brothers looked especially mournful, in harmony.

After the funeral procession had left the cemetery the cashier from the village store came up to Novosiltsev Junior, took him by the hand and said, "I understand that this isn't the right time, but still."

"Why 'still'?" Novosiltsev asked her.

"A few days ago I sold your father a lottery ticket."

"So what?"

"The 'what' is that he won."

"How come you know for sure my father's ticket won?"

"I write out all the tickets."

"Is that so you can collect your cut later?"

The cashier smiled coquettishly in reply.

"And what did he win?"

"A car—a Moskvich."

"All right!" Novosiltsev shouted and comically waved his bandaged fist. "But, then, now there's the question of where to find the ticket. Where should I look?"

The cashier shrugged her shoulders and walked away.

The next day Novosiltsev requested a day off and started searching for the winning ticket. In the course of the working day he managed to ransack all the drawers, cupboards, boxes and other out-of-the-way nooks and crannies, and even in some places peeled off the wallpaper, but had no luck at finding the lottery ticket. That evening out of grief he went to the beer joint across from the bus stop, and there he let two or three friends know about his new calamity. Soon word of the lost ticket had spread through a territory equal to France and Switzerland combined.

For some reason the rumor reached the drifters first. The majority took it indifferently. Masha Shalyapina declared that if she should win a car, she'd sell it and buy herself a fake fur coat with the proceeds (in her naivete Masha assumed that fake fur was terribly expensive). Frenchy observed: "Fool's luck!", but Pasha the Saint responded to the rumor with the following words:

"As the philosopher Schopenhauer maintains, there's almost no one in this world except madmen and idiots; I'm afraid the philosopher is right."

But this piece of news paled very soon by comparison with the latest: Frenchy kept his word and made amends for his recent guilt by presenting Pasha the Saint with an excellent suit that he—Frenchy— ostensibly got in trade for an SS dagger that the street barber—a former chief of spies at the Romanian Embassy—had wanted. True, the pants turned out to be too long, but Masha Shalyapina cropped them off with her scissors and the overall result wasn't bad. Pasha got decked out in the new suit and walked around Drifters' Island for a long time with that not entirely graceful stride peculiar to people dressed up in something new.

Meanwhile, Novosiltsev Junior hadn't given up hope of finding the ticket. He rummaged through the house for another day, but the only result was that he transformed a habitable space into an all but uninhabitable one. Toward evening he decided to have a talk with the cashier at the village store; he came just before closing time, leaned his elbows against a corner of the cash register, and began sorrowfully:

"I didn't find the ticket. I searched everywhere, I even pulled up the floor boards. I could eat my heart out—there's just no ticket."

"But did you check your father's pockets?" the cashier asked him.

"Yeah," Novosiltsev confirmed.

"But did you look in that blue suitcoat? The day he bought the ticket he was wearing a blue serge suitcoat. Now, this is how I remember it: your father put the ticket in the breast pocket of the blue suitcoat."

With a heavy, heavy look Novosiltsev stared through the wall of the village store.

"Shee-it!" he said in a strange voice. "That's the suit we buried him in!"

The cashier shrieked and pressed her hand to her mouth.

The first thought to come into Novosiltsev's head was that the best thing to do would be to quietly dig up his father's body and get possession of the ticket that way, but thinking it through, he came to the conclusion that he wouldn't exactly be patted on the head for such a stunt and that he would have to act in accordance with the law. About an hour and a half later he was already in Sladkoe, in the regional office of Internal Affairs, where he had a friend—a sergeant of the militia, a jolly little guy with bushy grenadier whiskers who was always ready for a party. The sergeant heard Novosiltsev out and said:

"If you weren't such a blabbermouth, the two of us could've done it all on the q.t. As it is, we'll have to go through the rigamarole of the prosecutor's office."

And for emphasis he rapped his knuckles on his forehead.

Despite this prediction, there was no special red tape with the regional prosecutor's office: Novosiltsev's petition caused the deputy prosecutor of the Yagodnovsky district to become so flabbergasted and indignant that he wrote out the exhumation order on the spot and all but flung it in the petitioner's face, the way they used to fling kid gloves when challenging someone to a duel.

"What's with this guy of yours? Maybe he's not all there, you think?" Novosiltsev asked the sergeant, who was waiting for him in the hall.

"Yeah, something's missing," said the sergeant.

After midnight on August 15 the friends armed themselves with shovels, ropes, and pocket flashlights and set out for the mine cemetery, which was situated in a little larch grove not far from the Kartkhala riverbank. The night was bright and somehow watchful, concealing itself—a night-ambush, you might say.

The two friends got to Novosiltsev Senior's grave, spit on their palms, and started to dig. Because of the eternal permafrost, graves in these areas are dug very shallow, and before five minutes had passed the sergeant's shovel hit the top of the coffin with a thud. Novosiltsev Junior shuddered, straightened up, and wiped the sweat from his forehead with his hand. For a while he couldn't stop shivering, but finally he got hold of himself and started shoveling again. It wasn't long before they dug up the coffin, set it out on the adjacent mound and removed the top. What the friends saw surprised them in any case: the corpse was naked.

"Um-okay!" said the sergeant. "An obvious violation of article 229. We'll have to file a complaint."

The complaint didn't have to be filed, however, and here's the reason why. The next morning Pasha the Saint was squatting alongside the village store and telling the drifters about the battle of Poltava. At the most interesting spot he reached into his breast pocket for his cracked ballpoint pen to sketch out in the sand just how in 1709 the Swedes were encircled near the village of Yakovtsy, but along with the pen he pulled out a lottery ticket that carried a sharp earthy stench. For a full minute Pasha inspected the ticket thoughtfully, then got up and went off in the direction of the abandoned repair shop. Inside the shop he took off his new suit, changed into some rags spread out on the old joiners' benches, then set off to find the Novosiltsev work crew, which was panning for gold two miles up the Kartkhala.

Novosiltsev wasn't using the hydraulic monitor; he was splitting an over-size rock with a sledgehammer, but, sensing an intruder at his back, he turned around and gave Pasha a nasty look.

"What brought you here, dummy?!" he said, squinting contemptuously. "Doesn't any fool know that you can't come into the claim zone without a pass?"

"I'd like to see you for a minute," Pasha proposed in a conciliatory tone.

The expression on Novosiltsev's face changed immediately, as if he guessed what had brought the drifter there, and throwing his sledgehammer aside, he followed Pasha. They walked some fifty paces away and stopped simultaneously; Pasha squatted down, produced the ticket, and extended it to Novosiltsev.

"Take a look," he said as he passed it to him. "Isn't this your ticket?"

Novosiltsev took the piece of paper, turned it this way and that, and answered:

"Who the hell knows! You think I remember!? I wrote the number down at home, but of course I can't come up with it from memory."

"I'll drop by in the evening," said Pasha. "You check it with the registration. If the numbers don't match, you can give the ticket back."

That evening, a little after six o'clock, Pasha the Saint dropped in at Novosiltsev's and from the host's friendly demeanor he understood right away that everything tallied.

"Frankly, I just don't know how to thank you!" said Novosiltsev, leading Pasha inside. "Whatta you say, let's bend our elbows a bit? What do you relish most: vodka or wine?"

"I don't drink vodka," Pasha said.

"As for the winnings," Novosiltsev continued, "a quarter of it is yours."

"I don't need anything."

"Hey, you're crazy!.."

Pasha shrugged his shoulders.

"Listen, how'd you come by the ticket?"

"I found it," answered Pasha and lowered his eyes.

"In the breast pocket of the blue suitcoat?"

Pasha nodded.

"Fine," said Novosiltsev. "We're gonna flip this talk over to the happy side, only first tell me the truth: did you dig him up yourself?"

"Dig who up?" asked Pasha.

"Okay, that means it wasn't you. So much the better."

Novosiltsev went to the kitchen and came back in a couple of minutes with a jar of chopped squash for appetizer, a bottle of vodka, and two bottles of vintage wine in his arms.

"Tell me, why's your place such a wreck?" Pasha ventured. "It looks like Mamai's Tatar hordes have swept through here..."

Novosiltsev burst out laughing good-naturedly.

"It's what I did—looking for the lottery ticket," he said between laughs. "A couple more days of searching and I wouldn't of had a place to live. Okay, fine, take your glass. A good morning to ya, as they say!"

"But why 'a good morning'?"

"Well, you say that so it'll be more fun drinking. First, you say 'a good morning to ya' and afterwards, when you've drunk it all, you say 'had a drink

in the morning—the whole day's free.' It's sort of a saying. But what do you
guys do—just plain drink?"

"Just plain drink."

"You're boring people, you drifters, unimaginative. You've got no spark in
you!"

Pasha held his tongue.

"I'll say something else: you're scummy people—don't you take offense
now. But, judge for yourself: you're strong healthy guys, and you live like par-
asites, you collect empty bottles—it's a disgrace! Do you really like such a
shameful life?"

"People aren't usually drifters because they like it."

"Why, then?"

"Because they don't have any other way out. Once a person breaks away
from the way everybody else lives, I'd say what happens is that deep down he
cuts himself off for good, so that there's no way back."

"I don't understand it!" said Novosiltsev and banged his fist on the table.
"They've got legs, they've arms, their head's in place—they've got everything
they need to be able to go back to normal life!"

"Normal life—what's that?" said Pasha a little slyly.

"Go to work! You'll have some money, you'll get some kind of housing—
that's what!"

"But there's no place to go to work, that's the whole point. They're not
gonna take me on as a manager, they won't take me on even in some measly,
second-rate office."

"Get a construction job, they'll take you on in construction."

"Yeah, but on a construction job you'll surely have to do heavy labor, and
my arms can't hold a match box. And I'm a sick man to boot, all eaten up inside with something."

"Oh yeah, inside?" Novosiltsev observed in an unfriendly voice. "On the
outside you still look strong as a horse."

"I just look that way. I'll go on being a drifter for a couple of years, and
that's it—it'll be the cold sleep of the grave."

"In that case you're in deep shit. A clear case, as they say, of a total lack of
prospects. But here's what I wonder about: how did you get to such a state?"

"The usual way," said Pasha and gave a long, drawn out sigh. "In '78 I got a
sentence for embezzlement. I served it out in Kuteman. In '79 my wife di-
vorced me and immediately remarried. In '81 I got free and, to celebrate,
went on a binge in Sladkoe. When I came to in a week, I was naked as a blue
jay. Nothing to eat, no reason to get up and go, in fact, frankly speaking, there
wasn't any place to go..."

"You're weak," said Novosiltsev. "You're not a real man. That's the problem."

"Well, there's nothing to do about it, everybody's got his own internal constitution."

"Your internal constitution isn't worth a damn: you talk and whine at the same time."

"How can I help whining if I've had nothing but sorrow by the bucketful?"

"I just don't understand it! Look what kind of country we live in: all you've got to do is snap your fingers and you can eat, drink, and be merry, as they say, but he figures out a way to get a bucketful of sorrow!.."

"Nobody's obligated to be happy," said Pasha sternly.

"Yes, we are obligated!" Novosiltsev objected.

"No, we're not!"

"Yes, we are, because if it's possible to achieve happiness, then a human being is obligated to achieve happiness!"

"No, he's not, because for some people happiness is unhappiness and vice versa!"

"That's something I can't make out," said Novosiltsev, the very picture of blank bewilderment. "What are you saying? That somebody purposely forces unhappiness on you? But, hey, that's a joke! For God's sake don't let this get out to foreigners—they'll split their sides laughing!"

"It's not that it's purposely... It's all a lot more complicated than that, but to some extent basically, it's on purpose, too. You see, it's like this: we've got an enigmatic string in our temperament that constantly plays a certain obstinate, defiant tune. Among the folk it's called 'just don't do it the way people usually do it.' It's a very powerful string that in many ways defines the music of our life. Even when cars will be given out free here on every street corner, one person out of ten will still use public transportation on principle or make a show of walking. Even when we attain total, universal, maybe even unavoidable happiness, I assure you we'll still not be rid of God's fools, unrecognized geniuses and outrageous loners. And it's not because every tenth one of us is simply incapable of happiness or because the discordant string leads us astray—although, in part, both the incapacity and the string figure in. It's because our life is somehow determined from the start, programmed to give birth to various intentionally unhappy souls—types like General Uvarov, who one fine day stepped out, went for a stroll around Petersburg and disappeared..."

"Hold on," Novosiltsev said and started pouring another round. "We've let this conversation make us completely forget about our drinking."

"I even think," continued Pasha, "that without these people our life is impossible, without them we wouldn't be ourselves, just as Aphrodite with arms wouldn't really be Aphrodite. You ask why? Well, because universal prosperity is the same thing as sugar diabetes, and the nation's body—if it's healthy, of course—absolutely must excrete some element of misery that will keep the country from getting sick and, for no good reason, slipping into the grave. Look, it's a fact that there are no hungry and cold people in this country now. Really, all you have to do is snap a finger and you'll be up to your ears in refrigerators and carpets. But another time you won't be able to walk a block without some self-pitying whiner trying to bum twenty kopecks from you. Or another example: we've got, thank God, complete freedom for the family as far as divorce goes. Thank God, in divorce we hold first place in the world. And yet, you can't drink a glass of beer without having someone complain about his wife to you..."

"Well, a good mornin' to ya!" Novosiltsev said, drained his glass, sighed and added: "He drank in the morning, he's free all day!"

"You say 'freedom,'" Pasha started up again. "But just where's the freedom?! Actually, you're not only not free, you're an out and out slave, pure and simple. You're a living slave of industrial production, of your own needs and of social prejudices. The man who's truly free—that's me! You all but tore down your own house board by board just because of a miserable lottery ticket."

"Hey, my friend!" said Novosiltsev with a stony expression. "If you knew what lengths I went to for the sake of this idiotic ticket, you wouldn't even speak to me. I even dug my own father out of his grave on account of it!"

"Come on, now," Pasha said, waving him away. "You'll start saying..."

"Honest, hope to die, I really dug him up!" said Novosiltsev and banged the table with his fist. "That's just what a thick-skinned, cold-blooded bastard I am! And the main thing—what's the point? What the fuck did I need this ticket for?! Without any kinda ticket I could buy three Moskviches even tomorrow and still have something left over to get spare parts with! No, I probably am in fact a slave. Say, maybe I should...become a drifter too?"

"And why not?" said Pasha. "Don't look at us. There've also been outstanding figures among the drifters, for example, Khlebnikov, Gorky, Alexander Grin...* Finally, there was a certain Jesus Christ—perhaps the most confirmed drifter!"

"Hold on, let's have another drink," Novosiltsev said, taking aim at the bottles and ready to pour another round, but Pasha hastily covered his glass with his hand.

"No more for me," he said with some embarrassment at his own gesture. "To tell the truth, I really don't like wine. And I guess I'll be going home now. Not home, of course, but going—it's already very late."

---

*Futurist poet Velimir Khlebnikov (1885-1922), socialist writer Maxim Gorky (1868-1936), and writer of fantasy Grin (1880-1932) all spent time wandering "among the people."

"In that case, let me see you home."

"Like I said, I don't have a home to be seen to."

"Yeah, you're right..." Novosiltsev said. "Well, take care of yourself! And go on and wear that suit, let it be like a memento of our encounter. You're a nice guy, Mr. Drifter, I say you're an okay guy. The only thing is that your outlook on life is false—it's pure idealism. Don't be offended if I tell you frankly—you drifters are phonies, complete phonies and alcoholics. Did you really think Arkady Novosiltsev could actually become a drifter? No, he'd sooner dig up all his ancestors to the thir... hold it! ...thirteenth—uh—generator—generation, I mean—than ever—er—collect empty bottles and nurse a hangover with a shot of cologne!"

These words stung Pasha the Saint. At first he was about to retaliate and say something insulting to Novosiltsev, but then reconsidered and decided to explain it to him in a good way. That—phony and alcoholic as he may be— the ordinary drifter personifies a protest against the wild superstitions of prosperity. But it immediately occurred to him that all theories coming from a person in rags reeking of machine oil must definitely and inevitably ring false.

"And you gave the ticket back for nothing," said Novosiltsev suddenly with obvious hostility. "You're a fool, a fool!.."

"For nothing," Pasha agreed.

Translated by Byron Lindsey

Originally published in *Novyi mir,* June 1987

Vyacheslav Pyetsukh

Novy Zavod[*]

On the whole, life is good. In particular, it's good because every now and then pleasant surprises take us unawares. For instance, you're going about your own business when all of a sudden you stumble across a purse or catch the eye of a ravishing woman. And then the sun seems to rise inside you, setting you aglow with its caressing rays—you suddenly feel so joyful and breathtakingly good.

One day a young man named Komnatov had a row with his wife. The fuss began when Komnatov refused point-blank to go to the station and meet his father-in-law, whom he disliked to such an extraordinary degree that he got an upset stomach every time the father-in-law came to visit. Consequently, his wife really laid into him. Not only did she make some undeserved caustic remarks, several of which were quite unbearable coming from a wife, but after Komnatov had jammed his index fingers in his ears, she also thumped him twice across the back with her fist. This insulted him terribly. He went off to the bathroom, locked himself in and started to study himself closely in the mirror. He felt bitter. He gazed into his own eyes and felt so sorry for his insulted reflection that his nose began to hurt. He was thinking about how you could live half your life with someone supposedly very close to you, only suddenly to discover that this person is completely alien to you, like an idealistic outlook on the world.

He spent only ten minutes in the bathroom, but that was enough to make him so miserable that he suddenly made up his mind to go far, far away, to where people still wave farewell to birds and trains. In general, he was an eccentric person and had done more than a few foolish things in his time.

He set off from home for the station, where he bought a ticket for the Odessa Express and then for a long time languished, sitting in a compartment that reeked of stale bread, dust, coal, and something burnt.

[*]*Novy zavod* in English means "new factory."

The other people in his compartment were an unpleasant bunch: an old woman traveling as far as Kursk with a monstrous amount of luggage and an elderly couple, who were getting out at Novy Zavod. The old woman maintained an angry silence and kept munching salted cucumbers, and the couple immediately started up a dreary conversation nobody else could understand. The back of his head started aching because of this conversation, and because the old woman constantly stuffed herself with salted cucumbers and when two sailors started scuffling on the platform immediately after Kaluga, he started to feel terrible: his good mood soured and he grew utterly dejected. "Where am I going, and why?" he asked himself, feeling a nasty anxiety. He remembered his apartment: everything there smelled so peacefully and wonderfully of home, and through the curtain you could see the multicolored cups of his wife's bras and other lovely luxuries fluttering on the balcony. And he longed so much to get back home and lie down on the sofa with a book while the flies just buzzed sleepily overhead that he got a tickle in his throat. But the train was carrying him further and further away...

He crawled up onto the top berth, tossed and turned a while, and then started dozing. "Fool," he said to himself, half-asleep, "absolute fool!.."

...He woke up in the night. Outside only the occasional lights flashed by, the carriage rocked, something creaked, and he felt as heavy-hearted as you do waking up from a dream in which you have committed a murder. He could hardly wait for the next station.

The station was called Novy Zavod. Because of the early hour no one was on the platform and the deserted space filled by the cold morning made him feel unbearably lonely and sad. It was not yet dawn and he stood gazing in the direction of the bluish-gray clouds through which the sun, with its unsettling color, was already making itself felt, and even the sun, which had absolutely nothing to do with it all, seemed hostile.

Directly behind the station building a large cobblestone square stretched out before him. The stones glistened with dew, as though the square had just been washed down. In general, it was unusually clean and orderly everywhere. What struck him most, however, was that despite the early hour the square was full of life: the men were strolling about, clattering like horses, the women smiled at everyone they passed, here and there old women conversed politely, and from indoors you could hear hearty morning coughing. What surprised Komnatov most was that everything he could see on this side of the station building was so different from everything on the other side, as though he had accidently walked through a magic door into a wonderland. The place appealed to him at once, his depression vanished, and he eagerly awaited more surprises.

Sure enough, before he reached the square someone offered him a cigarette, another man asked for a match box, two others invited him to drink kvas, and someone else even suggested swapping shoes.

Next, he was stopped by three boys. One took him by the sleeve and asked, "Who are you visiting, comrade?"

Komnatov replied that he was here by chance. Then he answered the question that one of the others, a freckled little boy, put to him about what town he came from, and then about the type of work he did and then about whether he was famous, and finally, he had to promise on his Communist Party honor that he was not in the habit of lying. The upshot of it all was that Freckles said, "Well, if that's the case, why don't we show you our sights..."

Komnatov agreed with a shrug,

First of all, the boys took him to the local cemetery, which thy called "churchyard," in the old-fashioned* way. There Komnatov was shown the grave of a Full Councillor of State* by the name of Chekhmodurov, who turned up in this backwoods heaven God alone knows how, then the grave of some woman with a double-barrelled surname who had thrown herself under a train because of love, and then a haunted belfry and a monument embossed with silver plate to a sailor of the Caspian Flotilla. The sailor had been installing electricity in the town and was shot by rich local peasants.

"But why aren't you boys at school?" Komnatov suddenly remembered.

"We don't go to school," said the first.

"Come on, you're pulling my leg," said Komnatov.

"No, honest, we don't," confirmed Freckles. "We don't want to, so we don't bother. We can do as we please here. Of course, those who want to can, but we don't."

To tell the truth, Komnatov was astonished.

"Well then, how do you spend your time?" he asked after a short pause.

"Oh, everyone's different," the first boy replied. "I, for instance, read books. It's absolutely incredible how crazy I am about them! I'm just finishing off *An Introduction to Latin Epitaphs*."

"I'm not mad about books," said Freckles. "There're just so many lies in them. I'm crazy about anything you can build. You can't imagine how good my father and I are! We can build anything!.."

"And what does your father do?" Komantov interrupted him.

"Nothing in particular. He just works—that's what he's good at, you see. At the moment, for instance, he's building a hydrogen reactor for our electric power station."

"His father's a very skilled workman," confirmed the first boy. "You could say he works for the whole factory. During the last five-year plan, for in-

*One of the ranks in the tsarist Table of Ranks.

stance, he built a water-pipe—there's nothing like it even in Moscow—a water-pipe without pipes."

"How interesting!" marveled Komnatov. "But how does the water flow through it?"

"It doesn't," replied Freckles. "It condenses. In such conditions the saline coefficient is negligible."

"But I don't approve of your father's personal life," said the first boy. "You've really got to draw the line somewhere. I mean, getting married for the seventh time, imagine that!"

"Well, that's no concern of ours," Freckles said good-naturedly. "He can marry as many times as he likes. And what's this habit you've gotten into of criticizing everyone! You know what Mark Twain used to say about nobody having the right to criticize someone else on ground on which he himself didn't stand totally upright."

"What are you getting at?"

"At Akimova and Preobrazhenskaya, that's what."

"I see... Point taken," the first boy agreed amicably.

The third boy kept silent throughout.

While they talked, they came without noticing to the next place of interest, which turned out to be the local steam baths. At first glance, the only special thing about them was that they were in an old mansion with a columned facade.

"Here are the baths," said the first boy. "There are separate places to wash in, but everyone steams themselves together—that's the way we do things here."

"But aren't people embarrassed?" asked Komnatov warily.

"What's there to be embarrassed about?" asked Freckles. "Bodies are bodies. Besides, from an early age we get used to... well, you know what, and then there's no more fuss about it."

Komnatov stared at the boys and shook his head in astonishment, but said nothing because there really was nothing objectionable about the body.

After the baths they looked at a church, and then a small house where the famous revolutionary fighter Savinkov* had spent some time, and then another house occupied by a retired minister. When Komnatov asked why the retired minister had moved here, the first boy replied, "He just did. He said he wanted to spend the rest of his life among happy people. Apparently, he had never in his life met such happy people as here in Novy Zavod."

"Only everyone's really fed up with him now," added Freckles. "Whenever he gets the chance, he makes speeches and says things like: 'Comrades, you must work, and work for the sake of your conscience, not from fear!' Of

---

*An anti-Bolshevik Social Revolutionary leader, later killed by the Cheka.

course, he just gets laughed at. And sometimes he's interrupted and asked things like: 'Why does Comrade Ex-Minister reckon we should work?' 'Why?' he replies, 'why, to create better living conditions...' And then they just howl with laughter again."

"Wait a minute," said Komnatov, "but your father works, doesn't he, so aren't they laughing at him too?"

"My father works for his own enjoyment. What's so funny about that..."

Komnatov felt uneasy. He had felt uneasy earlier, but now felt really uneasy.

"There's one thing I don't understand, guys," he said. "If hardly any of you work, how do you get by?"

"Just fine!" said the first boy, sticking up his thumb. "We live ordinary happy lives here based on respect for the human personality. In other places they just haven't reached this stage yet, that's why some people just gawk like donkeys at our life here."

These words offended Komnatov, but he did not let it show.

"In any case, I've got a formula to propose," added Freckles: "'Soviet power plus respect for the personality equals ordinary happy life.'* That's why our people are obliging and kindhearted, and work purely for the love of it."

"You know what, guys," Komnatov said, "maybe it's a good thing, but it's premature."

"Of course, it's premature!" Freckles agreed. "We're just longing to live a little, that's all!.."

At this point the conversation broke off and Komnatov took advantage of the pause to work out exactly what the boys had told him. It was obvious that Novy Zavod had a strange and unusual way of life that even the young people shared, and it wasn't so much sharing—there was nothing odd about that— as supporting in every way, while normally young people neither support nor for the most part even share anything. But because he still had not fathomed this life and was shocked that people in Novy Zavod were flagrantly skipping work, he felt a kind of irksome antipathy towards them, as ordinary people often do toward "privileged idlers,"† heroes and sages. And to the point of a pain in the pit of his stomach he felt he could not stick it out here a moment longer and simply longed to go back home. He decided to go straight to the station and buy a return ticket , and told the boys as much.

They weren't at all surprised.

"He'll go with you," said Freckles, pointing at the boy who had said nothing. "We'd all go with you, but we haven't got time, we're in a hurry."

---

*An updating of Lenin's famous answer to What is Communism?: Soviet power plus the electrification of the whole country.

†An adaptation of a phrase from A. Pushkin's "Little Tragedy" entitled *Mozart and Salieri*, where Mozart refers to artists as the "lucky, idle elect."

They shook hands with Komnatov in an adult manner and strode off on some business or other. Komnatov suddenly felt like asking just what kind of business it was, but, afraid he might hear something totally fantastic, kept silent.

Back at the station Komnatov bought a return ticket, settled down on a bench standing by itself at the far end of the platform, and began to wait. The quiet boy sat down beside him.

"I've got an aunt in Moscow," he said suddenly. "I mean, in Monino,* not Moscow, but it's the same as saying in Moscow, isn't it?.."

And then he fell silent again, gazing sadly at something in the distance.

His friends turned up, after all, just before the train was due to leave. Eyeing the quiet boy suspiciously, they handed Komnatov a bouquet of bird-cherry blossoms, and once the train started moving, they waved after it for a long time until they turned into touching dots...

"Well, now, what a strange thing life is," thought Komantov, lying on his top berth. "If my father-in-law hadn't invited himself to stay, I wouldn't have had a row with my wife and left home, and then I'd never have discovered that a hundred or so miles from the dungeon I call home people live completely different lives..." And the interesting part about it was that a little later he began thinking that this way of life really was most enticing, that, by the look of things, life in Novy Zavod really was happy, and his home really was a dungeon where, incidentally, new scenes and his fool of a father-in-law were quietly awaiting him, and the best he could expect was to lie on his side. Only the counterpoint of the suspicious silent boy had somehow put Komnatov on his guard, but, generally speaking, this was such an unnerving notion that he suddenly felt desperately like getting off and going back on the return train. "Fool," he said to himself, "absolute fool!.."

Meanwhile the train had slowed down and soon stopped. Komnatov glanced out the window to find out what the station was called: it was Novy Zavod.

Translated by Jan Butler

Originally published in *Novyi mir,* June 1987

---

*A town outside of Moscow with a sanatorium nearby.

Alexander Ivanchenko

Safety Procedure I

People stand huddled against the walls of the train station. Hiding behind stone projections, columns, and water spouts, they peer out now and then and look somewhere into the distance, down a dirty, oil-covered track. They are all waiting for a train, but for some reason the train is not coming.

And soon they lose hope.

The last few pieces of baggage placed on the platform disappear into hiding places and not a single brave soul dares to leave his refuge any more. But maybe the wind is to blame for this.

Fitful and angry, the wind blows along the deserted platform, carrying cigarette-butts, paper wads, and the last leaves far away, to the ends of the earth.

A man walks into the wind. He walks interminably slowly, even though he is apparently in a hurry. He overcomes the wind inch by inch, but he is slow anyway, this man. And the wind catches his hand.

The wind catches his hand. In his hand he has an elegant little briefcase, and under his arm a little parcel. The parcel slips and unravels. In a flash the wind tears the newspaper off the parcel and wraps it around a lamppost. Someone will read it later.

There is still another, possibly blue, paper covering the parcel, and then another, probably the same color, and then another of a somewhat different, but maybe the same color (you can't tell for sure) and then another and, it seems, yet another, but it too will be torn off by the wind, no one doubts this any longer, and now there are only colored scraps left and they are carried off by the wind.

But the contents of the parcel remain in place. Something vague, flat and defenseless on the bare train platform. Probably a book, a stack of records or something else. You can't tell for sure.

The man (he probably knows what's in the parcel, but maybe not), the man (everyone leans out of their hiding places for a moment and looks after him), the man (the newspaper ought to be read today or otherwise it will be out of date), the man (hurry; it could also be carried off by the wind), the man (if it's a book, it's probably a gift edition), the man (it is so huge), the man (no doubt one of the classics), the man (the likes of him always fuss over classics), the man (and if it is a record, it's undoubtedly Schönberg), the man (on the other hand, maybe it's Penderecki), the man (the likes of him always hob-nob with Schönberg), the man (with Schönberg and occasionally with Penderecki), the man...

The man struggles to bend over his parcel, but the wind won't let him do it; but the man does not abandon his attempts and he is helpless, this man. And hope abandons the man.

He looks at the people in dismay, soundlessly moving his lips and spasmodically, like a fish on ice, he gasps for air and helplessly thrashes with his hands. He's probably asking for help, this man. But the people reject his pleas. Someone from among those waiting wants to help him, but he is held back by his sleeve: why?

After making a few more timid, unsuccessful attempts and having his desperate appeal refused, the man picks up his briefcase and again faces the wind.

He also faces hatred, because he is late, this man—he's late, but he will still manage—and, of course, because he is lightly dressed. Because of Schönberg and Penderecki, and because he is lightly dressed. And because he is leaving the parcel.

He travels light, this man. And it would be better for him not to leave his parcel. Without a coat, without his things, in a light-colored summer suit. The man doesn't even have a hat on. Apparently he's just gotten off a plane, from some warm countries. Where else could he have come from?

He fusses about; in the anxiety of impending guilt he continually adjusts his tie, holds down the flaps of his coat, and also looks at his watch. Why is he looking at his watch? It ignites hatred.

It ignites hatred. It dispels hope.

The man is approaching the station, the wind is more moderate, even significantly so; one could say that it has almost died down, but why is he so late, this man, and why does he walk into the wind?

Only the train can come toward him now and the train is still not here, only this unbearable, late man who, moreover, has left his parcel behind, and who, in addition, is still looking at his watch. It would have been better for this man to have come on time and it would have been better not to have left the parcel behind, and better without Schönberg and Penderecki—certainly better without them. And it would have been better if he had no watch. And better if he were to walk with the wind, this man. Then he would have come from the direction of these people's home, from the direction of the home-land, as hope, and not from the direction of the train, as one who dispels hope. Because whatever is from the direction of hope but is not hope dispels hope. And it ignites hatred.

Slower and slower, this man. It would be better if he didn't have a watch, better if he were to walk with the wind.

Everyone steps out to meet the man, they form a black semicircle, not even a semicircle, but a circle, a ring, a black oval of hatred left ajar to admit guilt. And the oval swallows the man.

He stands confused, this man. He can't bear the look of truth. Because the many always have the look of truth, the one always the look of guilt.

He stands confused, this man. He wants not to have a watch, he wants to walk with the wind. The wind starts up again and the man instinctively turns his back to it. But it's too late: the crowd closes its ranks tightly and, protected on all sides by its hatred, the man loses his sense of the wind's direction.

His guilt is obvious. The people come closer and closer; he doesn't deserve leniency. The one thing left is to clarify what was left in the parcel and then... Someone is sent for the parcel.

The people circle in closer and closer. He doesn't deserve mercy. The most energetic are women and the young; others are there only to support malice. A pale woman in black, apparently a widow, will take revenge for her own misfortune. She is already in the epicenter.

And he is confused, this man. A little island of despair and hope. He is searching for something in his pockets, he seems to have lost something there, this man, he probably wants to produce something, some impossible justification. With despair and hope he peers at the people and rummages and rummages, searches ceaselessly, he even guiltily turns his pockets inside out. What is he hoping for, this man?

What is he hoping for, this man? The widow has already laid a hand on his throat.

The courier is late, the crowd is panting with hatred. So where is this im-possible man? And where is this impossible Penderecki?

A warm quivering hand. A cold quavering throat.

Now he's already approaching the station, this courier (not the courier train, the courier; the courier train will arrive soon), and so he's already at the entrance, this courier, and he's joyously waving the parcel.

The hand that has found certainty no longer hurries, no one will take away its future. It is even prepared to toy with its sacrifice, that is possible now. It is even prepared to defend it before other, also warm, hands. There's even a certain kind of pleasure in this—to defend when you know that later you will give in anyway, that you want to give in. Anyway, why is it that he is so unshaven and why is it that Penderecki is so delayed?

Penderecki came. Not Penderecki, but the courier with the supposed Penderecki. If only it were he.

The crowd sweeps toward the courier (not the courier train, the courier; they will sweep toward the train later), the crowd sweeps toward the courier and waits for Penderecki to emerge into the world. They post a guard by the man.

The crowd greedily surrounds the obstetrician. And he continues to tear the paper off the parcel, his hands immersed up to the elbows—the parcel turned out to be unexpectedly large. Covered with sweat, he groans and tears away, and hurries, and gets nervous and changes hands, and blood, blood, a sea of blood, and callousness, and the lust of his assistants over the gaping womb of the mother. Finally, he turns something over inside—he has just felt the fruit—he turns it, tears it off, turns it over and grunts with satisfaction. Finally. He will find out before anyone else what's there (he's already felt the fruit), he will find out before anyone else who is there, and his hand will find out even earlier. Now he's ready to drag it out into the world. They all lower their heads modestly so as not to give the child the evil eye, and then—the still uterine but already half-earthly wail of the child.

The still uterine but already half-earthly wail of the train.

Who was it, then, who appeared in the world? Schönberg, or was it Penderecki, after all? Or was it some other composer? And maybe it was simply some pitiful little bastard, unworthy of attention, with a wolfish jaw and a harelip? They didn't have time to clear this up and they left Penderecki (since it was he, after all) to lie on the asphalt. Discordant, cosmogonic exclamations, at first uncertain and tormented, then more joyous and harmonious, accompanied the appearance of the approaching train.

And he was left alone—alone in the funnel of expanding hope, in the torment of a contracting guilt.

They all rushed toward their things. A blind green caterpillar reluctantly tracked its way toward the station. The passengers were seized by despondency. The corrugated, dusty sphincter of the rear wagon drifted past the man.

And he's still looking for something, this man. One can only hope that it's not the ticket, after all. Because no one will let him on the train without a ticket. He even forgot about Penderecki—and this is precisely the time he should remember him. But he continues to look for something, this man, and one can only hope that it's not the ticket, after all. Because no one will let him on without a ticket.

The train will stop for ten minutes. Quite possibly, a bit longer. During this time the man will have time to check his pockets more than once, to pick up his parcel and to look at his watch. Now he is quite proud, this man, of the fact that he has this watch. And of the fact that he is walking into the wind.

He is walking along the platform and is not even looking back at the parcel. He walks slowly, importantly, like a self-assured person, a passenger for whom this train had been especially prepared. But why is there, nevertheless, anxiety on his face, and why is he, nevertheless, not finding something in his pockets?

Everyone had boarded the train a long time ago. He alone lingers, this man. Maybe the tickets are at fault, after all (maybe they are at fault, after all)? At any rate, he leaves his pockets in peace. A stream of glassy indifference followed on his heels.

He walks along the platform, this man. Lightly dressed and also looking at his watch. Without a coat, without his things, in a light-colored summer suit. The parcel is forgotten. He throws out a challenge, this man, but the submissiveness of fulfilled hope will not accept it.

Final preparations. The cocked mechanism of the train is frozen in its tracks, preparing to shatter the red target of the semaphore. The conductors have gotten a yellow light.

Yellow on black, the conductors have gotten a yellow light. In vain: the train won't leave, the man has not been given a seat yet.

The people haven't been given a seat yet in the first sleeper car with bars on the windows. A car with reserved seats, a sleeper. Sleepless places: 58. (The man's friends will ride in the car's vestibule.) And the train awaits the people.

The train awaits the people. They have arrived. Six massive, streamlined trucks were prudently driven onto the platform and quickly, maintaining an interval, they began unloading from the back, then they started depositing people into the car. An unimaginable recount started. (The dogs participated in the count.)

The man comes closer. Curious to see what is going on. Through the narrow chink of trucks parked next to one another he observes the people unwillingly abandoning the inhabited expanse of the trucks. Only one step between the trucks and the car (over an abyss of uncertainty), only one step, but they are in torment taking it, abandoning their familiar space. Now the trucks are leaving, carrying the living space away. They are leaving now and a terrifying anxiety seizes the man.

A terrifying anxiety seizes the man and the engineer gives the signal for departure. The man runs alongside the train, turning out his pockets on the run. He waves a multicolored bunch of tickets—just like everyone else he had them, of course—he lifts them above his head like a banner, but for some reason he shows his pockets. He shows them, those insignificant, empty pockets as evidence of non-guilt and guilt. The guilt of innocence and the innocence of guilt. But the naked shame of his turned-out pockets touched no one.

The train starts moving slowly. The man loses hope. For the last time he shows his multicolored bunch; for the last time he lifts it above him like a banner, he even makes a bashful attempt to palm off a bribe—if only they would take him along on the train, he so badly wants to go—but the conductors sullenly shake their heads, indicating his empty pockets with their eyes. Madly, panting in despair and madness, he runs behind the train, which is gaining speed (the first car still hasn't passed the switch) and shouts something into the roar. The man's flat, desiccated shout is wound around the wheels of guilt.

And hope abandons the man. He watches despondently as the last car makes a farewell turn and leaves the switch behind.

And, suddenly, hope returns to the man. He sees that the last door of the last car is slightly open and that there is no one behind it! Strictly speaking, hope had already floated past the man (the redemptive inertia of hope), and he's just now become aware of it. Not letting hope pass into hopelessness (the redemptive self-sufficiency of hope), he rushed off after the departing train and in three jumps overtook the car. Having jumped into the half-open door (hope left him only now and turned into its opposite quality, although it had just been realized), having jumped into the half-open door and slammed it behind him with relief, as if severing from himself all possibility of impossibility, he finally took a breath and finally tucked in his pockets (the latter unmasked him in his own eyes). But fear before the future immediately took possession of the man, for hope is afraid of not being realized and, once realized, of being lost. And fear accompanied the man.

Fear accompanied the man, but he tucked in his pockets anyway. By this he hoped to delude someone, this man. He even brushed the dust off his shoes, imparting to himself a gentlemanly appearance, since this was an entirely legal man and one who even lay claim to loyalty. He even combed himself before the window and even adjusted his tie. Pity only that he doesn't smoke. Now he regretted this. Why, he could have taken a cigarette and pretended that he had come out for a smoke. Many do this, that is, go out when they have to smoke. There is nothing unusual in this. And it arouses suspicions in no one. But the suitcase would betray him anyway. Why would it be necessary to come out with his things? It's true that this was not a real suitcase, the kind with which every self-respecting passenger would travel, but only a small briefcase, a delicate, elegant attache case for everyday, cultural trifles. But even so, a normal passenger is not about to take it out with him every time he has to smoke. That would be just too funny. Why, it would be better if he had some sort of stuffed suitcase that had been around or a bag or, even better, a venerable coffer of imposing proportions—with stickers. They would give proper expression to his lawfulness and law-abiding nature. But as it was, his little case only emphasized all his frivolity as a passenger and, even worse, his illegality. Illegality was insufferable to the man.

The man made an effort to hide the case behind his back, but nothing came of it. The case now and then rode out into the open and somehow flippantly rattled against the wall. And, in fact, you just can't hold your hands behind your back the whole time—that would be too suspicious. No, it's better to just keep it out in full view. And he deposited the case directly on the floor, nearly in the middle of the vestibule of the car, challengingly, of course, and hysterically, yet he put it out, but the narrow bottom of the case didn't hold up under the braking and it toppled on its side.

Initially the man rejoiced. It seemed that chance had helped him. Here, one might say, lies my little case. It lies there, not afraid of anything; it just lies there as carelessly as anything, as befits the lawful things of a law-abiding passenger. But then he caught himself. To leave his case like that was unthinkable. Its new leather shine on the worn linoleum of the vestibule was just too challenging. No, the illegality of the case in this position was obvious. Then the man took it and placed it next to the wall, lightly pressing it with his leg. From the very start the man realized the unlawfulness of the case in this position. This was simply its temporary, in a sense, intermediate, state, a substantiation of a working hypothesis that would still require some future undertaking by the man. It was necessary to find a reliable and stable state for the case and the man plunged into tormenting thought. To begin with, it could be hidden under the folding seat, in the coal compartment, or squeezed in some way just under his coat. Ultimately it could be covered with an old newspaper. But all of this would mean that he had hidden the case and wished to evade its indictment, whereas the task consisted precisely in simply changing its position, while the case, and, consequently, the entire responsibility for its presence, remained where it was, etc.

And what if he were to place it upright (having gotten confused in subordinate clauses, the man decided to place the case upright), and what if he were to place it upright, or to shove it behind the grating of the glass, or simply to go and open it, lay it on the seat, demonstrating his indifference? Orororor? Possibilities followed one after one, but the man rejected them decisively.

Possibilities followed one after another and the man set to tormented thinking. Thought furrowed his gloomy brow until another accident helped him again. He noticed that a square plastic hatch made for some purpose in the ceiling of the vestibule suddenly opened and started banging in rhythm to the wheels. However, the hatch had probably been open from the very start; it is even certain that this was so and he had no doubts of it now, and these sounds... (That unconscious irritation with the railway authorities as soon as he had gotten used to this place [at first he had felt only gratitude for their carelessness], and a kind of incomprehensible, floating, vibrating knocking that merged with the swelling harmony of the dominant tone—now he discerned them clearly.)

Now he clearly made them out. He had only to raise his head to see the gray lid of the hatch, bordered by a duralumin strip, every now and then either contracting or expanding its mysterious ceiling slit (ceiling, not sexual), producing all the while unpardonable erotic sounds. Moreover the hunger of suppressed lust sought nourishment and sharpened his erotic senses. He felt again how the hardened fruit of his long-standing irritation sprouted an insecure and timid shoot of gratitude—and the case found its refuge. Pulling away the edge of the hatch (only one edge; the other was fastened by a mysterious tetrahedron), pulling away the edge of the hatch and stretching the mysterious sexuo-ceiling slit, he squeezed his finger in and felt a blessed emptiness.

Having expelled his seed, he felt a blessed emptiness. Under the weight of the case the door of the hatch was drawn back and stopped emitting sounds. The blessed sexuoripe slit hid within itself an ineffable treasure. The man calmed down. His disgorged desire, coupled with the destruction of clues, significantly diminished his agitation. Now he could attend to the externals (the concealment of the case seemed so reliable that he could declare his noninvolvement not only in its presence, but also in its absence). He again brushed off his shoes (they were already dusty) and loosened his tie. But he immediately buttoned up the jacket he had unbuttoned earlier—that seemed like an insult to loyalty. The loosened tie was perfectly sufficient. Besides, the color of his. . . But then it hadn't even occurred to him that a passenger might allow himself somewhat greater freedom. Even though every passenger is, unquestionably, also a citizen of his country, the shifting space of the train (but not the airplane) guarantees him somewhat greater freedom of action (an alternating loyalty usually suffers some loss). And the man unbuttons his coat.

The man unbuttons his coat, the coat has three buttons, the tie is loosened, the hand is shoved carelessly into the pocket. He is even whistling something, this impossible man, some catchy little tune which he invented just for the occasion—for the occasion of shifting guilt. The occasion of shifting space, the occasion of intermittent guilt.

And guilt takes possession of the man.

He feels anxiety, this man. His position, he feels, is not secure after all. Otherwise, why this tune and why the motif of constantly approaching guilt?

It's true that he has tickets. He even has a suitcase, the desire, and the need to travel—everything that determines the status of a passenger. Somewhere deep down, in the very depths of his soul, he knows that he is right, that his status is legal, that he has tickets—here they are in the inside pocket of his jacket, you can see for yourself—that he has money—he is ready to spend it, and this gives him additional confidence—and that, after all, he has the desire and the need to travel (in this instance desire and need coincide, though the latter outweighs the former). He has everything that characterizes a passenger; besides that, he has things (and they appear here as the substantiation of need). He has them, but nevertheless, somewhere in the depths of his soul, in its very depths, he feels that he is not right and that his status is highly undefined. If he is right, why did he unbutton his jacket, loosen his tie, hide the case—in general undertake everything possible to prove his rightness? This, after all, is not invention and there exists the presumption of the passenger's innocence. Let them prove their case.

It exists, but why, then, does he still feel guilt? What is this unheard of, senseless anxiety, this catchy, alternating little tune, this anxiety of buttons and hands?

The train makes a first stop. For the time being, it's not an obligatory one, but more like an unconscious striving for symmetry and rhythm. But this brings relief to the man. He feels that he is on the firm ground of legality while the train is not moving. Yet he's already seized with agitation at its impending departure. And he is already prepared to abandon the firm ground of certainty, prepared to jump out and push the train from the back, so that it resolve itself all the faster, this agitation, so that he might be on his way as soon as possible.

A sharp, intermittent, tracer-like shudder of the locomotive's jerk passed along the cars and the man burst into tears. (The man was at the very end of the jerk and took upon himself not only the summary result of the blow, but also the sum total of universal striving: each of the passengers now strived to depart as soon as possible.) The man burst into tears and rolled on the floor.

At the moment of falling, before he fell but already after he became conscious of the fact that he would fall, he saw the massive handle of the door leading to the car slowly begin to turn downward and the door about to open.

The man hurried to get up, dry his tears, and wipe them away with the sleeve of his summer coat. It was not necessary to provide additional evidence, and he tried his first smile on for size (as he fell, he evaluated the slowness of the turning handle, and assuming from this the slowness of the opening door, which was only to have opened, he decided that he would have time to try several on for size).

This one was unsuitable. It was too insulting and deliberate (but, even as he was getting up, he had time to grasp that for someone in his position any smile would look prepared and deliberate, and, of course, guilty in its preparedness and deliberateness in the draughty suddenness of the doorway, but then he somehow forgot about it.) Having hurriedly tried on all of them, and stopping finally on one that was rather formless but unassailable in its formlessness, he decided that it was time for the door to open (he even wanted to help it open, since he could no longer hold the formlessness on his face), he decided that it was time for the door to open, otherwise he would once again start the trying-on process and get caught in the middle of his changing. Though he should have known that any negligé (like any noted shortcoming) is always more excusable than... The handle, released from below, initially rose upwards slowly and then shot up like an arrow toward the ceiling and caught on something, emitting the short, dry crack of a tightly wound spring.

The man breathed a sigh of relief. Having been left with his wrinkled house clothes, natural and, therefore, comfortable, he tried to remember the motif (not the tune, the motif) of that basic and everyday behavior in which he felt good and which, as he now realized, he had not once tried on today since his appearance at the station. He had only begun to remember this when the handle again started a series of new transformations.

The series of new transformations consisted of:

(a) complex, rather confident, though graduated movements from bottom to top and exactly the same kind from top to bottom;

(b) sharp swings, visually indivisible into separate motions, also from top to bottom and from bottom to top;

(c) slow, insinuating, snake-like arcs, as if intending to delude the door;

(d) silent, smooth rocking, as if informed by long experience, in which a shadow of doubt could nevertheless be felt;

(e) and, finally, shuddering, completely despairing and panicky jerks in the horizontal plane of the door and in the shattered mechanism of the lock.

It goes without saying that from the very start the man realized his criminality. He realized it, and could do nothing with himself. His criminality (apart from the chief crime of illegal travel) also consisted in the fact that he did nothing to hide his criminality, i. e., to help open the door for the one who so persistently sought to do so. Finally, he realized that at some point the door would be opened anyway and then everything would be revealed instantly. And the longer these, so far unsuccessful, attempts by this incognito continued, the clearer and more obvious would be the success of his exposure later. He realized this.

He realized it and still did nothing to forestall this exposure. More likely he even sought it and only delayed the enjoyment of his final fall. (Having abandoned all hope, the handle continued its endless trans-formations.)

He again started redressing his face. To tell the truth, he no longer expected that this would prove useful. The more so since the handle, it seems, had reached total despair. Its waverings, at any rate, were lifeless and formalized. His redressing was also lifeless and formalized and resembled the dressing of an aging courtesan, limply and indifferently slipping off her peignoir and having neither the strength nor the desire to move on to daywear.

Slipping off one smile, he did not put on another for a long time. He scrutinized himself unclothed. And so he remained, either from forgetfulness (the waverings of the handle did not die down), or because he felt the pleasure of nakedness.

The handle suddenly trembled desperately, a sudden yawning of the door enveloped the man from head to foot and he staggered back into a corner. He didn't even have time to change. He was caught unaware.

A pale little pixie got up off her knees and with the curiosity of a developing woman stared at the man. She examined him with interest, appreciatively studying his naked body, its every separate feature, and slowly moving her eyes downward.

The man covered himself with his hands. He understood everything, this man. He understood that if this were to continue even an instant longer, he would be accused of corruption. Corruption of a minor is a punishable offense. A crime of no lesser magnitude than the one he was already guilty of. But what could he do? How to hide himself from her undisguised delight? How to conceal that which. . . It would be better to strip completely, not to betray his nakedness in any way, and to look her directly in the eyes. And he removed his hands.

In the defenselessness of shifting space, in the intermittent fever of guilt, he removed his hands from. The girl opened her eyes wide.

"Mommy, mommy!" she would shout were she able to speak. "Look at the funny man and his funny beard! "

"Let's get away from here, child," her mother would say if her daughter were not mute (not only from delight), "let's get away, my child, that's just a man... he just hasn't shaved for a while."

The terror of a safety razor slid across his bare belly and he clenched in agony (all this accompanied by the agony of her farinaceous face and the grain of the door revealing itself before his eyes). The door swung and closed. The man grasped his head in his hands and thought that he hadn't shaved for a long while. That meant even more evidence. But guilt was already abandoning the man: the train was nearing a station.

The man finally calms down. Something resembling a smile is on his face. A sensation of light. He breathes deeply and opens his eyes and ears wider. He releases them from a safety catch (his lecherously lingering hands also calm down). And he opens the door (not the one whose yawning enveloped him and not the one in which he corrupted minors); he opens the door and releases the safety catch from it. The broad air of the fields rushes into the man's cramped space and he joyously gulps it down.

The train slows down. This is the first obligatory stop. The man shyly peers out of his kennel and looks along the line of cars. His hair flies in the wind.

His hair flies in the wind, his tie flaps again in the wind, and again there is some sort of inconceivable noise near the train, by the first barred car with people. Everything was mixed together: people, confusion, four-legged creatures. Vague shouts intermingling with the threatening light of the semaphore; greetings intermingling with the anguish of parting. Not a single passenger got off at the station, nor even looked outside. Only a handful of prisoners proceeded onto the platform. (The dogs separated the clean from the unclean.)

The man rushed back into his cramped space. He pressed up to the window fogged over with fear. Poles, lamps and gloomy railroad workers floated by; a yellow signal flag with a red pancake on its head floated by; the prisoners who had been taken off the train floated by, a small group of ten, twelve people (the dogs prevented a count), a small group of ten, twelve people—greetings intermingling with parting.

Despair distorted the man's face. Grasping his head in his hands, he started running feverishly around his solitary cell, stifling his anguished wails.

What can he do? How should he act? Where is his salvation? Where did he go wrong? Can it be that they will soon get to him and then... No, it's better not to think about that. The whole horror of his illegal status presented itself to him.

Again he rushed to search his pockets. He inspected literally every finger length (alas!—this is the mercilessness of the language's helplessness, and not the impotence of rhythm lapsing into silence), he inspected literally every finger length...

"Finger length" to describe a pocket? Help! Commotion in the Institute of Beef Tongues, *chaos* in the Academy of the Tongue-Tied.

He inspected literally every *square finger length* of his trouser pocket, despising the purism of the tied tongues.

Halving his hope (only in regard to his trousers; his coat was also not pocketless), halving his hope in regard to his trousers, he started on the second pocket. A huge hole, the size of a man's *red* fist, was brought to light, and in spite of the fact that all hope in regard to his trousers was exhausted, the man's chances increased exactly by four (the number of pockets in the coat). For the time being he did not take the possibility of other volumes into consideration.

Alas! alas and alack, the dry logic of a rationalist. But his intuition whispered to him that his chances had fallen to the tune of a man's fist and that both his case and his coat with its four pockets were powerless against this fist. Fate was lowering the stakes. Pranks of the heavenly broker.

He took his jacket off timidly. To kill off the last glimmer of hope. He hung his hope on an improvised hook. He walked away to a corner. . . He didn't dare kill it right off—rather, it wasn't a question of daring, he just didn't want to—what good is there in killing an infant? Let it live at least till it comes of age (there is, after all, a special delight in killing a grown-up: it's already an attempt on a god and not a man; it makes sense). He will raise it on his own milk.

He raised it. What a huge, rosy-cheeked child, as chubby as Gargantua. How he radiates life! Can it be that the man will raise his hand?

He raised it. With pale, trembling hands the man went for his own child and strangled it as it coiled on the hook.

Hunched and devastated, he put on his hunched coat, hunched, stripped of money and hope (alas, again the helplessness of language, this time the helplessness of polysemy: why, the coat was stripped of its contents as well).

Having put on his coat, stripped of money and its contents, he descended to the very depths of his despair and collapsed to the floor of his solitary cell.

A thin, dusty ray of light broke through toward him. He opened his eyes. A black, lame spider, eternal toiler, wove its endless web. They were friends. Yesterday he almost lost the spider again. By evening the lame one had woven over all the corners and circled the ceiling in perplexity, looking for work. Finally, slowly, as if it were glancing over its shoulder, it headed for the window, sighing from old age and cares. It was possible that the same thing would happen as it did many years ago when the spider, bringing all activity to a close in its cell, set out on a long prison tour and years passed before it returned again. Were this to repeat itself, the man would be unable to bear his loneliness. Yes, he had a great scare yesterday. He wanted to stop it, no matter what, not let it get away at any cost, but the spider continued out of reach along the ceiling and then the window, a narrow vertical crevice, which was

also too high. And then the man threw himself on his knees before the crawling creature and began entreating it to remain. But the spider, after lingering
in indecision, crawled away. In a fit of despair the man threw off his heavy
prison shoe and flung it at his friend. No, he didn't want to kill it, only to
stop it, to hold it back, to force it to remain here for at least another moment.
But he missed, and his shoe flew into a corner and tore down the web. Either
the spider heard his entreaties, or it wished to check his work for the last
time, or it may be that it simply got frightened by the noise, but it returned
and, discovering an empty corner, it set to work. From that moment on they
were never apart. Now the man regularly assigns the lame one work, and as
the latter is finishing its final corner, the first already awaits it, empty. This has
continued for many years, and it is the man's innermost secret. He has no
other secrets. And he hopes that others will never find out about it. Because if
the other prisoners learn of this, they will definitely complain to the prison
authorities and justice will be restored. Because the spider belongs to everyone. But it's hardly possible that they guess the truth. No doubt they don't
count the spider among the living. Just so the overseer doesn't notice.

He propped himself on his arm on his cruel prison couch and turned to
the wall. Broken rows of days spent in prison covered the wall in fantastic
shapes. He had been building cities from these days, adding suburbs, laying
out new streets and alleys. Finally his creation took on a finished look. A brilliant layout. A marvel of architecture. Quarenghi and Corbusier.* Lately he
was busy with the reconstruction of the central street, but he constantly felt
that he had run out of days and surreptitiously stole them from eternity. He
was in everlasting debt to it, but nevertheless continued his senseless borrow-
ing. In the morning, the day having hardly begun, he would patiently scratch
out the next line, and in the evening, at the close of the day, he would add another as if he had completely forgotten the former one. That is how the huge
debt mounted up. Was he counting on the fact that in the end fate would
grant him these days: stolen from eternity? Perhaps; more likely he understood that by doing so he was only bringing his own end closer, and that this
anticipated happiness snatched from fate was only shortening his life.

Reluctantly he scratched on the wall the day that had just begun and got
up. He walked up to the window and, standing on his toes, he put his chin
on the stone windowsill (he no longer tried to get the prison's stool that was
bolted to the floor, though it took him a long time to get used to the idea that
it was bolted to the floor; at first this oppressed him most of all—the impossi-

---

*Giacomo Quarenghi (1744-1817). A Russian architect of Italian origins, an outstanding repre-
sentative of the classical style, for example, the Hermitage Theater and the Smolny Institute in
Saint Petersburg.

Charles LeCorbusier (1887-1965). French architect and theorist, a proponent of the aesthetics of functionalism.

bility of moving the furniture according to one's wishes [the table and bed were also immovable]. This subtle attempt to take away the prisoner's final freedom grieved him. Later he understood that the prison authorities in their infinite mercy were only forcing him to face himself and to find there that which he sought; he finally learned this).

He looked through the window. A narrow shred of sky appeared, crossed out by a thick iron bar. If he's lucky, he'll see today, as he did once in some forgotten alley of obliterated days, a soaring bird in the sky, or a cloud or a kite flown by boys. If it rains, one can hope for lightning. He had seen it rather often on almost every street of his huge city. But the day was cloudy and there was no use counting on the window. On such days it doesn't even rain.

He walked away. His legs were tired. He had learned the art of alternating standing with resting. His toes no longer ached as they had in the first days of incarceration. You simply had to walk away from the window in time and to sense in time that nothing would take place outside while you were resting; you only have to listen to yourself, your intuition won't deceive you. He used to spend entire days in this terrible self-torture and then his legs would torment him for weeks. Meanwhile it was possible that outside the window a bird or the boys' kite was flying by. This he couldn't forgive himself.

He looked up. The spider wove on, unraveling its endless thread. At times he hated it, this spider, and even though it was his only companion, he was ready to kill it. And he was perplexed by this duality (he didn't know that there are friends for loving and friends for hating). Freedom was accessible to this creature, but it scorned it. After all, it could have found itself a cool, damp corner somewhere in freedom, far away from these gloomy walls. And what does it feed on here? Even a fly won't venture in, yet how many of them are there on the outside? But, then, if it's not born in freedom, there's nothing you can do.

He suddenly remembered that long, long ago, at the very beginning of his countless days, a big, velvety bumblebee pierced by a piece of straw flew in. It flew around the cell for a long time and finally, weakened, it plunged to the floor. The man picked it up and pulled out the straw, but the bumblebee didn't revive. Somewhere beyond the high prison wall children were playing. At that time their joyous, spring voices would often reach his solitary cell. They undoubtedly had many such bumblebees and they didn't begrudge them their straws. But the bumblebee died and the children grew silent. Undoubtedly they grew up and dispersed. And, of course, such a thing never repeated itself, because the children of those children now played other games. He understood now that the bumblebee had been granted him as a memory. And he suddenly understood in general that the free, careless life now no longer had any value for him, and he was even afraid of admitting this to himself. Those verdant, joyous impressions, at one time so lush and bountiful, had now grown dull and somehow alien to him, remote and unreal, as if related to him by someone else, transmitted to him by some other person, not by one who had experienced them, but one who had received them third, fourth or fifth hand. It was some other, unreal, counterfeit life and no one would be able to convince him that he had lived then and not now. Because not a single free recollection *corresponded* to his present situation and, consequently, could not possibly be roused to life. After all, every recollection is born of hope, maybe minute, but hope nevertheless, and it was precisely hope that was lacking here. And he understood the munificence of fate, which had condemned him to this paucity of impressions. This paucity had been granted him to liberate a hitherto unknown space in his hitherto dead imagination, to disembody it, and to free it from his body. He felt free only here. He didn't even know whether he now wanted *that* freedom, that visible, external, disgusting freedom in which he would now feel like a prisoner. Wouldn't he be blown apart by the rarified space of *that* little freedom, since the difference in pressure between his inner and outer freedom would be enormous.

In a state of happiness each of our impressions is positive, localized, and is only what it is, while in a state of suffering the positive sense of the impression is joined by a negative sense, that is, by all that which it doesn't express and in a sense denies while it inevitably assumes it, just as the subtrahend assumes the minuend.

And he remembered how at some point long, long ago, also in the beginning of his countless days, he heard something glassy falling and breaking somewhere in the endless prison corridor, a kind of fine, flimsy phial of delicate, *light-blue* glass. It fell on its fragile oval bottom, frosted, almost silver, with tiny bubbles of air inside. Still silent, as if frozen in horror before itself, still intact and chaste, a hundredfold more intact before its disintegration, it pondered an entire inscrutable instant whether it should shatter into a thousand fragments or not. And he knew that it would shatter, it could not but shatter, he wanted this, after all, and it fragmented, flowed out, not, of course, from the blow (what nonsense!), but from his desire and his entreaties, from the fact that he wanted this. He knew that. And when it disintegrated and flowed out and surged in transparent streams along the steep steps of the prison, crumbling into innumerable pieces and multiplying on each step, he saw, he felt, he knew each little obstacle in the way of this shrill stream, each flat rock, twig, silt-covered stone, every quiet backwater in the jagged shore of the stream, the icily splashing fish, the shimmering spiderwebs drifting above the water, the delicate, intermittent trace of a water bug, a leaf floating to the bottom, the murmur of a vine skimming the backwater, and then a sharp, stormy turn when all the water in the stream arches and seems to want to splash out onto the shore, followed by still another, just as swift and sharp, with a fallen tree trunk in the waters, and then a smooth, deep, restrained bubbling of the waters, the glass has massed together, a narrowing of the stream, a dam, separate sounds are no longer distinguishable, a stealthy, oily discharge and, finally, the shoals, a broad, open expanse, flooded, green meadows, brooding and chiming herds, and the sound distends into a single iridescent, thin film, a keen silvery sound of endlessness ringing in the ears.

This sound is endless. He always hears it, even in his sleep. He knows that he can stop it any minute, he only has to turn the sound back and to lead it back to those hands which had released it. It was sufficient just to imagine the backward journey of the glass—doing this, he already started tempting fate again—step after step, from the meadows, the fields, from the brooding and chiming herds, from the distended iridescent film, back to the dam, into the narrow, oily channel, to the turns, the fallen, mossy trunk, to the backwaters, the shimmering spiderwebs, the leaf floating to the bottom, up along the endless prison stairs, the sound thickening and coarsening and the glass becomes more and more intact, it flows together as onto a magnet, what large fragments, but there are still other fragments in them, everything is still grouping together from atoms, and now there are already whole pieces, ten, five, four, two, the phial is whole, it rises, floats to the bottom, there is some resistance of forms, finally the creation is finished, again that senseless suspension above the precipice, he is now before the upward leap, now that flight has started, an inconceivable, incalculable curve, a rest on the landing (the final reunification with the bottom), tiny jumps along the stairs, precisely eighteen, cracked sounds that will no longer be delivered from the burden of song flow together into a din, again a landing, a grooving, an indentation, by dusty, worn-out shoes, a senseless circling, quickening, quickening, a few inconceivable somersaults, and now it stands on its bottom, a din, a piercing din in the whole prison, silence, it tears away from the ground, a tumbling senseless flight upwards, into a precipice, an abyss—into the nether regions of hands frozen in horror.

But the phial was not to know hell. It freezes at the very threshold of the nether regions. Again it conducts its endless flight, and now, once more, down along the endless prison stairs, and again the cramped channel, the backwater, turns, the dam, the broad expanses of the meadows, and endless is the flow of time, and fate is unrestorable, and endless is the sound of eternity in one's ears.

Now that sound is always with him. He's at one with it and sometimes he himself becomes the sound. The sound becomes more refined, dissolves in its causality; it drops down to the very bottom of consciousness and becomes unmanifested. But it's there, the man knows this, and he has only to desire it to hear again this endless symphony of blue glass. And again, together with the water, he savors freedom. For who can hold back water? It penetrates everywhere.

And how about the ray of sunlight, the dance of dust specks in it, and endless life, full of sense and motion? In that ray you can see that the earth is not dead, that it's not at all dust, as the poets say, but a living and feeling organism. And the inscriptions appearing on the walls? Patterns of dampness, the play of shadows? And the velvety tenderness of the lichens in the corner over the bed—soon they will be in bloom. He waters them from his meager prison soup. And the hoar-frost in the winter cold? And the pigeon down on the window? And the mysterious natural designs on the leg of the wooden table that he has quietly started to decode? And the mysterious procession of the sun on the wall that reveals the decorative pattern of the ancient brickwork?

He lay down to rest and closed his eyes. He had begun to tire easily. The least impression in the prison now expanded into the broadest scene, an endless flow of associations, which drained him to the point of exhaustion. The glassy sound that had once again come to life in his brain, which now horrified him by its inevitability, was interrupted by the jangling of bolts and the sorting of rusty keys. Someone was coming toward him. The phial was suspended in mid-air.

Apparently they were coming to feed him. Sure enough, the sunspot was in its usual position on the floor, precisely in the crack of the flagstone. But the spot was already emerging from the crack.

The door opened. A morose, pockmarked overseer with keys at his side stood by the door, silently indicating that he come out.

The man obeyed. He looked around his cell for the last time, the window, the spider, the lichens, and at the long series of his sad days. And this last, the *ultimate,* day, this as yet totally unlived today, stood out somehow too absurdly from the others and violated their deliberate symmetry somehow too vulgarly and coarsely. It was shorter than all the others and by this fact seemed to indicate its unlived nature.

Why had he hurried? He repented it now. Maybe they were leading him to his execution. At this moment, in the light of this insufferable supposition, already on the very threshold of the door and his consciousness (he had not noticed this in his cramped cell), he noticed not only this imprudently and insufficiently lived day, but also the entire last tier of his incarceration slipping down improbably toward the floor. Its curve was slow, but inexorable, almost without infringing on the strict parallelism of the remaining tiers.

It was strange that another thought, almost opposite to that of death, had not entered his head. Why, of all things, was it execution? After all, he'd spent years here and what absurdity to assume such an absurd cruelty in those who had granted him life for so long? One would sooner think that they would pardon him. That would be more natural, more human and ultimately more consistent, but this thought somehow didn't occur to him. What, then, made him think of it? Certainly not the overseer's usual moroseness, or his solemnity, which seemed to fit the occasion. And most certainly not the new rope on his shoulder, which was totally inappropriate to this occasion. He somehow immediately spotted that it was too long, this rope, too new and coarse and that it was barely rolled into a careless coil and still more carelessly looped under the armpit, and somehow too impractical in its newness and coarseness. But the main thing was that he was *aesthetically* incapable of contemplating his own end. The obviousness and the bad theater of this rope was too apparent and vulgar, and if he were a director... (its essential inelasticity and uncoilability, its *inflexibility* and, therefore, the *impossibility* of a sufficiently quick...); those fibers on his greasy shoulder (meaning, *later,* fibers on the dead throat—no, he decisively rejected this thought)—no, he decisively swept aside this thought. But the unrealized and therefore terrifying impression of the day he hadn't completed drawing—its careless, monstrous and frivolous brevity, the fact that it stood out so absurdly and pointlessly from the others, the seeming illegality of this act, the residence of this day among other, full-valued days certain of their length—all this frightened him. But the main thing was that the entire final, lowest tier of days was being dragged so unswervingly by degradation, by a slow but imperious parabola of death, toward the head of his mournful death bier. Another thing was the unconscious, violent movement towards the wall and the desire to straighten out, to change this unthinkable affectation of fate, to restore, to lengthen this last, deformed, stubby day, to lead it into a distance, a depth, an infinity, to lock it away into a single closed circle. Still another was the stern cry "Back!" which suddenly transferred blind conjectures into his consciousness and by this act, in a sense, made fast the reliability of his suppositions. And at the same time that the entire content of these suppositions was inserted into the consciousness and almost mastered by it (the cry had served as a catalyst for this process and simultaneously served as a cause for its disintegration), he understood that nothing was a threat to him precisely because he understood. It is amazing how jealous fate is of man's perspicacity. He only has to foresee misfortune and right away it packs up its machinations (doubling its energy in other sectors), as if it were striving to strike us not with misfortune itself, but with its unforeseen nature and suddenness. Even if we retrospectively introduce the foreseen into something that has taken place, we separate the unexpected from misfortune, by virtue of which we deprive suffering of half its power. For all serious reflection on our trials reveals the legitimacy of suffering, convinces us of its judiciousness and, consequently, its inevitability. And it gets easier to live.

They passed a small corridor, the last branch before the dead end of his solitary cell. The man hunched over and drew his head into his shoulders. He felt uncomfortable in his abbreviated prison garb, as if this were already the beginning of freedom. At home he felt superb in these clothes. Yes, this was, in fact, the beginning of freedom and he was gradually seized by a fear of open spaces. For he understood that freedom, strictly speaking, consisted not in being deprived of something, of some vaster space, rights or privileges, but in being condemned to a defined space, rights and privileges, and, from this point of view, the millionaire condemned to his million is as unhappy as the poor man condemned to his poverty. In the dialectics of the free person, both things are indistinguishable and one flows into the other, but in the dialectics of the prisoner they are considered separately. He knows that freedom is the freedom to choose. And to even interpret freedom—something which the incarcerated person is deprived of from the first, and this, it would seem, more than anything else—means to choose it according to your own wishes. In actual fact freedom is not realized anywhere and the best possible way of attaining it lies only in interpreting it

The turnkey stopped before the door. He turned his rusty six-sided key. Letting the man go in front, he slammed the door and they set off down the corridor.

It was a long, straight corridor with cells on the righthand side. It was strange, but they were all standing wide open. It was possible to go out into the corridor, to get water by yourself, even to talk with your neighbor. The man was envious of these people. He thought in pain of his own gloomy solitary cell. He wasn't permitted so much freedom. But very few of the prisoners availed themselves of this right to go into the corridor and nobody availed himself of the right to go into other cells. And did they, in fact, have this right? It was possible that the open doors meant nothing.

Each of the cells had a few people. They were cramped and emitted the stuffy air of cellars. The entire place was suffused with a dank dampness. A scant, sepulchral light barely bled through the dirty glass.

He often encountered children. Pale prison children with pale, breaking voices. They argued quietly among themselves, not daring to burst into tears and not daring to look in each other's eyes. There were women in even greater numbers; apparently communal living was permitted here. The latter were rather cheerful. And, in general, the adults, as the man had managed to notice, were much more carefree and happier than the children. They were all occupied with their affairs, muttering something under their breaths to each other, and paid no attention to the man. They ate, played cards (intellectual games were forbidden); some were engaged in reading prison regulations. Only now the man noticed the great number of prison regulations encased in glass on the walls. They were posted literally everywhere. The prisoners would go out into the corridors and read them listlessly, noiselessly moving their lips. Apparently they were trying to memorize them.

In a cell especially designated for these purposes children were being taught. Some of the children silently tormented each other with pinches and safety pins, others recited diligently, tracing with a pointer on a map of the prison. It was huge, covering an entire wall, with innumerable channels of corridors, zigzags of stairs, and squares of windows. The smallest children read poetry composed by prison poets. A strict educator from among the adult prisoners disciplined the ones who disobeyed.

The man liked it here. He was envious of these people. He remembered his gloomy cell, in which even the window was four times narrower than theirs; his hateful spider, whom he had so naively pampered; his lichens, the bumblebee, the phial, and the whole useless play of his refined imagination, which now was ruthlessly rescinded in view of this magnificently rich life.

But something elusive suggested to him that these people had never known freedom. From gray-haired old men to babes in arms, they were all born here: their faces were pale and emaciated and their hands spectral and half-transparent. But they were so unconcerned about their non-freedom, so sincerely carefree and joyful, that for an instant the man doubted his surmise. Yet it was precisely their behavior that betrayed their origins. Truly, he thought, pausing by the door, non-freedom is to know, while they didn't know another life. And the man felt pity for them. He was free-born, this man, and therefore none of the advantages of prison could attract him.

And so they walked for a long time along the endless corridors, passing countless doors; he, pursued by his double, and the double pursued by the man, for they often traded places. Traversing one corridor, they entered another and the shadow walked behind the man and the man walked behind the shadow. And the echo of rusted doors accompanied them.

Finally he sensed that they had arrived. The overseer, who had fallen far behind, caught up, with a nod of his head indicated an empty cell, and withdrew. That meant it was simply another cell. The man silently submitted to his lot and went to the indicated spot. He did this almost with gratitude and wasn't surprised at himself. In the course of his long incarceration he had grown accustomed to his own obedience.

He began pondering his fate. Now, for some reason, it frightened him. Of course, this was a great improvement. It was much roomier, brighter and drier here. Besides, they'll probably move in other prisoners with him (the cell was for four), otherwise why these additional beds? (All the furniture was firmly fastened to the floor here as well.) But, most importantly, his door will always be open. For the time being he hadn't received any instructions or restrictions regarding it and he could probably use it to go out into the corridor. He wondered if it was locked for the night. Probably not, otherwise why keep it open during the day? He will soon know. But what if this is only a ruse of the jailers, an especially subtle piece of mockery designed to breed in the prisoners an illusion of freedom? In a sense hinting at it and constantly inciting flight. Or, on the contrary, they don't close the doors in order to keep them here even more securely?

It was clear that the door was fraught with some sort of danger. Yawning space oppressed him and evoked a feeling of defenselessness in him. Any change for the better made the man sense danger. He always thought that any attained level of misfortune was a blessing, and its integrity, stability, and the fact that it was not subject to fluctuation were perceived by the man as the greatest possible level of well-being. He considered any change in his fate, especially a positive one, to be a threat to the well-being of his customary misfortune. And, indeed, any change in one's lot is undesirable, since it is fraught with a threat (possibly illusory) to the level of suffering that has been attained, for happiness is always fickle, unstable, and abandons us at the first chance it gets; even as we fall back to a former level, to a condition of blessed pre-happiness, we already see it in the light of lost happiness and, consequently, we suffer doubly.

When will they bring him something to eat? From morning he hadn't had a crumb in his mouth. Maybe they were going to starve him to death? This also produced misgivings. However meager the prison rations, they were, nevertheless, guaranteed without fail, and, moreover, at the same time and twice a day. At times it seemed to the man that they'd sooner let him go free than not feed him. He thought of his lot with alarm. He even tried to recall his distant crime. Had it taken place? When? What did it consist of? It was astonishing that at times he would forget completely why he was here. He simply didn't remember and refused to remember. There was no memory of anything. And, naturally, there was no repentance either. They wanted to condemn him here to eternal penitence, but this was precisely what was always missing. That is, it was there initially, but not later. It disappeared right after sentencing. And even earlier, at the moment of his arrest. But here in prison it was absent. He remembered that at the time he even sought his arrest and then experienced untold relief. For it is precisely in prison that the criminal seeks deliverance from repentance, this unique form of retribution and conflict, since repentance is merely the unbearable conflict within the criminal arising from his criminal consciousness and the consciousness of his illegal use of freedom. Prison liberated one from repentance. He now knew that if they would cease prosecuting everyone who was guilty of crimes, and not only prosecuting, but also instituting punitive measures in their laws (steps by means of which three-quarters of the repentance is removed), all criminals would come forth and confess. Prison is amoral not because it deprives man of freedom, but because it deprives him of the torments of conscience. In prisons he had seen a number of cheerful, red-cheeked rapists, thieves, and murderers. On the outside they were pale, bilious outcasts. Here they all enjoyed healthy appetites; on the outside such appetites were unknown to them.

The hungry, powerful dream exhausted the man; he dropped off into a heavy slumber. The horror of yawning space dragged the man off and he set out to cope with it in his sleep. In fact, the need to cope with it prompted the sleep; a consciousness that is awake would have been unable to deal with it for anything in the world. But the man himself, of course, guessed nothing of this; he thought he guessed nothing, though the guess was to become knowledge at any moment. He will wake up in *his* cell. Sleep will make it dear to him.

He awoke from intense hunger. His throat was gulping convulsively. He walked out into the dirty, worn corridor and got some water. The sullen, cross-eyed conductor who had led him there immediately waved him away with his hands as if asking him to take his assigned seat. The man submitted gladly. This informality calmed him; it hinted superbly at his legality. Now even his hunger seemed to have left him in peace. The man walked into his compartment and took a seat. The train was nearing a station. The conductors got ready to enter the station.

The train slows down, its air brakes hissing. The power of inertia runs through the standing cars and the man descends to the ground.

The man takes his first step. He stretches his benumbed extremities and takes his first breath. A moist, easternly wind fills his famished chest and he breathes and breathes. The first drop of rain has fallen. The first person from the first car with barred windows has been taken off. The man goes closer.

The man goes closer, right up to the ring of armed guards, to people in equal measure with the four-legged. They don't drive him away, the guards have no time for him, they are now occupied with unloading and counting. Gloomy people, disfigured by the onslaught of sudden freedom, unwillingly abandon their habitable expanse and jump to the ground. Without any orders they line up by twos and take their neighbors' hand. Six gray striped pairs with eyes fixed on the heavens. Six gray young dogs with pupils fixed on the prisoners.

People are still standing, bidding farewell to their friends, huddled up in the piercing wind. Uncertainty awaits the ones and the others, but those who remain have an advantage: the habitable expanse of the car. It's warmer, more familiar, and they no longer feel like criminals there, while those who were taken off are made uncomfortable by the cold as well as by the space. And they huddle up from an expanse of guilt.

The train starts pulling out. Somewhere far away in the sky a bird is flying. (Of course, at first there was the bird, and then the train, in imitation, only copied its motion; at the same moment a windmill started revolving.) The train starts pulling out. Somewhere far away in the sky a bird is flying. The wheels of the train and the windmill are seduced by revolution. Infected by the general movement, the convicts take the first step. Infected by the movement, the dogs pull on their leashes. But the guards are not asleep. First roused by the universal movement, they nevertheless, manage to overcome this impulse and hold the procession back. This will cost them dearly. For later, striving to make up this delay, they will unconsciously begin to hurry, by virtue of which they will simultaneously cause two misfortunes: flight and death. (Having held back the common desire and waited it out, they will ultimately move anyway and then they will rush madly, submitting to the rhythm of an unconscious desire; they will move so quickly, almost at a run—amble, trot, gallop—that even the dogs will ask for mercy, their weapons will become covered by perspiration, drink, drink, if there were only a sip of water, half the world for a sip of cool, spring water, but there is no stopping—forward, forward, striving to delude destiny—and somewhere at a crossing, soon already, at some time designated by fate, they will again encounter this train (the train will make a detour, but it won't skirt fate), and they will have to stop before the railroad crossing barrier, even though desire will continue pleading to go *beyond, beyond,* as if knowing that beyond the railway bed it will run dry (getting beyond the railway bed was precisely the goal which, alas, was not fated to be). They didn't make it. The inconceivable mass of the train, cleaving space, hung over them, and the severe, straining guards and the hot breath of the prisoners, and the blind flash of someone's desperate flight right under the wheels of the locomotive, and the lightning reaction of the dog, dragging its handler under the train, and the body severed in half, and the senseless shooting under the wheels, and the engineer off washing his hands, and the exaltation of sudden freedom, and the impotent zeal of the dog dragging behind itself half of its young master. They didn't make it. Why did they fight it? There was, after all, a sign from the anonymous bird that was, moreover, decoded by the train.

The train starts pulling out. A guard winds the leash more tightly around his hand. Tightly, more tightly, marked one, cut off the circulation till it turns green. Already his gaze and waist are numb and there's already mortal anguish in his eyes. So young, he's just a boy, his mother's only son.

The train starts pulling out. And the bird flies in the sky like a stone, and freedom flashes in the eyes of the fugitive, and a green paleness surrounds the eyes of the corpse, and his mother already seeks new conception, and the engineer is ready to stain his hands with red, and the machine gun already wants to fire.

The train starts pulling out. The man jumps on the moving train and waves his handkerchief to the unfortunate ones. No one answers him; only the fugitive hails him as a future liberator, and the guard hails him as a future murderer. The final, unfree smile of the fugitive. The final, beaming smile of the victim. (And all this amid the seductive cacophony of the revolving wheels and accompanied by the creaking of the seduced windmill.)

The train gains momentum. It hurries after the sinking sun. Twilight swiftly falls outside. The man enters the compartment.

Again he rummages despondently through his pockets, giving himself hope only for formality's sake. There is, of course, nothing in them and the man falls into despondency.

What did he hope to find in them? That remains a mystery and if it hadn't been for the man's returning hunger (now needed for reasons of composition), and if it hadn't been for the returning compositional hunger of the man, the mystery could be exposed. For every mystery seeks exposure and all reality concealment.

The man set off through the car. The feeling of approaching hunger made his attack of guilt more remote and he set off through the car. Even a crumb of food, even the smallest crumb. The passengers were dozing with their hands on their suitcases, but vigilantly looking after the man. As if they were afraid of him.

He walked to the end of the car. A dirty, slovenly child playing by the toilet in the corner looked at him trustfully. The boy was slurping on a piece of candy. With fear, with trembling hands and fear, now and then looking back timorously, the man stroked the boy with his hand and drew the candy from his mouth. He sucked it out of his mouth. Swallowing it, the man fearfully rushed back. The child followed him with his eyes, but for some reason didn't start crying.

The candy satisfied his hunger only a little and in exactly the same amounts it added to the man's repentance. Even its magnificent sweetness (of the guilt-candy and the candy-guilt) could add nothing to it.

Again a stop and again they are unloading prisoners. The remaining ones. They are cleared out completely. Indistinct, incomprehensible shouts, shouts of resistance and threats. Fog, and the heavy pounding of rain mixed with the barking of dogs. The retreating light of lamps on endless, wet rails. A fog, a heavy fog and the raging light of lamps. Finally everything quiets down. The train gains momentum.

A new burst of guilt flooded over and possessed the man. A new burst of despair and hope. Painfully clenching his teeth, he plunged into his pockets, examining literally each millimeter. It was as if he didn't notice the huge red hole in the right pocket of his trousers and he just worked on, whistling, *around* it.

The little watch pocket of his trousers that he suddenly discovered sooner filled him with surprise than with hope. Somehow he hadn't noticed it earlier. Alas. Alas and alack, the pocket was, of course, empty. And to pin one's hopes on this pocket would have been an abstraction: what he hoped to find there wouldn't even have half fitted in it. He knew this. He knew and, nevertheless, shoved his two—the middle and index—irresponsible fingers and even wiggled them inside. He knew this himself long ago, much earlier than his fingers, but the fingers still didn't believe in the emptiness and continued their senseless tenure. Dividing himself (for a time) into fingers and all the rest, and continuing his separate existence in this way, the man weighed in his mind what could have happened to the lost articles, picking over in his memory all the possibilities, while his fingers continued to examine the emptiness. He couldn't have forgotten and left them home, that was excluded. The object was too vital and necessary, even more necessary than a toothbrush (the fingers stumbled onto a piece of tobacco and froze in surprise; a mistake; they became convinced of this immediately and didn't even bother to convey this insignificant information to the brain and dealt with it by themselves; a caraway seed). Maybe he left it in his parcel? No, that was also excluded. The parcel contained only records that he had gotten not long before boarding, while he, as he recalled, discovered his loss earlier. He remembered this. So he'd lost it? (The man had been aware of the red fist's threat from the very beginning; even though latently, but he was aware, and now, finally, it had come out, this threat, though, of course, the fist still remained in the pocket); but the hole was huge, even too huge for that which he searched (in view of the metallicity and compactness of the sought-for object and, consequently, its capacity to slip out, it increased further in size), and though, of course, it could easily have lost that which was entrusted to it, something told him that nothing was entrusted to it after all. One should not put one's trust in the obvious: it is always illusory. But was the hidden hole obvious (and consequently illusory)? Yes, for all that, it was, for it would immediately have discovered its obviousness, had the man only wanted to entrust something to it. No, his leg didn't recall anything falling. He concentrated on a narrow strip of flesh running along his left leg from the hip to the sole, but the first-rate memory of the body produced nothing. Then he tried by force to impose on the leg the notion of a cold, metallic sliding, and a muffled blow on the ankle bone, but the leg stubbornly resisted. No, the leg couldn't detect it. Thus the fist's threat was unreal, and, as a result of this deliberation, seemed to be a mere fiction (but the fingers continued their senseless frictions, though one, the middle, later dove out of the darkness; the frictioner/freeactioner still stayed in).

A gloomy, indistinct desire came over the man. He shifted his fingers to their normal position and calmed down, having become united with himself. The reunification was accompanied by a receding rumble of wheels and the rush of a pacifying rhythm. Feeling a wholeness within himself and in possession of his entire being (as well as the presence of an unejected desire), the man was rejoined with his fingers, which had partaken of sin, and walked out.

The train had almost stopped when the man opened the door. A powerful searchlight shone along the row of cars and some dark figures walked in its beam. They walked slowly, afraid of nothing, with their hands deep in their pockets. They wore long black topcoats and black hats. Silently walking around the first, by now empty, car, and satisfying themselves that it was empty, they just as silently left the light and headed down along the cars. There were some forty or fifty of them, they walked slowly and in a disorderly fashion, but in this very disorder could be discerned direction and purpose. They all got in the last car and the train immediately started. They did not have any kind of baggage. None of the passengers had gotten off.

The man shut the door in fright and pressed up against the window. Little night animals of some sort and a crowd of glowing insects froze on the periphery of the light; with a muffled groan a bat struck the light as if the light were glass. Unable to overcome the beam of light, after a few more attempts it fell unconscious on the periphery of light, belonging to it only with one wing.

The man was seized by an inexplicable fear. These dark people—who were they? Who could they be? Where were they from? And how long did they intend to stay? The danger lay in their darkness, and in the fact that they kept their hands in their pockets. And in the fact that they had turn-down collars.

Just in case, the man patted his pockets, but cheerlessly and without any hope. His whole attitude was one of total indifference. Apparently, he was drained of all hope. Strictly speaking, he was killing the infant in the womb, not letting it develop even a little. In fact, he hadn't even conceived it. What did he expect, this man? He was using birth control.

He sat down and hugged his knee. He pulled his foot off the floor. He let out a false whistle, intended to sound independent and cheery, but immediately become embarrassed at his cheeriness. What alarmed him about these people (he tried to be calm about this whole matter), what could it be?

To begin with, they were dark, these people. To the last man. And they kept their hands in their pockets. They also had turn-down collars. Long black coats, black wide-brimmed hats. And black kid-skin gloves. Of course they kept their hands in their pockets, but they kept them there in gloves. That was clear from the very beginning. And this is precisely the point: the man was convinced of this from the very beginning, otherwise he would not have become so frightened. After all, it was impossible to imagine turn-down collars without the gloves. That simply could not be. If the collars had been turned up, then this would directly suggest the absence of gloves. That's clear. (His refined aesthetic sensibility, which he applied unwaveringly to all of life's situations, brought to light not only such mysteries as this [the bad theater of the rope; a blunder or a coarse allusion on the part of the director?]; he even believed that any crime can be investigated *aesthetically*, not counting those, of course, which are committed by esthetes. An esthete will never blunder and will never permit himself a lapse in taste, even in cases of murder. In cases of suicide by hanging, he empties his bowels and strings himself up only with the help of a silk cord.)

Of course, they also had ties on, given that their coats were tightly buttoned. The ties followed logically from the coats being all buttoned. Then there was the matter of the collars. . . They were, of course, there, but what kind? They were hardly woven or woolen. They were most likely smooth oilskin, those turn-down collars.

Now let's try to check ourselves and to compare their appearance (accessible, visible, visual) (as far as the internal is concerned, the man is also no longer mistaken), their visual aspect with the absence of ties, and, particularly, gloves. First, in regard to ties. Had the ties been missing, it would also have to be assumed that the uppermost button of every one of these men's shirts was unbuttoned (there was no sense in buttoning the shirt if there were no tie). The assumption that follows is the color of the shirt. The color of an unbuttoned shirt would be non-official, not pale blue, and most certainly not white. That's clear. For wouldn't it be too absurd to think of wearing a white shirt without a tie, and unbuttoned, at that? Thus the color of the assumed shirt would be gray, dark-blue (green) or a temperate, sparkling burgundy. But most likely, the unbuttoned (and we've already decided that the shirt was unbuttoned, since it had no tie), but most likely, the object most in keeping with the unbuttoned state of the shirt would be a checked flannel (let's not forget that it was autumn outside) consisting of comfortable, swamp-brown checks. It would follow directly from this that these people were not wearing suspenders, since, without doing violence to matters of taste, it is impossible to imagine suspenders on a checkered (with comfortable, swamp-brown checks) flannel shirt. And further. After this, it would be necessary to assume that these people were not carrying firearms (the absence of suspenders was equal to an absence of guns), and this would be followed directly by humaneness.

Now let us compare the intermediate and final results of our investigation (humaneness as absence of weapons and the absence of weapons as humaneness) with the external appearance of these people. Version one. Black hats, tightly buttoned black coats, hands in pockets, turn-down collars, plus a checked shirt without suspenders (consequently, without guns), and humaneness. The ridiculousness of such assumptions was obvious. Version two. Black hats, long black coats (tightly buttoned), hands in pockets, turn-down collars, starched, white shirts, suspenders, a gun. This all added up. (The infinity of associations prompted by the gun—cruelty, amoralism, criminality, etc.—were consciously brought to a halt by the man so as not to anticipate the results of the subsequent examination; the disinterested scientific approach.) The man grunted with pleasure. The picture of these people was now aesthetically convincing. And the color of the conceptual shirts helped him in this.

So much for ties. Now, regarding gloves.

If the gloves had not existed, then there would have been no need for coats and hats. And, most important, the turn-down collars. The absence of one would presuppose the absence of the other. Pale bared hands (even reddish hands look rather pale against black) would hardly have been in keeping with their appearance and with those turn-down dollars. Besides, if these people smoked (and among them there definitely had to be at least one smoker), besides, if these people smoked, it would be impossible to imagine them without lighters (one mechanized image evokes another—the gun). And to imagine a lighter in the *bare* hands of a man in black would be simply impossible: only in gloves (the glitter of a nickel-plated lighter also assumes the presence of shining cuff links, but the glittering buttons of the gloves are assumed to be even more essential). Consequently these people were criminals (weapons and gloves), and now the whole question is what kind: State or *State* (alas, alas, again impotence [polysemic, not polyspermic], again the semi-debility of the language, because what did the man have in mind? Against the State or of the State; in the name of the State and empowered by it?). We'll examine both possibilities.

So then, dark people with guns and wearing gloves. In addition, wearing hats and with lighters. Plus turn-down collars. (To facilitate the investigation, he would deal with only one man.)

The elegant kid gloves clearly evoked an image of lock picks being sorted out coolly, the night, darkness, a full moon, someone's unforeseen corpse and, finally, a safe. (The safe, properly speaking, arose even earlier, together with the lock picks being sorted out coolly) (just as a quill pen always arises together with the image of the poet), but the unforeseen corpse suppressed all this at the very beginning (together with the pen, by the way, arises not only the poet, but also guttering candles, an unfinished sonnet, someone's dear little foot drawn in the margins, a brace of dueling pistols, growing slander, betrayal, conspiracy by the seconds, a shot, short torment in the snow, a secret burial and, finally, the oblivion of centuries-old fame before the ultimate oblivion of time.) But the unforeseen corpse rescinded all this from the very beginning.

But the man still didn't know what the safe contained, and continued investigating the flow of his criminal associations.

Initially the safe contained only money (the lock pick easily came to terms with the secret). Not a lot, only one or two bundles. The remaining space of the safe was huge. The inappropriate nature of this mise-en-scène was immediately discovered and noted by the director, not only as a result of its inappropriateness but also its unconvincingness. The unconvincingness expressed itself in the bad theater of the scene: the unquestionably comic insignificance of the sum, the European collection of lock picks, the full moon (the full moon effectively parodied the crime: the safe was empty) and now, the no longer unforeseen, but simply absurd corpse. The second version was more acceptable. The same safe and lock picks and the same unforeseen corpse. There was no full moon, but there was a lighter. The storm clouds now and then covered over their pale traveling companion, the blizzard was rising to the sky, and the lighter flickered. The presence of the lighter prompted the sudden appearance of the clouds, the snowstorm, and even the season.

Now the safe contained super-secret documents. And thus the two mechanical objects, the lighter and the gun (three: the man didn't count the fountain pen, given the ordinariness of the object; but this ordinariness participated in a series of causes which prepared for the appearance of a certain apparatus...) with full consistency paved the way for the appearance of the camera. In addition, the necessity of the lighter in this mise-en-scène was also underscored by the fact that if needed, it could be used to destroy some unpleasant document. And this intensified the very potential for crime.

So everything tallied: the night, the sudden appearance of the clouds, the sheen of the finest gloves, plus the four mechanical objects, and the by now mandatory, though still unforeseen, corpse, whose foreseenness was well hidden by success (the crime was being carried out successfully).

But something rejected this possibility as well. The bad theater of the foreseen corpse, even though it was masked by the success of the crime, was too obvious anyway, even to the unpracticed eye. But the main thing, as he only now discovered, was that in both versions, the criminal operated with a standing collar. The consciousness simply balked at imagining the opposite, and the criminal had only to take a step before his collar stood up by itself. This was the condition of the burglar's motion, the condition for the commission of the crime, and even the condition for the very existence of the criminal. Besides this, the fact that the imagined criminal acted alone was dictated not so much by the necessity of simplifying the logical and irrational operations, as by the aesthetics of the crime, for it would have been impossible to imagine even *two* burglars (with raised collars), not to mention several, by the wide open and pillaged safe.

Consequently, both versions had to be rejected. There remained the possibility of a *State* crime and the man set about examining this possibility with a passion.

As such, the crime harmonized with the calm self-assurance of these people, with the fact that they were all in black and with their turn-down collars. Not all criminals can afford to dress so loudly, to button up so tightly, and, in addition, to turn down their collars. The main thing, however, is that there is always defiance, hysteria and constraint in the self-assurance of State criminals, while the self-assurance of the *State* criminals is incontestable and is always accompanied by a sense of limitless freedom. And, once again, the collective image of these people (let's not forget that they wore gloves) was totally at odds with this broken into safe, lock picks, standing collars, the flashing of lighters, an unforeseen corpse, etc. On the contrary, the things that really suited them were bunches of keys in protective covers, a sealed-up safe, the seal itself, scrupulously kept in a felt bag, handcuffs proffered to others, a bright (but not sunny) light, and, it goes without saying, tightly buttoned turn-down collars. And also an always necessary, and as though legitimized by someone, death. These people's whole route was littered with *foreseen* corpses. The whole matter rested in the collective nature of a given crime, something the man had at first failed to consider, but which quite specifically pointed to the State and to legality. And, again, these turn-down collars. They were what guaranteed these people a legal status.

The man thought about all this later, when he came face to face with these people. Until that time all these matters flowed below the threshold of his consciousness, which is why they were so dazzlingly real. In fact, his long journey through the entire train was specifically evoked by the necessity of transferring them into his consciousness. He wanted to check the validity of his deductions; therefore he strove towards this with full consciousness, though unconsciously. In his consciousness there was only agitation because it was incapable of grasping the logic of his movement toward danger, and in this movement there was just as little apparent sense for him as there was in the striving of a moth towards fire. The more so since he himself was this moth. In fact, he was simply trying to vacate his subconscious (the latter was already preparing to take within itself something more substantial; moreover, it was still preoccupied with the loss) and to loose on himself the consciousness of his subconscious.

He walked along an endless row of cars, sensing the rhythm of space and doors (in each car there were six connecting doors—we'll ignore the side doors, that is, the secondary, unnecessary ones, for now). Every now and then he would lose his rhythm, stumble, get his hands entangled and forget to close the doors behind him (this could also be held against him, he realized), and this added to his confusion and agitation. But he only had to change hands—the left forward, directed towards the future, meeting the unknown, the right backward, plucking off the past (the legs now synchronized the motion of the corresponding extremities)—and he would again pick up the rhythm, first of the doors, then of the space of the car, then of the car's motion (duplicating the beats of his own heart), then the rhythm of his measured breathing (which immediately evoked the image of a pendulum's measured swing, of waves rhythmically beating on a shore, the glimmering of stars, the bubbling of red-hot plasma, of the rhythm of the Universe transfigured into nonvisible form).

He walked through several cars, six or seven. On the rumbling, moving platforms he took respite from the rhythm that was taking hold of him. He tried not to fall in with it, to throw it off, to get away from it, but to do so he would have to bring his heart to a stop. The fading oscillation of his heart drove him forward. Now he knew that he could stop not only his own heart, this train, all the pendulums on earth, and the motion of all waves in the world, but also the glimmering of stars and the oscillation of the universe. But that would mean stopping his heart. And he moved on.

He left the past behind easily, surmounted the present, and entered into the future. The present and future were separated by only shaky, illusory little bridges (on which he took respite from the rhythm). And the future copied to the letter not only the present, but also the past, and soon he lost his sense of time. For this division of time was useless; time was only a condition of his displacement in space and constituted the endless flow of existence that he had entered and could get out of only by getting off the train. (We emphasize:

not by stopping the train [which would be equivalent to suicide], but precisely by getting off. But that was impossible for now.)

And then he saw those people. Black hats, button-down collars. And they kept their hands in their pockets. They didn't sit down, these people, and, strictly speaking, they were not real passengers. Having separated into two equal groups, they stood on either side of the car, cold, somber, and keeping their hands in their pockets. It goes without saying that everything in the car was under their command and, of course, they controlled the motion of the train and, had they wanted, they could easily have stopped it whenever they felt so disposed. But apparently there was no need for that now.

The man tried to look inside, beyond their thickset broad backs, but was pushed back. Inside everything was quiet. These people evoked dead silence by their presence. But not peace. They stood, sullen, impenetrable, indifferent, and they had turn-down collars. They kept their hands in their pockets. It was as if they were waiting for something, these people, and the passengers were waiting for something as well. And when the train started slowing down, the people parted and all the passengers, as if on command, got up and in organized fashion, not shoving or stepping on each other's feet, made for the exit. (The man drew back at this moment.) They were getting off. Forming pairs, they took each other's hands and waited for something. A few of the dark people separated from the group and, hurriedly counting the people, led them away somewhere. Those who remained quickly checked the car—quickly but quite scrupulously—and crossed into the next one. They pushed the man back. The train started.

Again they stood by the exits, blocking the doors on both sides, again the passengers made ready and rose from their places. And almost immediately the next stop came up. Again a few people separated from the group and, organizing the passengers in pairs, they led them away somewhere. Everyone submitted unquestioningly. And again the deserted car was examined quite thoroughly and the man was jostled.

And everything was repeated anew. The dark people lined up, the train stopped, the passengers were led away. And the train continued on its way.

In this manner they moved from one car to another and steadily neared the head of the train. Soon they were in the middle.

Only now did the man notice that, in essence, none of the passengers put their things out, they didn't occupy their places, and they didn't settle down to sleep. Even their bags were not stowed away, were not put on the luggage racks, but stood around at their feet. No one hurried, no one even dozed, and everyone tensely waited for something. They were even wary of eating, afraid of being taken unawares. With trembling hands they only took hurried bites from the food on their knees, spasmodically swallowing the pieces. They didn't even undress their children and didn't let them fall asleep. Everyone was watchful. As if everyone knew everything and, from the very beginning, from one second to the next, waited for someone to come. And when these people finally appeared—appeared, smiled, and sullenly stood at the entrance—they sighed with relief, grabbed their things and, not waiting for the order, rose as soon as the train started to brake. And many others rose to meet them. Meekly they all went off somewhere into the distance, accompanied by the people in dark clothes.

The man rushed back. Back, back to his own place. Maybe something could still be done. Back from the future into the past, into ignorance and the irreversible—back. The present had nothing to feed on—back.

He reached his car and quickly took off his coat, shirt, tie (the last slipped off together with his shirt), and feverishly started going through his clothes. It can be said that not a single millimeter remained unexamined. But, as before, there was nothing in his pockets. Finally, in despair, he even searched through his tie—even smelling it, in growing alienation—and even tore out the lining of his coat. Nothing. Despair, fear and pallor, together and in turn, disfigured his face. He threw his coat into a corner and burst into tears. Why had he been so thoughtless? He now cursed himself for his foolhardiness.

And the people continued their advance. They came and came in a black wall, advancing inexorably towards the man, and soon they were right at his side.

Coldly, almost impassively, the man took off his shoes, trousers and socks. He gave his trousers only a cursory examination, favoring his shoes. He inspected his shoes with special scrupulousness, even unlacing them and then taking out the laces. Then he turned them over and with clenched teeth shook the shoes above the floor. After this he tried to tear off the heel. The shoes were new and would not yield. So far, nothing. Only the socks remained now, but their drooping, insubstantial and somewhat otherworldly appearance hinted at emptiness as well. He picked them up (only so that he could dot the final i and impart completeness to his despair) and crumpled them, in the same way that dirty bills are crumpled. Alas. He threw the socks aside in disgust, but immediately became frightened of something and arranged them, folding them together. There still remained his balled-up handkerchief, which, even crumpled, sparkled with starchy whiteness. (The background of the handkerchief was finished in large blue squares.) But this freshness, and even more, a particular cheerlessness and hopelessness in the disposition of the crumpled squares, did not portend anything good. He looked at the handkerchief squeamishly, without even bothering to unfold it. It was all over. The passengers in his car were already getting up to meet the people.

In total despair, mocking himself, he lifted the top of the lower bunk and hid under it. And there, in the darkness, he continued to deride himself, tugging at his chin with his fingers. Soon the muffled shuffling of feet stopped and relative quiet ensued.

People entered his car. Apparently, the last check. A thin, dismal crack menacingly refracted the gloom until it was finally covered by something black. He breathed a sigh of relief. It was someone's legs. Strange, but now he felt protected. Though not for long.

The sullen trampling of feet stopped. They'd plunged into thought. Now he wasn't afraid of these people, he was only afraid of their legs. Their legs were huge, clumsy and malevolent. It seemed as if all the danger emanated solely from them, from those legs: from the dark, herringbone weave of the trousers, baggy under the knees, from the tangled ball of hair stuck to the cloth and making incredible efforts to hold on in the crease of the cuff, from the hardened, oily spot, covered with dust.

The legs lived an independent life. Only now did the man understand how terrifying and dangerous man was, how he hides in his physical and moral totality, wholeness and completeness, and if you examine someone separately, by parts, you'll immediately become horrified and understand. You only have to take a finger, or an eye, or an ear, for example, and examine each separately. Or only to think of some individual's internal organs. And each time that man's malice will become obvious to you—his bestiality, brutishness, and malice. And each deformity, the absence of hands, legs or a nose, is terrifying not because it disturbs the harmony of wholeness, but because it betrays the missing organ or quality, singles it out, focuses attention on it, and in seeing it, this missing organ or quality, you see the *entire* person.

The man tensed his anus and shuddered. Most likely by intuition he sensed that these people were now examining his clothes, squeamishly touching them with the toes of their shoes. He became embarrassed for his balled-up handkerchief; not for his socks, not for his trousers, not for his coat, but specifically for his handkerchief. Why had he balled it up? He wouldn't have to redden now (and his shame was muted by the darkness). He wouldn't have to be aflame now. An intimate thing, if it even dares to appear before someone else's eyes, should only be untouched and impeccably clean. But mainly he was embarrassed because he wasn't there. That is, by the fact that they assumed that he wasn't there. That is what was unbearable. And this feeling was aggravated by his discarded clothes. It was unbearable to feel that they take you to be naked, and this whole unfolding situation as the escape of a naked person. No, it would be better to turn himself in than to think that they think that he... He was already prepared to give himself away, but someone sat on his bunk and made the crack somewhat smaller. A piercing, crushing pain in his knees (especially the right) halted his repentance and again he wanted to avoid these people. Of course, he could try to change the position of his legs, to turn on his side (he was lying on his back) and free his legs. (On the other hand, hopes for success were minimal, his kennel was just too tight.) But that would mean changing the position of the bunk seat and completely closing off the crack. The person seated would immediately feel this change (and in the illumination as well, since darkness swallows light). And the man rejected this thought. But the pain in his knees was so unbearable (and it intensified because the person seated was humming some song), and his repentance was even more unbearable (it seemed to him now that all his shame and repentance were centered in one knee, the right one, in his kneecap, cracked from childhood), that he was ready to reveal himself—to announce himself, to shout, and beg for mercy—but the seat suddenly sprang up blindingly and light rushed in (no, as before; but its suddenness was blinding). The repentance of the right knee continued (the inertia of shame and repentance) and very nearly betrayed him. But the person seated retreated rapidly. The man breathed a sigh of relief.

He crawled out of his shelter. Not totally, of course, just halfway, covering himself cautiously with the top of the bunk. Something told him that these people would return. The first thing that struck him (the absence of the people is assumed) were his rumpled clothes, which had taken on a strange, alienated appearance after these people's stay. Of course, they touched them with their feet and. . . But it was not a question of their feet, but the fact that they had *looked* at them. Especially the intimate things, the handkerchief and socks, which it would be simply unthinkable to ever use again. The coat and trousers, owing to their intended external use, were still bearable (the coat, by the way, was of little use, given its turned-inside-out state, but the man didn't have time to note this in the moment of his reappearance; nor did he notice the hairy red fist threatening him from the turned-out pocket; yes, hairiness was now added to the redness, because the fist was now no longer simply menacing, but openly cried out about danger).

The heavy pounding of feet, slamming of doors, and muffled shouts of orders resounded again. The man hid in the wings. The heavy velvet curtain flew at him, threatening to cleave him in half. A cloud of dust raised by the curtain caught up with him and he almost sneezed. Repressing this desire (not fully; it threatened now and then to achieve satisfaction and for this reason he held onto his nose), repressing this desire within himself, he considered the situation that had arisen. They were looking for him, that was clear. They'll no doubt resort to a systematic search of the train now, and, of course, they won't let him slip by. They may even bring in a German shepherd (he had no doubts that the dossier with his fingerprints had already been transferred here from the Center: each one of them undoubtedly had a pocket photo-telegraph, computer, etc. ; and he had left traces everywhere). The man's finger pads swelled out (not only of his fingers but of his toes as well), and he almost cried out. Gritting his teeth from the pain, he tried to remember whether in his childhood, as was true for all infants, they had taken prints of his feet (for this he had to resort to intrauterine associations). It seemed they hadn't (an inconceivable blunder by the Center), and he felt relief in his feet. (Baby was able to avoid this at the last moment, though it was at the cost of an unbelievable sleight-of-hand: in place of rosy footprints, at his mother's request, prints of his rosy elbows were taken and from that moment on the wonderful comradely sense of marching elbow to elbow with others never left him.)

It grew still. Soon they will start the search. (Maybe they've already started; no doubt they are tapping on every square inch, and the man thought about percussion; then about druggist's scales weighing emptiness [the pans on the scales were wavering]; the silent suffering of a couch covered with oilcloth; a starched, white coat with the rubber tube of a stethoscope; the sterile horror of a clinic; the all-pervasive smell of medicine, which produces this horror; and, finally, just before the curtain comes down, again the fine nickel-plated hammer aimed at someone's submissive knee—and his leg jumped to the ceiling.)

He tensed with fear. He blew on his bruised knee. Just so they wouldn't notice anything. Anyway, there seemed to be something wrong with his nerves.

And so, soon they'll start the search. That means they will start with the outermost, the last car. The man was sure of this, because: (a) they only had a few people left and they wouldn't examine each car separately (and simultaneously); (b) nor would they start with the middle or head of the train, that would be a violation of the system (not so much the system itself, as their conception of it); (c) moreover, they had just been here, in the first car, and just their very presence here would have made them search elsewhere. But they would start with the last car chiefly because they had done so earlier. It was precisely from there that they had started their activity (i. e., to arrest and lead away the passengers) and not for anything would they be able to depart from the stereotypical behavior they had imposed on themselves. This was his salvation.

And so they will start with the last car. Loads of time will pass before they get here. That means that he'll have time to crawl out of here, get dressed, get his proper bearings, and, if he's lucky, even make it to the next station. And then... Why, he had a superabundance of time. In addition, according to his calculations, they were now only on their way to begin the search (and before that, along the way, so to speak, they'll undertake nothing—they'll give in to stereotypical behavior); they are now on their way to begin the search, somewhere in the middle of the train, therefore, he was being granted extra time (after it had elapsed, they would charge him with a penalty shot on his goal). Such huge reserves of time pacified him to such a degree that he even decided to have a tiny nap. He decided that he had a right to this, but an imperceptible director pushed him out from behind the wings, finding that the public had long deserved it and that to abandon the stage and the mise en scène for protracted periods threatens the entire play with failure.

The man came out from behind the wings and looked around. The public met his reappearance silently. They didn't greet him at all. The man was seized by a feeling of incomparable loneliness.

How should he play this mise en scène? Where should he begin? Where should he put those endless hands? Will his fellow players be coming out soon? Yes, the public was punishing him with its silence. But this pitiless silence was still in his power and it was empty, like a virgin's womb, and it was up to him to impregnate it, whether with success or failure. Another second, a moment, an instant... No, he forgot all the words of the monologue. And without words he felt especially defenseless. Bare, undressed (let's not forget that he came out onto the stage only in his shorts), he looked for any redeeming gesture, hoping to hide behind it, but no, no, no. Naked, and nobody to rescue him. In a desperate attempt to escape his lot, clasping his hands to his head, he again threw himself towards the wings (registering the fact that his despair was acted totally falsely because it was unfeigned) and again stumbled against the director's grimace...

He walked around the stage, whistling. He saw someone's discarded clothes. With exaggerated squeamishness, using two fingers, he picked up the handkerchief. Throwing it aside, he burst out laughing theatrically, grabbed someone's rumpled socks, turned them inside out (there it was, finally, that saving, that original gesture, since he wouldn't have been able to hide behind banality anyway, and would have felt even more undressed behind it), he grabbed someone's rumpled socks, turned them inside out, slipped them on in a flash, and raised his hands heavenward.

The silence lifted. A roar of sincere applause drowned out the noise of the approaching fellow actors (and also the actor's fright); a deformed, immature fetus, oozing blood, rolled down the entire length of the auditorium and the man, jumping out a side door, ran down the corridor, leaving fear, success and despair behind him.

Why was it that he chose the socks? Not the coat, trousers or at least the handkerchief? (It's just too terrifying for us to even think about the tie, even though he had tried it. There, in the darkness, in the light of his shame and the slit, he had tried it on—on his bare neck, but had immediately thrown it aside with a wail, since he didn't want to be hanged by these people; and they would have hanged him without fail had he left the tie around his neck: the absence of the tie among the strewn-about clothing would undoubtedly have hinted at it to them; it was simply amazing, given their undeveloped imagination; but that was all right, let them imagine him without a tie.) And so, why was it that he chose the socks? And not the coat, trousers, or even the handkerchief? The coat, as has already been noted, was unbearable as a result of its turned-out lining. The trousers also, since the pockets were picked clean (they had been searched); and, since the pockets had been turned inside out, the man was seized with shame for the huge red hole that had undoubtedly been perused by the *State* criminals. The handkerchief was rejected because of its lack of freshness. And, ultimately, all of the clothes were rejected because they were all COMPROMISING (not as clothes, but as clues), and each of these items taken separately and, even more so, together, would give evidence of his absence if he wanted to use them again. Not one of the described items of dress—the trousers, coat, shirt, tie, handkerchief, shoes, or even the laces consisting of knots—could be removed from the wholeness of this picture without immediately destroying its unity, authenticity and anonymity; the nonrelativity and the nonqualitativeness of the universe; the strict regularity of chaos; and in the score of these chaotic signs the heavenly eyesandears perceived a secret harmony. The wholeness of this picture consisted not only in the presence of all these objects (an absence of even one of them would point to someone's presence) and not only in their convincing and casual position, but also in their disposition in relation to one another and of all to the Universe. The laces, for example, had gotten so hopelessly tangled together that the man, with his perverse notions about harmony and order, would have been unable to move them from their place without immediately changing their configuration and subjecting them to some sort of an artificial position (which did, in fact, happen with the socks); moreover, the laces had been flattened by someone's heavy tread, hammered out even in the knotted parts and trampled into the pliant, light-blue linoleum. Given this, and the specks of dust glued to them (and the gradual ungluing of these specks), they represented an unsurpassed example of the elemental and the unpreconceived. One shoe was turned over, but in such a way that it had stopped at some essential point (seized by the shoe itself). Strictly speaking, it hadn't turned over, but only wanted to turn over, or, even better, it could have turned over, or, even more to the point, it wanted to, but couldn't, or it could, but didn't want to, and the equality of these contradictory states ("to want" and "to be able to" are always opposite and are equal in their polarity) (we only want that which we're unable to do and able to do only what we don't want), their non-difference and self-cancellation were, in fact, the center of equilibrium, they necessarily assumed it and composed it, to the point that the shoe rocked in time with the train, balanced on the narrow strip of its welt, without, however (as has been said) falling into inertia and toppling over. The role of the other shoe consisted of its standing simply and boorishly in its usual position, staunch and unwavering, as is only fitting for a philistine, as if merely serving its double by its antipodality (now imposed not from the outside, but internally, from the very essence of objects), but too exhausted by the primitive and sham antipodality of right and left. One of the coat sleeves, hurriedly turned inside out earlier, was somehow inconceivably shoved into the pocket of the coat, which would have pointed to the artificiality of its position, had it not have been for that essential degree of carelessness (which literally permeated the entire composition), had it not been for that essential degree of carelessness and that essential degree to which the sleeve was shoved in, by virtue of which artificiality immediately turned into its antipodality (but if one were to go further into the very heart of the matter, both these qualities—artificiality and naturalness—manifested themselves here as *appearances,* as the usual optical illusion of displaced lines in a cube; both were activated by this illusion and negated by it and together with them matter was also negated). The position of the trousers could also have appeared totally stage-managed were it not for the button of the fly, which had been torn away in a hurry, and which was still deliberating if it should roll onto the floor from its seat (which it shared now and then with fingers). But the inner "Method"* of the given micro mise-en-scène consisted not so much in the button's alienation as in the inconceivable color that sharply distinguished it from its peers. In addition, even though it belonged to a man, it was clearly two-sexed, that is, it was distinct from its heterogeneous friends by the fact that it could have belonged to some intimate part of a woman's garment (the button was inexcusably small and, in essence, useless and in parasitic relation to the utilitarianism of the others).

And so, the bisexuality of the button was out in the open. The handkerchief, on the other hand, while its position was, in fact, questionable, simply expressed the necessity of its presence in this composition, like, let us say, the pit of a plum in a barely started still life, without which the entire canvas would look implausible. And all this taken together sounded like an indissoluble coupling of all things that couldn't fit a single other thing within it.

---

*The reference is to the cornerstone of Konstantin Stanislavsky's theory of theater, whereby the artist's ethico-aesthetic principles find lived expression on stage.

There remained the socks. Their position was questionable and premeditated and it would have been impossible to find a place for them in the given composition. (Let's not forget that the position of the socks had been corrected from the very beginning.) To simply paint them into the composition without transposing all other details of the still life would have meant to explode verisimilitude and craftsmanship. He no longer had the time for redoing the whole canvas anyway, he was painting it intuitively, *alla prima.** To approach his creation rationally would mean to doom it. And he threw aside the brush.

And so the socks were out of place here, there was no longer time to repaint the canvas (the panel of judges was approaching), and inspiration had been exhausted. That they may have simply been superfluous didn't strike him at first. The misplacement of the socks grew with every minute; they literally were being crowded out of the composition not only by a uniquely proper positioning of them on the canvas—one which had not been found—but also by their intimacy and the defenselessness of intimacy, not to mention (as he just now caught on) by their irritatingly characteristic odor of new shoes (the shoes had been bought just before he'd boarded together with Penderecki, though the old laces had been left in—Penderecki had insisted on that), by their irritatingly characteristic odor of new shoes, one which with each instance more powerfully and distinctly revealed the rationality of the given composition and more powerfully banished the socks from it. And he threw the brush aside and put on the socks (though it would nevertheless be more accurate to say that he pulled them over his feet; an example of the anti-stylistic function of grammatical rules).

The canvas only gained by this. Now the composition took on a finished look. And even if someone were to notice the absence of the socks, even then their absence would suit the man, because it would give a good hint of suicide (something the man counted on from the very beginning). In this sense the value of the socks could only be matched by the value of the tie, but the latter, as has already been pointed out, was rejected because the man did not want to be hanged. It was precisely the absence of the socks from among the strewn-about clothes, and, consequently, their presence on his feet, that evoked an animated image of a suicide (without which it would have been impossible to count on the convincingness of the imagined suicide), an image of his utter despair, confusion, biting of lips, pallor, trembling hands, mumbling, an imprint of socks darkened by sweat, tiny stones pressed into the sole of the foot, and even of water, prepared to receive the future victim of drowning. Firearms were rejected because of the impossibility of imagining

---

*A technique of painting (used for the first time in the 19th century) in which the picture is completed in one session so that all under-painting is obliterated.

the toe of the foot encased in a sock placed on the trigger of a rifle—there were no guns here (at the very least the sock should be torn in *that spot*, but we've said nothing of this earlier; the socks were whole). Death beneath wheels was also rejected, again because the picture was unconvincing: a naked man under the wheels! Just as in the first, firearm, instance, this suicide would demand the most complete foolhardiness and a truly perverse imagination on the part of the investigator (both criminal and scientific) to imagine something like it. It's just too... What about under the wheels of a train? No, too defenseless: *a naked man on the rails.* Dangerous to the imagination. But maybe under rubber wheels? It's true that they were less inhumane, but even they were too dangerous. Moreover, the suppressed suicide under rubber wheels directly suggested an image of a huge city, summer, a scorching pavement, blue-gray smog, a gorgeous, aging brunette behind the wheel. All of this had to be rejected, not only because of its inappropriateness in terms of the season but also because of the brunette, who may have seen a thing or two in her day, but never in such a public place. This incident of the suicide *en déshabillé* would undoubtedly have shocked her. Well, and what about jumping out the window? No, this death could not be prescribed for the imagination either. Again those sharp, tiny stones and a naked man on the stones. The inhumanity of this picture was again obvious (let's not forget that the man would have fallen on these stones alive). The only case in which a falling out could have been permitted (though it would be pushing it) would be if this falling were to be out of a skyscraper (one imagines that the naked man, because of a weak heart, would hit the stones already dead), but there were no skyscrapers in this country. Of course, there still remained hanging (the chances for which decreased significantly with the removal of the tie; they were not, however, eliminated totally, given a sharply convincing detail: socks with wet soles and legs swinging above the floor). But while hanging was initially a possibility, given the convincingness of the dirty socks, it was immediately rejected for the same reason, because the socks by that time would have become sweaty, and the odor of socks reeking of sweat... No, suicides, as has been noted, guard their post-mortem smells jealously. And so, both because of the absence of insufficient reasons for the imagination (there was no tie around the neck), as well as because of the indecent odor of the socks, hanging was rejected. There remained drowning, which would allow with aesthetic impeccability the appearance of someone naked in socks and shorts, a shore, a sandbar, silt, water stinging with cold and finality, a prolonged and indecisive wading in, hesitation, a last and final "forgive me," sudden decisiveness, immersion, a few reappearances on the surface, alternating with self-irony and a struggle for life and, finally, the ultimate disappearance and an end to everything—including the odor.

No, to have his socks on was better in all respects. Because he was indifferent to the kind of death these people would ascribe to him in their imagination. Moreover, he didn't feel defenseless in his socks. Not as defenseless, at any rate, as he would feel in just his coat, or just his trousers, or just his shoes, though they may be laced, or in whatever, or in all these things together, but sockless (there was even no question of putting on all his things and hiding, because for the sake of ending the chase he had to simulate suicide). The horror of feet, of bare feet arrayed in shoes, the horror of his whole being, of his whole makeup, was incomparable and the man knew this (you can kill a man by taking his socks away and forcing him to put on his shoes and hat).

But the socks also protected him well *morally*, and the man understood this. Moreover, he had very tender soles and the socks provided partial protection. But like this, he felt as if he were wearing armor. And he squared his shoulders.

Now he was ready to meet them, not himself, of course, but through this unparalleled composition. Because it expressed everything that was essential, namely, his absence not only here (here above all), but also on the train and, perhaps (the man counted on this), even in this world in general. Only the last clue remained to be eliminated. And he was that clue.

The man walked out onto the platform of the car (the voices were getting closer). He opened the outer door. He took a deep breath. A solid, stagnant, vertical smell of water struck the man: the train floated slowly above the river in the silver of the supporting structure. The cars carefully surmounted one junction after another; you could say they were proceeding by feel.

Abruptly shouted orders resounded close by, and they squeezed the man out of the train. Slowly and smoothly, as in a dream, he abandoned his refuge and landed on a box with sand and there and then hid behind a red emergency enclosure with buckets and grappling hooks. (His legs, by the way, would have been fully visible to people, they were a lot lower than the lowest level of the enclosure, if it hadn't been for the salutary fire-red color deflecting all suspicion. He could probably have hidden an elephant behind the copper shield).

Now he'll wait things out here (no, no, he'll go further), now he'll wait things out here and come to grips with his thoughts. He'll get warm (there in the car in the face of constantly threatening danger there was somehow never any time to get warm, the very thought had not occurred to him, but here, in freedom, he could finally work on it in earnest). He'll get warm. He'll pull up his socks and maybe even turn them the right way out. He'll start his inconceivable calculations (the intent here was one of computation and secret observation of train windows through a hole), the observed and calculated later to be divided by ten (the doors were added for ease of computation), and ultimately to be converted into the number of cars. He didn't want just to count the number of cars, either because of the primitive nature of such calculation, or because the meager possibilities of the hole did not afford a proper mathematical panorama (properly speaking, it wasn't even a hole, but just a nail hole; at any rate, not a knot hole). At the precisely calculated place (he had in mind the last car, but to make it he'd have to emerge three windows early, meaning that an additional computation of subtracting would have to be performed that would also take up some time), he'll come out of his shelter, straighten his back, throw his shoulders back (this is what those three anticipated windows will be spent on) (he relished this thought especially) and lightly, confidently, with a mocking smile, he'll jump into the dear, infinitely precious door and continue his journey. And he didn't allow for a second the thought that he might stay behind the enclosure and not go on.

Swallowing, he greedily pressed against the hole and began counting fervently. His hiding place was totally safe, even pleasant and cozy, and the old unpainted bottom of the enclosure attested to this.

He began counting. The row of cars was endless (no, for the time being he only counted the windows and wasn't converting them into cars), the row of cars was endless, and observation through the tiny dimensions of the opening intensified this endlessness. What could he do? To tell the truth, he dozed off for a little while. But later he quickly restored the windows that he'd missed, as well as the gap in the rhythm while he slept, then continued his count with redoubled enthusiasm.

The monotony of windows flashing by was soon replaced by the simple monotony of uninhabited space. The train had already passed long ago, but the man counted and counted, rocked by the rhythm. Apparently the cause of this was an enthusiasm that eternally outstrips events (though in the given instance outstripping had turned into its dialectical opposite). Or is it possible that he was simply adjusting the problem to the answer (after all, he knew the number of cars to begin with) and that he continued behaving in a manner that was contrary to obvious fact? Realizing this, he slapped his forehead and jumped out from his shelter. The train grew catastrophically distant and, not having given himself the satisfaction of throwing his shoulders back and straightening his back (the windows were now at minus nine and he bent over three more times, regretting what had just taken place), he gave chase.

He ran, he put his hope in the dear, near doors, in their salutary refuge, in their absolute safety. No doubt these people are now far from them and no doubt they won't return there anymore. For those who trust nobody believe excessively in themselves, thereby adding to the deficit of trust at great cost to others, and all of their behavior in their own eyes is absolutely infallible. The car had been searched and, consequently, it's completely safe, maybe even safer than it was before the appearance of these people (so the sky seems cleaner right after the passage of a storm cloud); deliberating in this way, the man increased his speed and soon overtook the train. From a desire to prolong his pleasure, he even ran for some time alongside the train, simulating the danger and rechecking his deliberations, and only then did he jump on the footboard and grasp the door.

From a desire to prolong his pleasure, he even ran for some time alongside the train, rechecking the movement of his deliberations, and only then did he jump on the footboard and discover that the door was locked. Alas, alas, he was also a captive of stereotypes. Why did he think that the door would be open to him again? Because he wanted it to be? Didn't he know that to guard against foreseen misfortunes was even more difficult than against unexpected ones (didn't he know that only one's own shortcomings are noted in others and that this very fact prevents us from seeing them; to other shortcomings, that is, those that have nothing to do with ours, we are profoundly indifferent). Intimations of all this flashed but momentarily in his face, never to become clearly conscious thought.

He jumped off and again ran alongside. It was imperative to think over the new situation. He could, in fact, have occupied himself with this on the footboard, but the door discouraged him to the point that he lost his head, jumped down, and even fell behind a bit from bewilderment. It was essential that he do something.

It was essential that he do something. The train was already leaving the darkness of the bridge. At any rate, it was clear that the door was closed. And not only this one, but all of them on the entire train. Those people, of course, had seen to that. This last door, which had seemed so dear and constant in its unlocked state, emphasized that fact clearly. There was no use rechecking it. He could only return to the beginning of the train and attempt to find a solution there. For the time being the train was moving slowly (at the moment its front was floating by some sort of a striped marker). The man jumped on the footboard again, having decided to ride up to the marker and thereby immediately to find himself at the head of the train and there to switch to the first car, but he came to his senses in time, blushed to himself at his slow-wittedness and to the marker (which he reached anyway), and again jumped off and fell behind a little from embarrassment (falling behind from bewilderment was significantly more remediable than falling behind from embarrassment).

This was an unbelievable blunder. Recovering from his embarrassment, he plunged in chase after the train, striking his detested dear door with his fist on the way, and hurling a curse under the wheels. The door opened in welcome and called the long-distance runner to itself. He became conscious of this only later, when he was far ahead, but in revenge (and in revenge for his presuppositions) he didn't return and he didn't even want to thank it for its hospitality.

He moved only twice as fast, and half his speed was in vain. Nevertheless, the other "half" shortened the distance and brought him closer to his goal. He ran, he got out of breath, he got closer to the train, breathing in the hot air of the rails and the smell of water that was catching up with him. The rush of oncoming trains buffeted his naked body with warm air and coal dust and the difference in the two air currents tore his body apart (internally his body was also torn by contradictions: he felt an intermittent impulse to jump onto the passing train); the trains' opposing motion would cancel all velocity and hope and then everything would come to a standstill. And in the midst of this dead realm of annihilated motion a horrifying silence would burst out and, seizing his head in his hands, he would plunge into this silence and feel defenseless in it. But the train would rush by and the man would run again at redoubled speed but only gain half the distance.

Now he was running even with the door, which he had left not long ago (left to be shielded by the shield of the enclosure), and, of course, he could pass it, or he could, if he so desired, fall a bit behind, but the nearness of the door warmed him. He ran, and pondered, and deliberated. He thought about those people. Where are they now? Had they gotten off? Vanished? Disappeared? No, surely not. Illegality of any sort was not one of their characteristics and since that time, it seems, there had been no stops. Did they spread out again among all the cars or gather here in his car to discuss the new situation? Yes, precisely in his car and precisely in his compartment. Now they're looking again at his strewn-about clothes and imagining him naked again (he modestly covered his chest with his hands) and maybe, even though he'd taken the tie off long ago, even hanged. He started panting (from the rope, not from fatigue), strangulation marks appeared on his neck, but the hanging was to be cancelled again on account of the all-pervasive smell of water. A victim of drowning, after all. He tensed his sphincter and prepared to jump in the water. The unbearable contradiction between reality and these people's assumptions almost compelled him to end it all and to realize their misanthropic scenario, but the inertia of shame and motion saved him yet again and they (he and the train) were already leaving the zone of the supposed suicide. Now they (these people) will undoubtedly leave him in peace and forget him forever. There was no longer any smell of water, nor was there any water. These people, whose conclusion about the nature of this suicide was thrust on them by the entire course of events, had no more reason to think of him. The waters of the river now concealed from view (and concealing his supposed corpse), now also concealed the true location of the man quite nicely and he grew considerably bolder.

He thrust out his chest and became bolder (not forgetting, by the way, to pursue his door). He jumped on the footboard and almost opened the door: he had put so much trust in the stereotype. He thought that these people upon seeing him would not believe the obvious (but they would believe the victim of drowning). He even started opening the door, he even opened it slightly, but then he changed his mind, reasoning that if among them there was even one sensible person... No, it was better not to tempt fate. And he jumped down once more.

Again he was running with his—his no. 2—doors and the train was picking up speed, and soon the man was running at triple speed, but he only made up half the distance. His heart beat madly against his ribs, there was a wheezing in his throat and something was twisting his liver. No, he can't take any more of this, the train's speeding up (and the people again started doubting the suicide because one of them accidentally stopped the swaying motion of the shoe, immediately disturbing the convincingness of the entire composition), it is time to rest up, and he's got to look for a permanent refuge (it was amazing that the relativity of his location increased as a result of his new hopes for permanence), he had to look for a new refuge and to hide finally from the ever-increasing suspicion of the dark people.

What should he do? What steps should he take? Excuse the original door and accept its hospitality? No, only not that. It was not in his makeup to change a resolution; besides, he still felt unavenged. Grasp the handrail and break into the door under cover of their imagined stereotype? No, that would be equivalent to turning yourself in and an admission of guilt (in view of the ever-receding smell of water, the changed position of the shoe and in view of the ever-increasing suspicions). The option of giving himself up, by the way, was something that he clearly underestimated: to have had the opportunity of escaping and not to have made use of this opportunity... He might be forgiven. Moreover he would give them a reason to show their mercy. They just might seize this opportunity. He was so taken by this sincere idea that he again grasped the handle of the door, but he immediately remembered the stereotype (the stereotype of the supposed suicide, which, though it was drowning in the waves of ever-increasing suspicion, nevertheless continually exerted a powerful presence), but he immediately remembered the stereotype and thought that these people would not forgive him any allusion to it (and even less any comprehension of the allusion). And he jumped off again and saw the train jerk desperately and race forward. It appeared that the train got tired of his vacillation and wanted to get away from his indecisiveness (vacillation and indecisiveness are infectious). And then, passing his dear door (simply because it had now stopped being that) (and because there was no longer any other way out), he jumped on the footboard of the electric loco-

motive, lifted himself up, and confidently opened the door. Simply because
he believed in harmony and rhythm and simply because he believed in fate.
He was convinced of a double symmetry: the symmetry of the train and of
the electric locomotive; if the last door of the train was open, it meant that the
first door of the first car (i. e., of the electric locomotive) was also open; if one
door of the electric locomotive is open (obviously the engineers aren't going
to lock themselves in), it means that the second door will also be open (the
first was open because the last was open); but while the second symmetry
was beyond reproach, the reasoning concerning the first was somewhat
strained (a shift from the green center of the color spectrum): the last door of
the last car corresponded in this symmetry to the door before the first one
(and because of this strained interpretation, the door still hadn't opened), but
he made no adjustments for this and while such a fact could ruin all his
hopes, he believed in fate.

The door opened and concealed the man, hiding him in the locomotive's
twin cab (enervated by the symmetry forced on it and by the preestablished
harmony of cabs). Now, pleased to receive within itself something unenvis-
aged and to infringe upon a pseudoharmony (the reason, as a matter of fact,
that it opened), the door hospitably proffered him its comfort.

There were two seats in the cab. The man sat in the one that was closer
and sighed contentedly. Having sat like that for a while, he felt a sudden agitation, moved to the other seat, and the agitation left him. Because initially he
occupied the assistant's seat and only then the engineer's, and to be in any
submissive position oppressed him. And so he occupied the engineer's place
and now he was comfortable.

He looked around. Right behind him there were clothes lockers, under
them, built-in refrigerators. On the side there were diagrams of electrical circuits and of the main air lines. The instrument panel, shining dully, emitted a
hidden strength. He checked the containers with sand and was pleased to note
that they were filled to overflowing. Then he put his left hand on the controller
(the reverse handle was missing), and his right on the auxiliary brake (in case
of emergency braking, he could also use this hand to activate the sanding apparatus). He moved the warning handle of the automatic breaking gear further
away so that he could focus greater attention on operating the train in an increasingly complicated situation. The warning handle served to check if the
engineer was looking after the movement of the train carefully as the train
passed between the home signal lights of separate points and the yellow and
red lights between two stations. In case of need an auditory signal comes on,
signifying that air from the brake lines has started entering the atmosphere. To
discontinue the signal, the warning handle is depressed, otherwise in six or
seven seconds auxiliary braking of the train would take place and the braking

gear recorder would lock in (it is also necessary to depress the warning handle after passing a red light between two stations).*

...To decrease longitudinal impact on the train, a transition from downgrade to upgrade is accomplished by the gradual engagement of the controller and by stretching out the head of the train in the area before the start of the upgrade. Turning down the controller after crossing a pass is also accomplished gradually in order to avoid jerking between individual cars. If sharp breaks occur between sections, it is essential to slightly brake the locomotive when half the cars enter the downgrade.

On passenger electric locomotives of the Ch S type, an increase in tractive force is achieved by a clockwise turn of the wheel on the controller. Each turn of the controls to the next position can be achieved at a current of 500 volts. Should wheel spin take place, the control wheel is quickly switched to a lower position, and with the cessation of wheel spin, as sand is dropped on the rails to control skidding, it is again turned to a higher position. The engineer makes his judgment on wheel spin according to the oscillation of the needle on the ampermeter, an auditory signal, or when the light of the wheel-spin trigger tube goes on.

Abrupt breaking should not be employed without dire need, since the electromagnetic brakes assure such an abrupt deceleration of the train that it could cause injury to passengers (!).

On numerous railways passenger trains are driven by electric freight locomotives with lowered gear ratios that insure great tractive force at great speeds. The starts of these electric locomotives are characterized by reduced tractive force, but it is fully adequate for starting and gathering momentum of trains weighing in at 1100 to 1200 tons. In driving light (!) passenger trains by electric freight locomotives with alternating current and external temperatures above zero centigrade, one is able to operate with only five or even four traction motors, that is, to save on electrical energy.

But the man grasped all this more by intuition than by reason, or by simple knowledge that he now recollected. In the meantime his intuition grasped more and more and right now it also understood the sequence of a transition to regeneration, the termination of the latter, the utilization of a braking resistor, taking the train on an open track, operating the electric locomotive with some of the traction motors shut off with damage to the rectifying plant, etc. etc., but the activity of his intuition was brought to a halt in time. A small factory plate (so unexpectedly coinciding with the external cast-iron brand) stated: 70K, and for some reason he thought about despotism. But this for-

---

*Those wishing to become further acquainted with the sequence of operations can consult the Ministry of Communication's "Instructions in Safety Procedures for Electric Locomotive Engineers."—Ed. [author's note]

bidden thought (it's criminal even to think of tyranny) was again swept away
by a wave of intuition, which this time gave him the basic technical specifica-
tions of the electric locomotive:

Type of service: .... Freight
Type of current .... Alternating
                                                                                                         50 Hz
Voltage .... 25,000 V
                                                                                                         +16%
                                                                                                         -25%
Running gear formula .... 3_0 - 3_0
Gauge 1520mm
Hourly rating of traction motor shaft .... 4590 kW
Continuous rating of traction motor shaft .... 4070 kW
Gear rating of gear drive 3.826
Hourly rating of tractive force .... 31860 kcs
Continuous rating of tractive force .... 26400 Kcs
Hourly speed rating of electric locomotive .... 52 kmph
Continuous speed rating of electric locomotive .... 55.6 kmph
Speed design of undercarriage .... 100 km
Continuous rating efficiency of electric locomotive in 33rd position 0.84
Continuous rating of power coefficient in 33rd position 0.85
Mass of elec. locomotive (c^2) 3 reserves of sand .... 138 ±2%
Axle load on rails .... 23T.S. ±2%
Load difference on rails of wheels from one axle .... no more than 0.5
Axle height of automatic coupler from rail head,
     with new tread bands .... 1060 ±2mm
Height from rail head to the working surface of
     the runner of the current receptor:
          in a lowered position .... 5100 mm
          in the "on" position .... 5500-7000 mm
          Diameter of wheels .... 1250 mm
          Smallest radius of traversed curves with speeds at 10 kmph .... 125 m

He then confidently pulled on some sort of handle, thereby instantly causing the entire train to shudder. This was strange: the train wasn't supposed to
be operated from this cab, the cab was non-functioning. He let go of the handle in alarm and immediately moved to the subordinate chair, since he
wanted to avoid responsibility. When the former sequence of motion was
reestablished, he took a deep breath and felt hungry.

He felt hungry. The portable refrigerator mounted into the back wall
turned out to be disgustingly empty and cried out with an impossibly edible

smell. The man closed off this smell as quickly as possible and again thought of recuperation. This made it easier for him to struggle with his hunger.

With trepidation he awaited retribution for his anti-railway activities. But gradually the thought of non-punishment took possession of him. To tell the truth, enough time had passed for this to occur, but it looked as if no one was coming. And he fell asleep. He no longer thought about those who were crowding around the platform of the car and who seemed not to notice him, because he was too high up and they too low and, besides, they were looking down. In addition to this, they were again in the power of the stereotype. They thought that if there was even any reason to look for him, it was there in the cars (and he was not there), in a place for passengers, and not here in the electric locomotive, a place for engineers. Of course they noticed him, not him, but some other him, they thought that it wasn't he and they didn't keep looking at him. And since he was riding in an engineer's cab, they took him for an engineer, even though he was operating the train with his back to the front. But in spite of this obvious absurdity, they were unable to free themselves from this stereotype imposed on them by the railway (and by their own nearsightedness). He fell asleep, and even though he felt secure as far as these dark people were concerned, the threat from the train engineers was still present and so that he wouldn't be caught unaware, he set the Warning Handle.

When he awoke he once again examined the refrigerator, this time even more thoroughly and scrupulously than before, but since it still contained nothing his scrupulousness only made him hungrier. Lamenting his fastidiousness, with his little finger he carefully touched the nozzle of the carbon dioxide extinguisher and sighed. He undertook no other active railway activities, only silently, moving his lips, he read from the diagrams of the electric circuits (pusillanimously, he disregarded the diagrams of the brake conduits), mentally moving to the very heart of the electric locomotive. Once again: he now felt totally safe. Danger could only come from the rear, from the train engineers (they could come here because of work-related needs), but the train was traveling at such a magnificent speed that their appearance here was absolutely excluded. As far as *those* people were concerned, he no longer thought about them, since he now felt protected.

How many of them were still left? About eight or twelve. They continued to crowd around the platform of the car; he saw them clearly from where he was. They were waiting for something or someone. But not him. He was separated from them by the thick, tempered, windshield glass of a perfect, streamlined form. (It was surprising that the man derived his sensation of safety specifically from the streamlining of the glass and its perfection of form, and not from its thickness and strength.) He saw them. It goes without saying that he also did not go unnoticed. But they, of course, suspected nothing. Again

they were in the power of the stereotype (inborn tracking reflexes, innate pre-
dispositions), and according to them, he didn't merit attention. Yes, of course
they saw him, and they saw him naked, nude, defenseless, and, of course,
they juxtaposed this fact with the discarded clothes (but earlier, with his absence; his nakedness was the second part of the syllogism). They had seen
him, they had engaged in the process of juxtaposition and in fact they had
juxtaposed correctly, but they were no longer capable of rejecting the very
principle they themselves had thought up. Who told them that only engineers ride in cabs for engineers? Engineers, assistants and railway workers in
general? But for them all special places existed only for specialists, and they
allowed no exceptions to this principle. They didn't even have faith in the obvious, even though he often got up, slept, looked after no instruments, did
without an assistant and, as was already stated, operated the train with his
back to the front. They saw all this, but they could no longer liberate themselves from the stereotype imposed on them by the State, the railway system,
and their own stupidity. No, these people did not want to notice him and by
their presence they only roused within him a feeling of safety. He grew so
bold that he even decided to take off his socks, dirty and torn to shreds, so
that he could once again verify his feeling of safety: will it leave him after he
takes them off, will it betray him and may it not change into its opposite?

No, without his socks this feeling looked even more magnificent. These
people simply didn't allow themselves to notice him. But the main thing that
sold him on a sense of safety (sold him *on,* not *out,* though this feeling would
soon sell him out), but the main thing that sold him on a sense of safety (together with streamlined glass) was the sense of height that completely separated him from these people, since the seating of the electric locomotive was
significantly higher than the seating in any car. And here was his main source
of safety and he drew from it with cupped hands as he had earlier drawn from
the socks. The dark people would be unable to surmount this height. He was
unreachable. And he waved to them through the window. They turned away
from him helplessly, concealing tortured grimaces.

But maybe he was dreaming all this (the windshield was encased in ve-
neer), but maybe he was only dreaming all this? And he was sorry about the
discarded socks. The thing with the socks was no dream.

Having studied the diagram of the circuits (again he felt that he was not
free), he opened the door to the engine room and let in a roaring noise. But in
the roar he gained additional certainty that nothing threatened him. It was a
sense of safety.

He stepped into darkness. He saw a long, narrow corridor that was half-lit,
a fact that seemed especially strange (and made the corridor even darker),
given the abundance of electricity. Carefully entering this electric abode, he

dragged himself along the corridor between shuddering walls, registering an ever-nearing warmth and a growing vibration of the floor with the soles of his feet (his hearing now no longer recorded what was going on, entrusting the care of his body to more reliable senses). Reaching the middle, he felt that he was in a familiar situation. Again everything repeated itself miraculously, but in reverse order, like a film running backwards. The warmth and vibration of the floor abated (the soles of his feet didn't forget to report this to him). His mood was improving considerably.

He moved in the dusk and the otherworldliness of the movie house, groping with blind hands and feeling his way along. But he didn't forget to keep an eye on the screen. Now the frame of the film showed a cab, exactly like his, but with two broad-shouldered men on the peripheries of the frame. Too bad that he was late and wouldn't see the newsreel. The film had already started.

There was a large crowd and all seats were taken. There was one place in the first row and he took it (only later did the man notice another seat and tried to get to it, but people shushed him. Banished by the displeasure of others and his own embarrassment, he went back).

In front of the screen a barrier of plexiglass had been erected against the displeasure and the indifference of the viewers, but, in moments of psychological contact between the actor and the viewers, it was removed automatically.

The man stared with interest at the screen. The plexiglass came up. Two tall uniformed men drove the train. They did this standing up, moving only their hands, their far-seeing gazes fixed somewhere in the distance. They did this in silence, and only rarely did the man on the right, apparently in charge, issue abrupt orders to his assistant. The assistant carried out these instructions precisely.

Twice they ignored a red light. The audience got excited, expecting an accident (each frame of the film now anticipated the image of an imagined oncoming train), but the composure of the engineers instilled hope. Apparently they were in a great hurry, these people; no doubt they were behind schedule. Not once did the public get a good look at their faces. They didn't even see them in profile. The entire film was a contemplation of backs and backs of heads. This inspired horror. But it was precisely this that instilled hope: straight, broad shoulders, a firm set of the head, carefully pressed uniforms, and the total psychological anonymity of the proceedings averted a catastrophe. It was strange, but the meager expressiveness of these frames kept the viewers in a constant state of tension.

The train braked abruptly. Some kind of compulsory stop. But they continued getting a green light. The engineer looked at his assistant in perplexity, but the latter refused to meet his gaze. Now the viewers got a good look at them. The assistant was significantly younger than his partner. He had a gray, marmorial face, a firm chin and metallic teeth. All his movements seemed mechanized. Guiltily placing his hand on the engineer's shoulder (a guilty, apologetic gesture: I don't want to do this, but I have to; and this imparted some warmth to his appearance), he pulled out a gun and aimed it at the engineer's chest. The engineer smiled, and in the course of this brief, forced smile, some dark people, but not those who were crowding around the car platform, quickly climbed into the cab. Handing over the engineer to them, the assistant moved over to his place and started off. Now he would drive the train on his own: the engineer had turned out to be unreliable.

Slowly stretching out the train, the assistant started off. The viewers, holding their breath, waited for a resolution. Getting the train up to speed, the assistant broke off the Warning Handle, abandoned all controls, and started rushing about the cab. The viewers' alarm grew. The train rushed forward heedlessly, paying no attention to the warning signs, and soon left the boundaries of the contact network and continued moving by its own inertia. Having given a drawn-out signal, the assistant released the sanding gear, preparing to brake. Smokestacks, crossing barriers, and suburbs flashed past. At full speed the engineer burst into a huge iron-beamed station, ramming with his bumper into a passenger train that hadn't left yet. The assistant took a deep breath. It was all over. After a thorough (and final) clean-up in the cab, he took a careful look around, wiped his hands on a towel and filled out some railroad documents. Then he gathered up his little leather case, released the reverse handle, let the air out of the braking system, shut off the sanding gear, and walked out.

They were already waiting for him. A small group of five or six people, very dark. Again these strange people, even darker and more dangerous than those. Keeping their hands in their pockets up to the elbows. They made way for him, ready to seize the criminal.

He walked up to them meekly and handed over the handle, his little case, and the documents. Then, placing his hands behind his back, he moved off, accompanied by these people. And the brims of their hats almost covered their eyes.

The man tensed with fear. Again these State collars, again these hands in pockets. What's going on? Where is the danger? Why should everyone be arrested? Why don't they resist? The huge train station was completely empty, and its ominous emptiness was vividly emphasized by the fact that all of the numerous platform clocks suddenly started up (prior to this, they stood still as if waiting for some essential flaw in the ceaseless stream of eternity, and, having poured into eternity., they started showing the correct time.) The man checked them against his watch and gave a cry. He was transfixed by the horror of precise time.

Trains arrived and departed, the electronic time tables constantly showed new information, everything was being done precisely according to schedule, electric baggage-cars scurried elsewhere, but the trains were completely empty, and red lights shone everywhere. The clocks froze again.

The man threw himself toward his cab. What dead town was this and why were the clocks here not running? This especially puzzled him. Again he ran to his cab, but he didn't occupy either seat. Both submission and power were now equally hateful to him and he sat down on the floor right between the two seats, still sorry about his lost socks. A feeling of defenselessness, now clearly emphasized by the perfection and the streamlined nature of the glass, took possession of the man. He put his head between his knees and burst into tears.

He got up. From his cab he looked at the platform of the car. What on earth were they doing there, these people? They were all standing around, these people, waiting for something. Those State collars. Those State pockets. Yes, they were still standing there, these people, on the platform of the first car, indecisive, somehow suddenly pitiful, almost dear, and warily whispering something to one another. No doubt they were waiting for others. And the darkness of these seemed gray in comparison to the darkness of *those*. It was apparent that they now definitely had no interest in the man. Now they needed help themselves. Then why aren't they leaving? Could it be that they sought protection from him? Certain dark people were afraid of other dark people and the color black, he'd heard, has thirty-six shades.

Finally, urged on by their own indecisiveness, they came out and gathered in a small circle, consulting each other about something. And suddenly they stretched out into a line, a long file of eight or twelve people. And they all held their hands in their pockets. And then they formed a circle. And suddenly one of them, with a radically turned-down collar, and up to now holding his hands in his pockets with special care, pulled out a bright yellow leather identification card and presented it to everyone. And immediately, almost without a pause, almost in an instant (and even sooner, in a split second), they all started pulling out their yellow identification cards, pulling them out and presenting them to each other, and this doubly consistent, unbroken betrayal was lightning quick and the circle closed and each was arrested by the next one. But they were all prisoners of one, of the first one, whose face was especially impenetrable, whose hands were held especially deeply, and whose collar was most fastidiously turned down, but not because of the hands and collar, but because he was the first of those who had shown their loyalty. Drops of sweat glistened on his repulsively legal forehead. And when the circle closed and identification cards were hidden away and they all started moving away escorted by this man, the last of those who had shown his loyalty took out his identification card and made the first one last. And everything was repeated again. So they moved away, holding onto each other, slowly retreating, betraying and carefully watching one another, not letting the others out of their sight. Some of the dark people betrayed other dark people; the color black has thirty-six shades. And in this atmosphere of ever-widening betrayal the man emitted a foul shout of despair and jumped out of his shelter. But he was heard by no one, because the dark people were absorbed in one another and they were already far away. He was left alone. Alone with his feeling of fellowship. And he placed his head on the rails.

How long did he lie like this, ready for death? Hardly less than twenty-four hours. There was a dead silence and the train no longer moved. The wheels quietly rusted beneath the rain. He climbed up to his car, walked into his compartment and got dressed. He again searched himself with anticipation. Alas, his clothes were still empty, even though he didn't expect this (emptiness that often repeats itself is always quickly filled psychologically). He dressed, put on his shoes, and went to the platform of the car. He had a gloomy look. He was seized by a horror of bare feet, intensified now by damp shoes and by the bright tastelessness of a tie he had gotten as a gift. It was a good thing that he didn't wear a hat.

Now he stood indecisively by the exit. The doors were wide open. There was no one around, he had arrived at his destination long ago, and nothing more was preventing him from leaving the car. Then what in the world was keeping him here? No doubt the usual inertia of space made habitable.

Making a few timid attempts to get off, even getting to the last step of the footboard (and to the ultimate point of his vacillation), he fearfully went back to his original position, to the platform. An inexplicable sense of leaving something behind, of deprivation and loss, which often accompanied the man in his travels, intensified with every abandoned step, and he returned. And suddenly he remembered. Well, of course, it was because of it, his little, elegant briefcase for small, everyday trifles. How could he have forgotten about it? It was the case that instilled a sense of alarm in him.

The man cheerfully slapped himself on his forehead and rushed back. Back, back to the last car, to the beginning of this terrifying journey. He hoped that it was still there. Well, of course it was there, where else would it be, what could interest anyone about his stupid case, everyone has his own worries.

He rushed through the cars, hurrying terribly, entangling his legs and hands, every now and then bringing the pendulum and his breathing to a halt, transgressing against the rhythm of the universe. He was in an incredible hurry, his blood pressure rose, and his masculine strength was prepared for action. He undressed as he ran, overcoming dozens of doors, and finally found himself by his dear crack. Without any erotic preparation, hurriedly, he copulated. Having gotten his little case, he did himself up. He checked his buttons. These disorderly sexual relations thoroughly exhausted him. He was pleased anyway. And the case was there. The bliss of emptiness and the emptiness of bliss held sway over him. And together this was called appeasement.

He opened those dear (No. 1) doors, just like that, to be on the safe side, to check his assumptions. He noted with satisfaction that they were still open (not his assumptions, the doors; his assumptions meanwhile shut down with a bang). Of course, he could just as well get off here (he was prompted to do this by the stereotype), but he'll go back, prompted by duty and symmetry. Anyway, his lawful place was there and there he would get off.

He set out on a backward journey. He didn't hurry. Everything had turned out well. The case was in its place. The libido was satisfied. No one was pursuing him any longer. The train arrived on time and at its scheduled destination. The clocks were working. He only had to pass through to the first car and walk out as befits a passenger. And no problems.

Without hurrying, he walked out onto his platform. He tightened his tie and dusted off a shoe. But now he was sorry about something. How quickly he had arrived! Sighing, he gestured in farewell and climbed down. But even as his leg was poised over the station platform and as he had almost parted with his fears in midair, his doubts started again and he rushed back. He had almost allowed for something irreparable. Cold beads of sweat appeared on his illegal forehead.

He is confused, this man. A little islet of despair and hope. He is searching for something in his pockets; he lost something there, this man; he probably wants to present something, some sort of an impossible justification. With despair and hope he looks around and gropes and gropes, searches endlessly, and even turns out his pockets guiltily. What is he hoping for, this man?

What is he hoping for, this man? Fate has already placed its hand on his throat.

A cold, quivering hand. A cold, quivering throat.

He travels light, this man. Without a coat, without his things, in a light-colored summer suit. The man doesn't even have on a hat. Apparently he's just gotten off a plane from some distant countries.

He fusses about; in the anxiety of impending guilt he continually adjusts his tie, holds down the flaps of his coat, and also looks at his watch. Why is he looking at his watch? It ignites embarrassment.

It ignites embarrassment. It destroys hope.

And suddenly he remembers. Well, of course, that was it, his small, elegant case, his briefcase for everyday cultural trifles. How was it that he hadn't thought to look inside?

He quickly opens the case, bares its vaginal interior, and unfolds the fan-shaped compartments. He carefully inserts his hand (he will be the first to find out what's in the little case, and even earlier—his hand, and before his hand—his fingers, and before his fingers—his nails, and before his nails—a presentiment, but earliest of all...), he will be the first to find out what is in the little case. Already the nail knows it, the finger of his hand, the hand itself, and finally, his entire self, and his face brightens, lightens, dissipates clouds and storms.

And his hand pulls out handcuffs, small elegant handcuffs made of titanium or some other light metal. And his face brightens, lightens, dissipates clouds and storms. He'll adjust his tie one final time, tuck in his pockets, and look at his watch. And he adjusts his tie, tucks in his pockets, and looks at his watch. And having adjusted his tie, tucked in his pockets, and looked at his watch, he pulls on the handcuffs, small, elegant handcuffs made of titanium or some other light metal.

And again he dissipates the clouds, adjusts his tie, and looks at his watch.

And having dissipated the clouds, adjusted his tie and looked at the watch, he smiles slightly, checks the reliability of the handcuffs, snaps them on one hand, then the other. He helps himself with habit, agility, and the case; he pulls them to the side and with a motion from top to bottom, he pinches his wrists with them, smartly lifts up the case, nods his head to himself approvingly, opens the door, straightens his chest, shoulders, and back and, replacing his approving nod with a grin, a smile, and self-derision, internally composed, he takes a deep breath and boldly places a foot on the station platform.

Thus in renowned parabolas,
in teachings about safety procedures,
in a book about style, parables about man,
is proclaimed the first parabola, called
SAFETY PROCEDURE ONE.
Let us turn to "Safety Procedure Two."

1979
(Manufactured on paper from the N paper factory).

Translated by Jerzy Kolodziej

Originally published in *Ural,* January 1988

About the Authors

BORIS EKIMOV
(b. 1938, Siberia)

About his roots Ekimov has written: "My Russia is the Don, its unique language, way of life and natural environment." In his work we feel an almost mystical attachment to the Don region (his family moved to the small town of Kalach-on-the-Don near Volgograd soon after the war). Ekimov is one of the most accomplished short story writers in contemporary Russian literature, unusual in his brevity. He has published more than ten books of collected stories, beginning with *The Girl in the Red Coat* in 1974. In their sketchy but poignant topicality, many recall early Chekhov, and the timely sociological and economic questions they pose have generated controversy.

Ekimov's mode of fiction is classically realistic, enhanced by a laconic, understated lyricism. A major quality of his appealing, arcadian depiction of the village landscape is the exactitude of detail, presented with the keen, dispassionate eye of a naturalist, and this gives a convincing authenticity to his distinctly southern Russian settings. His characters, for the most part villagers, are, unlike Chekhov's, too stereotyped morally, however, and this is his most serious fault as a writer. Ekimov shares a conservative vision many critics associate with writers from the Don, perhaps under the literary influence of Mikhail Sholokhov—the supreme socialist realist of the region.

Ekimov has avoided the nationalistic pamphleteering of many of his fellow writers during glasnost. Although he publishes regularly in their journal *Nash sovremennik*, his stories also appear in the centrist *Novy mir* and liberal *Znamya*. He has used the freedom brought by glasnost to enrich his stories of the Don countryside with details of social and political corruption that could not have been included previously.

B.L

DANIIL GRANIN
(b. 1919, Volyn, Russia)

Daniil German (Granin, a pseudonym) was born in central Russia during the Civil War—a chaotic time and place. When his father, a forester, was sent to Siberia, his mother made her way to Petrograd, where she established herself as a seamstress. Granin grew up in the rich cultural and literary atmosphere of the old capital. As he himself suggests in an autobiographical essay (1980), compromise may be the determinate feature of his life. As a student during the Stalinist terror, like many, he turned to the new technology as more promising and probably safer than literature, his avowed first love. He studied electrical engineering at the Leningrad Polytechnic Institute, finishing as a specialist in cables, a prestigious profession at a time of intensive industrialization. When the war began, he asked that his deferment be annulled and soon he was laying cables at the front. In 1942 he joined the Communist Party.

After the war, inspired by science and technology, Granin wrote a story called "The Second Variation," the first of his many works to use fiction to examine the conflicts between science and ideology, individual consciousness and political demands. A series of successful novels followed—*The Seekers* (1955), *After the Wedding* (1958), and *Against the Storm* (1962). The latter two were adapted for the stage and their success permitted him to leave the world of science for fiction. Granin moved quickly from the technology of electronic cables to the cabal of the Writers' Union, where he became a prominent mainstay and was frequently published in the Brezhnev period. As pragmatic in his second career as his first, Granin always stayed well within the framework of the politically prudent and never pushed the limits of socialist realism. His plain style was frequently marred by platitudes and party clichés, but he nevertheless succeeded in depicting moral dilemmas of people who are torn between conscience and social expediency.

Granin's novella *The Bison,* was one of the first controversial works of early glasnost. It relates the life of a gifted Soviet biologist who is trapped in Nazi Germany while working in research and returns to Russia after the war only to be arrested and exiled to Siberia. Recently Granin has publicly lamented his own and his generation's timidity and conformity during the years of Communist repression. "The Forbidden Chapter," published in this collection, is a good indication of what we can expect from Granin, now that censorship has been removed.

B.L

ALEXANDER IVANCHENKO
(b. 1947, Krasnoturinsk)

As a young, creative, non-conformist writer, Alexander Ivanchenko met total rejection under the Brezhnev regime, but he survived discouragement to find acceptance under glasnost. He has not been widely published, but he has gained critical recognition and professional support.

At the time he submitted his novella *The Fish Eye* to *Novy mir* in 1975, by the then dominant conventions Ivanchenko's credentials were impeccable—a graduate of the Gorky Literary Institute who had worked as a plumber, a metallurgist, a lumberjack and a fireman. The work itself, however, did not meet the requirements of socialist realism. It was published only in 1987 and in quite a different journal—*Rural Youth.*

The late dissident writer Yury Dombrovsky, who read the work in manuscript, wrote that the story's central character lived and worked "as a biological being, not a social one." This lack of a social context for his characters—a sine qua non for publication in the Soviet Union at the time—is characteristic of Ivanchenko's introspective, acutely personal fictitional world and makes him one of the most interesting, autonomous new voices in Russian literature.

His *Self Portrait with Great Dane,* a satirical, philosophical novel reminiscent of Italo Svevo's *Confessions of Zeno,* appeared in July 1985 in Ural, Sverdlovsk's excellent, venturesome literary journal, and it remains Ivanchenko's most ambitious published work to date. Chameleonesque in nature, the novel has been called alternately an "existential" and a "family" novel. In an afterword Daniil Granin lauds Ivanchenko as a writer whose work is "suffused with artistic thought and the diversity of contemporary culture, the technology of art in which man exists."

"Safety Procedure I" appeared in the "experimental" issue of *Ural* (January 1988), which became a literary benchmark and succès d'estime that provoked irate letters from conservative subscribers. The least provincial of writers, Ivanchenko continues to live in Krasnoturinsk, the small, remote city in the Urals where he was born.

B.L.

VYACHESLAV KONDRATIEV
(b., 1920, Poltava, Ukraine)

Kondratiev was a first-year engineering student in Moscow when he was drafted into the Red Army in 1939. He fought on the front lines until 1944, when he was discharged as a disabled veteran after being severely wounded. He resumed his studies, finished a graphics institute, and worked for 30 years as a draftsman and poster designer before his major career as a writer began.

Kondratiev's first and perhaps best work, *Sashka*, an autobiographical war novella, appeared in 1979 when he was fifty-nine. Initially published in the journal *People's Friendship (Druzba narodov)* with a warm introduction by Konstantin Simonov, *Sashka* was one of countless works about the war—a genre that was exhausted by that time but politically very safe. True to Simonov's prediction, however, Kondratiev's work became an instant favorite of critics and readers alike, mainly because it was so different from Simonov's own work as well as that of his epigones. The latter portrayed "heroes," emphasized courage, stoical self-sacrifice, and the unquestioning execution of orders—all in a highly charged language. Kondratiev's war, on the other hand, is not so much hell as limbo. His protagonists are dreamers more than warriors, more concerned about love, doubt, and the development of consciousness than valor and national pathos. Sashka is a somewhat wooden, idealized character, but he has an individual mind and conscience, and refuses his commander's order to shoot a German prisoner.

Kondratiev followed with a cycle of short fiction that he adapted into popular stage and screen scenarios. His spare, lyrical style, which emphasizes dialogue at the expense of social background, lends itself to dramatic adaptation, and in interviews Kondratiev confirms that he first thought of fiction as theater. Critic Natalya Ivanova places him among a group of writers who, during the late and post-Brezhnev period, wrote in an "honest, direct" style, raising questions without violating the fundamental political taboo that forbade drawing conclusions.

"At Freedom Station," which belongs to Kondratiev's stories depicting World War II from the Soviet side, was "delayed" until glasnost because it casts a sidelong glance at the war's concurrent Stalinist terror. *By Blood Redeemed,* another war novella (*Znamya,* December, 1991), was his first new work of fiction in several years. Throughout the glasnost period Kondratiev has concentrated his work on essays and articles supporting reform and democratic values. Asked recently which two contemporary writers now published in Russia seem most significant to him, he answered: Solzhenitsyn, the traditional Russian moralist, and Valeriya Narbikova, an innovative young (post) modernist.

B.L.

VITALY MOSKALENKO
(b. 1954)

Born into a family with a tradition of military service, after brief stints in an air force school and a polytechnical institute, Moskalenko trained as an actor. Graduating in 1977 from the Lunacharsky Theater Institute (GITIS) in Moscow, he joined the Moscow Theater on Malaya Bronnaya, where he stayed until 1988.

His thespian aspirations did not interfere with the writing he had begun in the early 1970s, which eventually displaced his acting career. Although he completed the sequence of courses that formally conferred upon him the status of playwright (1979), his plays remained unperformed and his stories unpublished.

Moskalenko broke into print after Gorbachev's accession to power and the 27th Congress of April 1985. His plays were staged, journals accepted his stories, and the publishing house Soviet Writer printed his collection entitled *District Center (Raitsentr)*, which includes the story "The Wild Beach." Intent on pursuing his literary activities, Moskalenko left the theater. Natalya Ivanova, the sophisticated literary critic who heads the poetry section of the journal *Druzhba narodov*, has championed him as one of the few truly talented young prosaists of the 1980s.

Married to a painter since 1980, Moskalenko is the father of two girls who, according to him, provide the sole tangible purpose to his life. Although he professes utter skepticism and rarely attends church, Moskalenko nonetheless also volunteers the information that he is a member of the Russian Orthodox faith who hopes for some miraculous salvation from humankind's own self-destruction. The impulse to maim or destroy, in fact, is disturbingly entrenched in his fictional world. Avowedly influenced by Pushkin, Chekhov, Platonov, Bunin, Faulkner, Whitman, Albee, and Ionesco, Moskalenko identifies himself with the generation of writers who, like Dostoevsky at one stage, naively believed, in Moskalenko's own words, that beauty will redeem the world. The emphasis in his fiction falls on the stark need for redemption from the viciousness of human behavior. An environment devoid of spiritual certainties and supports licenses the irrational impulses that prompt unspeakable acts. "The Wild Beach" harshly dramatizes the bleak aimlessness and moral incertitude that fundamentally isolate individuals cast back on their own inner resources by a seemingly indifferent universe. It exemplifies Moskalenko's symbolic use of space and objects; revelation of psychology through physical detail; Chekhovian exploitation of simultaneous dialogues that interpenetrate each other; and predilection for repetition, colloquialisms, and vulgarisms.

H.G.

VYACHESLAV PYETSUKH
(b. 1946 in Moscow)

A former history teacher and graduate of the Lenin Pedagogical Institute (1970), Pyetsukh published his first story in 1978. During the following decade he produced four collections of prose, including *The Alphabet* (1983) and *Good Times* (1988). He has attracted widespread attention, however, only with his more recent works, especially "Rommat" (1989) and *The New Moscow Philosophy* (1989). "Rommat" (short for "Romantic Materialism") constitutes Pyetsukh's contribution to the swelling tide of fictional treatments of history inundating contemporary Soviet publications. In it, Pyetsukh analyzes how history is constructed by elements from all social levels.

The New Moscow Philosophy, Pyetsukh's longest novella to date, explores the relationship between literature and life, as well as the nature of evil, the Russian "national character," and the role of tradition in culture. The death of an old woman from a communal apartment supplies the minimal plot interest of the highly self-conscious, discursive narrative dominated by the speeches of characters who express a wide range of ideas derived from Russian literary and philosophical sources. Concepts rather than language, character construction, or description clearly intrigue Pyetsukh, who interweaves into the text extended quotes from Dostoevsky's *Crime and Punishment,* ideas embraced by such thinkers as Konstantin Leontiev and Pyotr Chaadaev, and a wealth of echoes from the full spectrum of nineteenth-century Russian authors. *The New Moscow Philosophy* shares with Chernyshevsky's *What Is To Be Done?* a seriousness of intention, rather wooden characters, an arch exposé of novelistic conventions, and an uneven, bumpy development. Both implicitly and, at the novella's conclusion, too explicitly, it insists on the powers of literature to mold morals. Provocative ideas rather than narrative skill hold the reader's interest in a work that is ultimately flawed.

Like his longer fiction, Pyetsukh's short stories concern themselves with life's absurdities, banal cruelties, and unexpected twists. Their numerous intertexts enable him to convey his major perception of life as an essentially literary phenomenon. His express conviction that "Literature is the clean copy, life is only the draft, and not even a particularly worthwhile one at that," may account in part for the somewhat stilted air of his fiction. If his irony thwarts readers' expectations through a technique of deflation, those expectations proceed from recollections of familiar texts rather than lived experience: the ironic effects in *The New Moscow Philosophy* depend on a knowledge of *Crime and Punishment*, in "The Flood" (1988) and "Novy Zavod" (1987), on *The Decameron* and a combination of *Anna Karenina, The Brothers Karamazov,* the conventions of utopian literature, and the clichés of Soviet propaganda, respectively.

H.G.

LEONID SHOROKHOV
(b. 1946, Kobrin, Belorussia)

The destructiveness of man is one of the major themes that emerges from Leonid Shorokhov's works. In his first novel, *The Black Rainbow* (1989), he examines alcoholism; in the short story "Tomato," a psychological character study of moral consciousness in a contemporary Soviet slaughterhouse, he recalls American muckraker Upton Sinclair, and in *The Lifeguard,* the prize-winning novella translated in this collection, he reveals the complex interconnections of material greed, political corruption, environmental destruction, and murder.

Shorokhov's writing is realistic in style and sociological in theme—his fiction is somewhat journalistic, but unlike many of his contemporaries he writes with a convincing combination of technical expertise and moral commitment.

Shorokhov's parents belonged to the professional intelligentsia (his mother, a physician; his father, a teacher); he graduated from the Leningrad Institute of Mining and worked as an engineer in many different parts of the Soviet Union. He began writing twenty years ago, but his work was accepted only upon the advent of glasnost. He raises contemporary social issues and shows in naturalistic detail the brutal consequences of man's crimes against his fellow man. Shorokhov's fictional portrait in "Evening at Yasnaya" of Leo Tolstoy as an aging moralist can be read as a counterpoint to his contemporary concerns, but it also poses the question: how can we change?

Shorokhov has forsaken engineering for writing and lives in the small town of Bekabad in Uzbekistan. Except for *The Lifeguard*, which was first published in *Znamya,* all of Shorokhov's works have appeared in the Tashkent literary journal, *Star of the East (Zvezda vostoka).*

B.L.

NIKOLAI SHMELYOV
(b. 1936, Moscow)

Nikolai Shmelyov combines two careers: those of writer and economist. Since graduating from Moscow State University in 1958, he has worked in various economic institutes in the Soviet Academy of Sciences, gaining considerable national fame as a professor and author of books on problems in world economy. His fate as a writer, however, has suffered the vagaries common to many literati in the Soviet Union.

After the publication of Shmelyov's first story (*Odoviannye soldatiki,* 1961) in the journal *Moscow (Moskva),* none of his fiction appeared for over two decades. This long silence ended in 1987 with his novella *The Pashkov House* (*Pashkov dom*), which attracted considerable attention from critics and readers. So did subsequent pieces, notably his novel *A Performance in Honor of Mr. First Minister* (*Spektakl' v chest' gospodina pervogo ministra,* 1988).

Shmelyov's fiction is firmly grounded in the tradition of realism, favors rather simple plots, a straightforward style, and characters caught in crises arising in part from their own weaknesses and mistakes. In tracing the circumstances that have led to their moment of reckoning, Shmelyov reveals the psychology of acquisitiveness, accommodation and fear. His flawed protagonists customarily experience a degree of self-awareness through the soul-searching naturally prompted by personal catastrophe, as demonstrated in "The Visit" and "The Fur Coat Incident" Shmelyov occupies a middle position on the contemporary literary scene, somewhere between the neo-modernism of alternative prose and the fatigued realism of more conservative exposé fiction. His preference is for clarity, simplicity and immediacy of effect.

A similar clear-headed directness marks his publicistic writings, e. g., the articles "Advances and Debts" (*Avansy i dolgi,* 1987), "New Worries" (*Novye trevogi,* 1988) and *The Turning Point: Revitalizing the Soviet Economy* (New York, 1989). In his capacity as economist and publicist, Shmelyov has visited the United States and consulted with American specialists, many of whom consider him one of Russia's foremost economists.

H. G.

NATALYA SUKHANOVA
(b. 1931)

Although Sukhanova has been writing for over a quarter-century, until the publication of her story "Delos" in 1988, she remained unknown even to her fellow authors in the Soviet Union. Viktor Astafiev, a conservative representative of the village prose contingent, admitted as much in his laudatory preface to the text.

Like countless Russian literati, Sukhanova has held a bewildering variety of jobs. Upon graduation from the Moscow Law Institute, she worked as a notary, as first secretary of the local Kosmosol committee, an organizer of exhibits at a resort, and as a newspaper correspondent.

Sukhanova's early, unsuccessful attempts at poetry led her to fiction, particularly the genres of the short story and novella, to which she has adhered throughout her long career. Her first publication, in the arch conservative journal *The Young Guard* (1961), consisted of stories. It was followed by such collections as *Neighbors* (1966), *The Moon's Sharp Sickle* (1974), and *A Tale about Iuppi* (1984)—all published in Rostov-on-the-Don, where she has resided since leaving Taganrog in early 1961.

Those critics who have responded to her fiction have commended her powers of observation, her ability to penetrate the psychology of her characters, her good taste, subtlety, and gently lyrical narrative manner. They have noted her ties with a tradition that harks back to Chekhov and that produced the so-called Paustovsky school of prose. Among current writers, Sukhanova's values and manner have closest affinities with the village prose group. She shares their conservative ideology, their devotion to traditional habits and customs, and their disinterest in aesthetic experimentation and avant-gardism. In "Delos" that conservativism manifests itself in the story's strong pro-natal stance (aided by mythological precedents); its glorification of maternity and family; and the authority implicitly vested in male doctors to decide complex issues in the politics of reproduction.

H.G.

VLADIMIR TENDRYAKOV
(1923-84)

Tendryakov was born in a village north of Vologda, an area that ethnographers value as a repository of ancient Russian folk culture. His family were true believers in the new Soviet rule. His father, a village clerk, had seen Lenin at the Finland Station and during the Civil War became a Red Army commissar. Tendryakov's life reflects the extremes present in his childhood—the strong values of traditional Russian culture and Soviet political orthodoxy.

After finishing school, Tendryakov fought at the front in World War II until he was wounded and demobilized, whereupon he taught military affairs in a village school in the Urals. He later served as secretary of the regional Komsomol committee, and in 1948 he joined the Communist Party. In 1951 he graduated from the Gorky Literary Institute in Moscow, and in the next few years produced works undistinguishable from other Stalinist literature.

During the Thaw Tendryakov emerged as a writer with a voice of his own. He was a major talent in the first wave of village prose writers, which included Evgeny Nosov, Fyodor Abramov, Vasily Belov, and Viktor Astafiev. His stories and tales, usually set in the isolated North, emphasize moral conflicts between the smug bureaucracy and beleaguered individuals. The sharp tensions between his profoundly flawed characters and his idealistic, self-sacrificing heroes and heroines, emerge in fast-paced yet lyrical narratives about log drivers ("Three, Seven, Ace," 1960), pig feeders ("Creature of a Day," 1965), and the like. Morality in Tendryakov's world is complicated by his emphasis on primitive characters in extreme situations. His sensitivity to youth and its high aspirations, as contrasted to the more pragmatic older generation, likewise found expression in a series of stories concerned with upbringing, ranging from "A Topsy-Turvy Spring" (1973) to "The Night after Graduation" (1974).

The series of works published posthumously during glasnost, including this collection's "Donna Anna," reveal quite a different aspect of Tendryakov. Here he draws devastating, Goyaesque portraits of state-sanctioned chaos and cruelty during those years that orthodox Soviet texts have presented in heroic hues. *The Hunt*, a sui generis novella mixing historical fact with fiction and memoir with essay, is a masterful evocation of Stalin's post-war, anti-Semitic terror.

B.L.

YURY TRIFONOV
(b. 1925 in Moscow, died 1981)

Trifonov's early sketches, stories, and first novel, *Students* (1950), which won a Stalin prize, evidence little of the subtlety and narrative sophistication manifest in his mature prose. His unwieldy "production" novel, *Quenching a Thirst* (1953), reflects the official de-Stalinization policies of the Thaw ushered in by Khrushchev's strategic speech against the cult of personality and its attendant horrors.

With his subsequent series of "Moscow novellas," however, Trifonov became a writer worthy of serious attention, one preoccupied with history, memory, ethics, and the role of the intelligentsia in Russia's past and present. On the surface, *The Exchange* (1969), *Taking Stock* (1970), *The Long Goodbye* (1971), *The House on the Embankment* (1976), and *Another Life* (1976) treat such mundane matters as apartment exchanges, marital infidelity, academic squabbles, familial discord, materialism, and "midlife crises" in the modest terms of everyday domestic conflict. Yet all are concerned, on a more profound level, with moral choice and history, with the role of memory through time.

Those issues persist and acquire greater complexity in Trifonov's later novels, *The Old Man* (1979), *Time and Place* (1981), and *Disappearance* (1987). As in the Moscow novellas, metonymically, through characters formed by and representative of an earlier age, Trifonov persistently revives the tormenting dilemmas of the Revolution, the Civil War, the purges of the 1930s, and the Stalinist period.

Although Trifonov insists on the crucial relevance of the past to the present, he acknowledges the labile nature of historical events and their documentation, and recognizes people's impulse to block out or rearrange the past. Most of his works from the 1970s on are fueled by a passion for tracing roots, pinpointing beginnings, and identifying both causes and consequences. The unarticulated question presiding over Trifonov's fiction is: "How did Russia become what it is today, what forces were at work at decisive moments in its history?" That question requires painful confrontations that many of Trifonov's fictional characters prefer to avoid or memories that they labor to transform into less disturbing scenarios. Hence the retrospective movement of Trifonov's narratives and his skillful use of multiple viewpoints that juxtapose several versions of bygone eras or earlier occurrences in an effort to reconstruct the "truth."

"A Short Stay in the Torture Chamber" condenses the chief features of Trifonov's longer fiction: the subjective narrator whose recollections of the past determine his current judgments and reactions; a conflicting perspective from another source as a corrective to that dominant point of view; prosaic moments that are nonetheless loaded with ethical significance; and a "realistic" unfolding of events presented in a carefully subdued style free from imaginative leaps, poetic devices, and a colorful language.

H.G.

LYUDMILA ULITSKAYA
(b. 1943 in the Urals)

The only child of a biochemist and a specialist in agricultural machinery, Ulitskaya from the start had her loyalties divided between literature and science. Even before attending Moscow State University, where she majored in genetics, she had started composing poetry. After graduation in 1968, she spent two years in the Population Sector at the Institute of Genetics under Dubinin before moving on to other jobs in her field. She eventually abandoned the sciences, enjoyed a brief but successful stint managing a Jewish theater, then turned to literature.

Her output includes short stories, plays, filmscripts, and articles. Although a collection of her stories (*Poor Relatives*) is scheduled to appear, her publications thus far have been confined to several stories in *Krestianka, Ogonyok* and *Novoe russkoe slovo*. Among the filmscripts on which Ulitskaya has concentrated recently is the adaptation of her own "Bronka" for the screen.

Part of Ulitskaya's thematic originality stems from her focus on Jewish life, with its ancient traditions, lacerating losses, and stigma of exclusion—all rendered simply yet subtly through oblique references, as in "Lucky." The human impulse to retain dignity under conditions of inconceivable deprivation, whether material or emotional, often constitutes the mainspring of her characters' conduct. Spiritual vitality, resourcefulness, a stoic capacity to endure, and a continuity with those aspects of the past worth preserving elicit respect in Ulitskaya's fictional world. That respect casts a humanizing light on the disenfranchised, marginalized, enfeebled, or maladjusted, in whom her stories abound ("Bukhara's Daughter," "A Chosen People," "A Poor Relative"). Ulitskaya manages to infuse compassion and understanding in narratives that simultaneously evidence her lack of illusions about mankind. She does not flinch from physical detail or what by Soviet standards could be called risqué sexual situations: the seduction of a middle-aged man by a long-time acquaintance roughly his mother's age ("Gulya"), the impregnation of a virginal young woman by a man practically old enough to be her grandfather ("Bronka").

Terseness, sly irony, precision, and direct simplicity characterize Ulitskaya's authorial manner. Her succinct stories move briskly, often tracing two generations within a few pages, and avoid moralizing, rhetorical devices, and obvious dramatic effects. Perhaps her experience in the theater accounts for the authenticity and naturalness of her dialogue.

                                                                        H.G.